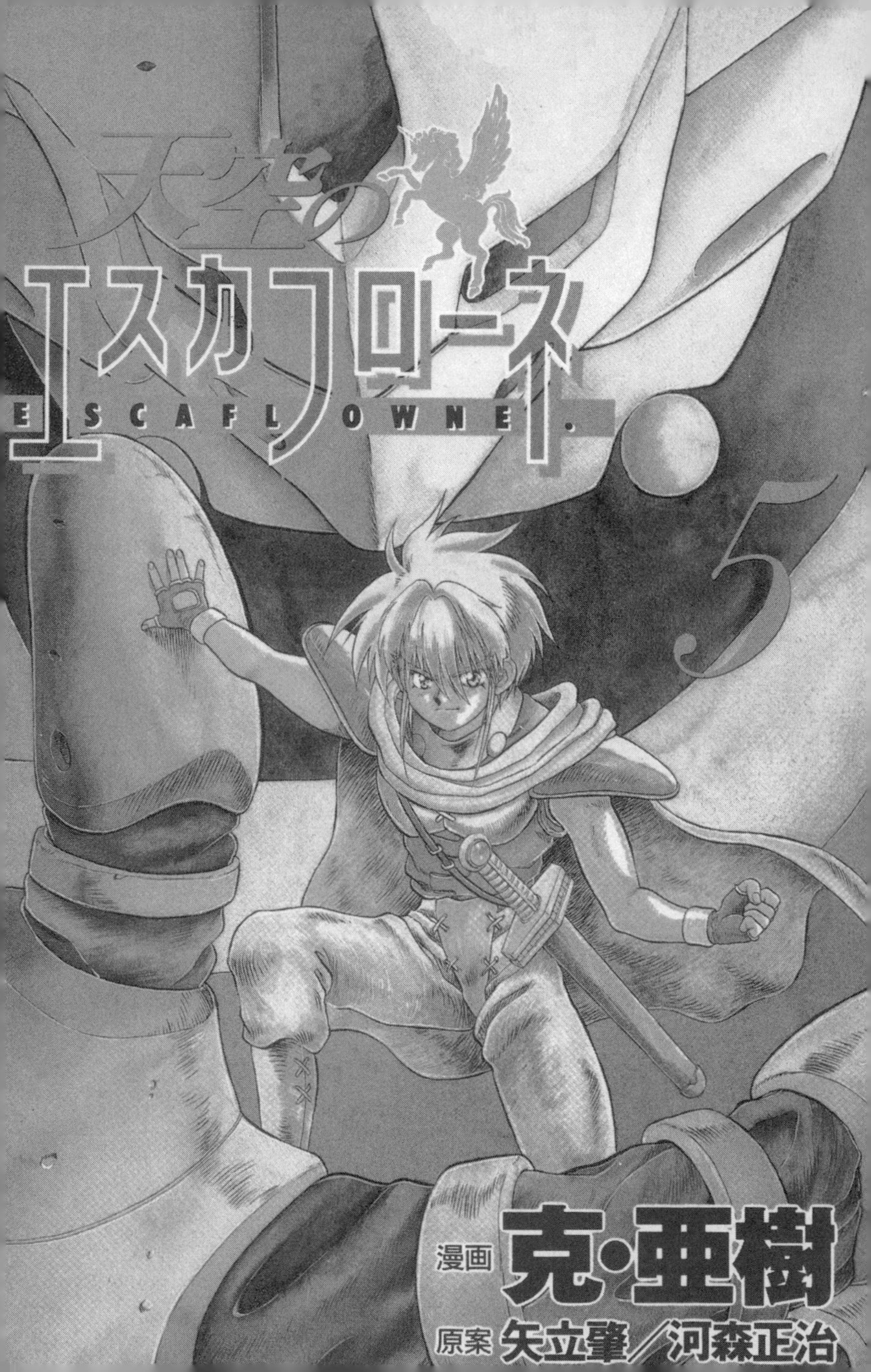
天空のエスカフローネ
ESCAFLOWNE
5
漫画 克・亜樹
原案 矢立肇／河森正治

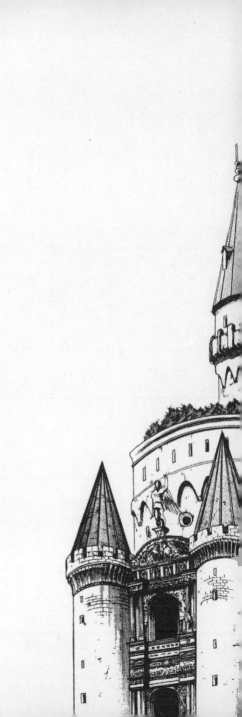

THE · VISION · OF
ESCAFLOWNE

Volume 5

By

KATSU AKI

Original concept
by
HAJIME YATATE
SHOJI KAWAMORI
(STUDIO NUE)

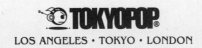

LOS ANGELES · TOKYO · LONDON

Translator - Jeremiah Bourque
English Adaptation - Lianne Sentar
Associate Editor - Tim Beedle
Copy Editor - Aaron Sparrow
Retouch and Lettering - Eric Botero
Cover Layout - Raymond Makowski

Editor - Rob Tokar
Managing Editor - Jill Freshney
Production Coordinator - Antonio DePietro
Production Managers - Jennifer Miller, Mutsumi Miyazaki
Art Director - Matt Alford
Editorial Director - Jeremy Ross
VP of Production - Ron Klamert
President & C.O.O. - John Parker
Publisher & C.E.O. - Stuart Levy

Email: editor@TOKYOPOP.com
Come visit us online at www.TOKYOPOP.com

A 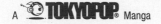 Manga

TOKYOPOP Inc.
5900 Wilshire Blvd. Suite 2000
Los Angeles, CA 90036

The Vision of Escaflowne Vol. 5

ISBN: 1-59182-450-8

First TOKYOPOP printing: March 2004

10 9 8 7 6 5 4 3 2 1

Printed in the USA

THE · VISION · OF
ESCAFLOWNE

INTRODUCTION

"Tenkuu no Escaflowne" ("Escaflowne of the Heavens," or "The Vision of Escaflowne" in North America) began as a story in the minds of Hajime Yatate and Shoji Kawamori, brilliant creators who planned Hitomi's epic tale to appear as an animated television series. While most anime series begin as manga, Escaflowne's two manga series were built off the ideas developed for the anime. Yuzuru Yashiro's shojo, or "girls'" manga, is two volumes in length. In contrast, Katsu Aki's shonen, or "boys'" manga, is much longer and happens to be the version you now hold in your hands.

Aki-sensei handled both the art and writing for this title, and it was actually the first version of Escaflowne to reach the public. While based on the concept of the anime, it began its serialization before the anime was complete. This version of the Escaflowne tale has a different flavor from the television series, with more action, tweaked character design, and an altered story. As a result, it is difficult to closely compare the two—they are simply two different versions of Hitomi's adventures. Escaflowne's versatility has always fetched great praise over the years. Its manga counterparts only expand the work's reach and deepen its universe. With that in mind, please put aside all preconceptions you may have as you sit back, relax, and enjoy this new look at the world of Escaflowne as you've never seen it before.

Lianne Sentar, April 2003

Special thanks to Egan Loo and his Escaflowne Compendium
(http://www.anime.net/escaflowne/)

ESCAFLOWNE VOL.5

CONTENTS

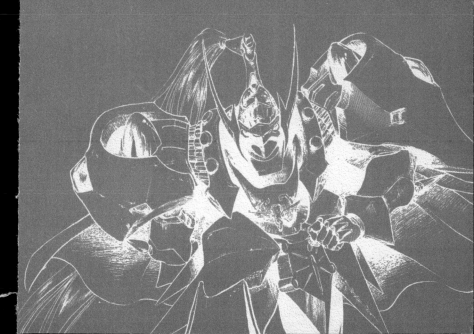

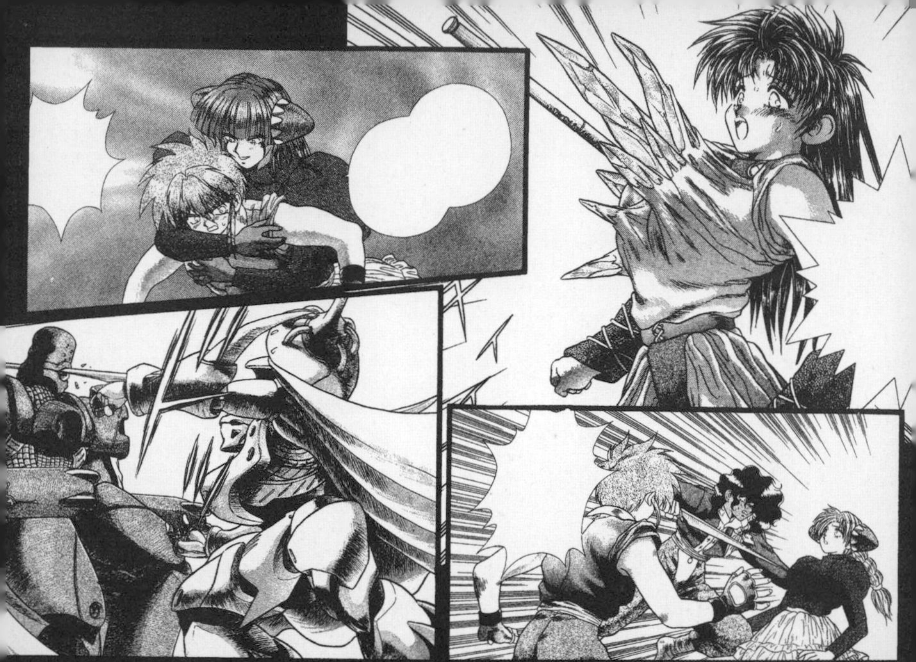

The Story Thus Far

In hot pursuit of the kidnapped Queen Escalina, Prince Van, Fanelian warrior Shian and schoolgirl-turned-Energist Hitomi Hoshino reached the Forest of Deception--only to discover Dilandau had already murdered the Queen. Unfortunately, Van was left with little time to mourn before Zaibach's shape-shifting warriors, Colt and Shilha, attacked the group, impaled Hitomi, and somehow sent Hitomi's soul reeling back to Earth. Before Van or Shian could react, Colt and Shilha made off with both the Energist crystal that housed Hitomi's soul and the mechanical deity Escaflowne.

While Hitomi tried to readjust to life on Earth, Van, Shian, and the Asturian knight Allen Schezar returned to the Holy Spring Ubdo to perform a ritual that could summon Hitomi back to Gaea. All went well until the spell was mysteriously deflected and Hitomi found herself deep in the Zaibach Empire, right in Emperor Dornkirk's clutches. However, the Emperor's interest in Hitomi waned when he discovered that her body is an Ubdo Energist housing an ancient soul. Van and Allen managed to rescue Hitomi and regain Escaflowne, but not before Zaibach Admiral Zongi arrived to detain them...

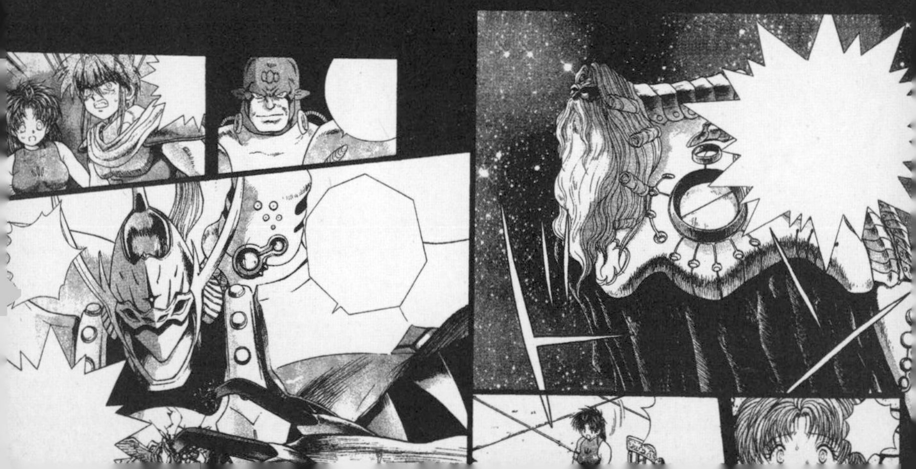

CHARACTER INTRODUCTIONS

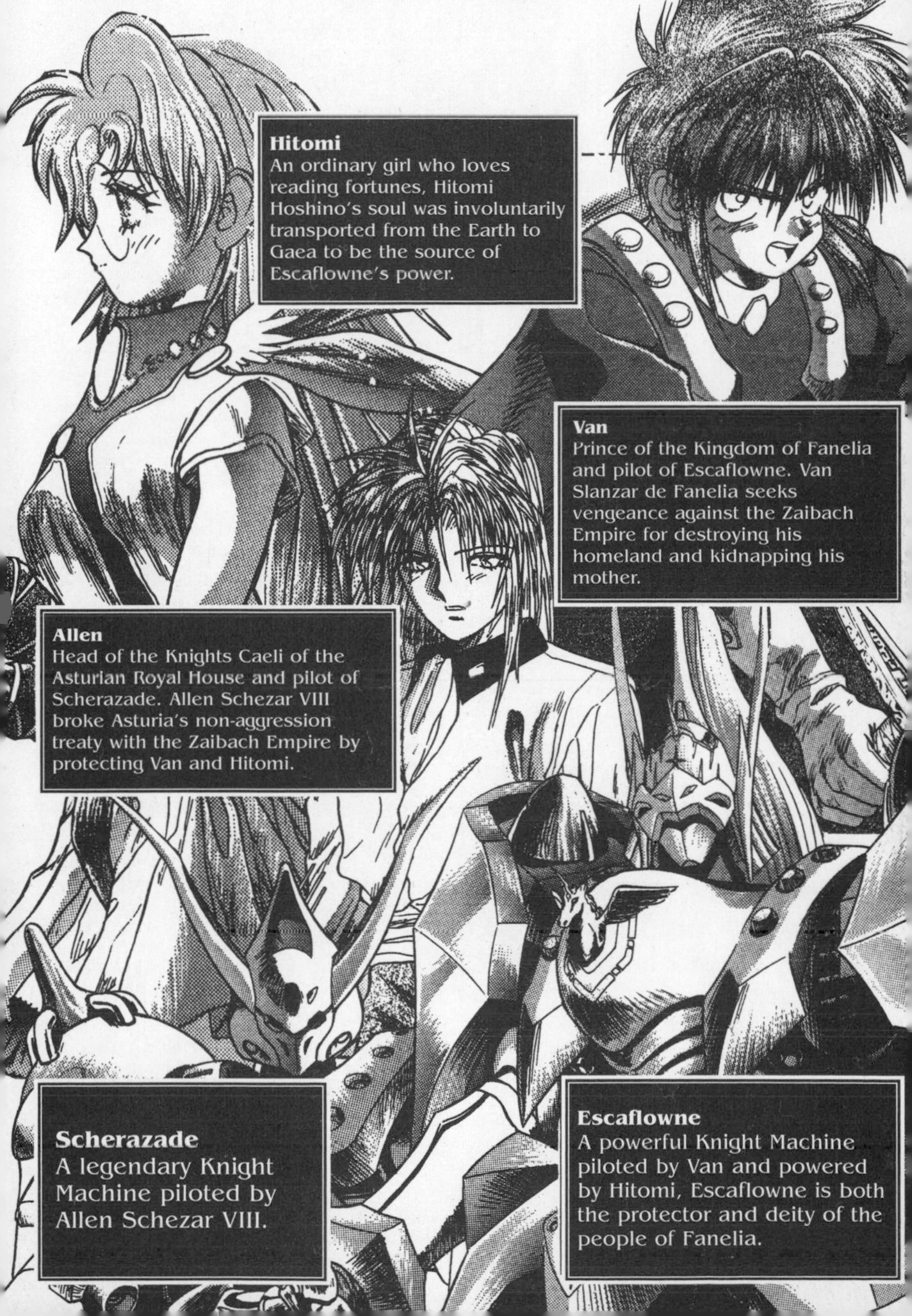

Hitomi
An ordinary girl who loves reading fortunes, Hitomi Hoshino's soul was involuntarily transported from the Earth to Gaea to be the source of Escaflowne's power.

Van
Prince of the Kingdom of Fanelia and pilot of Escaflowne. Van Slanzar de Fanelia seeks vengeance against the Zaibach Empire for destroying his homeland and kidnapping his mother.

Allen
Head of the Knights Caeli of the Asturian Royal House and pilot of Scherazade. Allen Schezar VIII broke Asturia's non-aggression treaty with the Zaibach Empire by protecting Van and Hitomi.

Scherazade
A legendary Knight Machine piloted by Allen Schezar VIII.

Escaflowne
A powerful Knight Machine piloted by Van and powered by Hitomi, Escaflowne is both the protector and deity of the people of Fanelia.

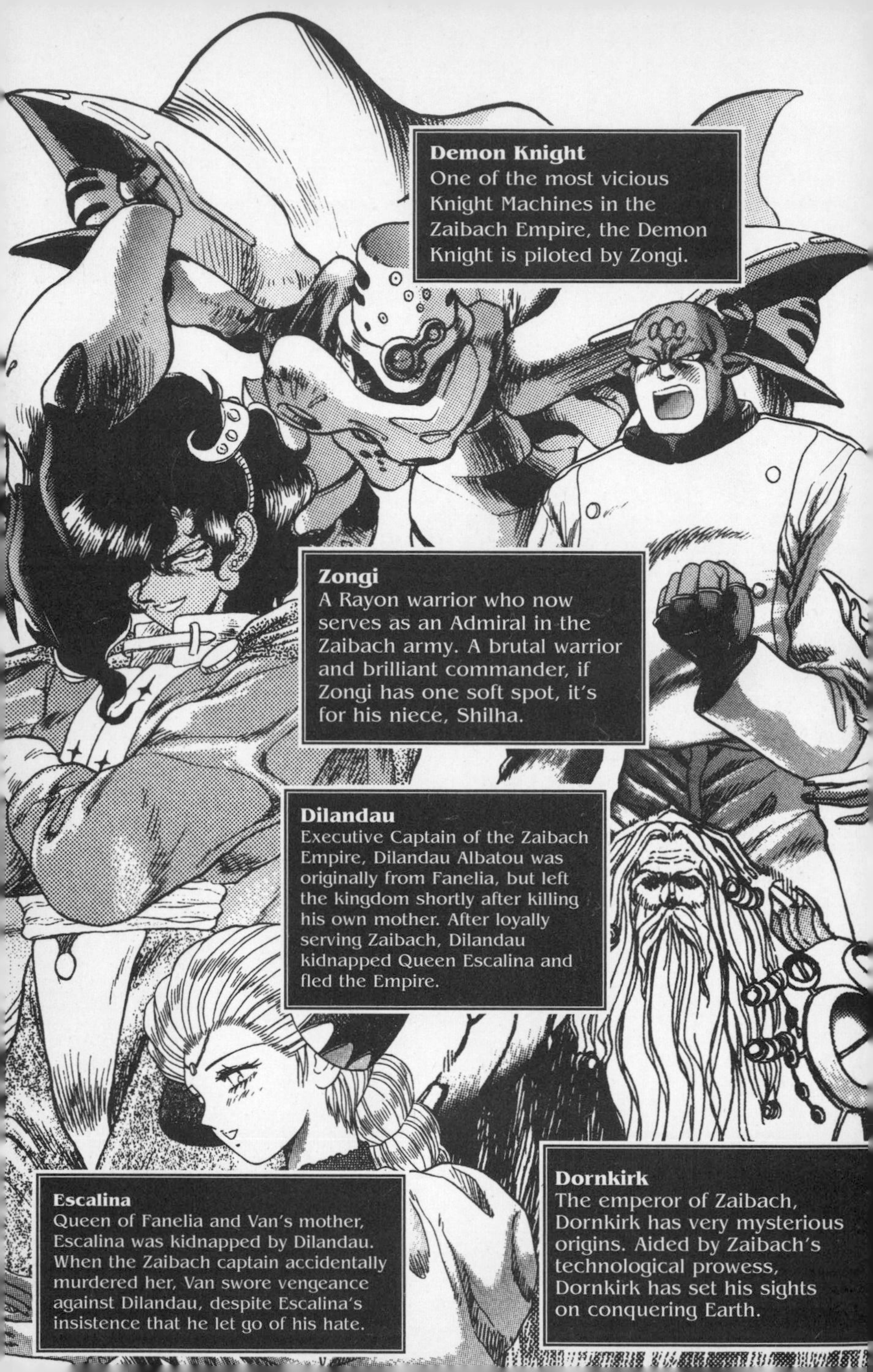
Demon Knight
One of the most vicious Knight Machines in the Zaibach Empire, the Demon Knight is piloted by Zongi.
Zongi
A Rayon warrior who now serves as an Admiral in the Zaibach army. A brutal warrior and brilliant commander, if Zongi has one soft spot, it's for his niece, Shilha.
Dilandau
Executive Captain of the Zaibach Empire, Dilandau Albatou was originally from Fanelia, but left the kingdom shortly after killing his own mother. After loyally serving Zaibach, Dilandau kidnapped Queen Escalina and fled the Empire.
Dornkirk
The emperor of Zaibach, Dornkirk has very mysterious origins. Aided by Zaibach's technological prowess, Dornkirk has set his sights on conquering Earth.
Escalina
Queen of Fanelia and Van's mother, Escalina was kidnapped by Dilandau. When the Zaibach captain accidentally murdered her, Van swore vengeance against Dilandau, despite Escalina's insistence that he let go of his hate.

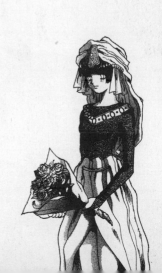

VISION 19:
SUICIDE BOMBING

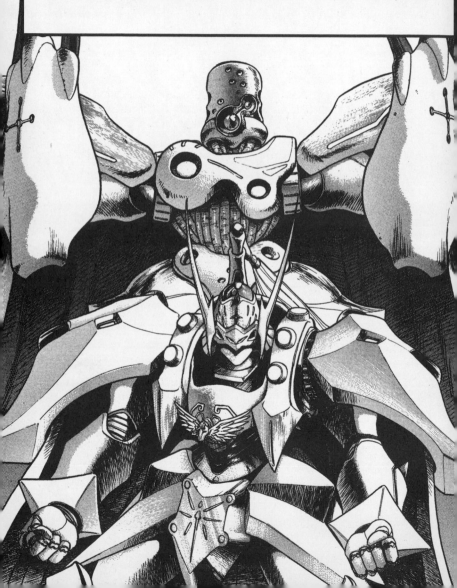

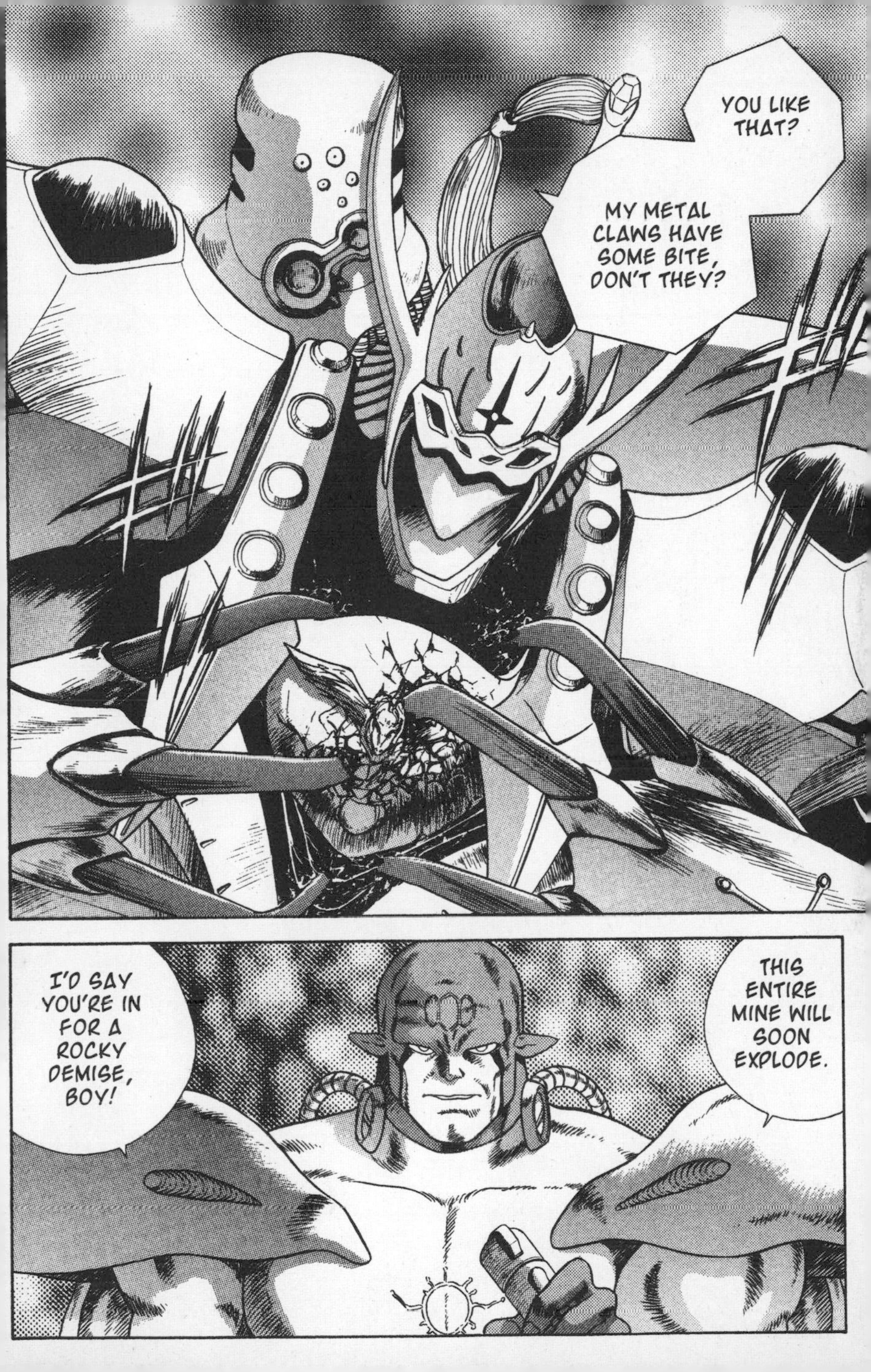
YOU LIKE THAT?
MY METAL CLAWS HAVE SOME BITE, DON'T THEY?
THIS ENTIRE MINE WILL SOON EXPLODE.
I'D SAY YOU'RE IN FOR A ROCKY DEMISE, BOY!

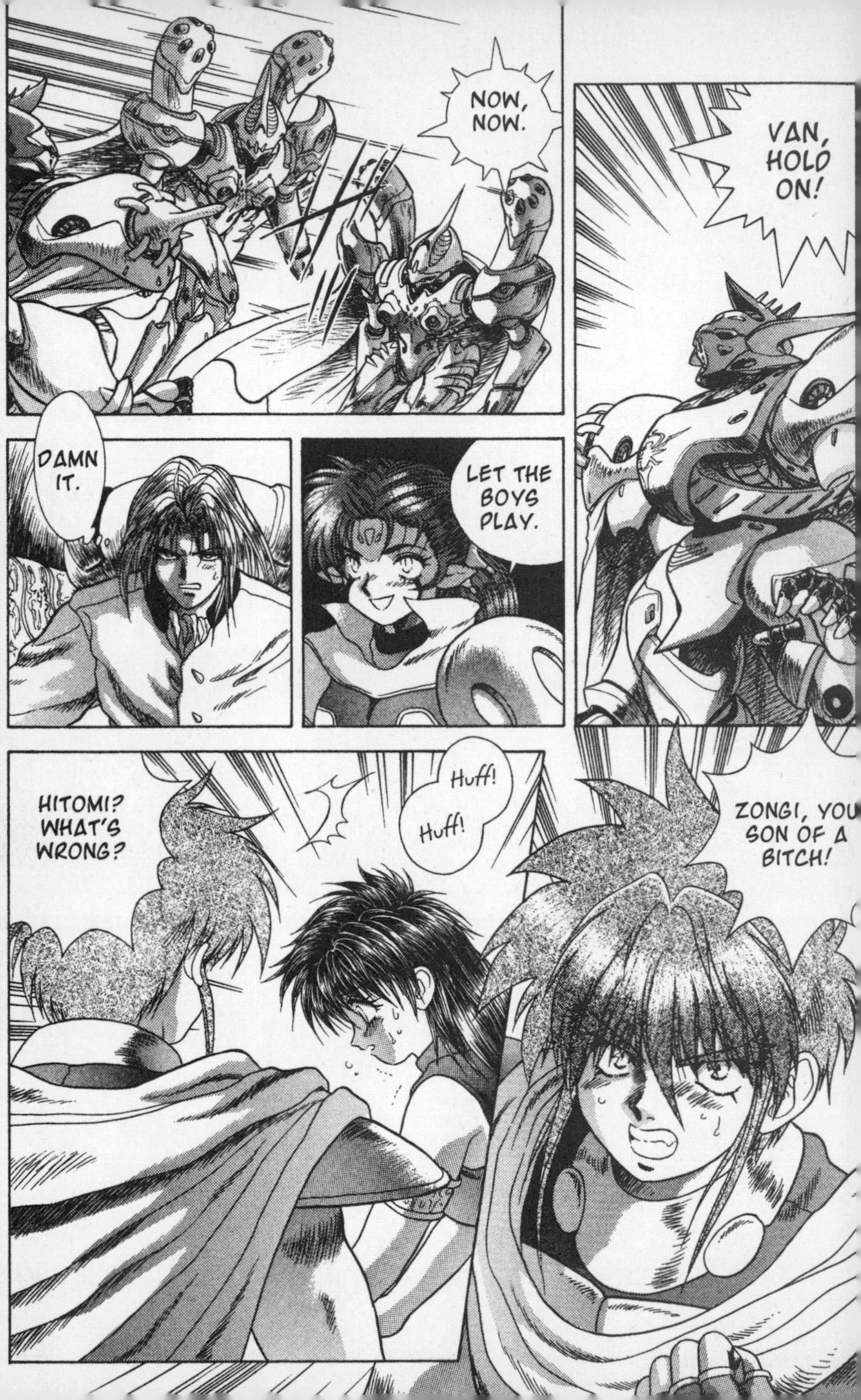
VAN, HOLD ON!
NOW, NOW.
LET THE BOYS PLAY.
DAMN IT.
ZONGI, YOU SON OF A BITCH!
Huff!
Huff!
HITOMI? WHAT'S WRONG?

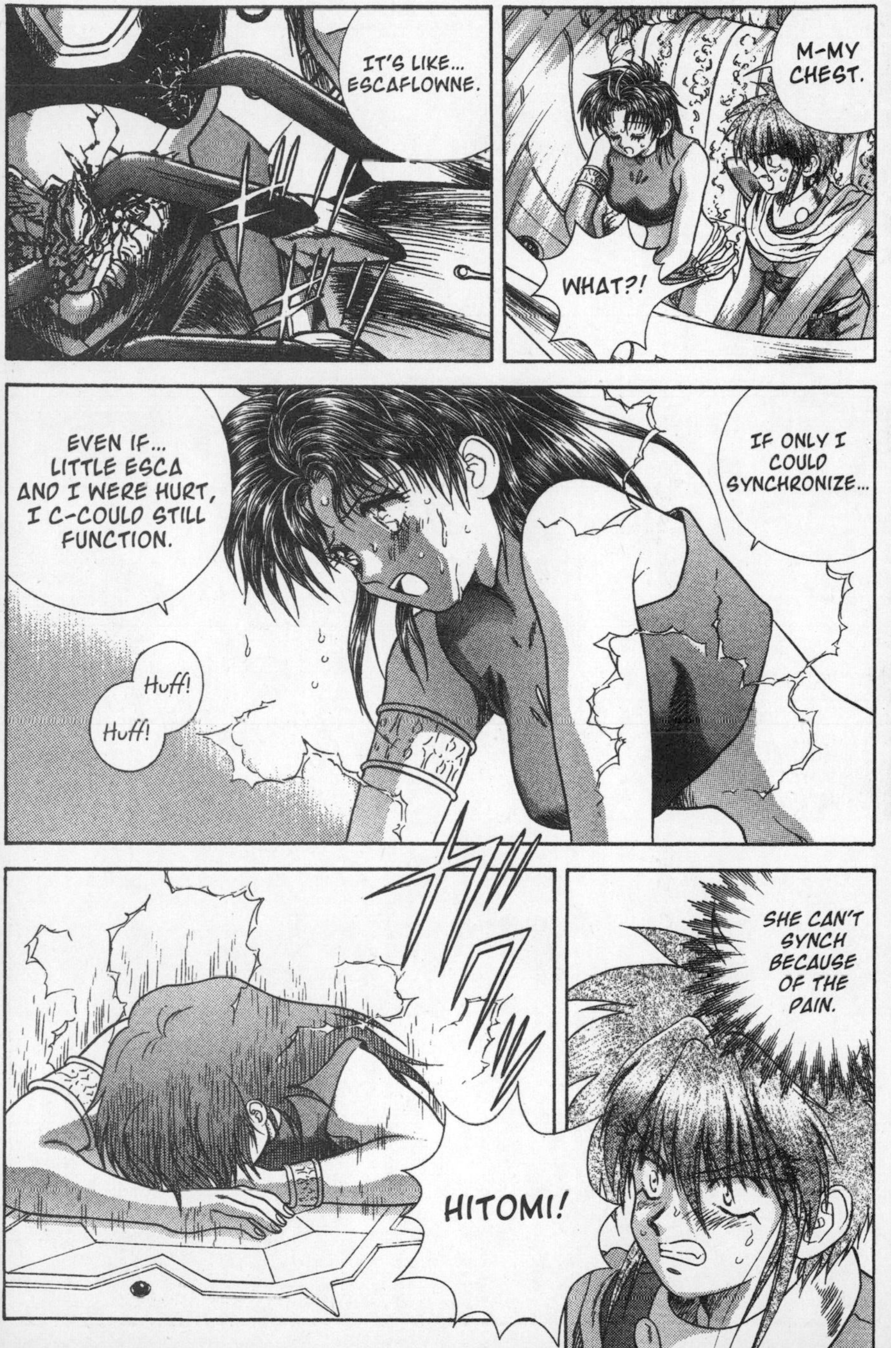
M-MY CHEST.
WHAT?!
IT'S LIKE... ESCAFLOWNE.
IF ONLY I COULD SYNCHRONIZE...
EVEN IF... LITTLE ESCA AND I WERE HURT, I C-COULD STILL FUNCTION.
Huff!
Huff!
SHE CAN'T SYNCH BECAUSE OF THE PAIN.
HITOMI!

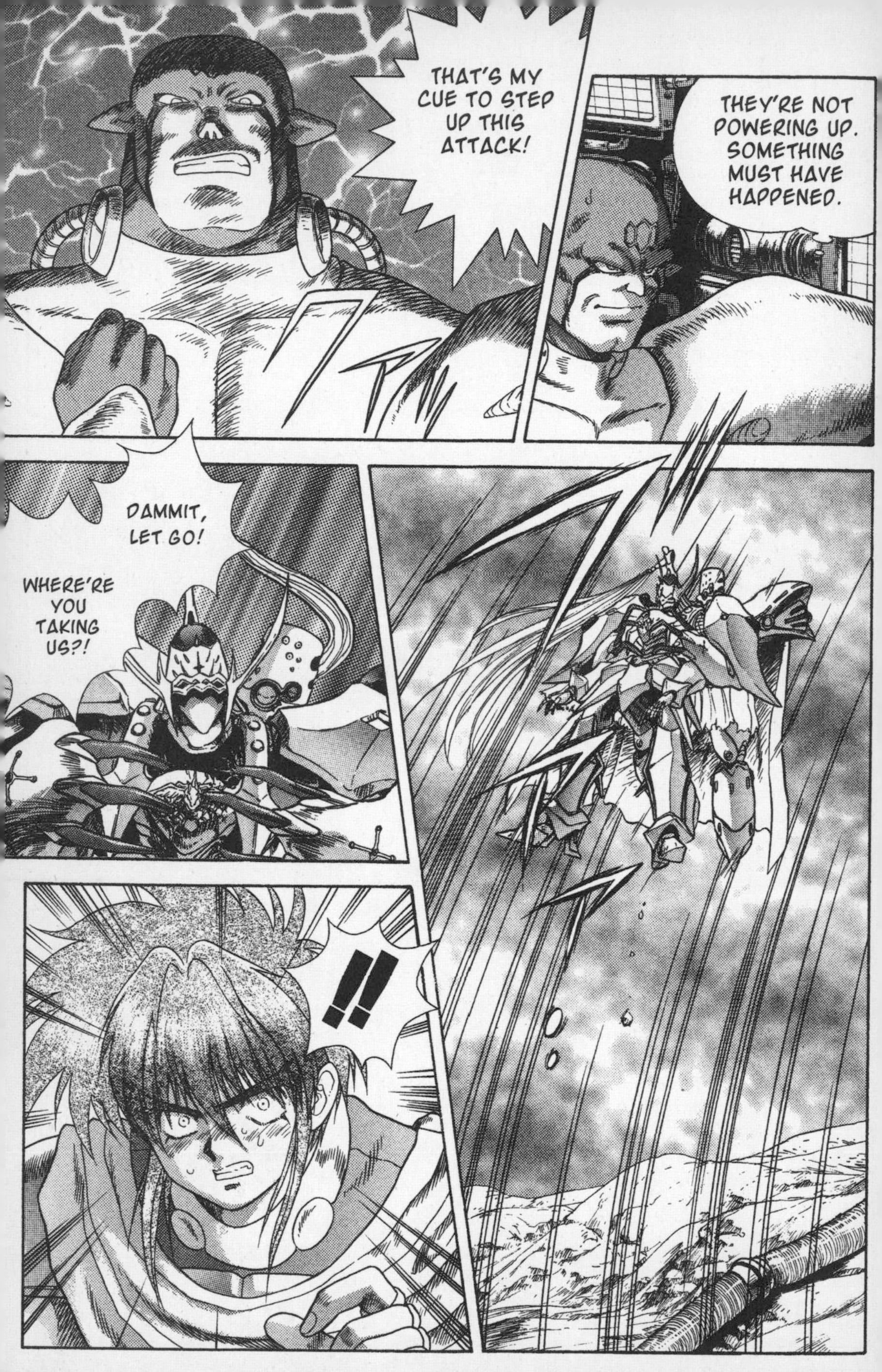
THEY'RE NOT POWERING UP. SOMETHING MUST HAVE HAPPENED.
THAT'S MY CUE TO STEP UP THIS ATTACK!
DAMMIT, LET GO!
WHERE'RE YOU TAKING US?!
!!

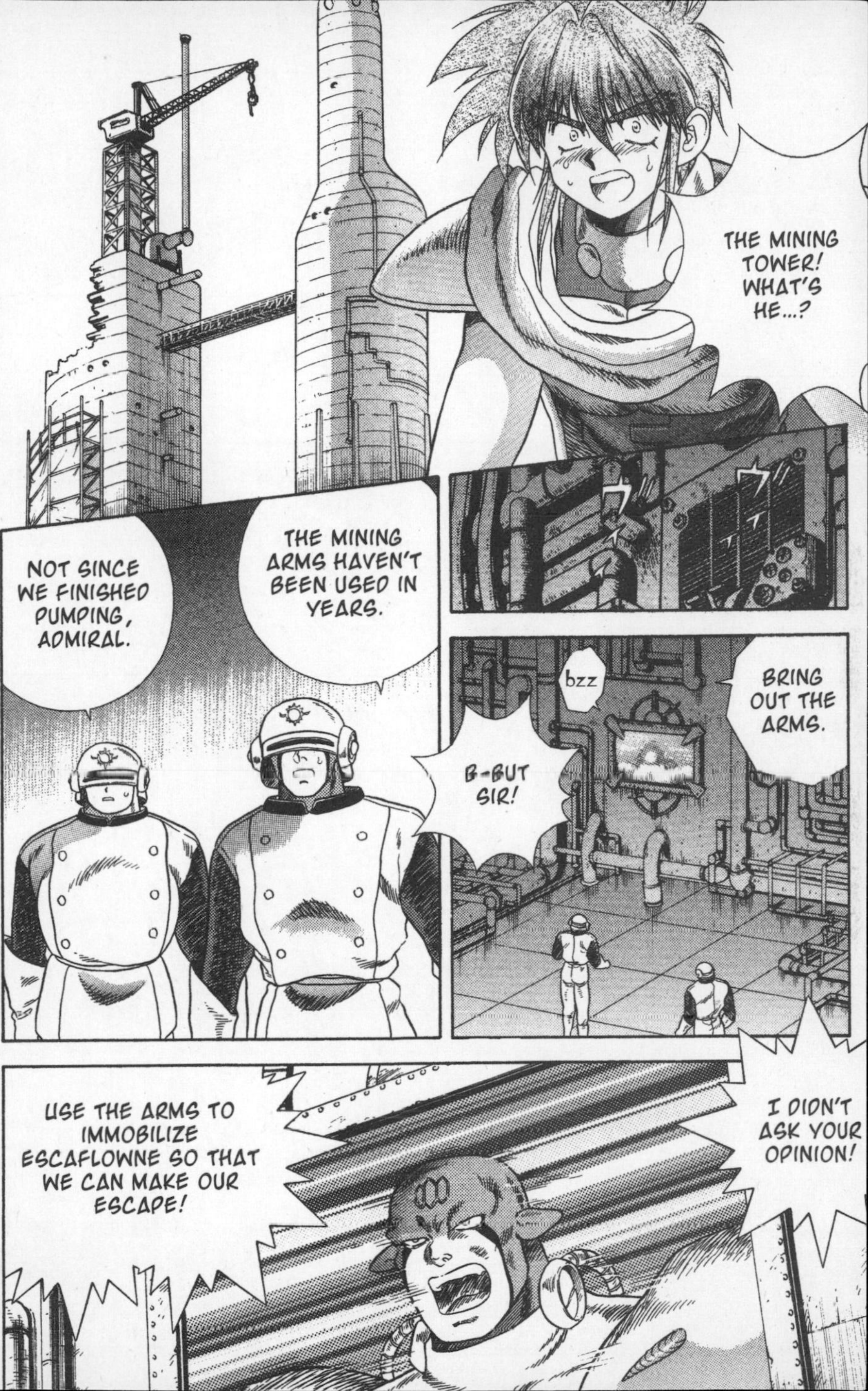
THE MINING TOWER! WHAT'S HE...?
bzz
BRING OUT THE ARMS.
B-BUT SIR!
THE MINING ARMS HAVEN'T BEEN USED IN YEARS.
NOT SINCE WE FINISHED PUMPING, ADMIRAL.
I DIDN'T ASK YOUR OPINION!
USE THE ARMS TO IMMOBILIZE ESCAFLOWNE SO THAT WE CAN MAKE OUR ESCAPE!

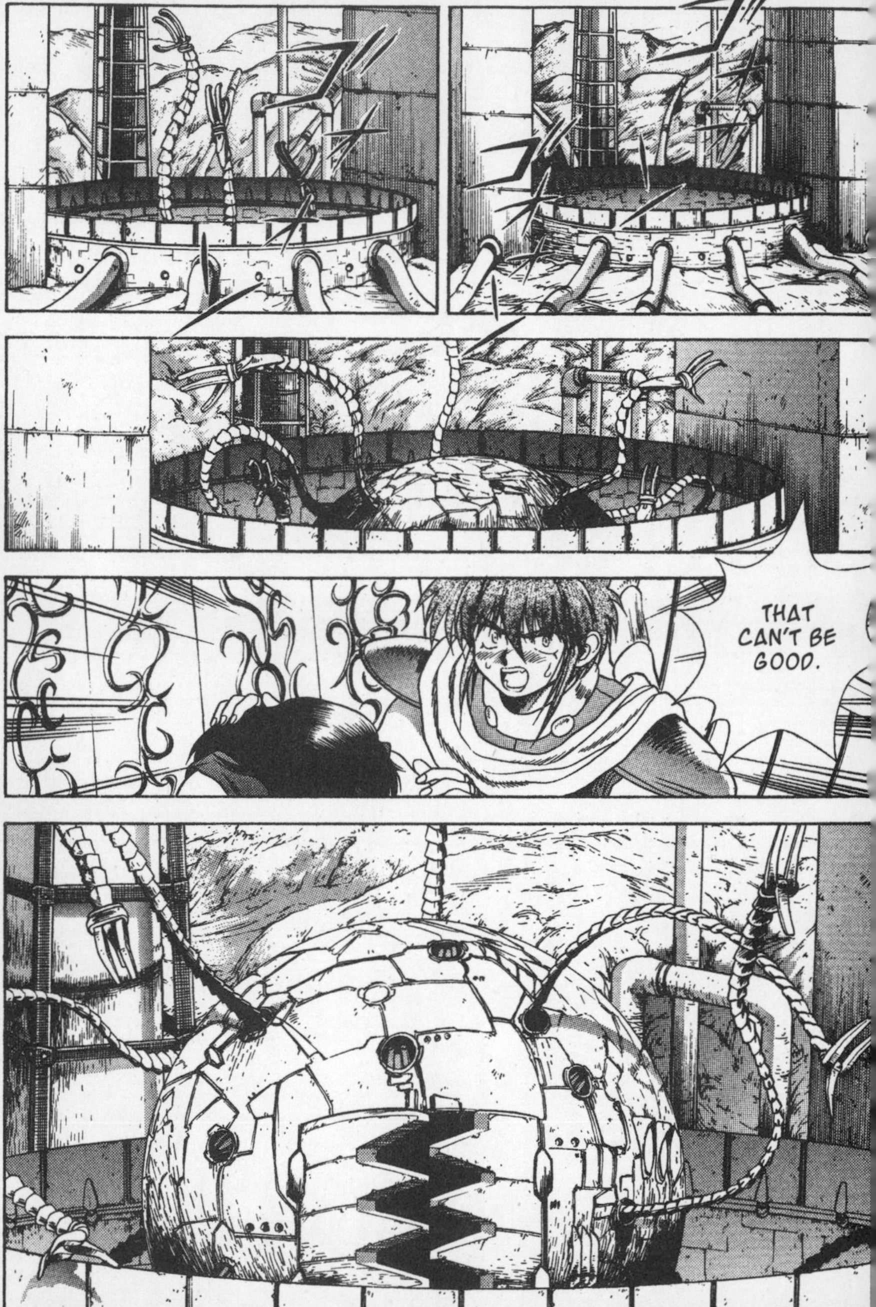
THAT CAN'T BE GOOD.

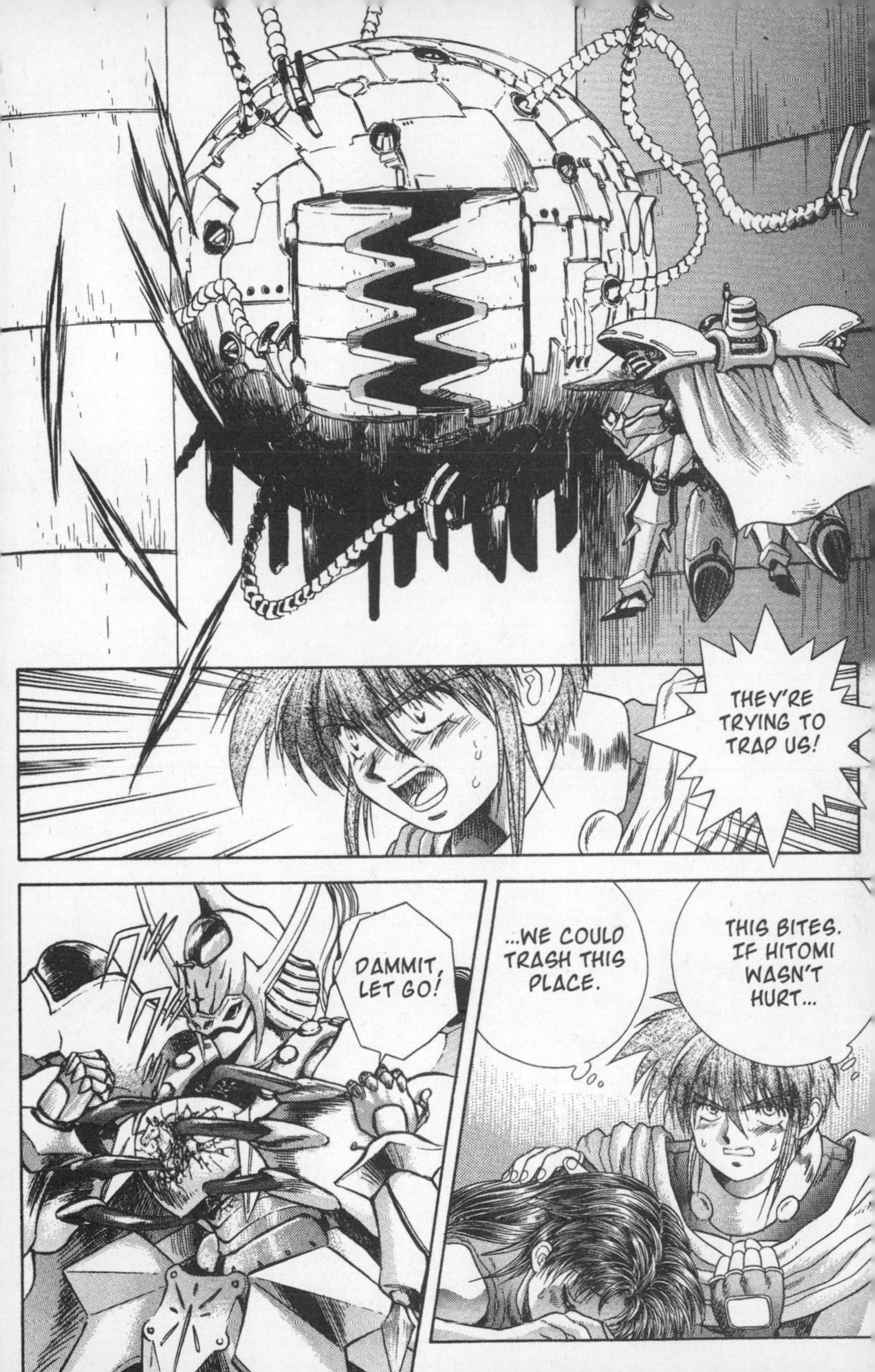
THEY'RE TRYING TO TRAP US!
THIS BITES. IF HITOMI WASN'T HURT...
...WE COULD TRASH THIS PLACE.
DAMMIT, LET GO!

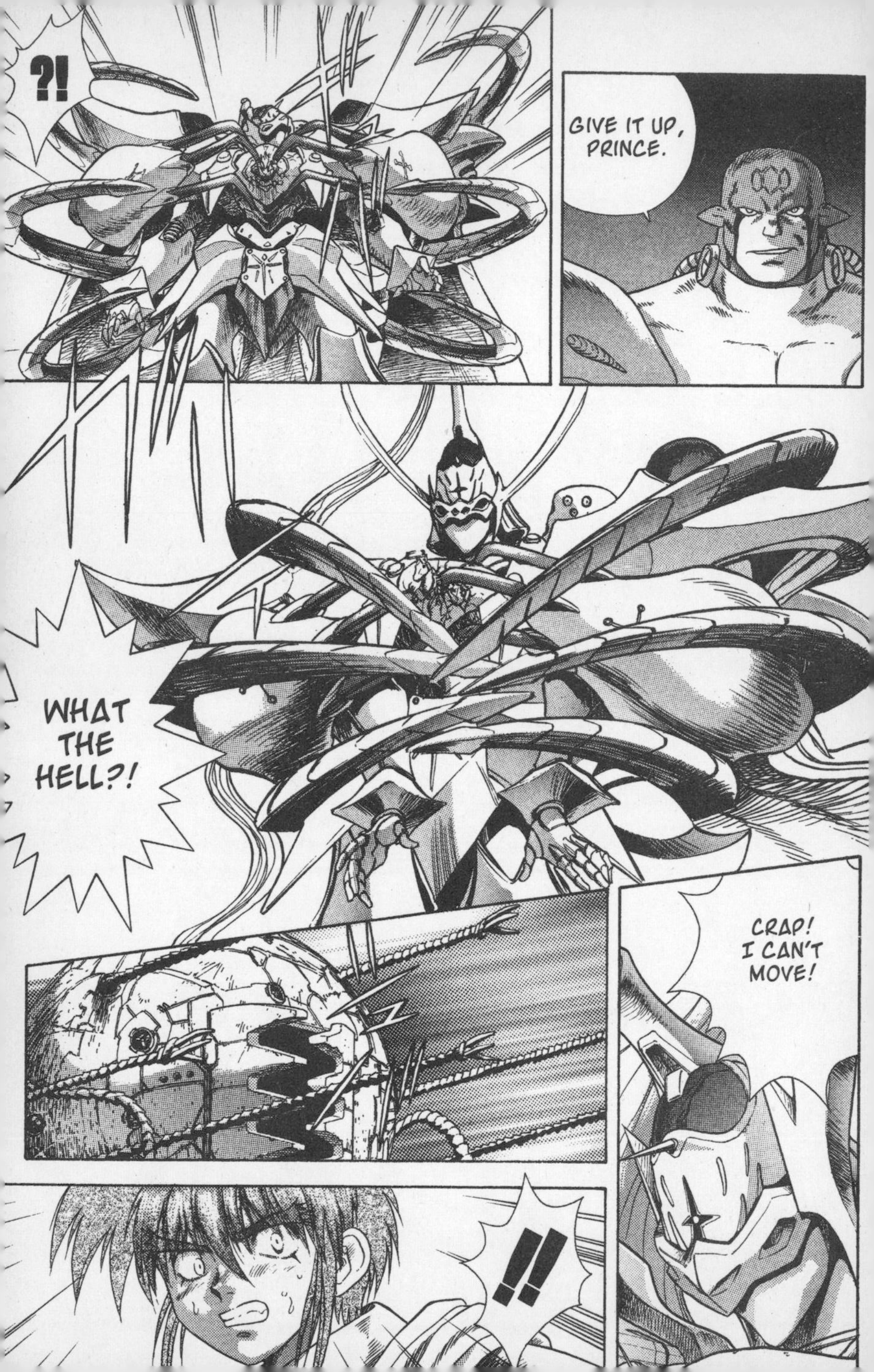
GIVE IT UP, PRINCE.
?!
WHAT THE HELL?!
CRAP! I CAN'T MOVE!
!!

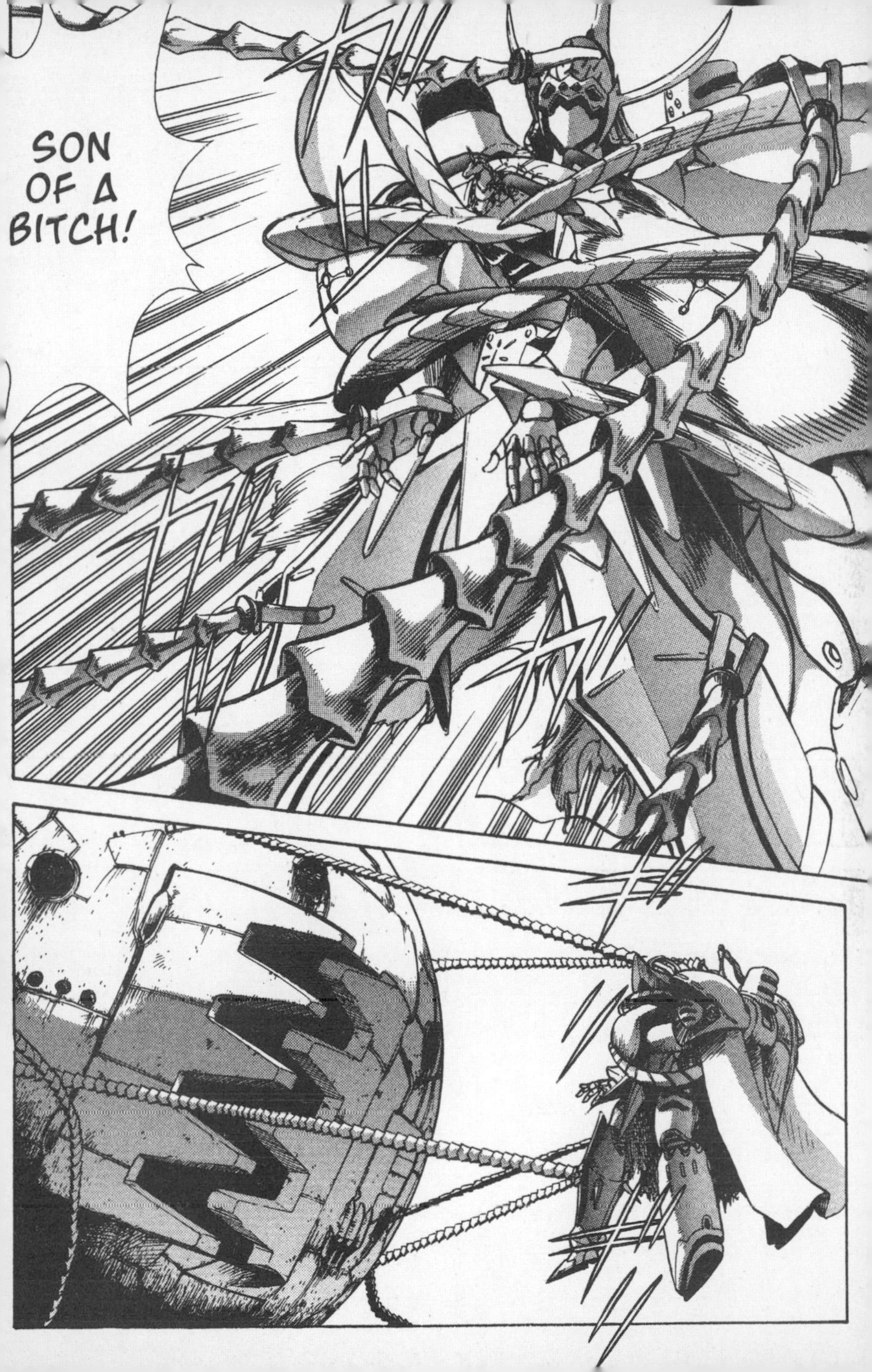
SON OF A BITCH!

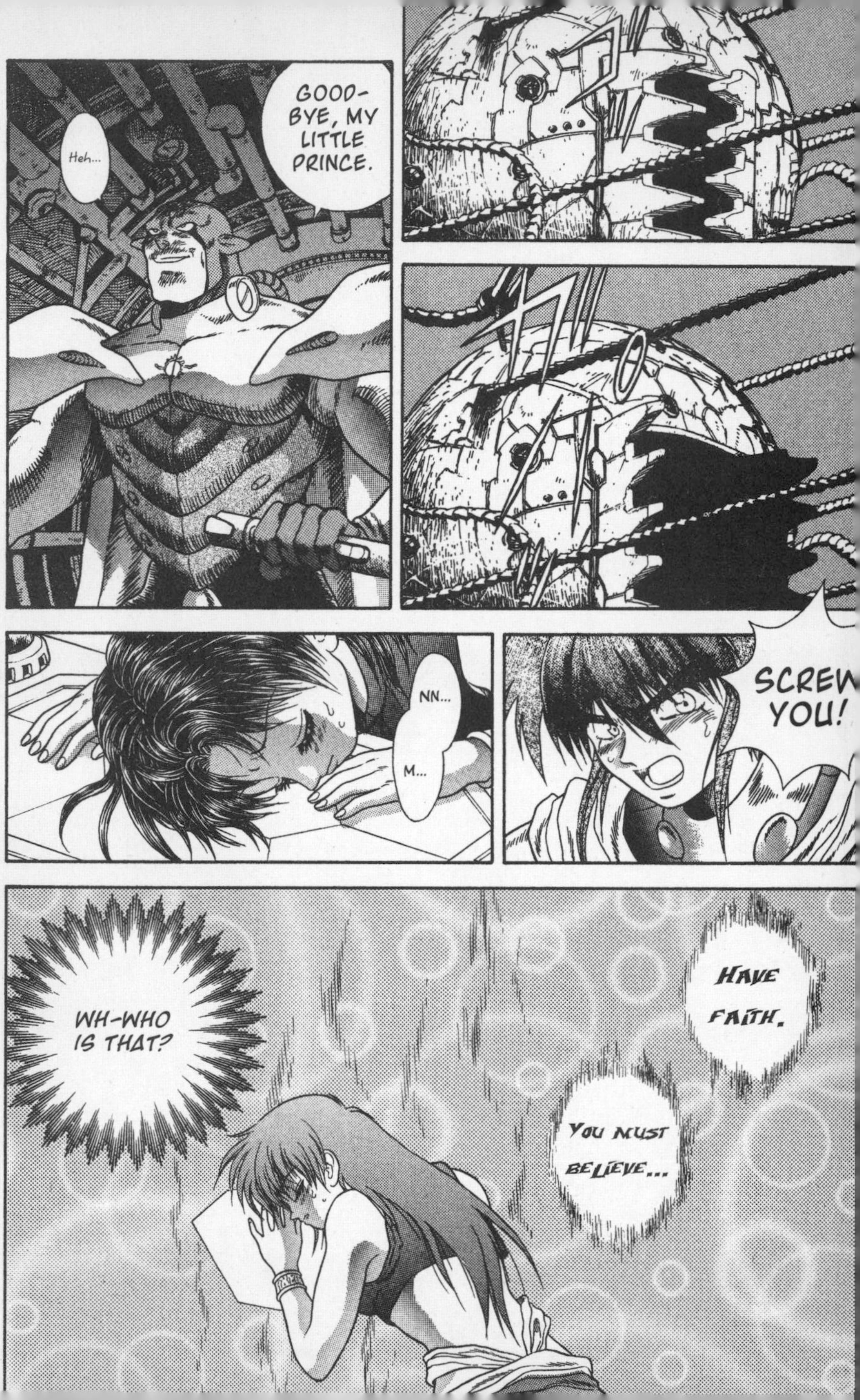
GOOD-BYE, MY LITTLE PRINCE.
Heh...
SCREW YOU!
NN...
M...
HAVE FAITH.
YOU MUST BELIEVE...
WH-WHO IS THAT?

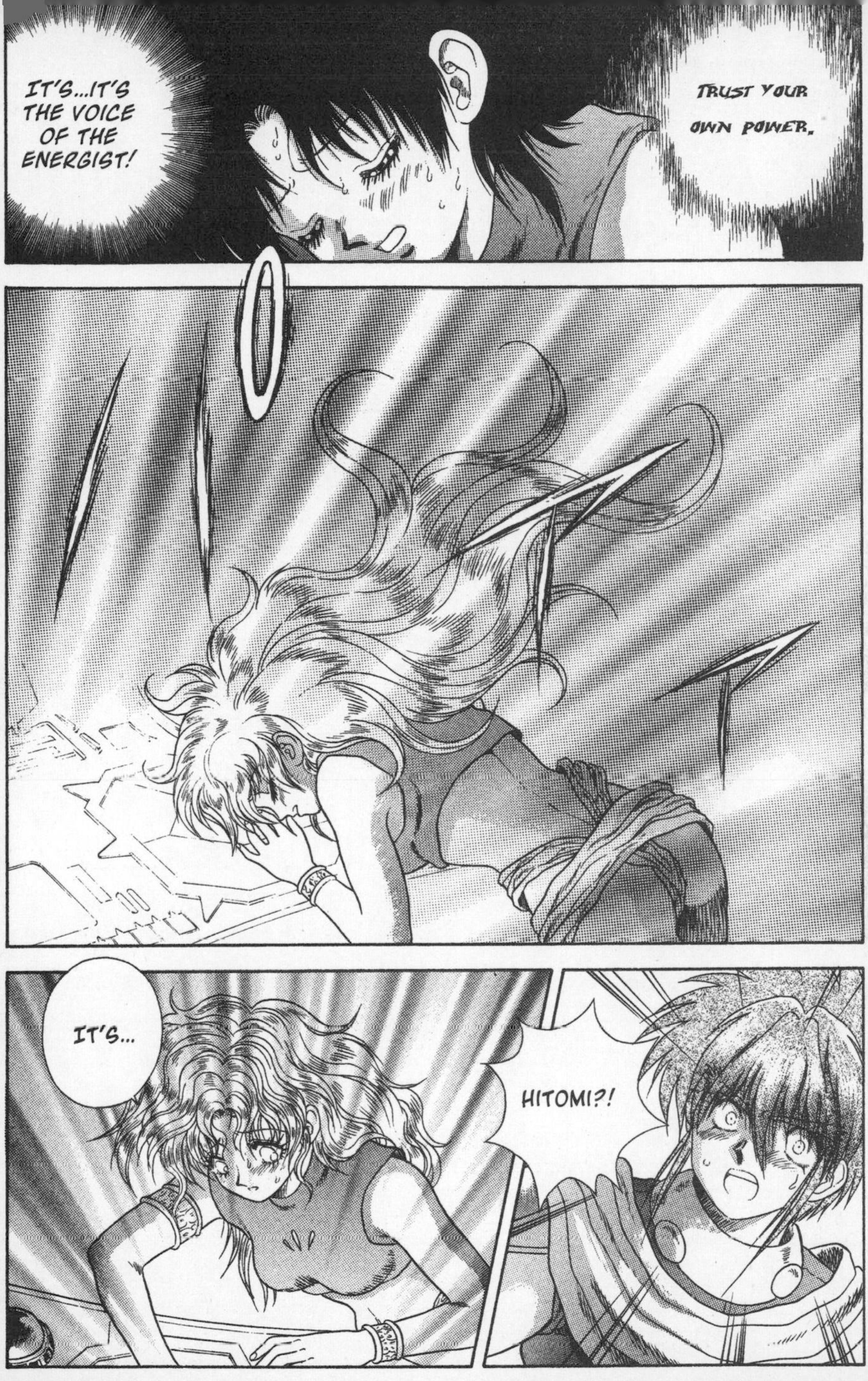
TRUST YOUR OWN POWER.
IT'S...IT'S THE VOICE OF THE ENERGIST!
HITOMI?!
IT'S...

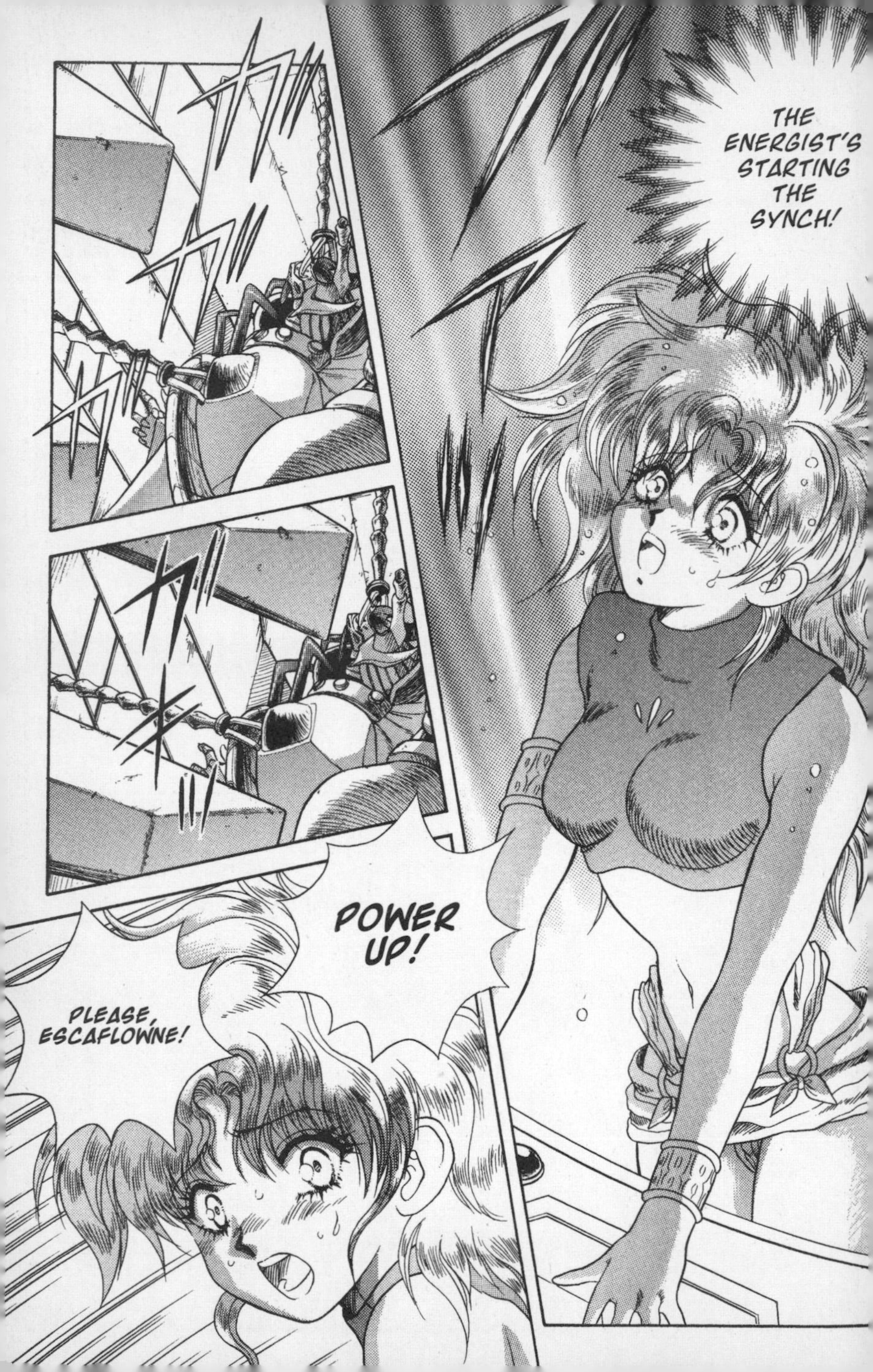
THE ENERGIST'S STARTING THE SYNCH!
POWER UP!
PLEASE, ESCAFLOWNE!

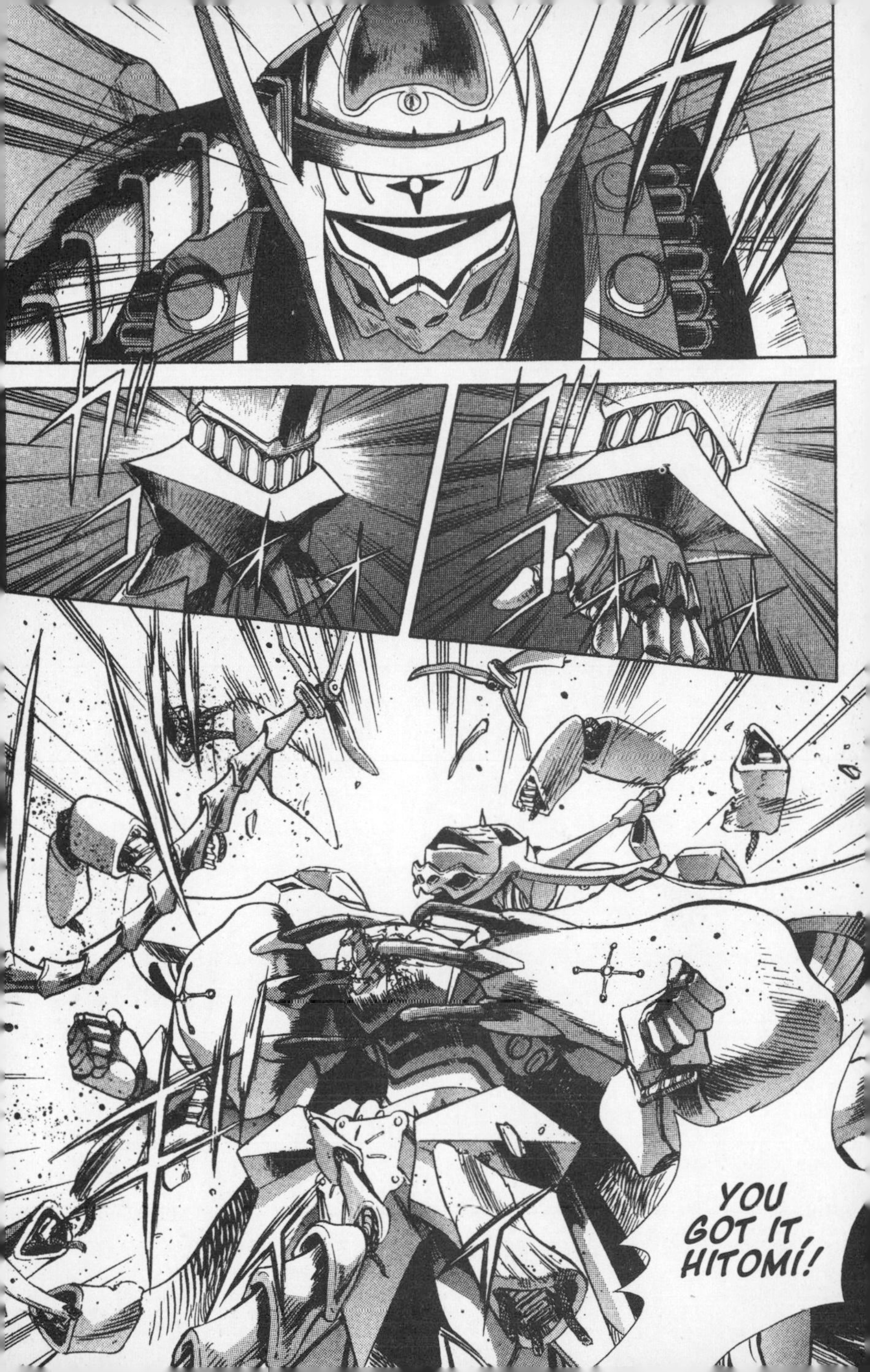
YOU GOT IT HITOMI!

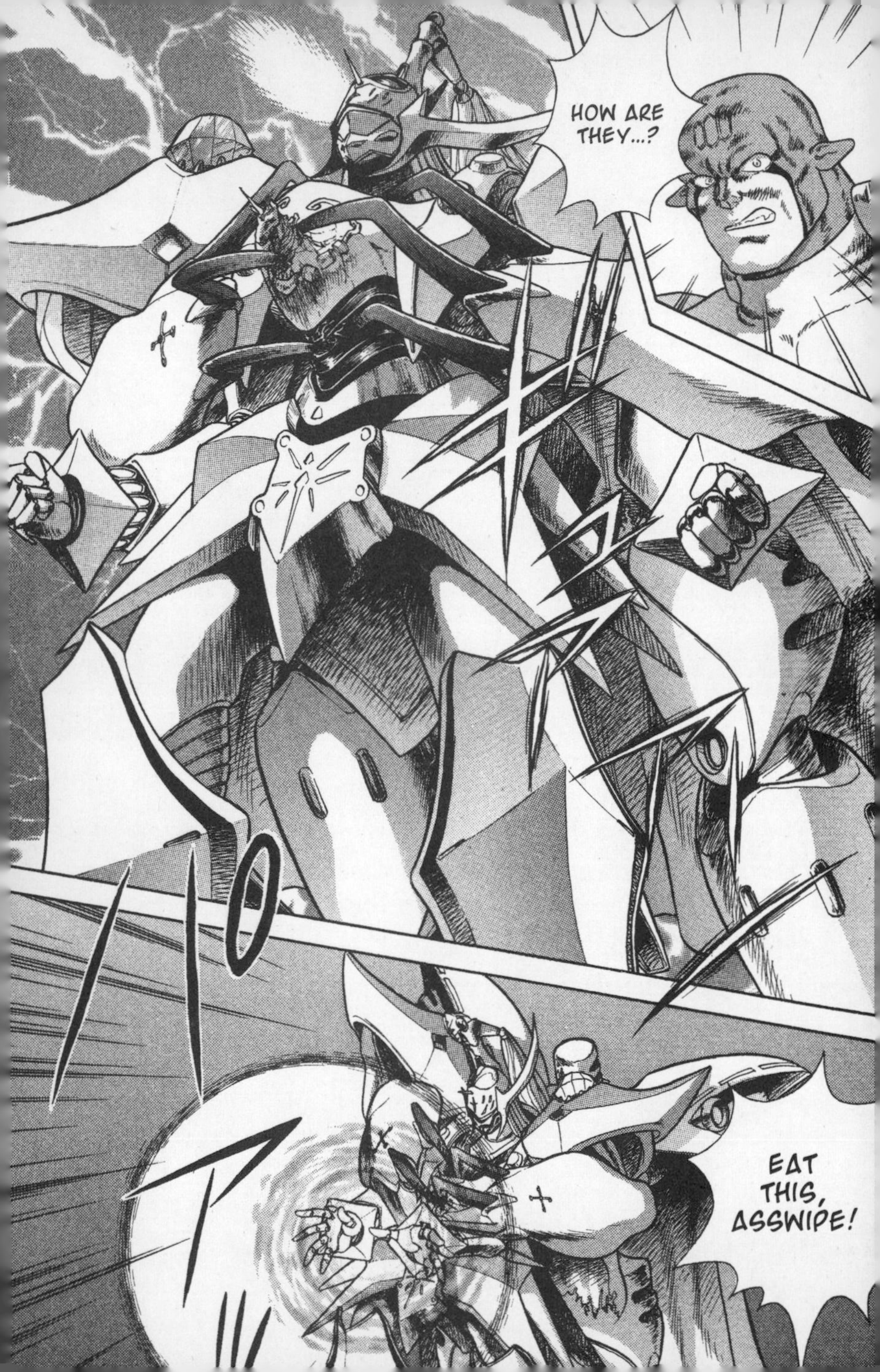
HOW ARE THEY...?
EAT THIS, ASSWIPE!

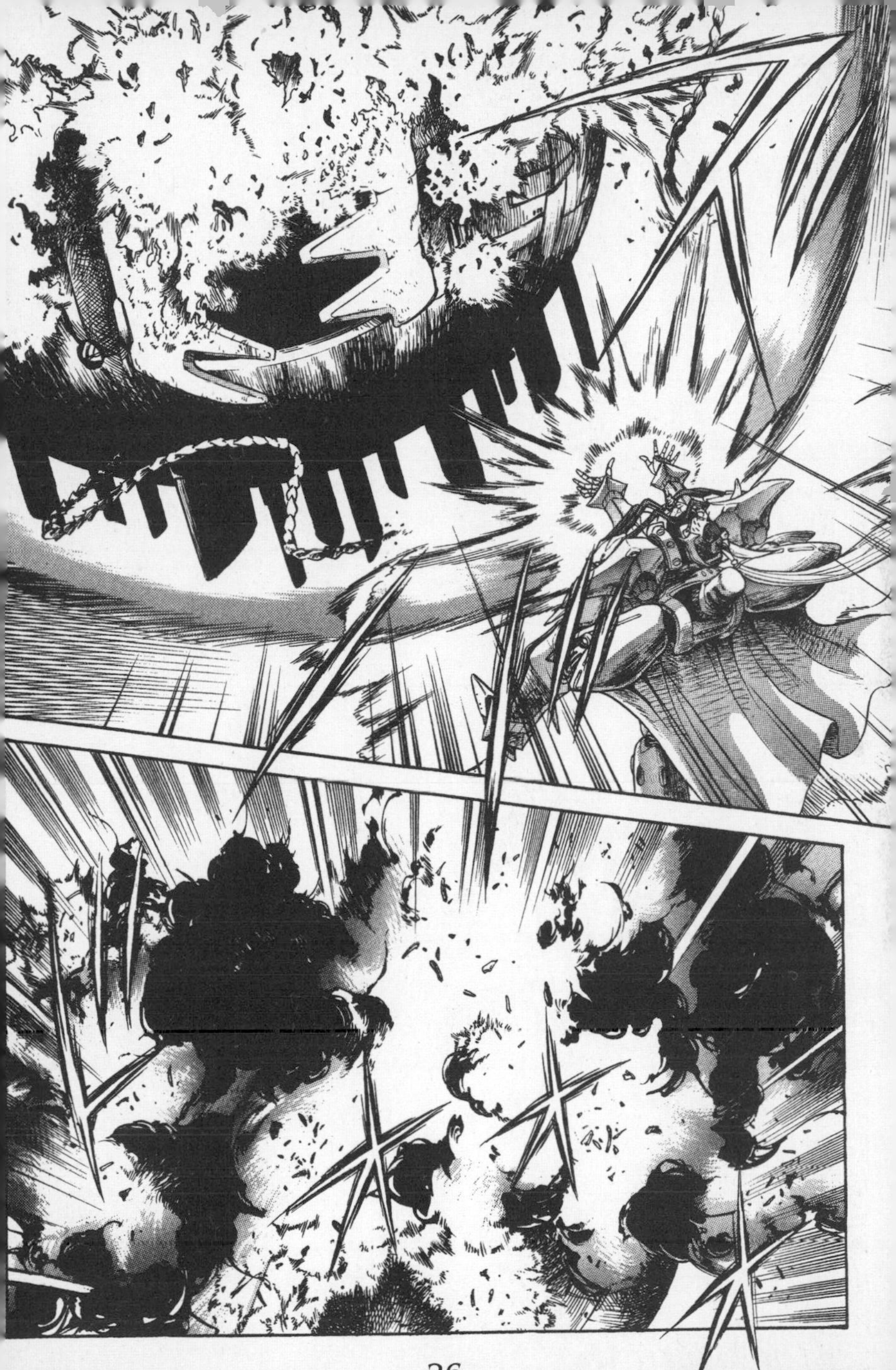

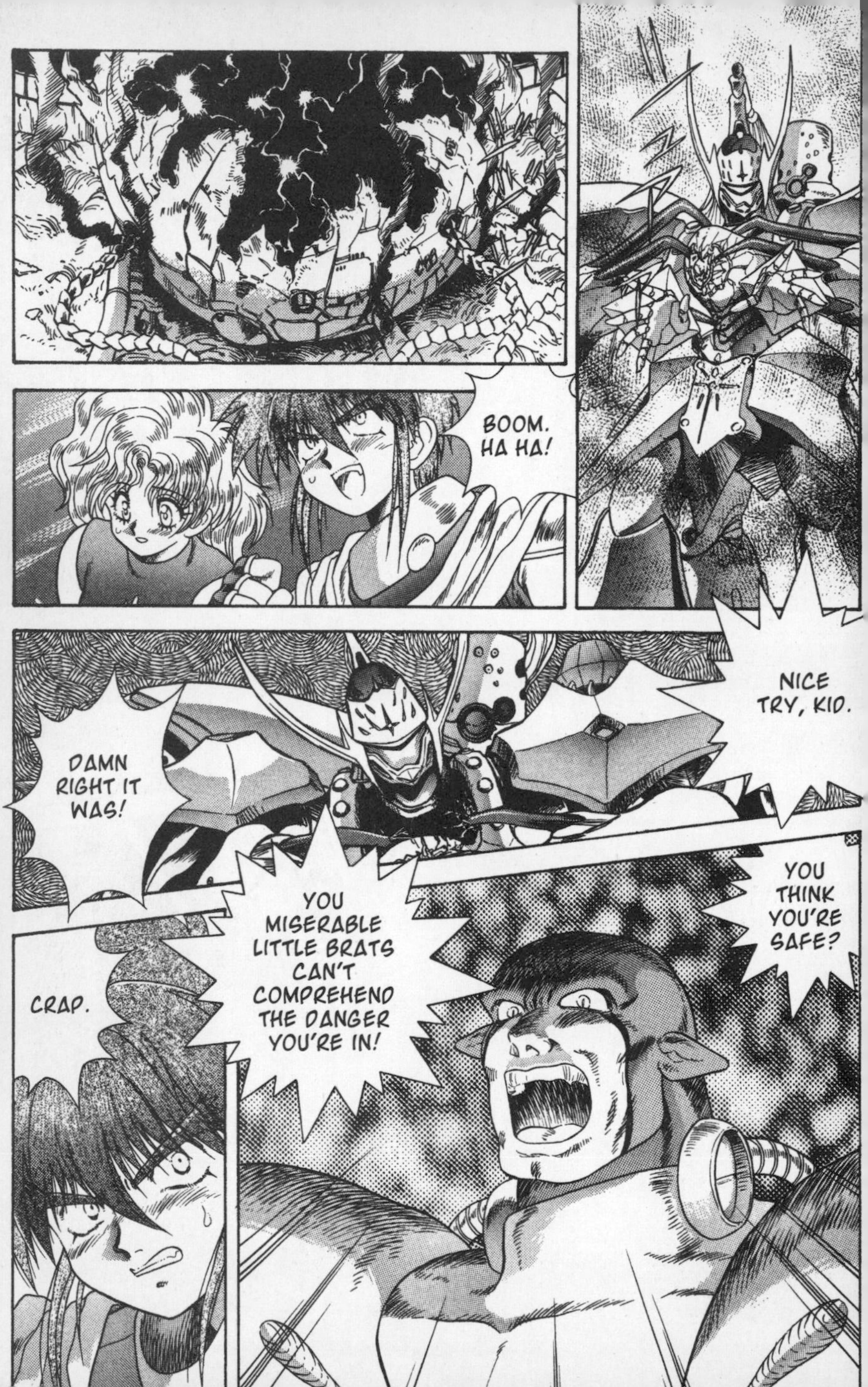
BOOM. HA HA!
NICE TRY, KID.
DAMN RIGHT IT WAS!
YOU THINK YOU'RE SAFE?
YOU MISERABLE LITTLE BRATS CAN'T COMPREHEND THE DANGER YOU'RE IN!
CRAP.

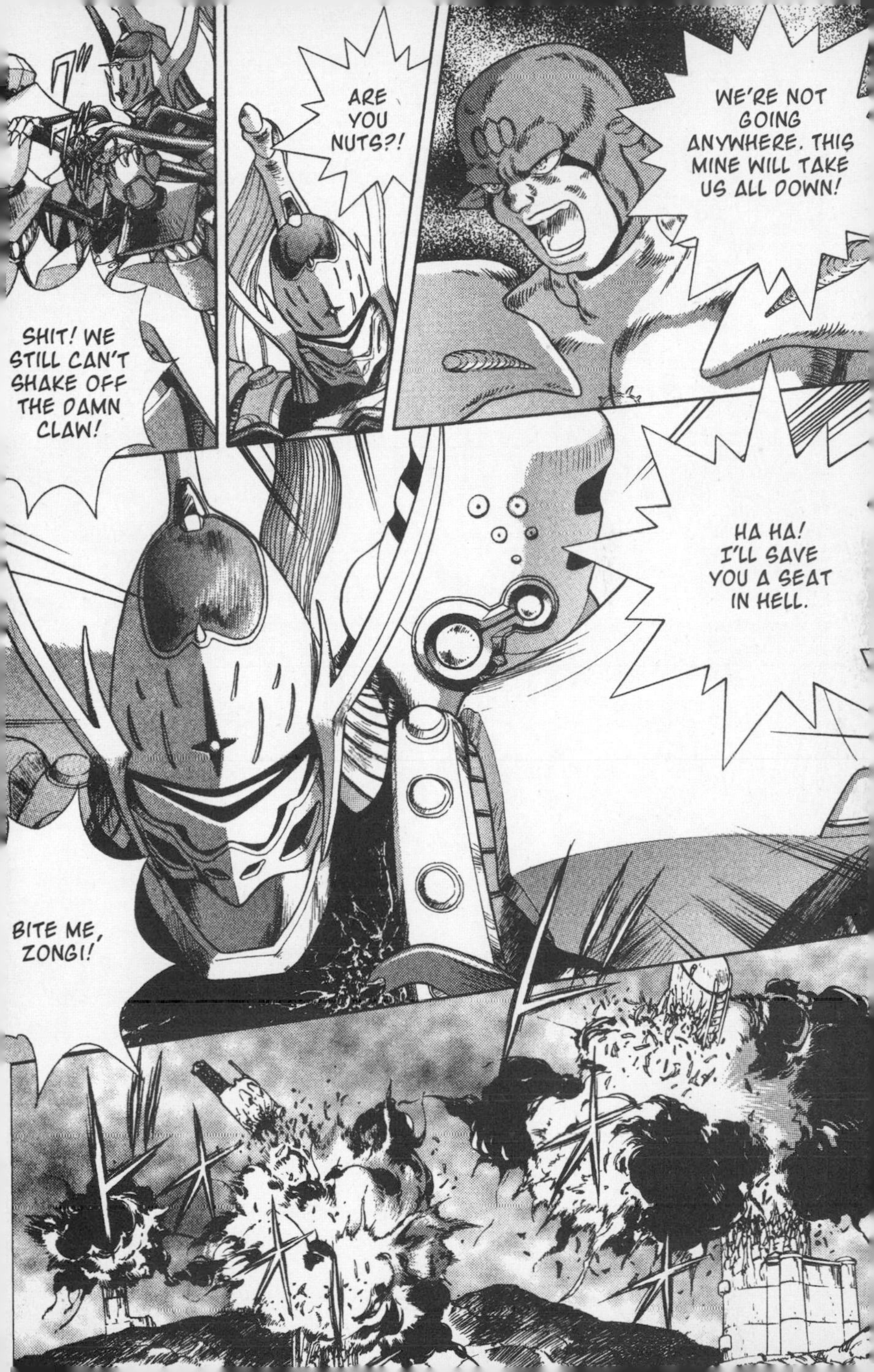
WE'RE NOT GOING ANYWHERE. THIS MINE WILL TAKE US ALL DOWN!
ARE YOU NUTS?!
SHIT! WE STILL CAN'T SHAKE OFF THE DAMN CLAW!
HA HA! I'LL SAVE YOU A SEAT IN HELL.
BITE ME, ZONGI!

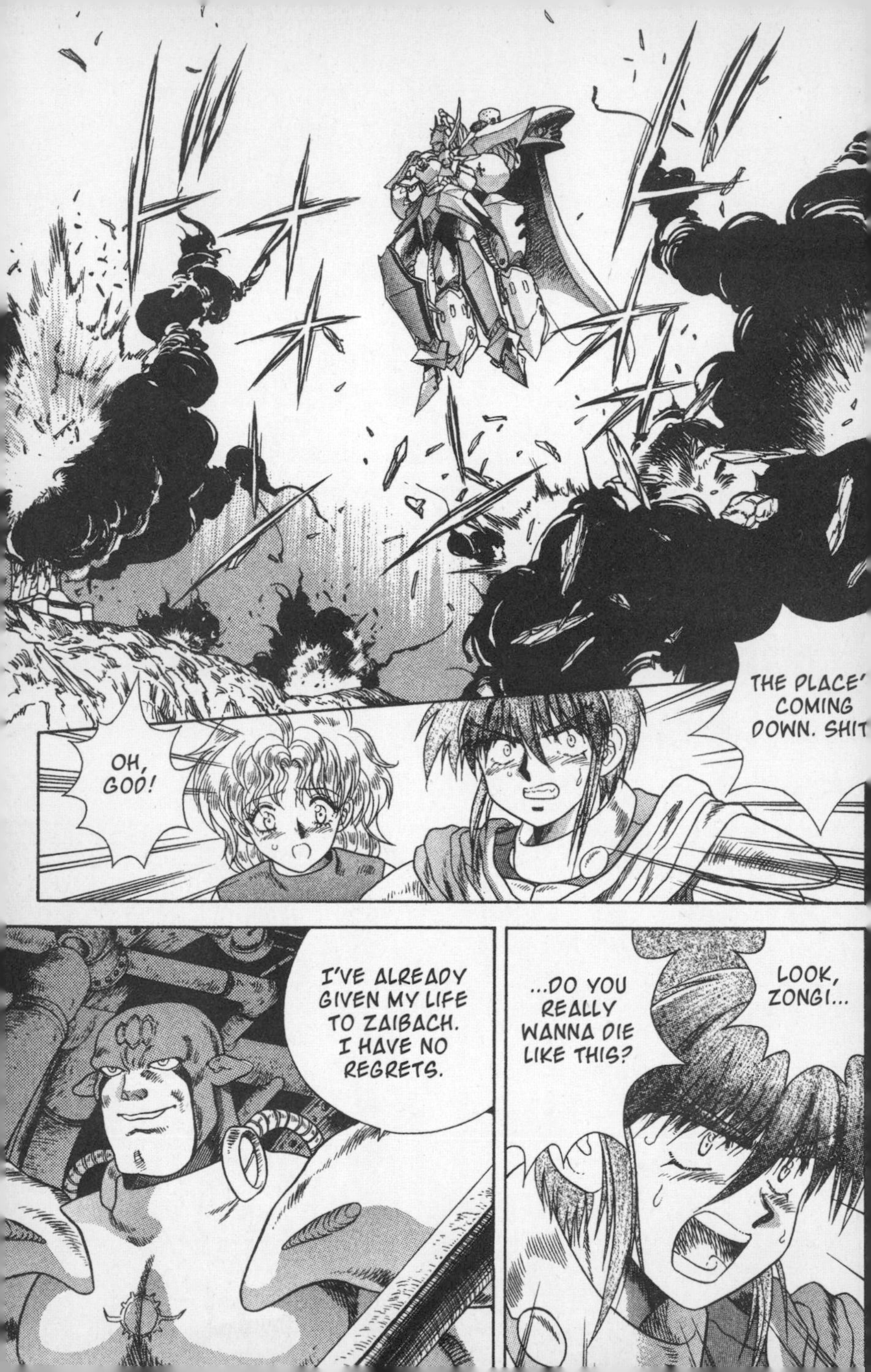
THE PLACE' COMING DOWN. SHIT
OH, GOD!
LOOK, ZONGI...
...DO YOU REALLY WANNA DIE LIKE THIS?
I'VE ALREADY GIVEN MY LIFE TO ZAIBACH. I HAVE NO REGRETS.

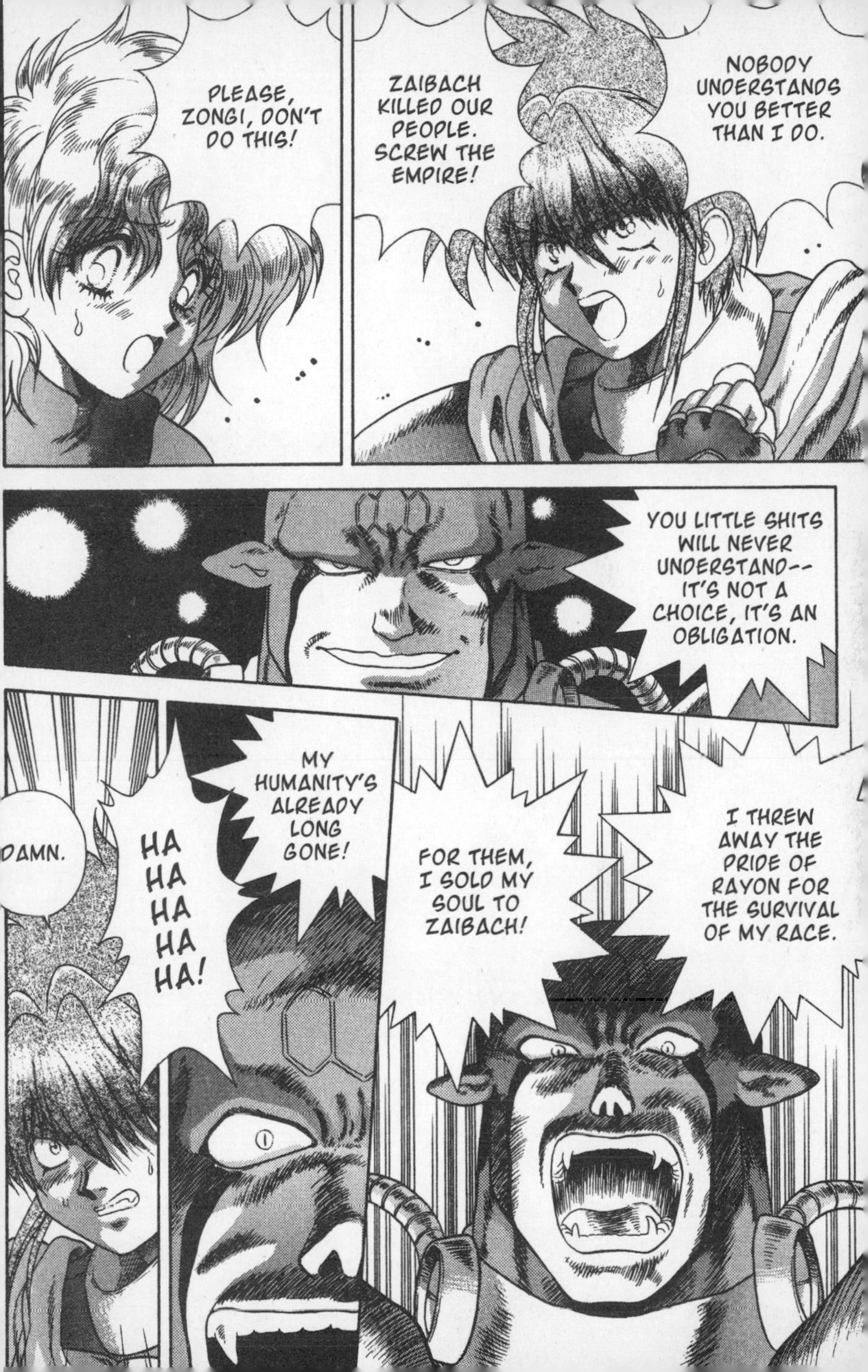
NOBODY UNDERSTANDS YOU BETTER THAN I DO.
ZAIBACH KILLED OUR PEOPLE. SCREW THE EMPIRE!
PLEASE, ZONGI, DON'T DO THIS!
YOU LITTLE SHITS WILL NEVER UNDERSTAND-- IT'S NOT A CHOICE, IT'S AN OBLIGATION.
I THREW AWAY THE PRIDE OF RAYON FOR THE SURVIVAL OF MY RACE.
FOR THEM, I SOLD MY SOUL TO ZAIBACH!
MY HUMANITY'S ALREADY LONG GONE!
HA HA HA HA HA!
DAMN.

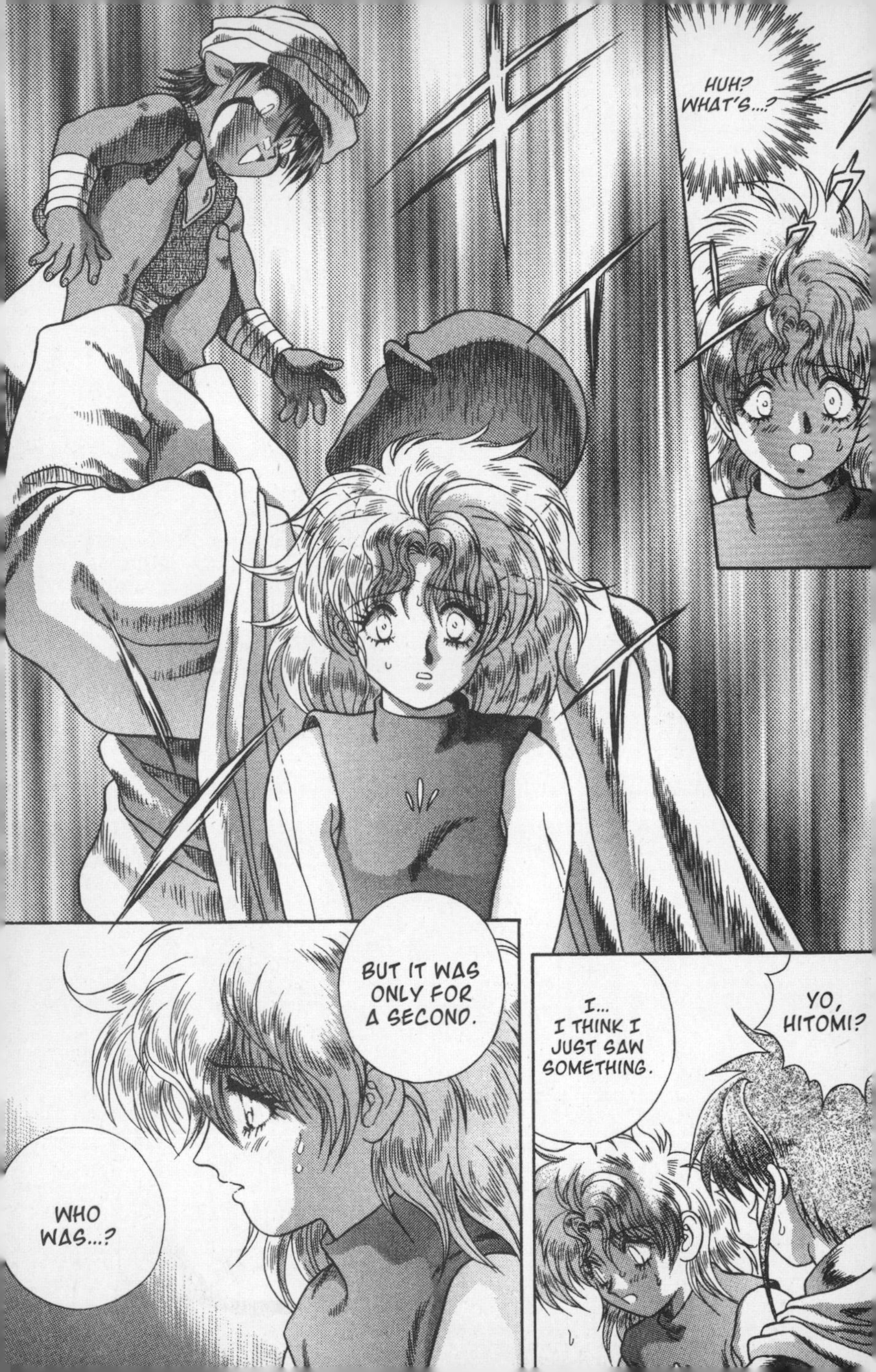
HUH? WHAT'S...?
YO, HITOMI?
I... I THINK I JUST SAW SOMETHING.
BUT IT WAS ONLY FOR A SECOND.
WHO WAS...?

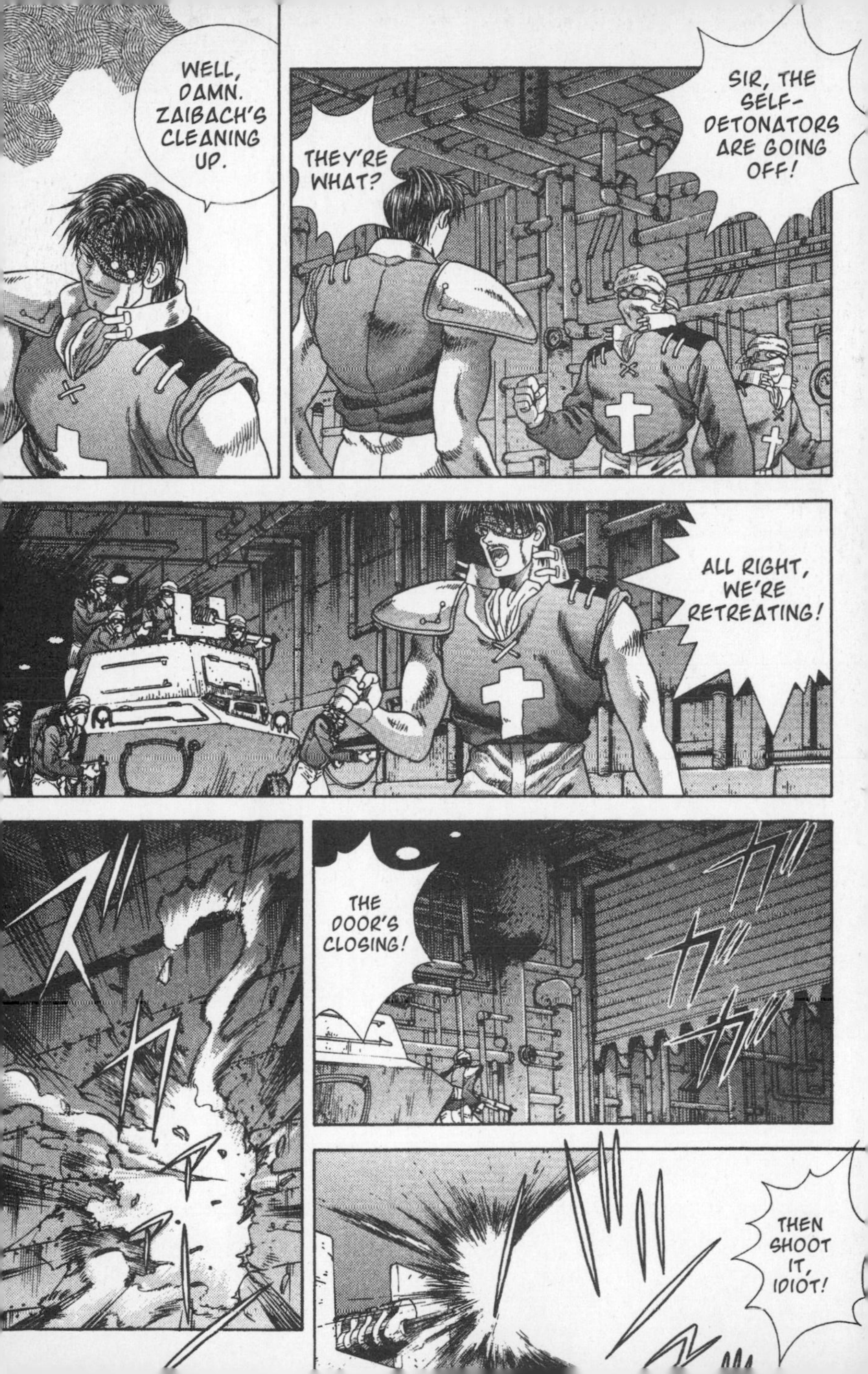
SIR, THE SELF-DETONATORS ARE GOING OFF!
THEY'RE WHAT?
WELL, DAMN. ZAIBACH'S CLEANING UP.
ALL RIGHT, WE'RE RETREATING!
THE DOOR'S CLOSING!
THEN SHOOT IT, IDIOT!

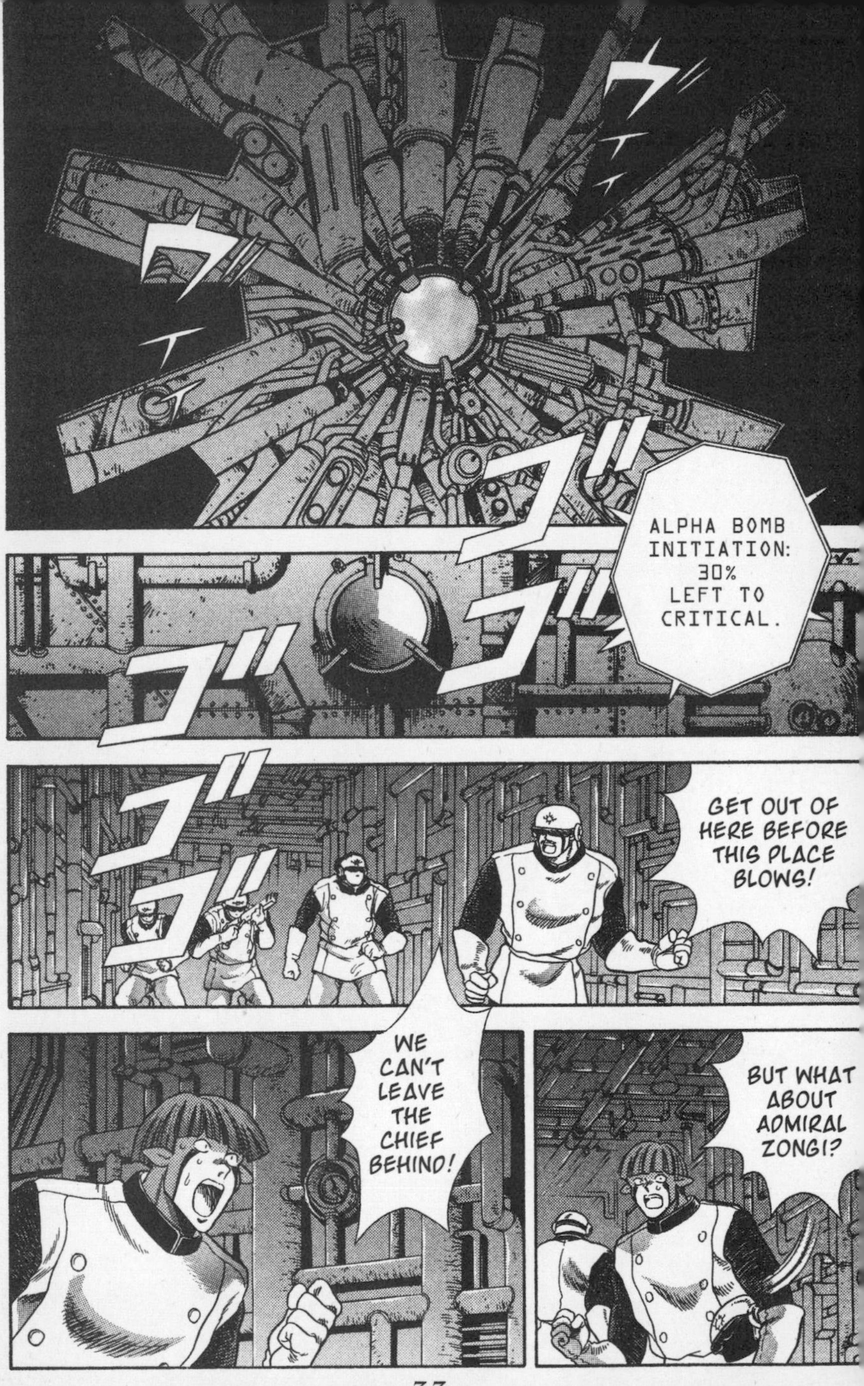
ALPHA BOMB INITIATION: 30% LEFT TO CRITICAL.
GET OUT OF HERE BEFORE THIS PLACE BLOWS!
BUT WHAT ABOUT ADMIRAL ZONGI?
WE CAN'T LEAVE THE CHIEF BEHIND!

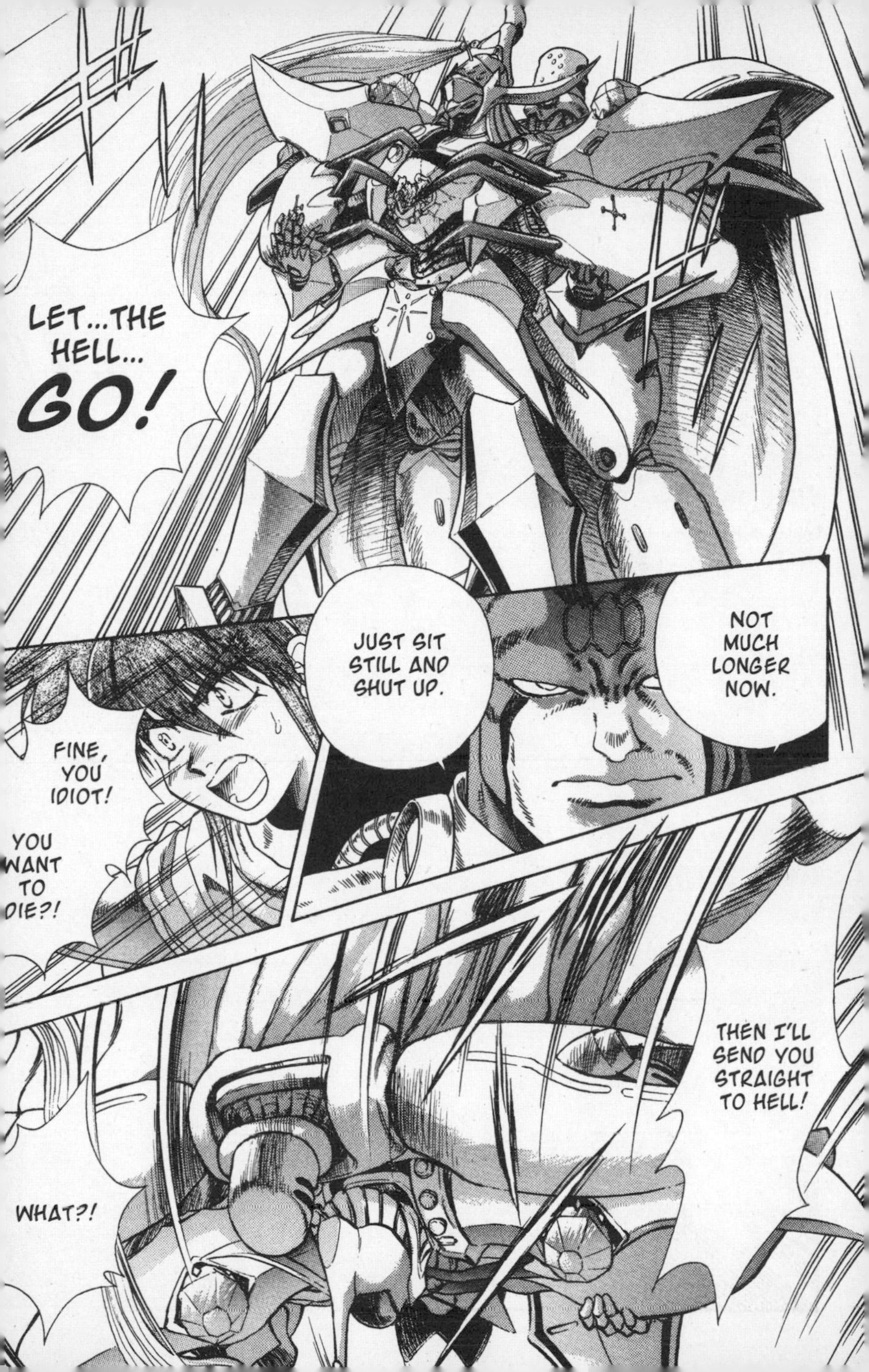
LET...THE HELL... GO!
NOT MUCH LONGER NOW.
JUST SIT STILL AND SHUT UP.
FINE, YOU IDIOT!
YOU WANT TO DIE?!
THEN I'LL SEND YOU STRAIGHT TO HELL!
WHAT?!

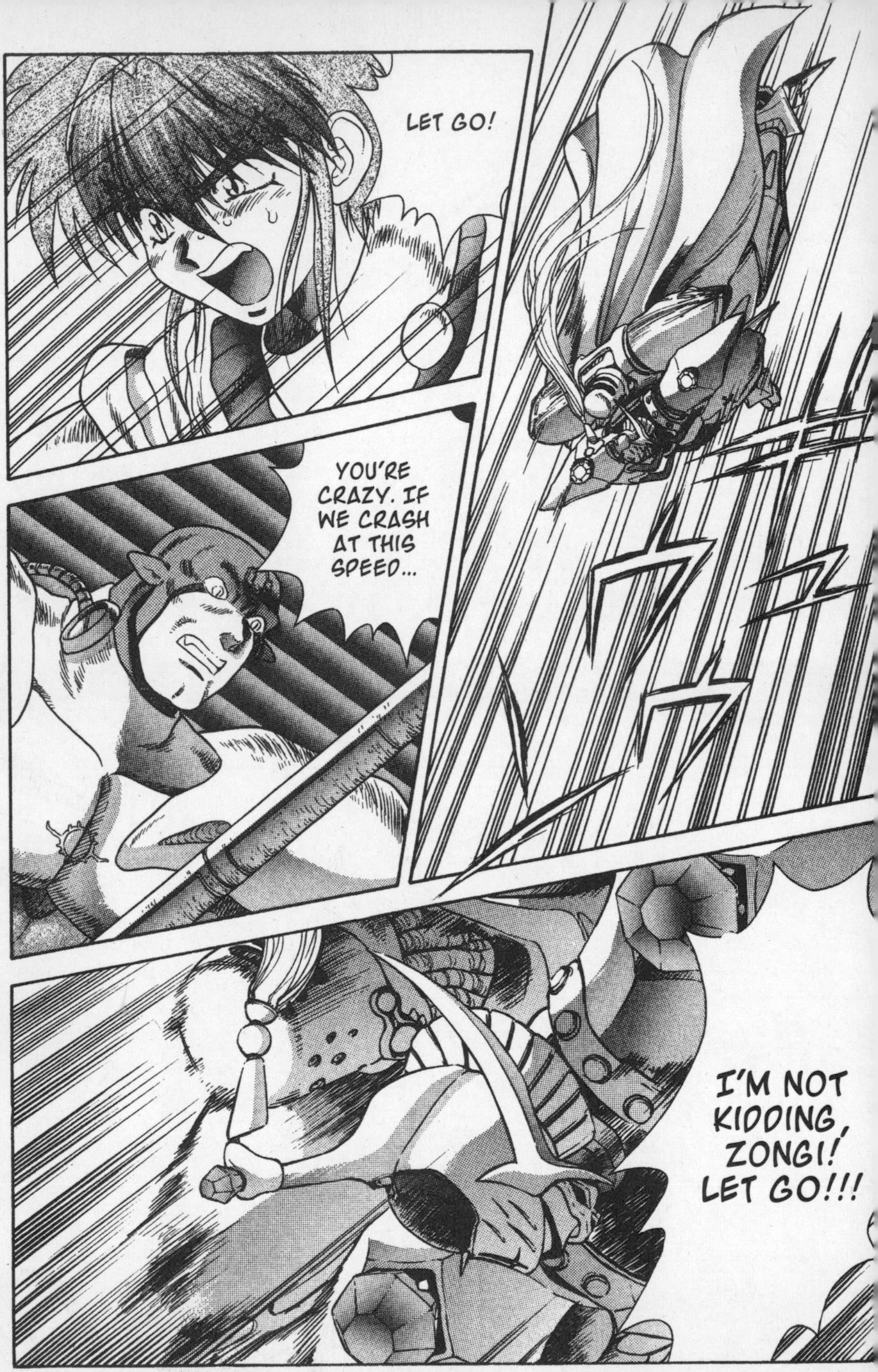
LET GO!
YOU'RE CRAZY. IF WE CRASH AT THIS SPEED...
I'M NOT KIDDING, ZONGI! LET GO!!!

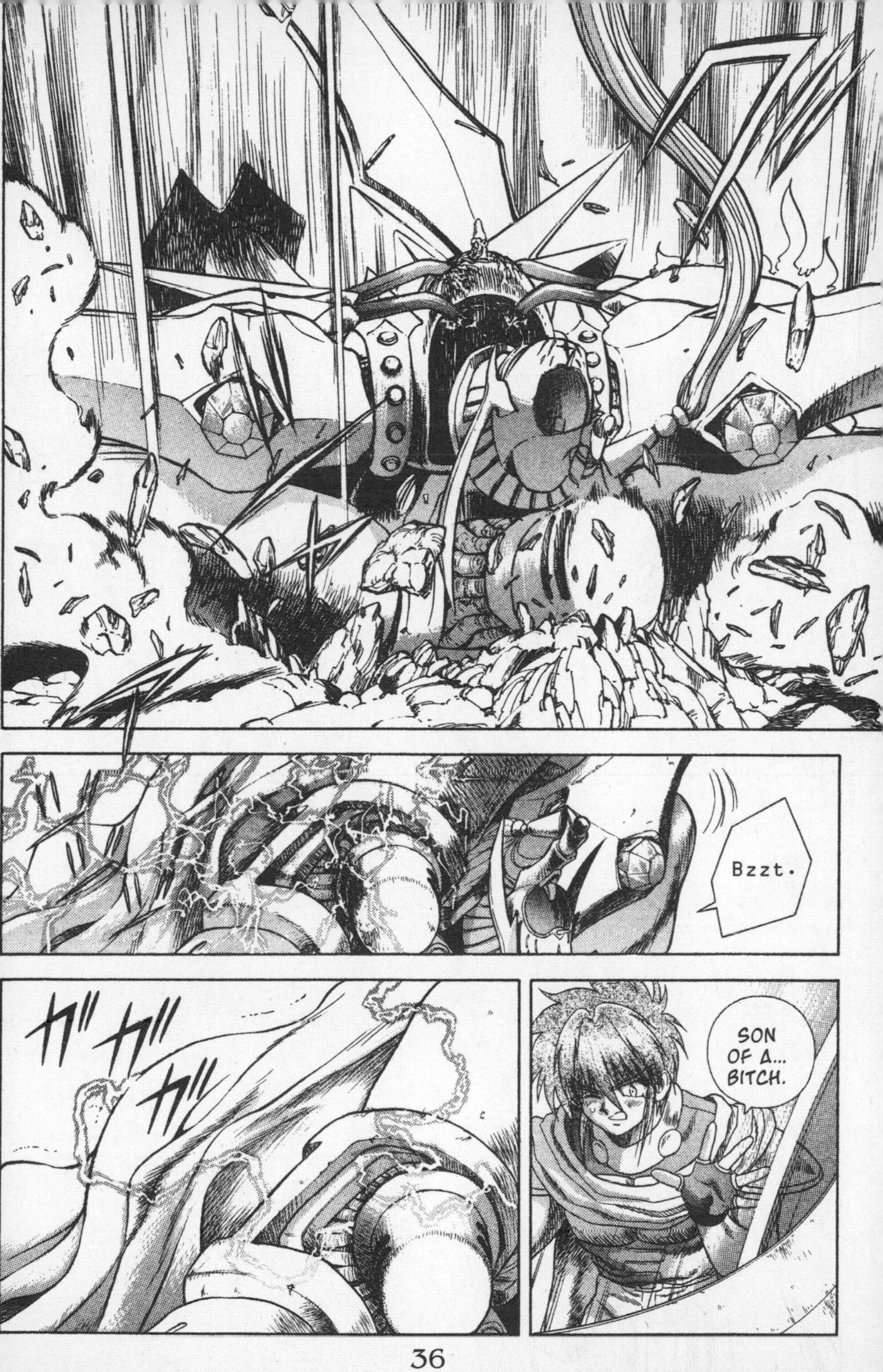
Bzzt.
SON OF A... BITCH.
ガ ガ ガ

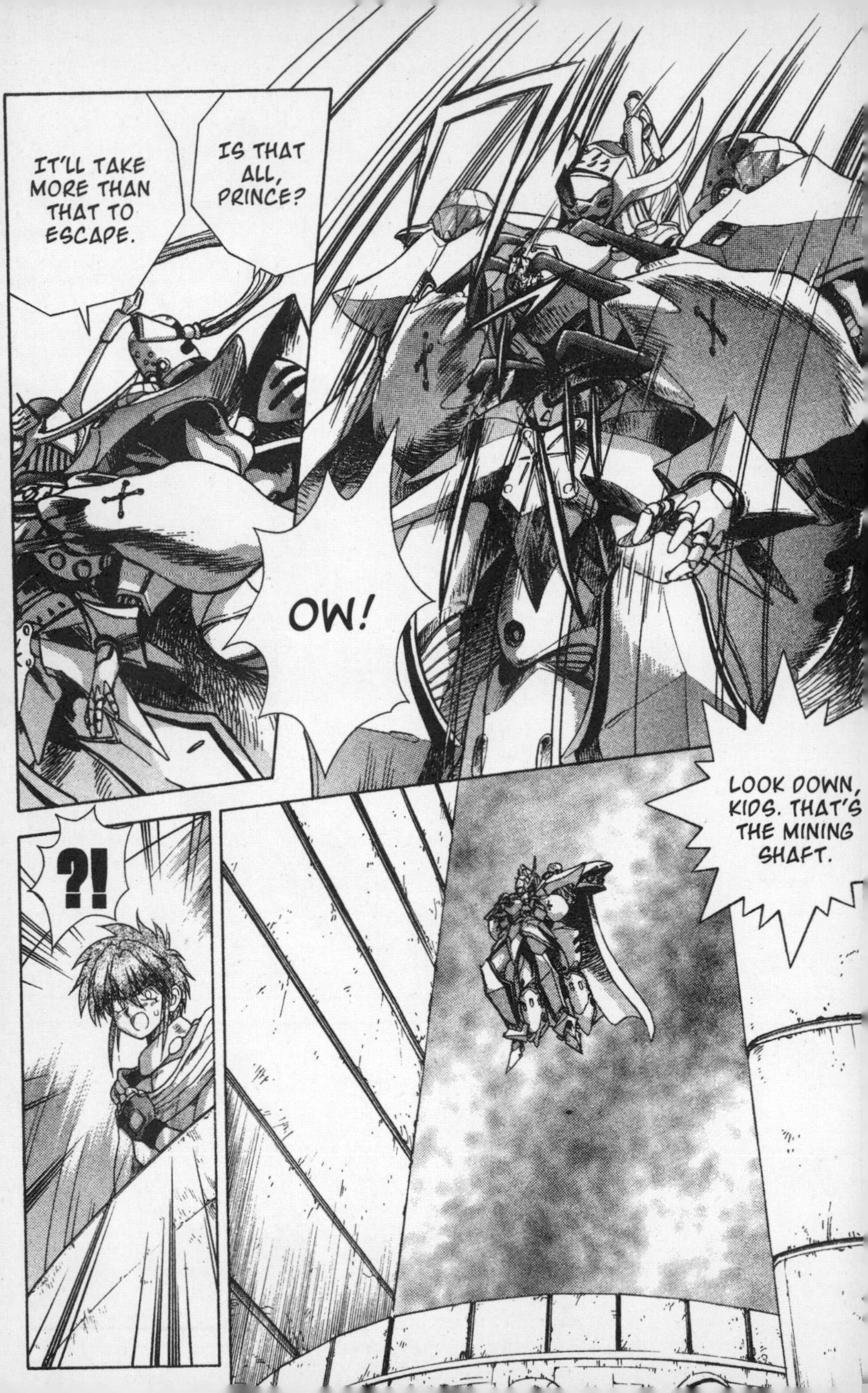
OW!
IS THAT ALL, PRINCE?
IT'LL TAKE MORE THAN THAT TO ESCAPE.
LOOK DOWN, KIDS. THAT'S THE MINING SHAFT.
?!

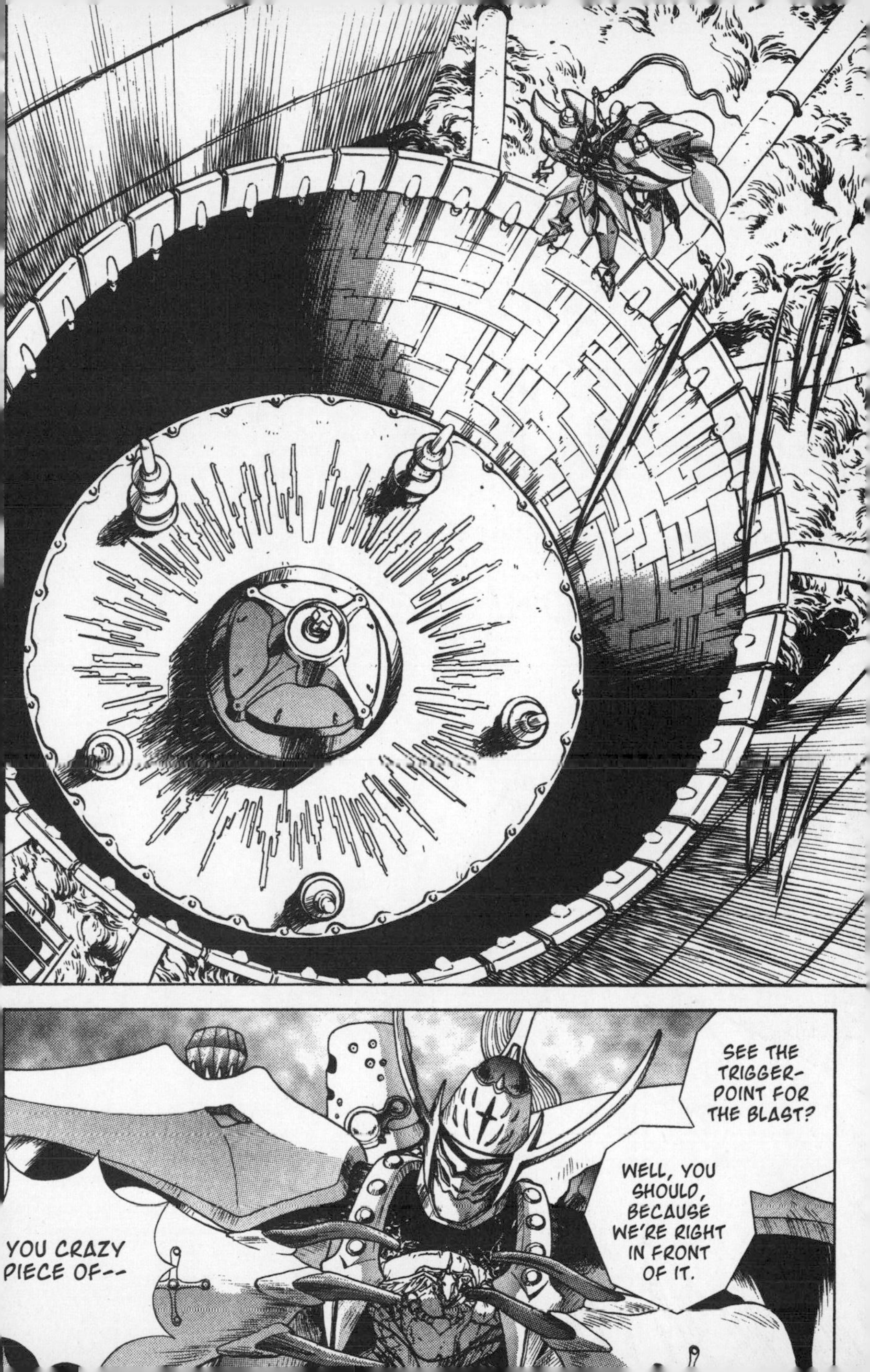
SEE THE TRIGGER-POINT FOR THE BLAST?
WELL, YOU SHOULD, BECAUSE WE'RE RIGHT IN FRONT OF IT.
YOU CRAZY PIECE OF--

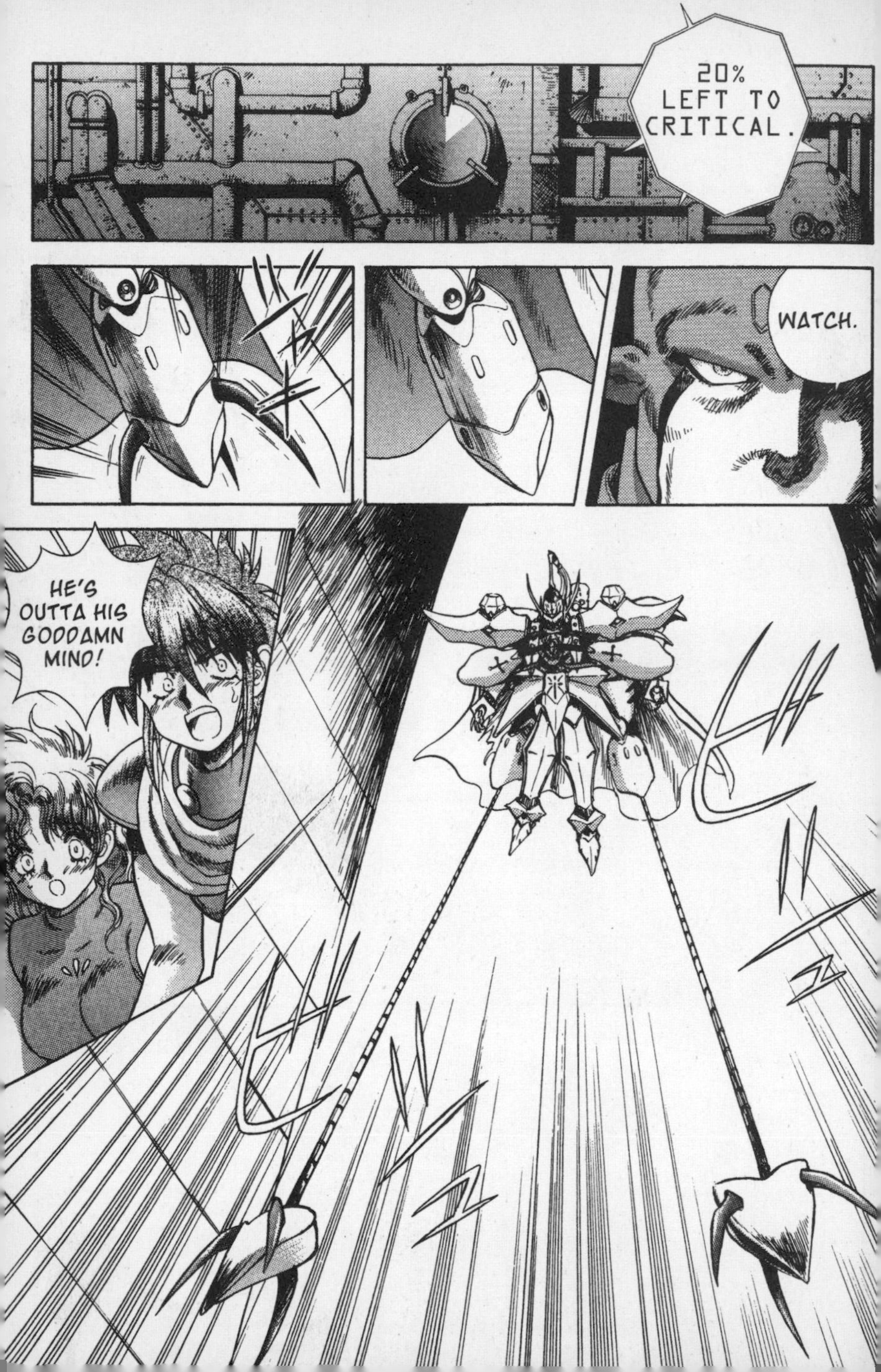
20% LEFT TO CRITICAL.
WATCH.
HE'S OUTTA HIS GODDAMN MIND!

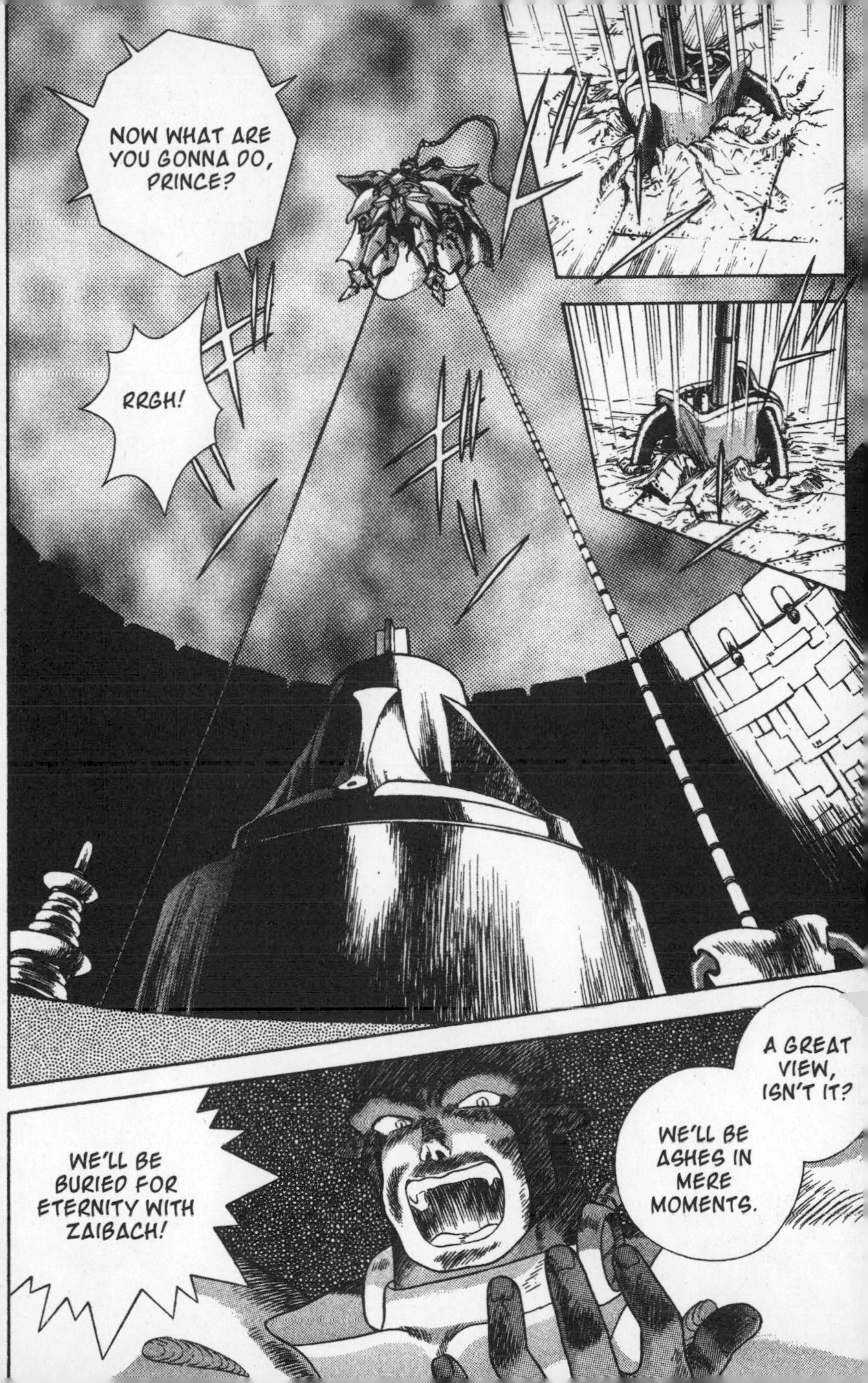
NOW WHAT ARE YOU GONNA DO, PRINCE?
RRGH!
A GREAT VIEW, ISN'T IT?
WE'LL BE ASHES IN MERE MOMENTS.
WE'LL BE BURIED FOR ETERNITY WITH ZAIBACH!

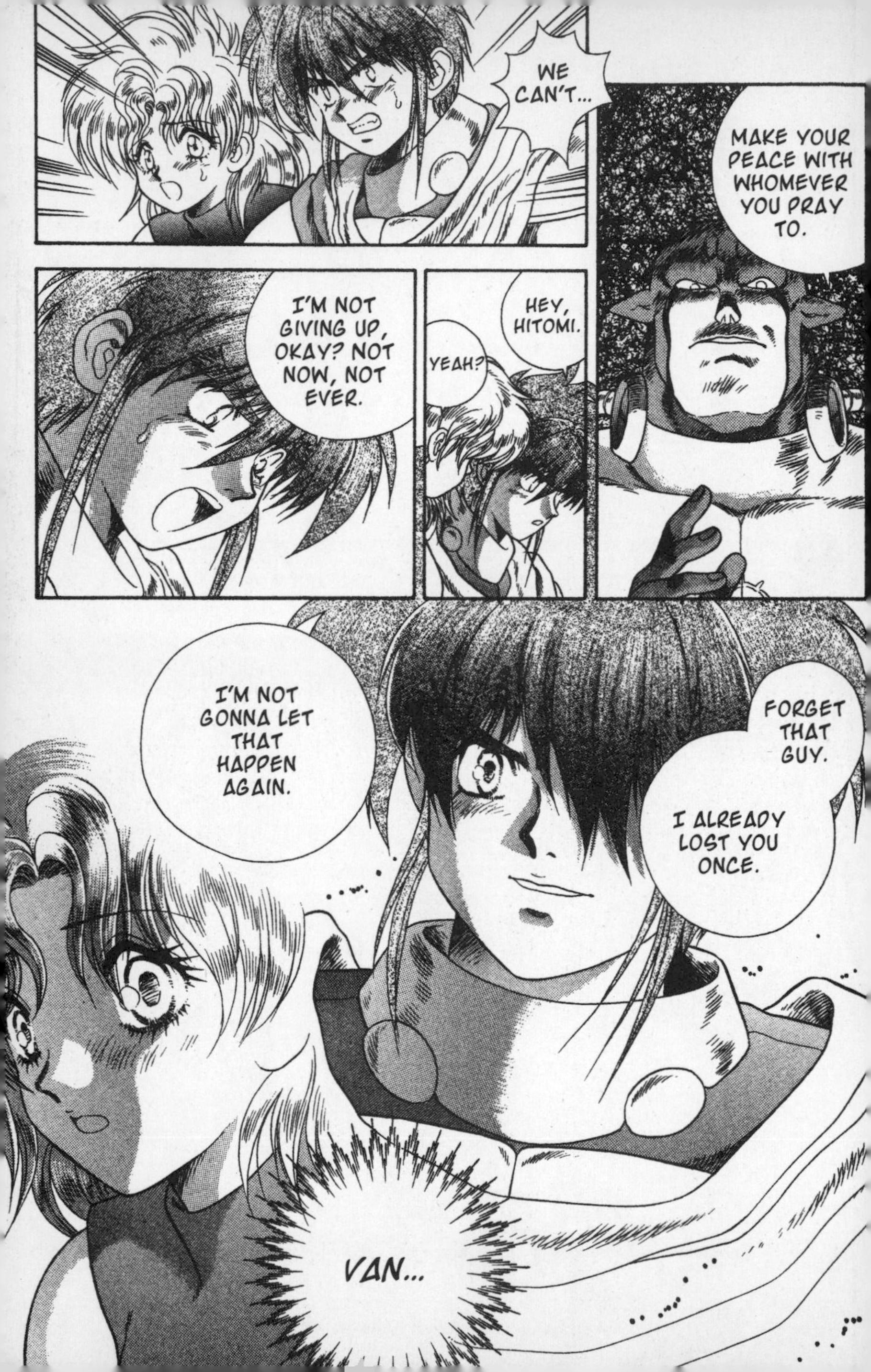
MAKE YOUR PEACE WITH WHOMEVER YOU PRAY TO.
WE CAN'T...
HEY, HITOMI.
YEAH?
I'M NOT GIVING UP, OKAY? NOT NOW, NOT EVER.
FORGET THAT GUY.
I ALREADY LOST YOU ONCE.
I'M NOT GONNA LET THAT HAPPEN AGAIN.
...
VAN...

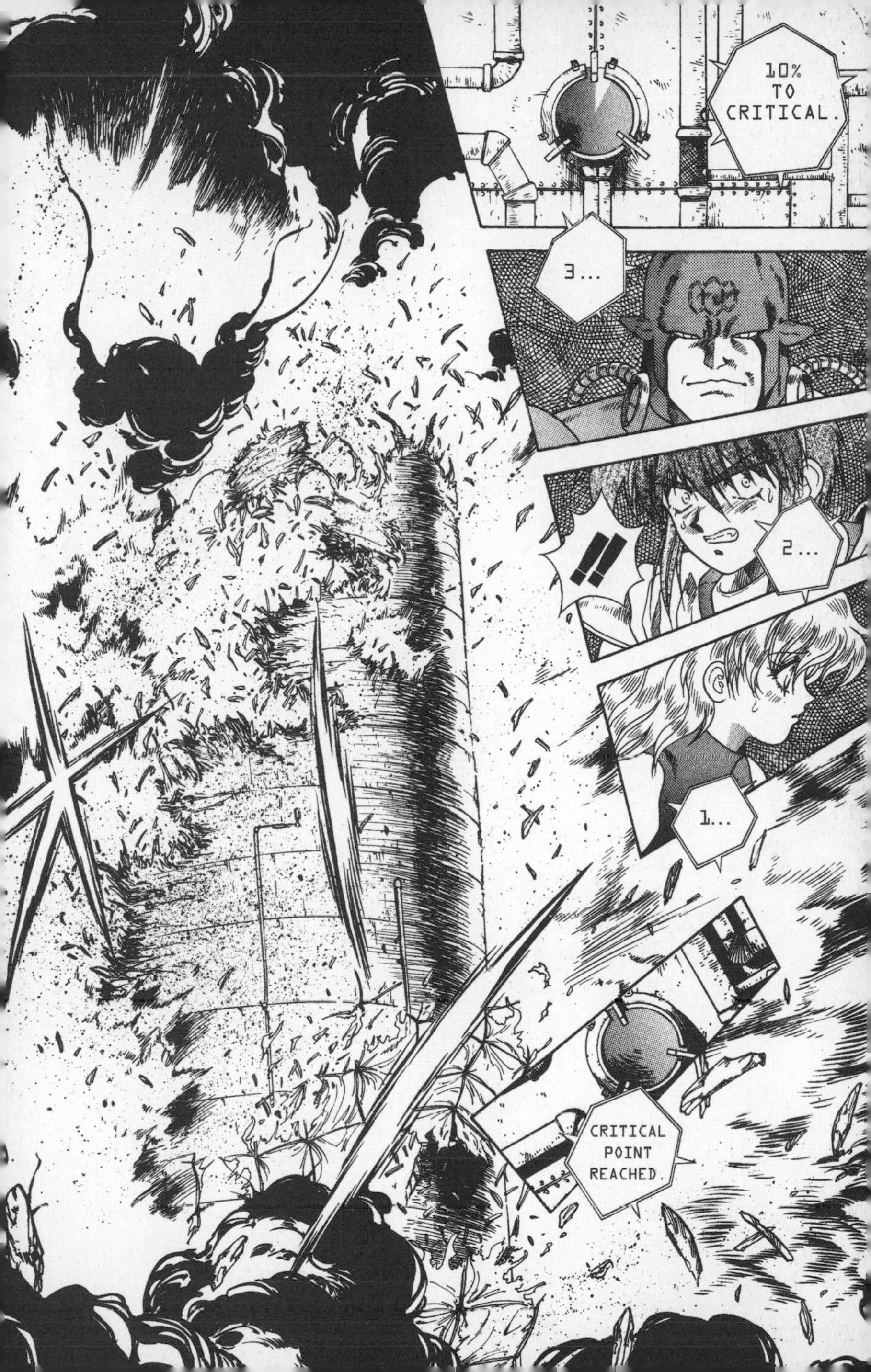
10% TO CRITICAL.
3...
2...
!!
1...
CRITICAL POINT REACHED.

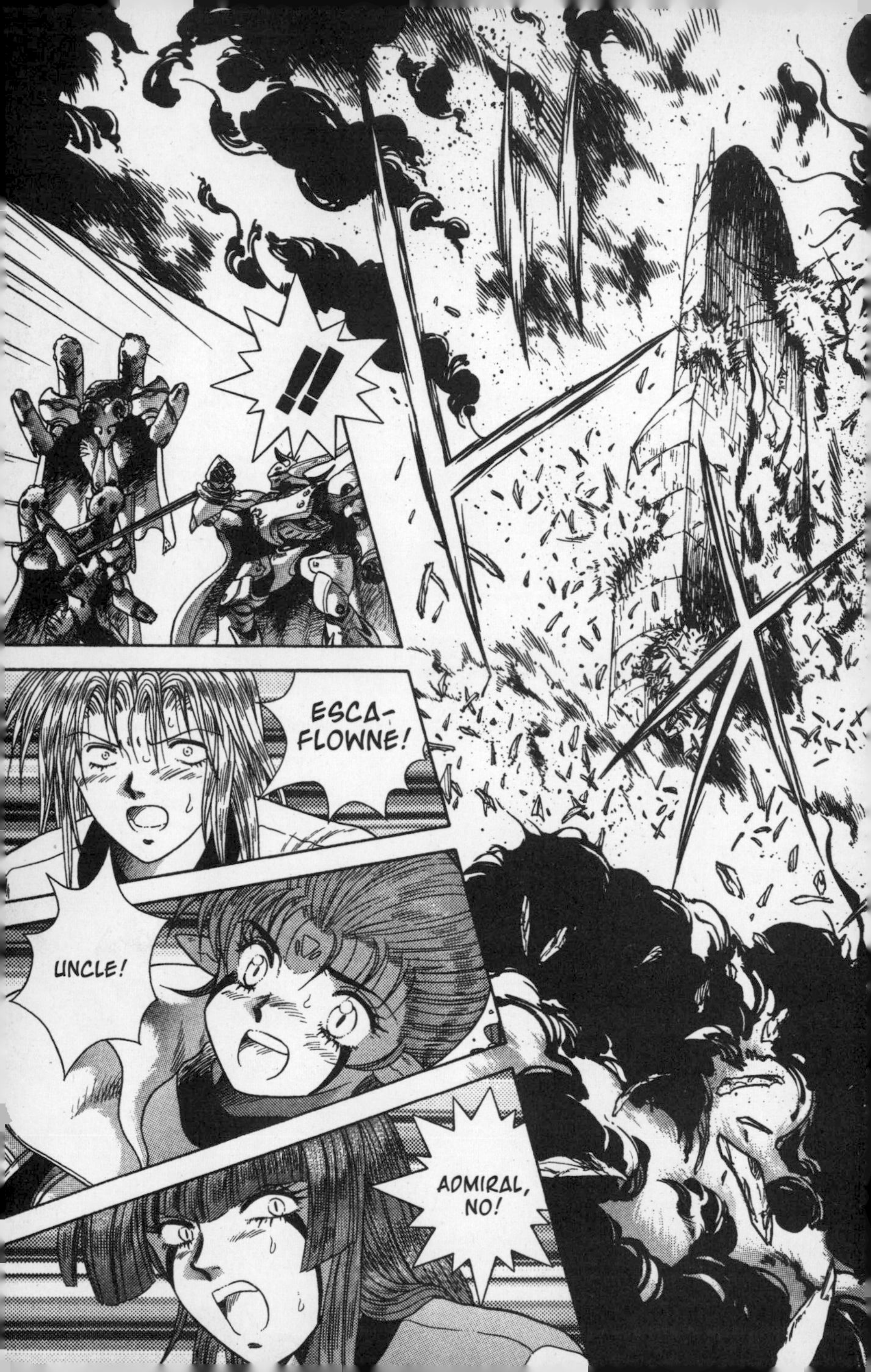
!!
ESCA-
FLOWNE!
UNCLE!
ADMIRAL,
NO!

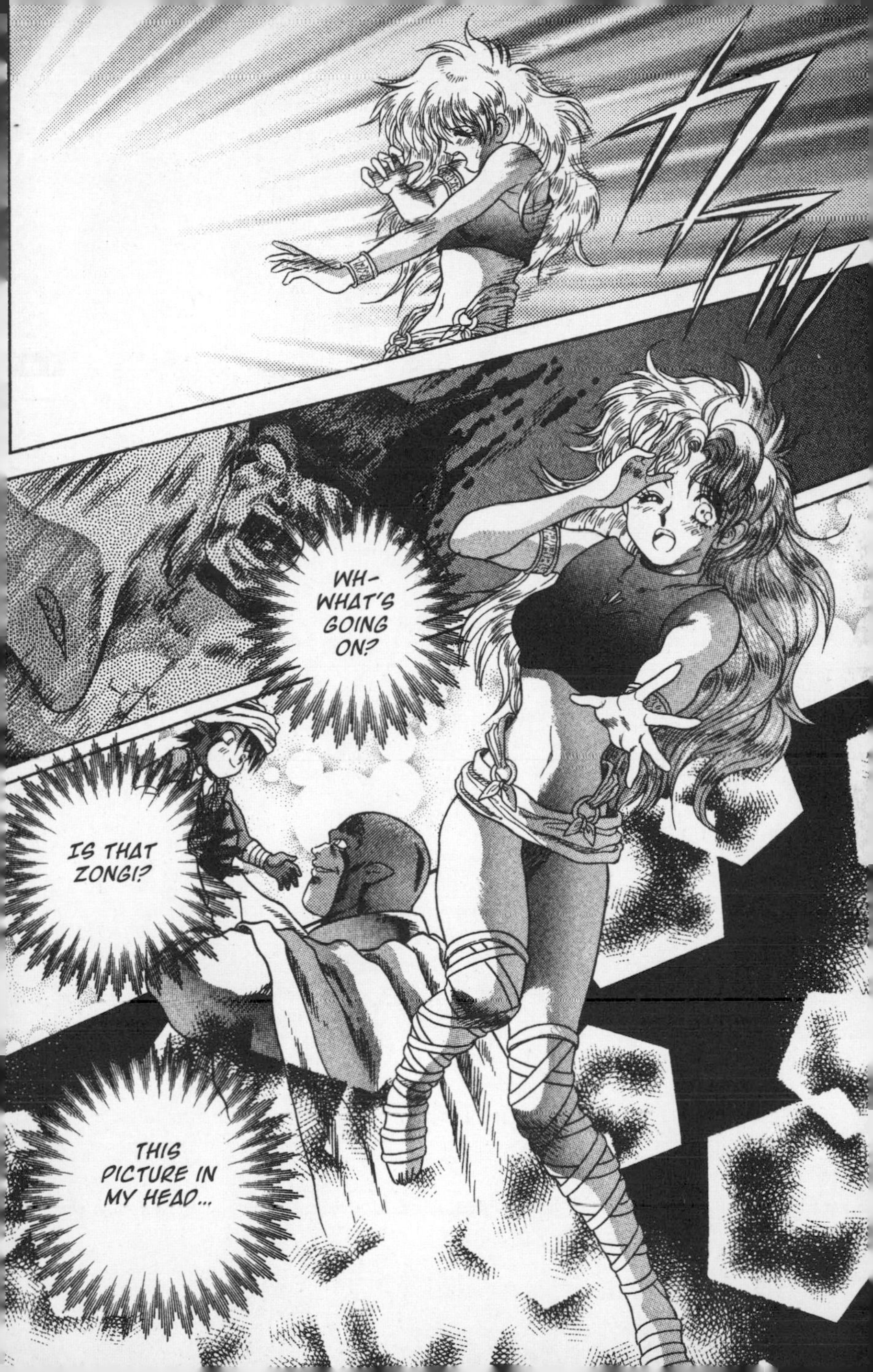
WH-WHAT'S GOING ON?
IS THAT ZONGI?
THIS PICTURE IN MY HEAD...

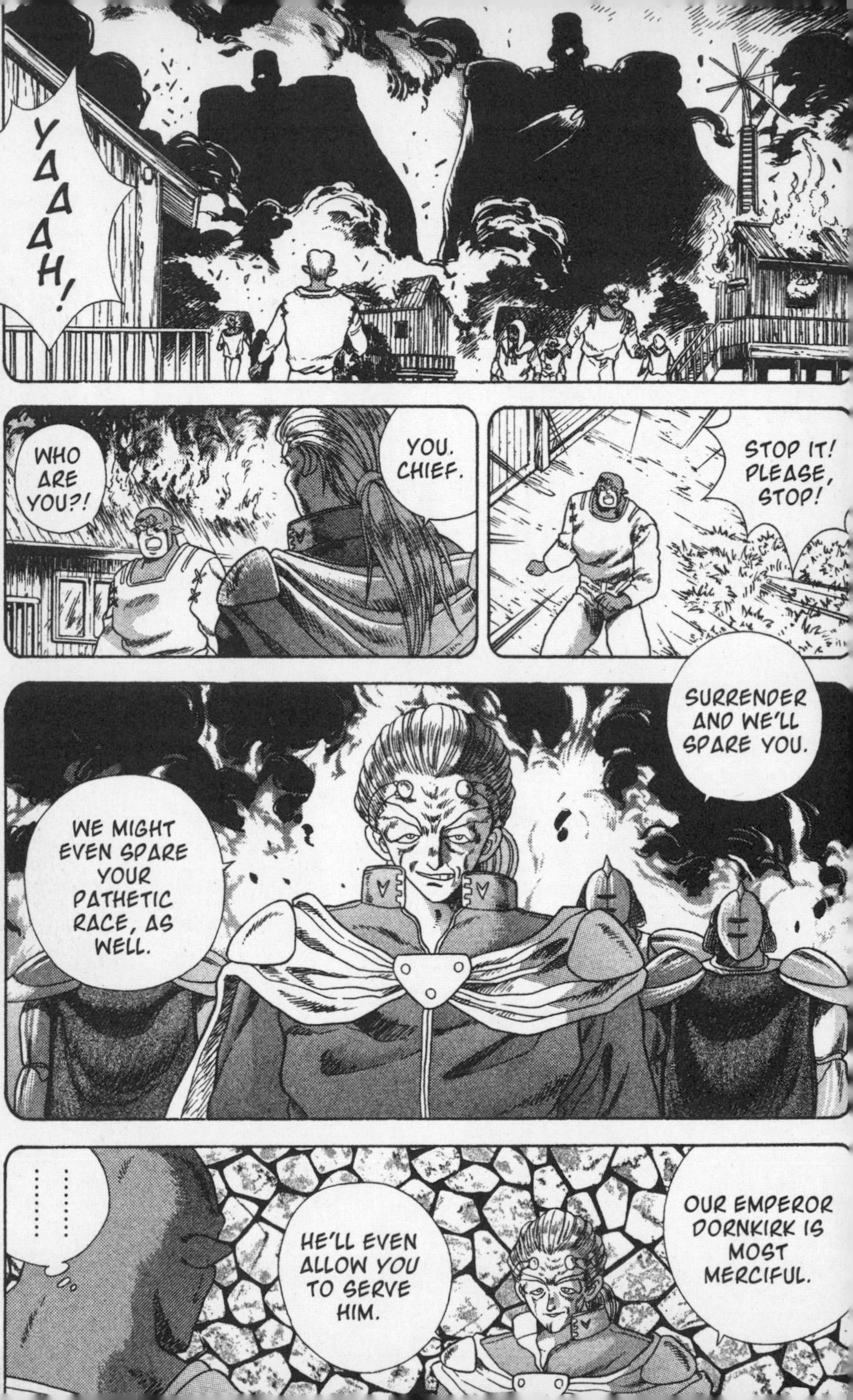
YAAAH!
STOP IT! PLEASE, STOP!
YOU. CHIEF.
WHO ARE YOU?!
SURRENDER AND WE'LL SPARE YOU.
WE MIGHT EVEN SPARE YOUR PATHETIC RACE, AS WELL.
OUR EMPEROR DORNKIRK IS MOST MERCIFUL.
HE'LL EVEN ALLOW YOU TO SERVE HIM.
......

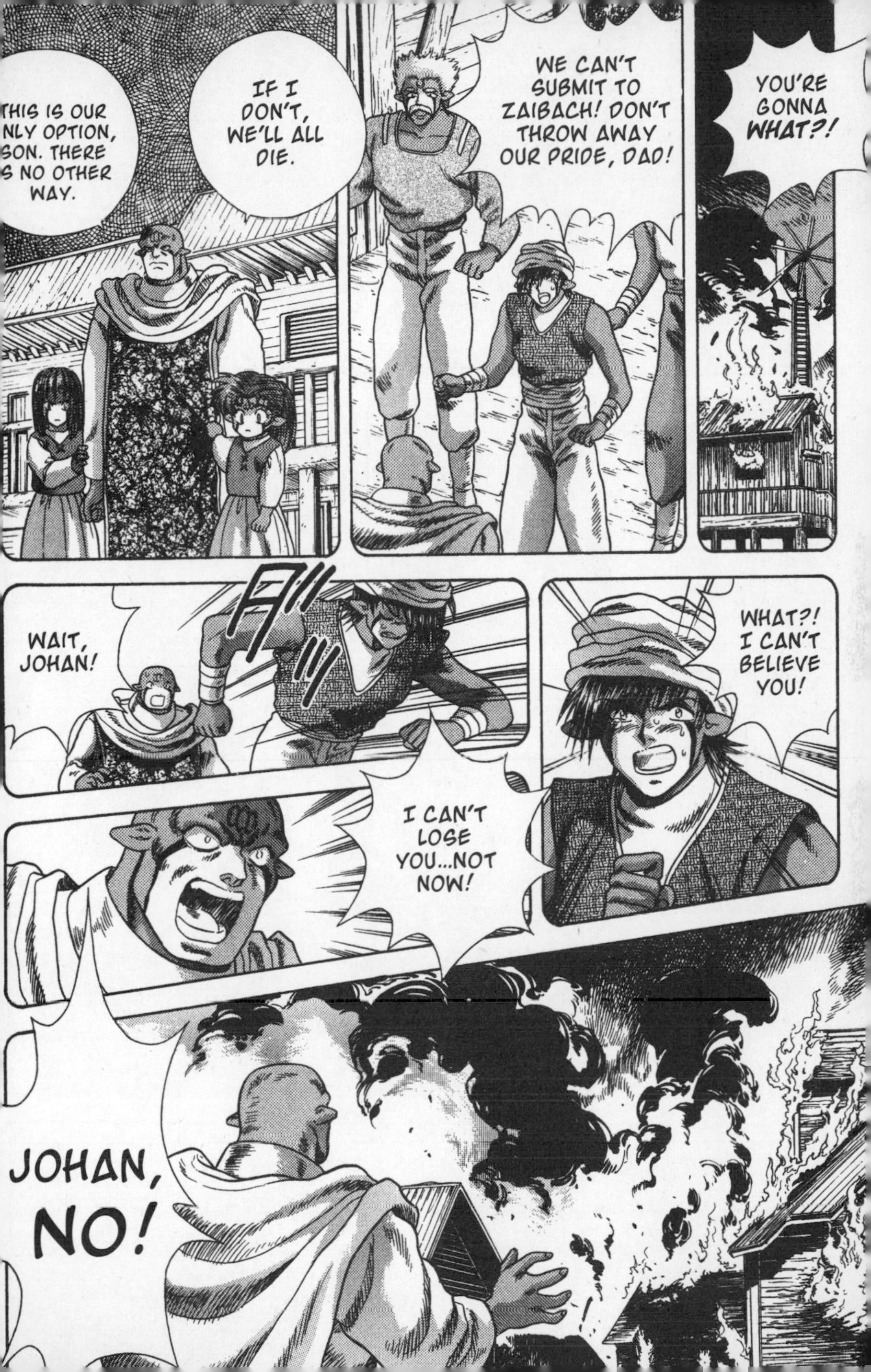
YOU'RE GONNA WHAT?!
WE CAN'T SUBMIT TO ZAIBACH! DON'T THROW AWAY OUR PRIDE, DAD!
IF I DON'T, WE'LL ALL DIE.
THIS IS OUR NLY OPTION, SON. THERE S NO OTHER WAY.
WHAT?! I CAN'T BELIEVE YOU!
WAIT, JOHAN!
I CAN'T LOSE YOU...NOT NOW!
JOHAN, NO!

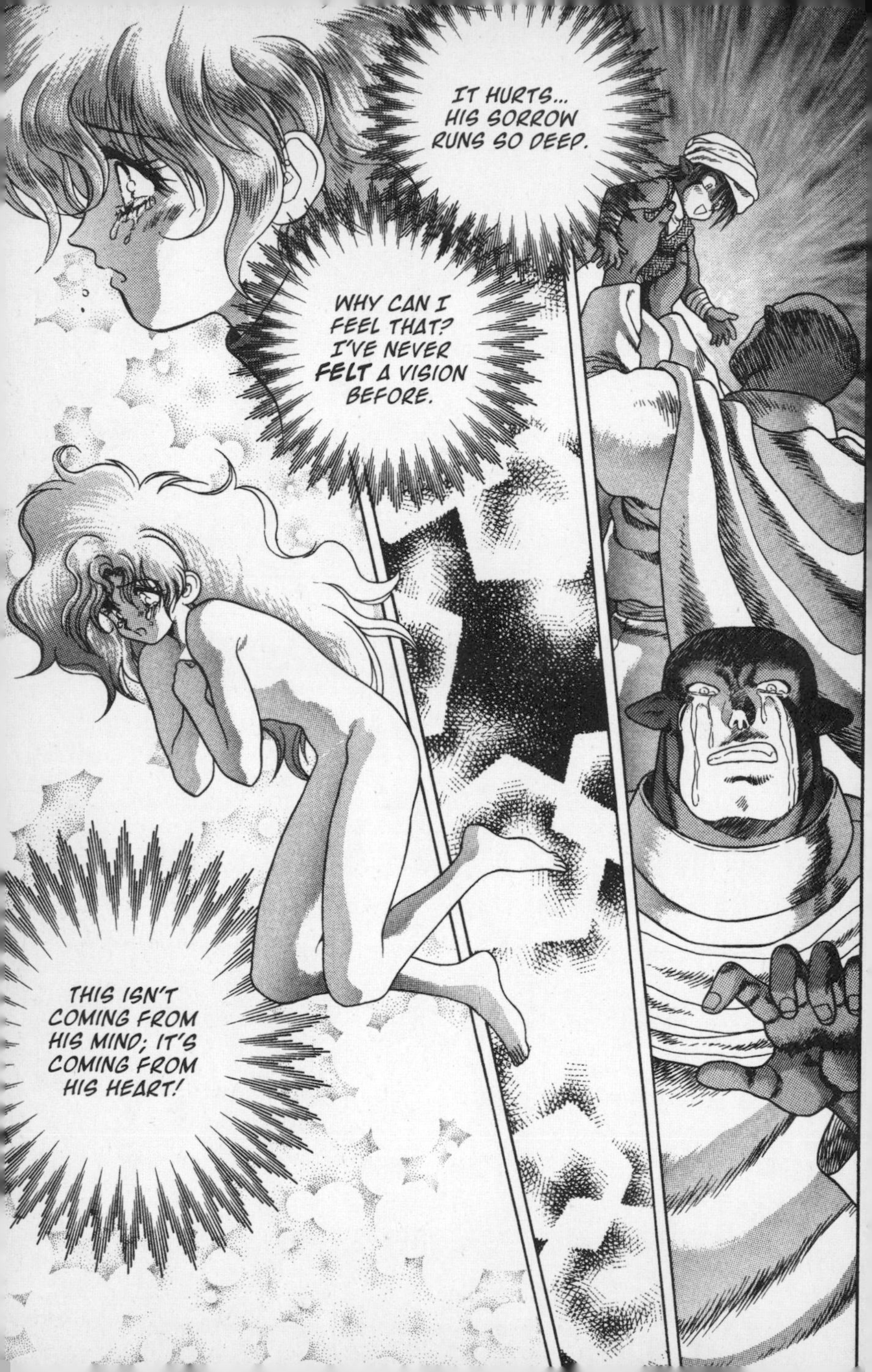
IT HURTS... HIS SORROW RUNS SO DEEP.
WHY CAN I FEEL THAT? I'VE NEVER **FELT** A VISION BEFORE.
THIS ISN'T COMING FROM HIS MIND; IT'S COMING FROM HIS HEART!

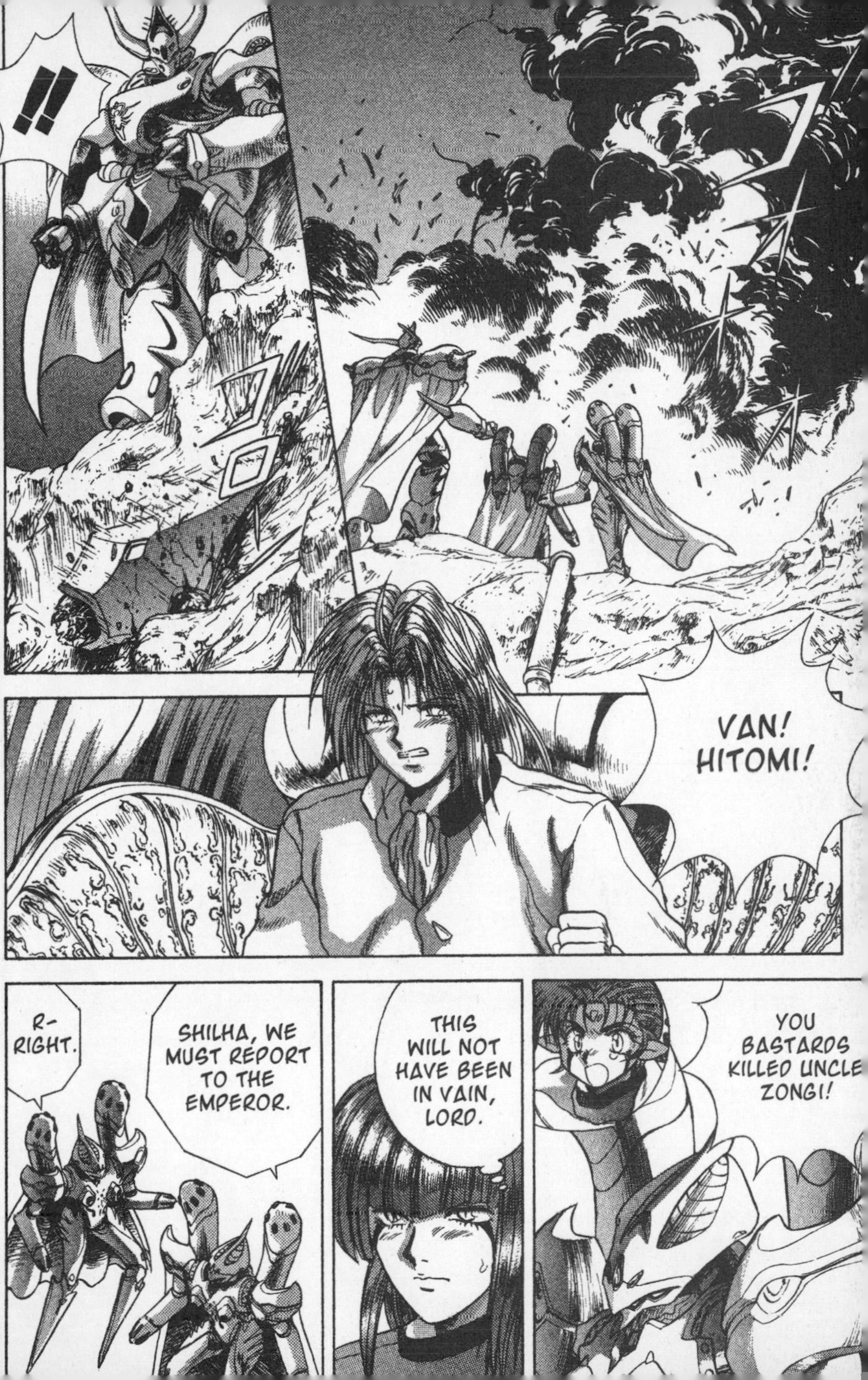
!!
VAN! HITOMI!
YOU BASTARDS KILLED UNCLE ZONGI!
THIS WILL NOT HAVE BEEN IN VAIN, LORD.
SHILHA, WE MUST REPORT TO THE EMPEROR.
R- RIGHT.

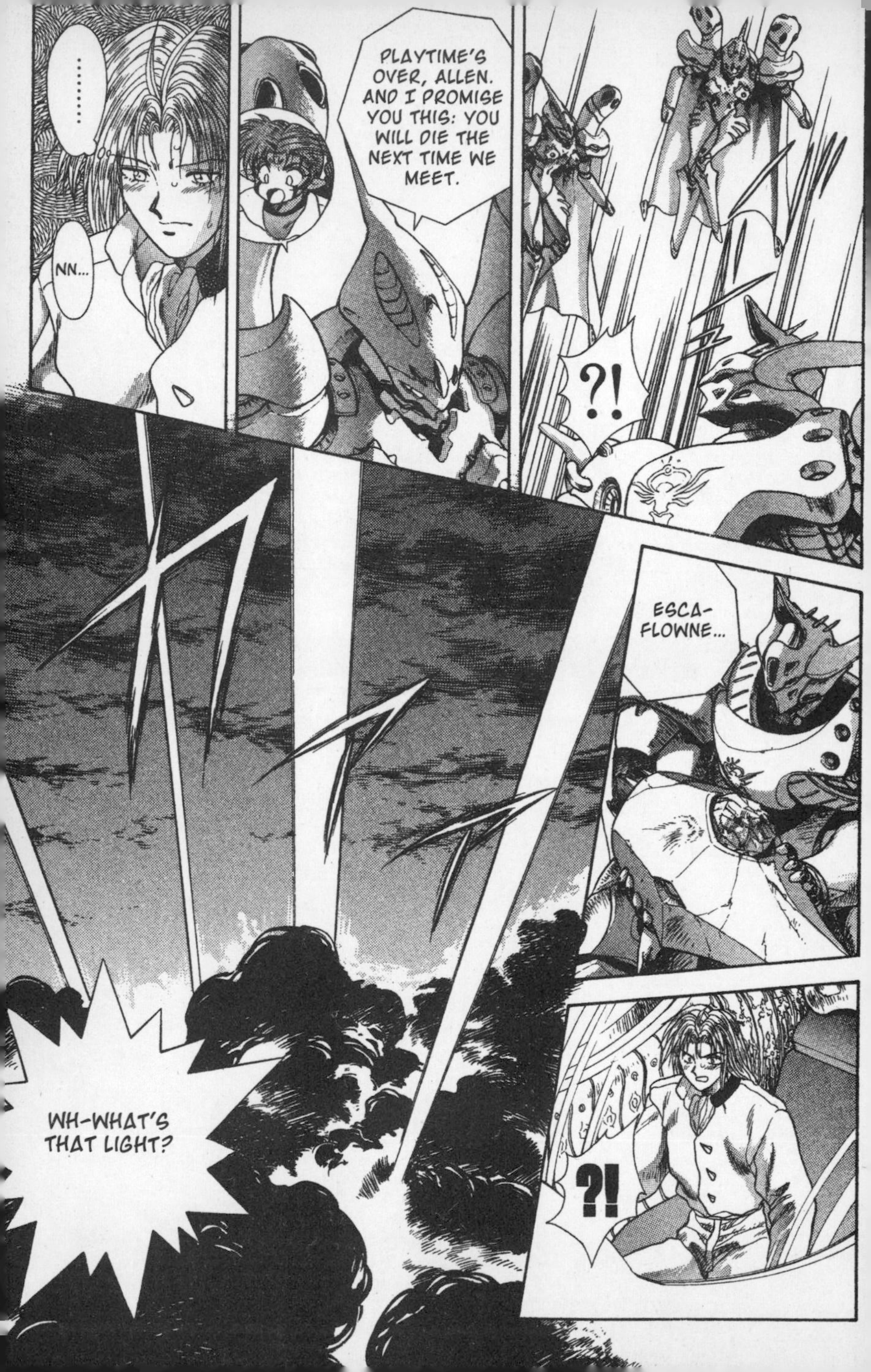
?!
PLAYTIME'S OVER, ALLEN. AND I PROMISE YOU THIS: YOU WILL DIE THE NEXT TIME WE MEET.
......
NN...
ESCA-FLOWNE...
?!
WH-WHAT'S THAT LIGHT?

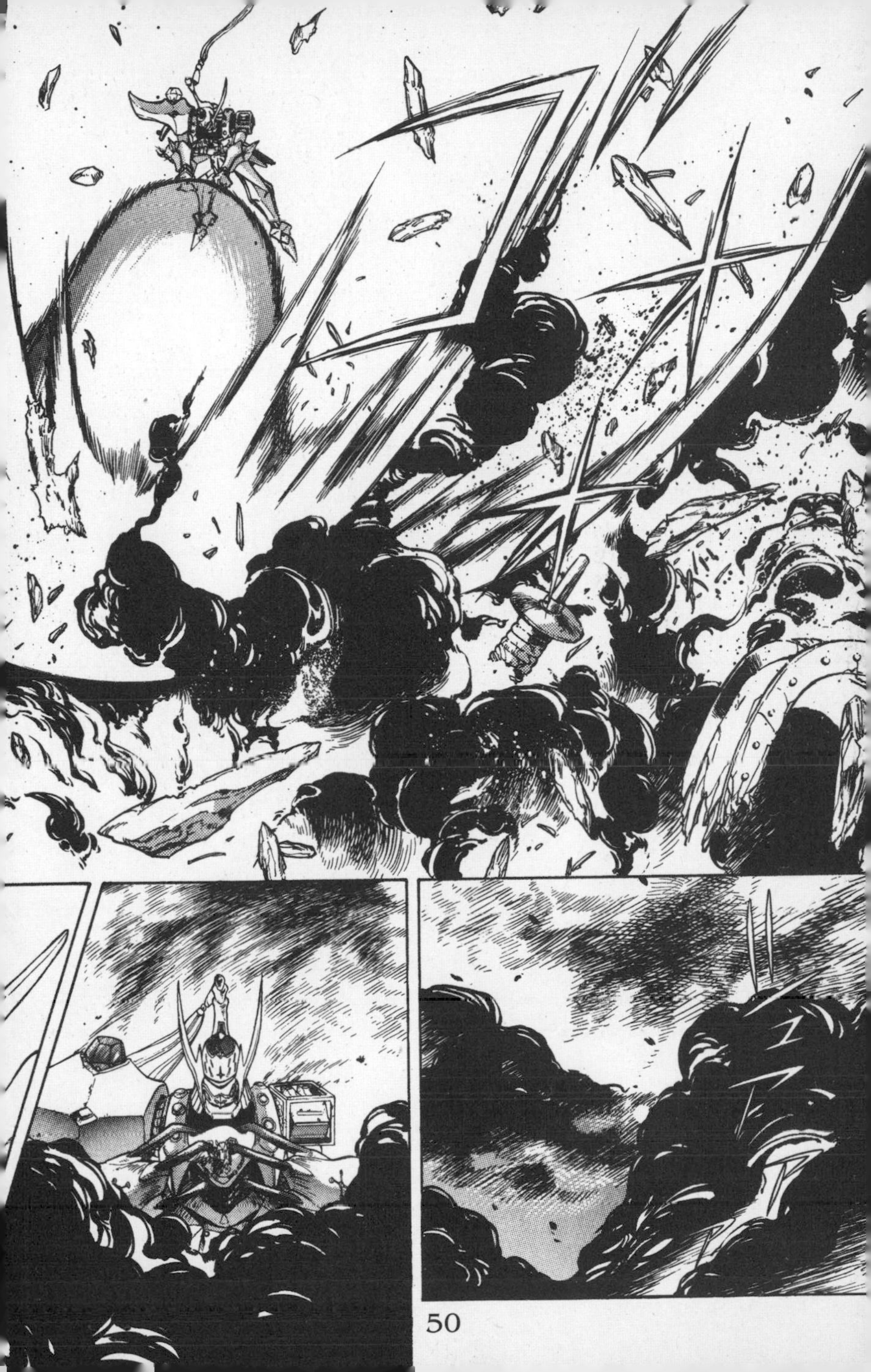

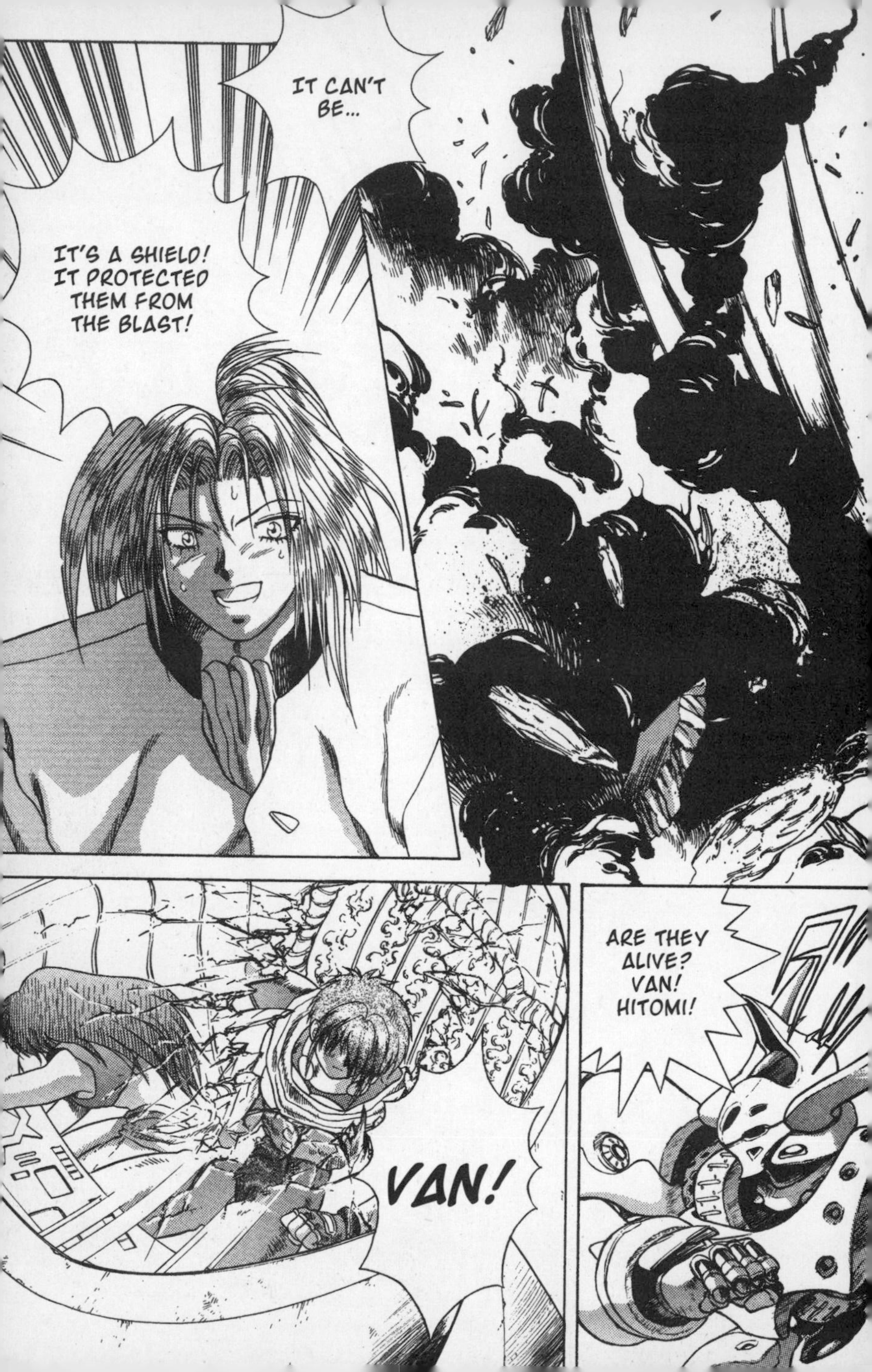
IT CAN'T BE...
IT'S A SHIELD! IT PROTECTED THEM FROM THE BLAST!
ARE THEY ALIVE? VAN! HITOMI!
VAN!

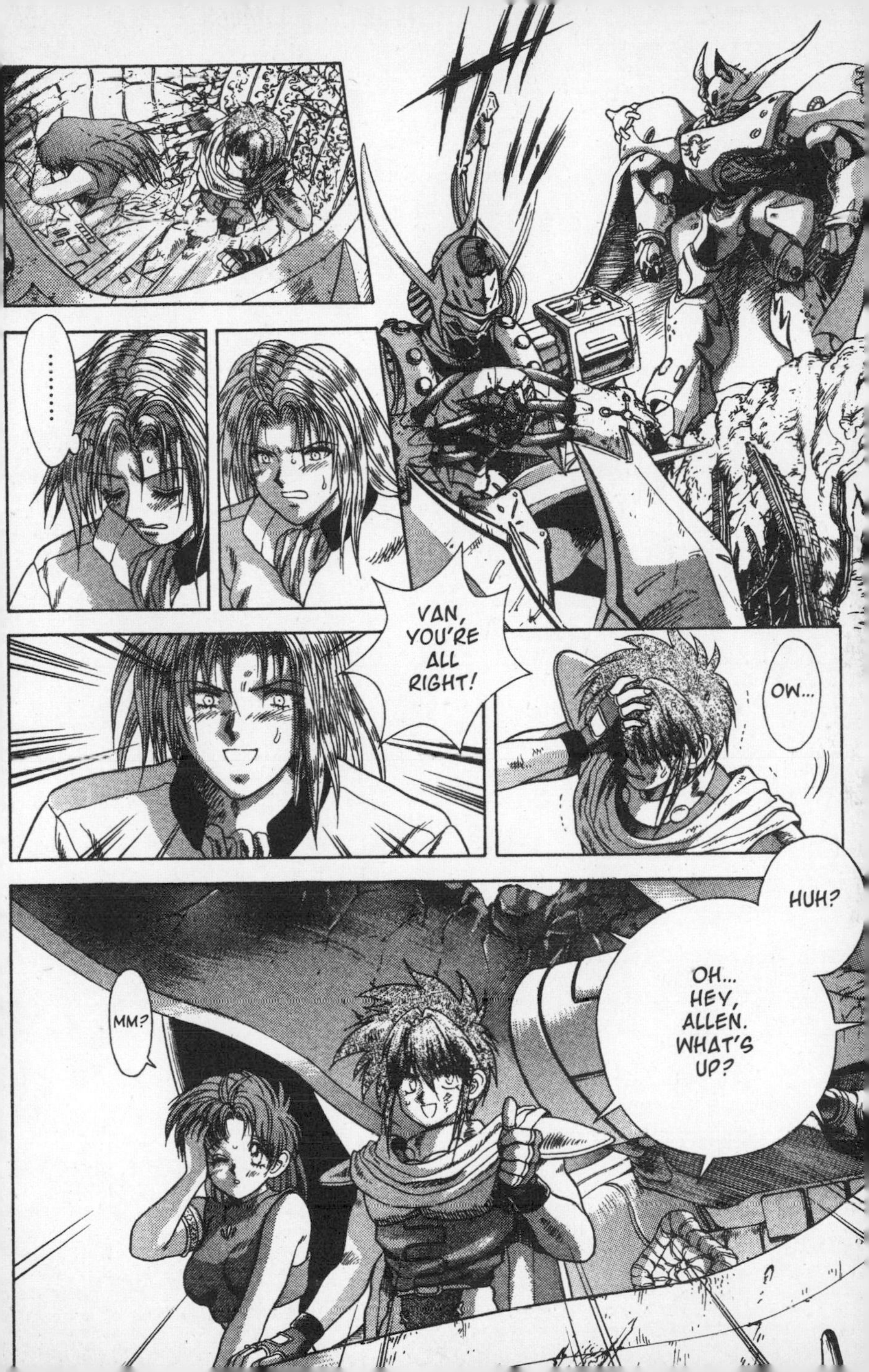
......
OW...
VAN, YOU'RE ALL RIGHT!
HUH?
OH... HEY, ALLEN. WHAT'S UP?
MM?

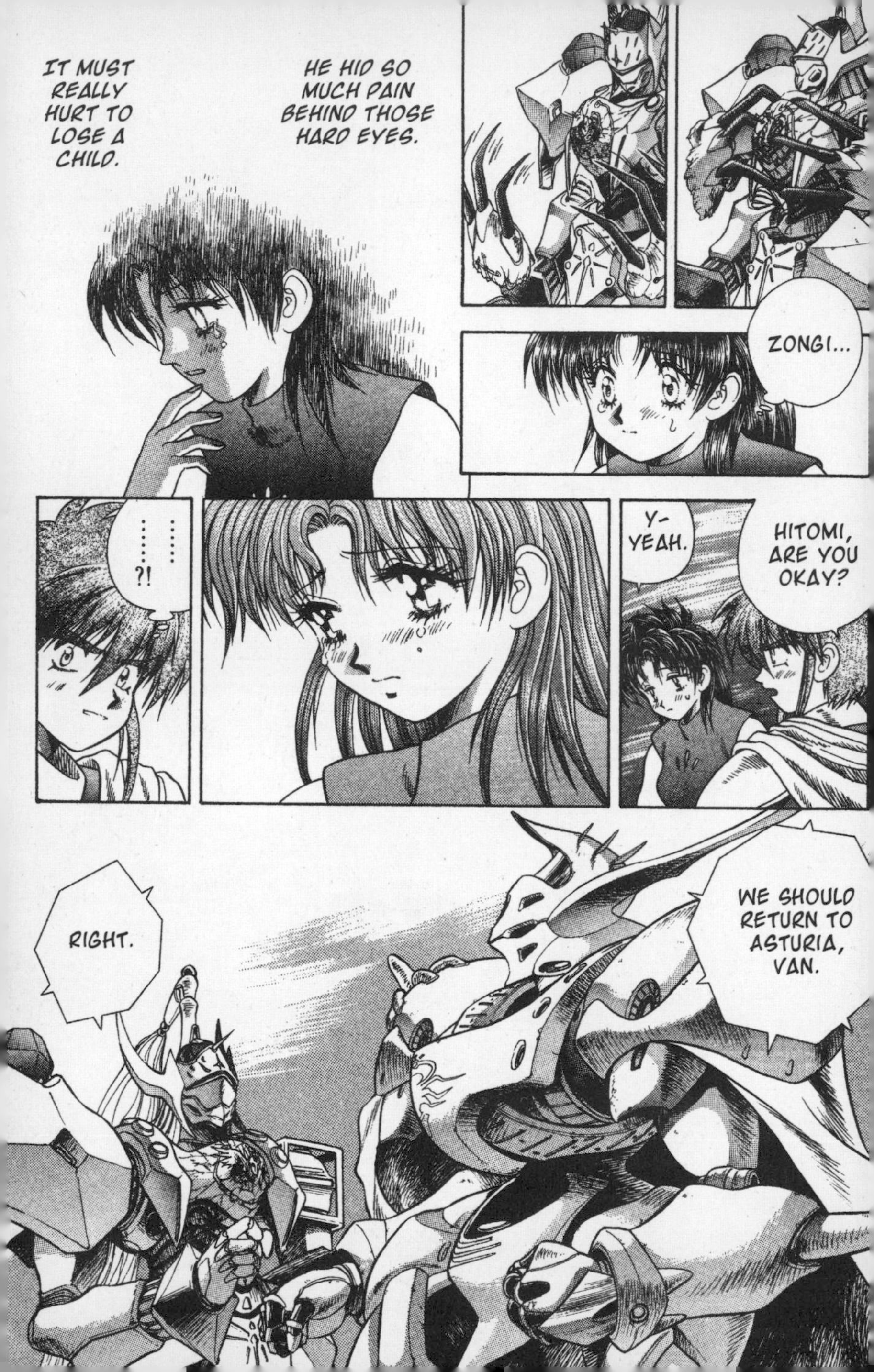
ZONGI...
HE HID SO MUCH PAIN BEHIND THOSE HARD EYES.
IT MUST REALLY HURT TO LOSE A CHILD.
HITOMI, ARE YOU OKAY?
Y-YEAH.
......?!
WE SHOULD RETURN TO ASTURIA, VAN.
RIGHT.

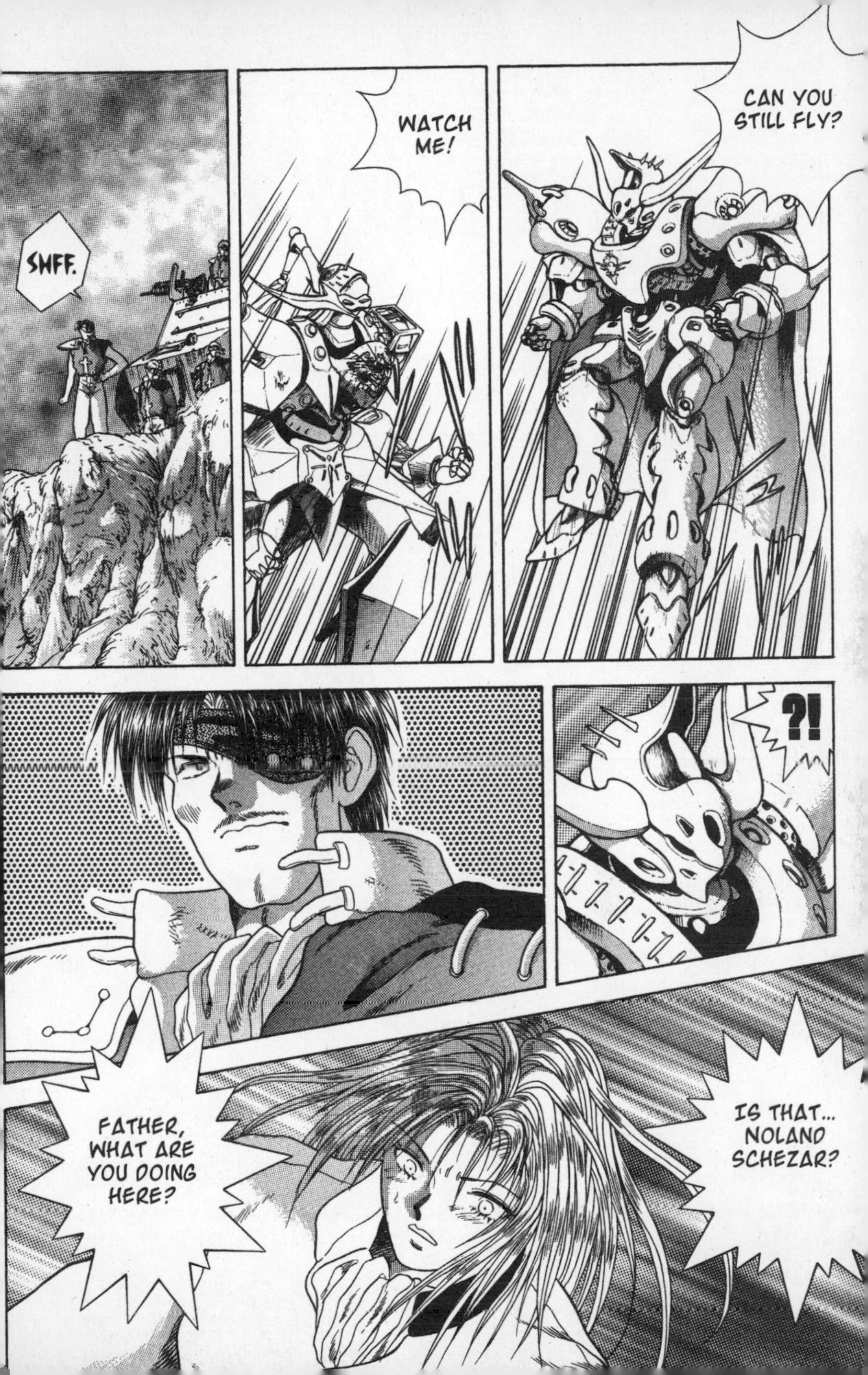
CAN YOU STILL FLY?
WATCH ME!
SNFF.
?!
IS THAT... NOLAND SCHEZAR?
FATHER, WHAT ARE YOU DOING HERE?

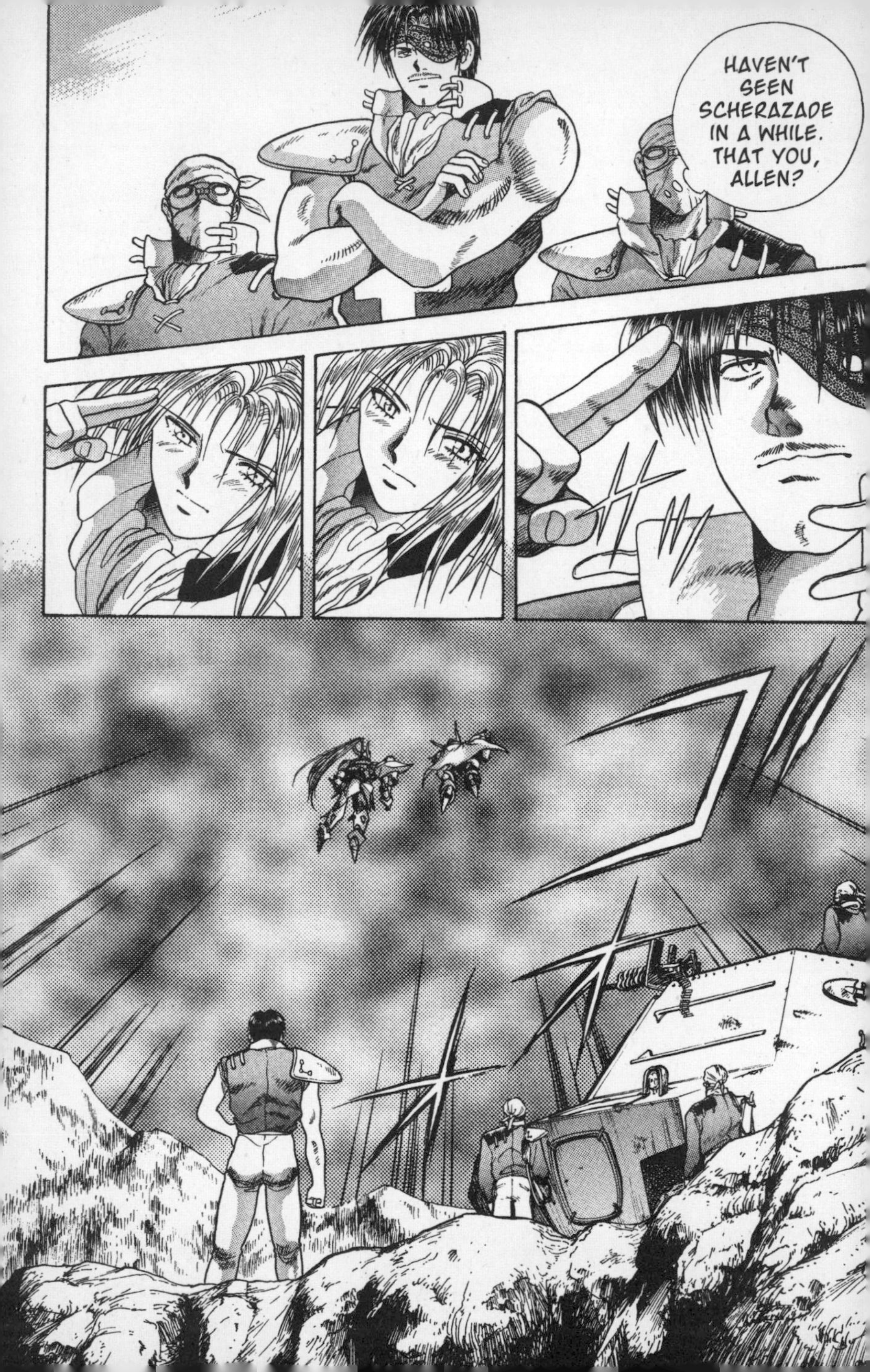
HAVEN'T SEEN SCHERAZADE IN A WHILE. THAT YOU, ALLEN?

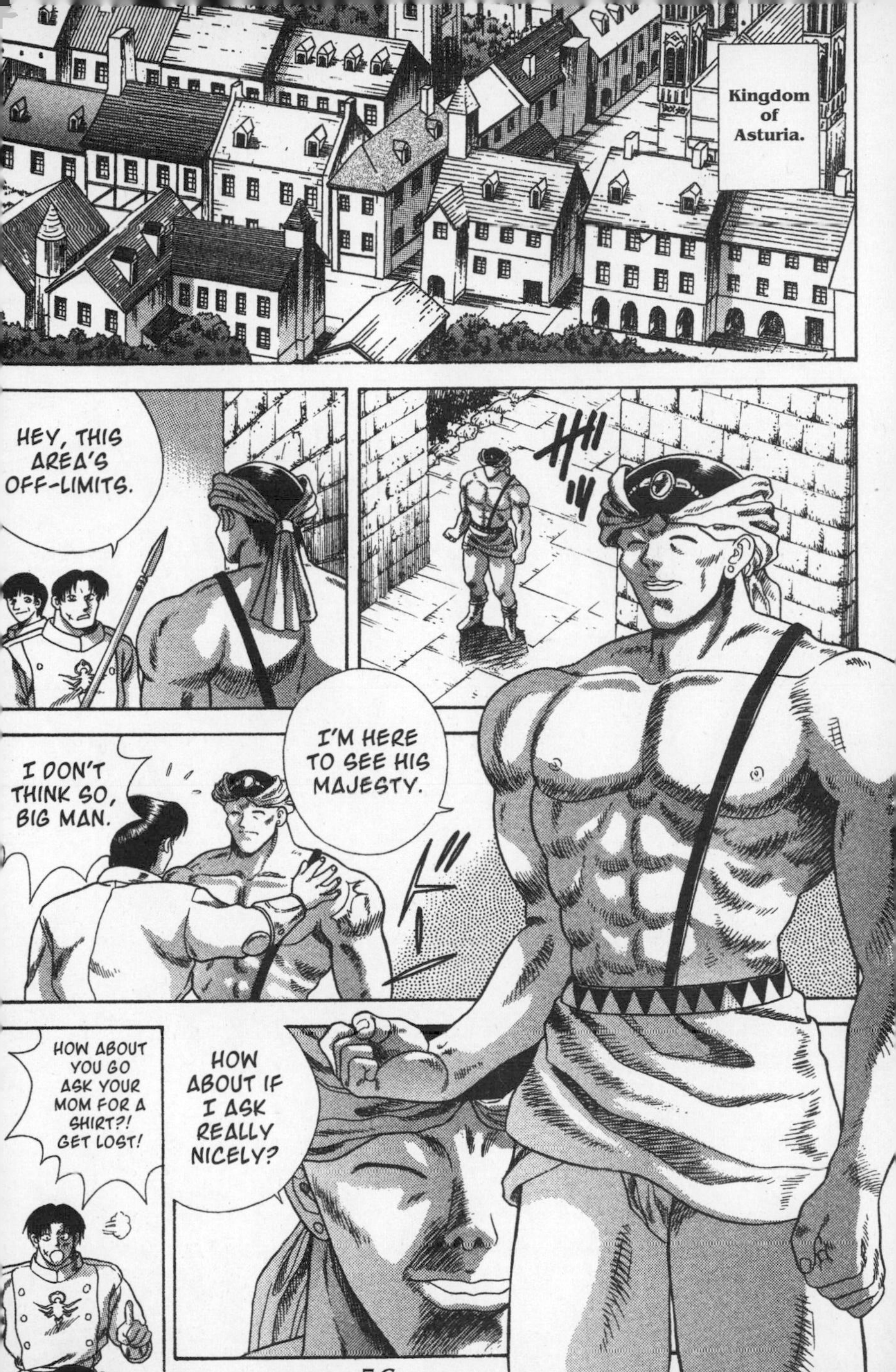
Kingdom of Asturia.
HEY, THIS AREA'S OFF-LIMITS.
I'M HERE TO SEE HIS MAJESTY.
I DON'T THINK SO, BIG MAN.
HOW ABOUT YOU GO ASK YOUR MOM FOR A SHIRT?! GET LOST!
HOW ABOUT IF I ASK REALLY NICELY?

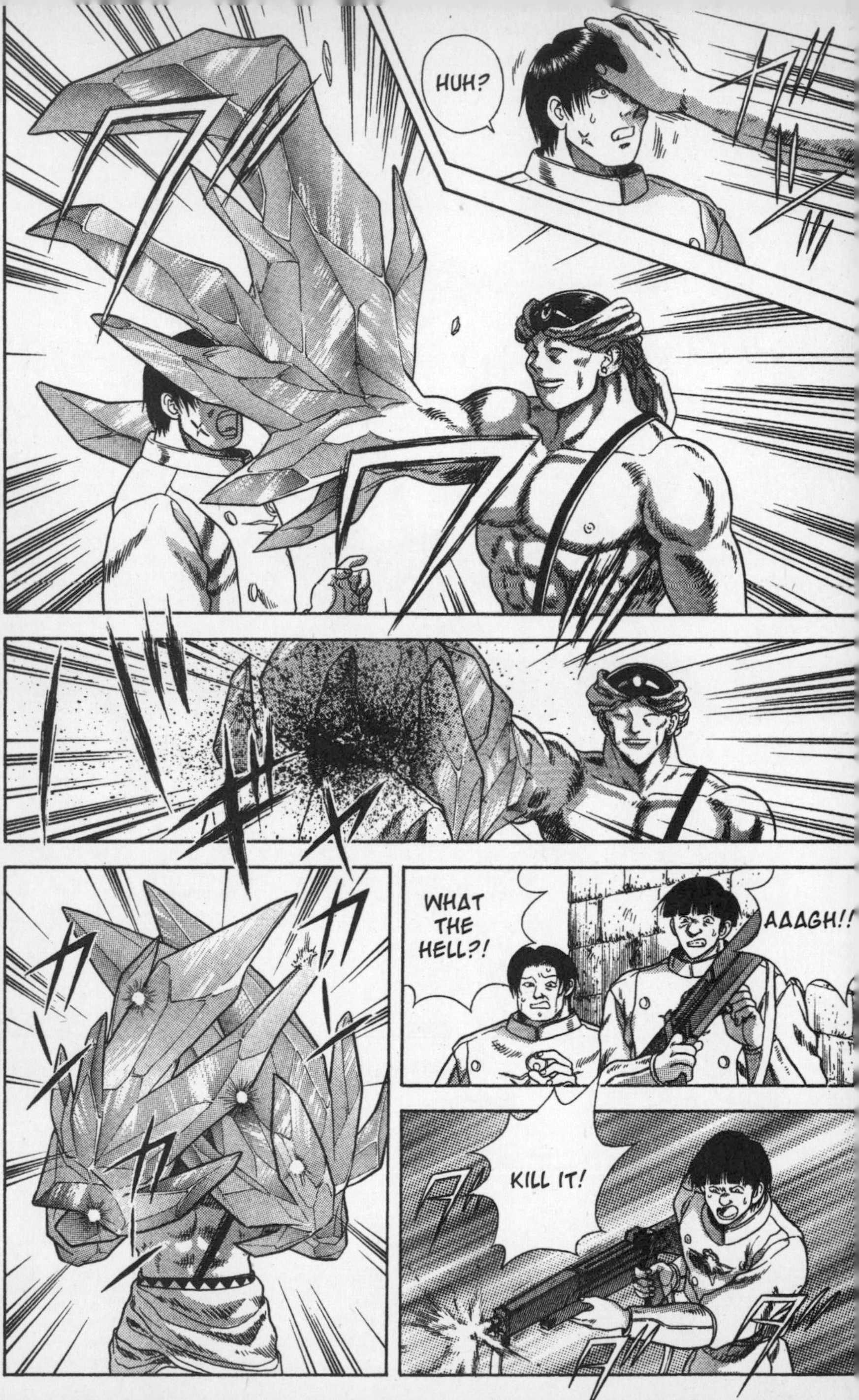
HUH?
AAAGH!!
WHAT THE HELL?!
KILL IT!

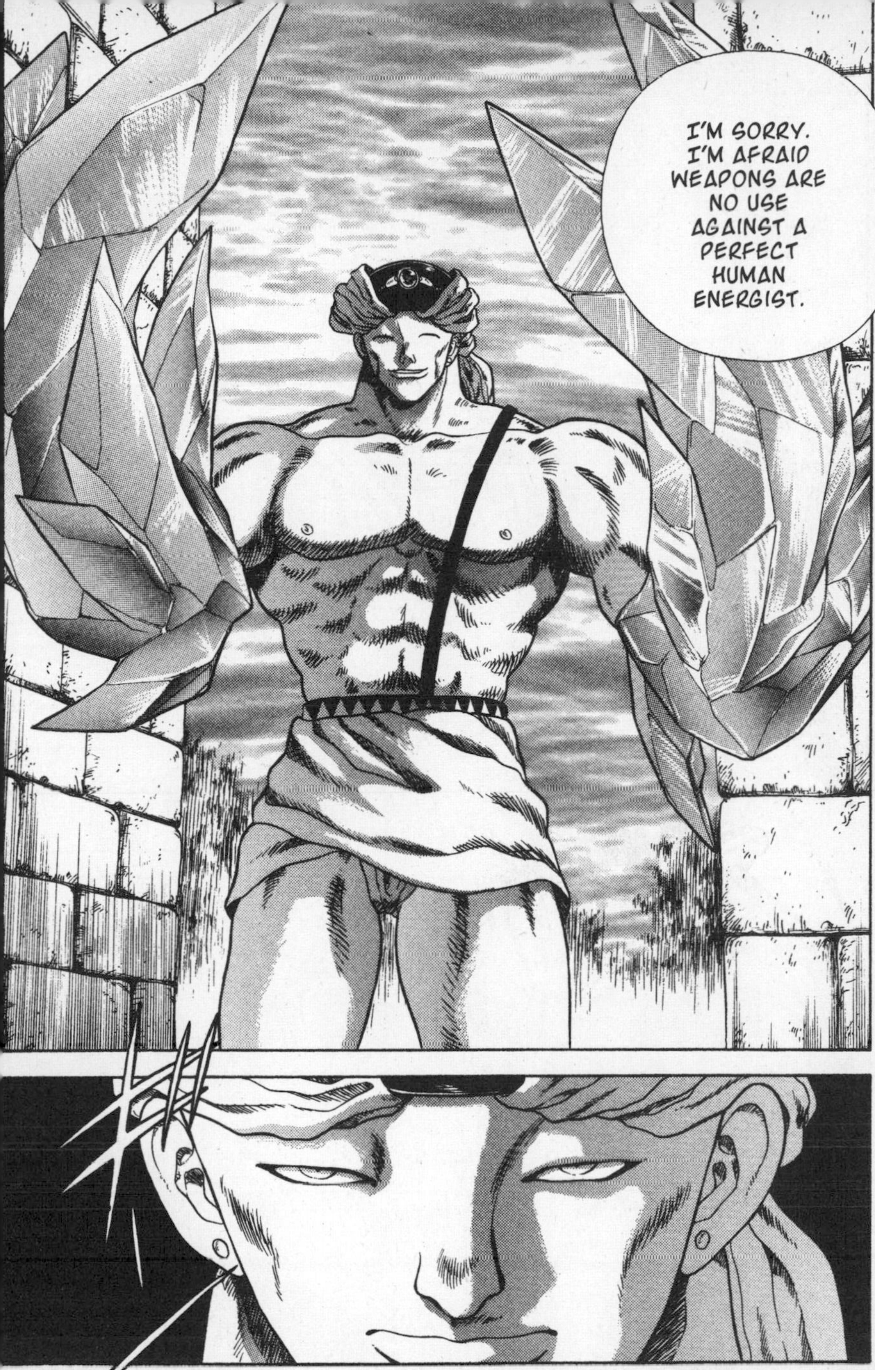
I'M SORRY. I'M AFRAID WEAPONS ARE NO USE AGAINST A PERFECT HUMAN ENERGIST.

VISION 20: MILLERNA'S CHOICE

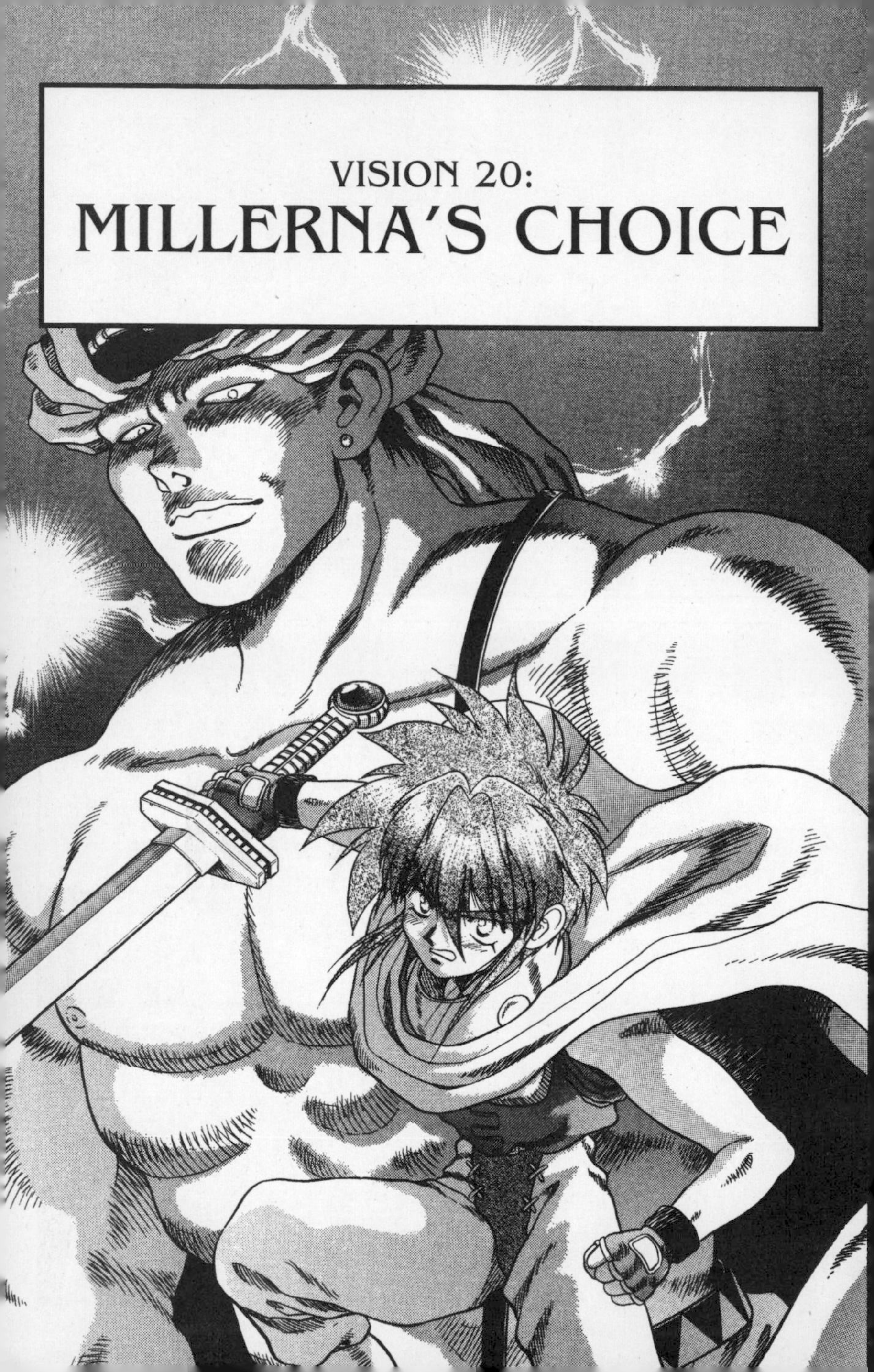

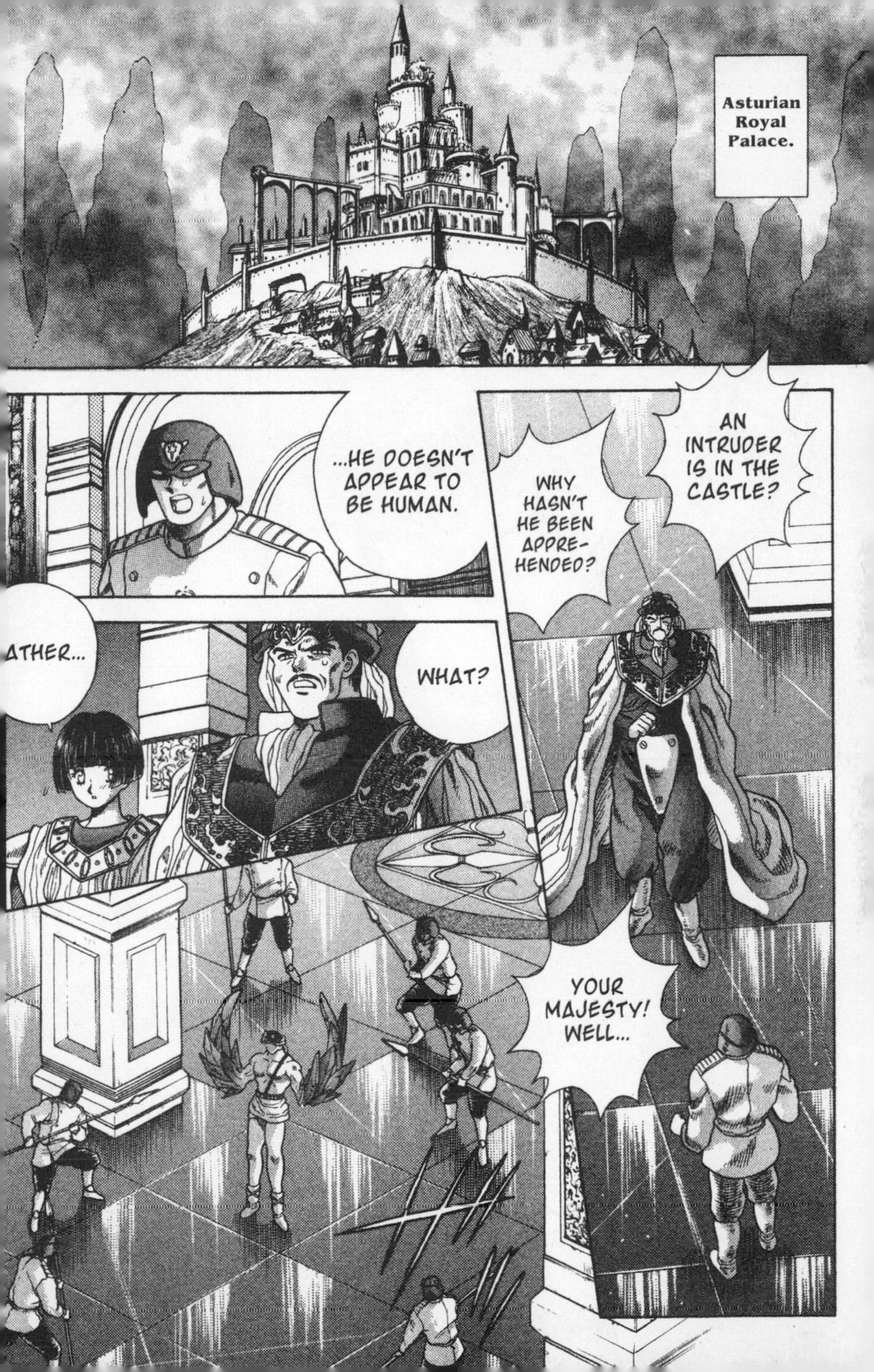
Asturian Royal Palace.
AN INTRUDER IS IN THE CASTLE?
WHY HASN'T HE BEEN APPRE-HENDED?
YOUR MAJESTY! WELL...
...HE DOESN'T APPEAR TO BE HUMAN.
WHAT?
ATHER...

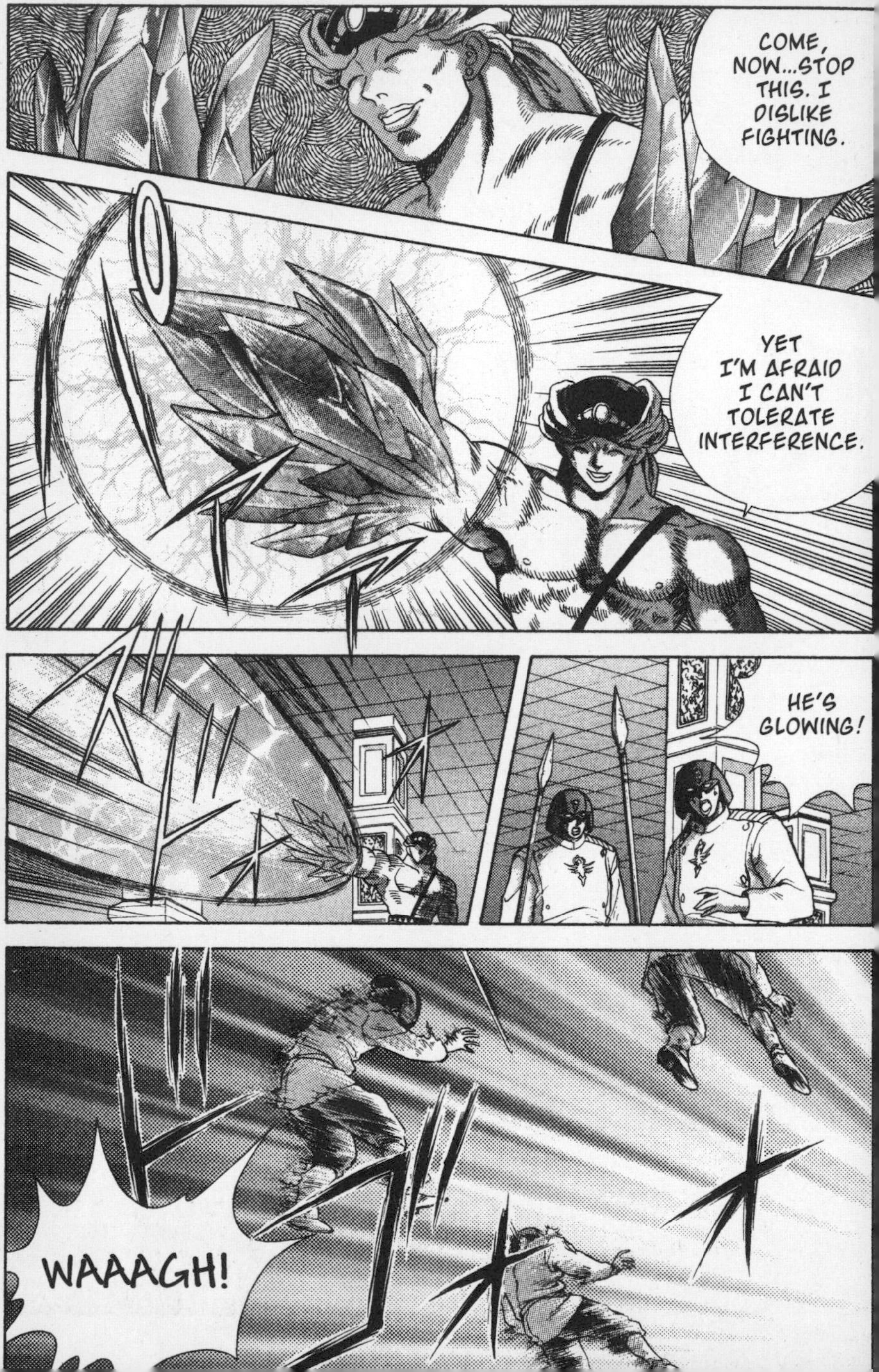
COME, NOW...STOP THIS. I DISLIKE FIGHTING.
YET I'M AFRAID I CAN'T TOLERATE INTERFERENCE.
HE'S GLOWING!
WAAAGH!

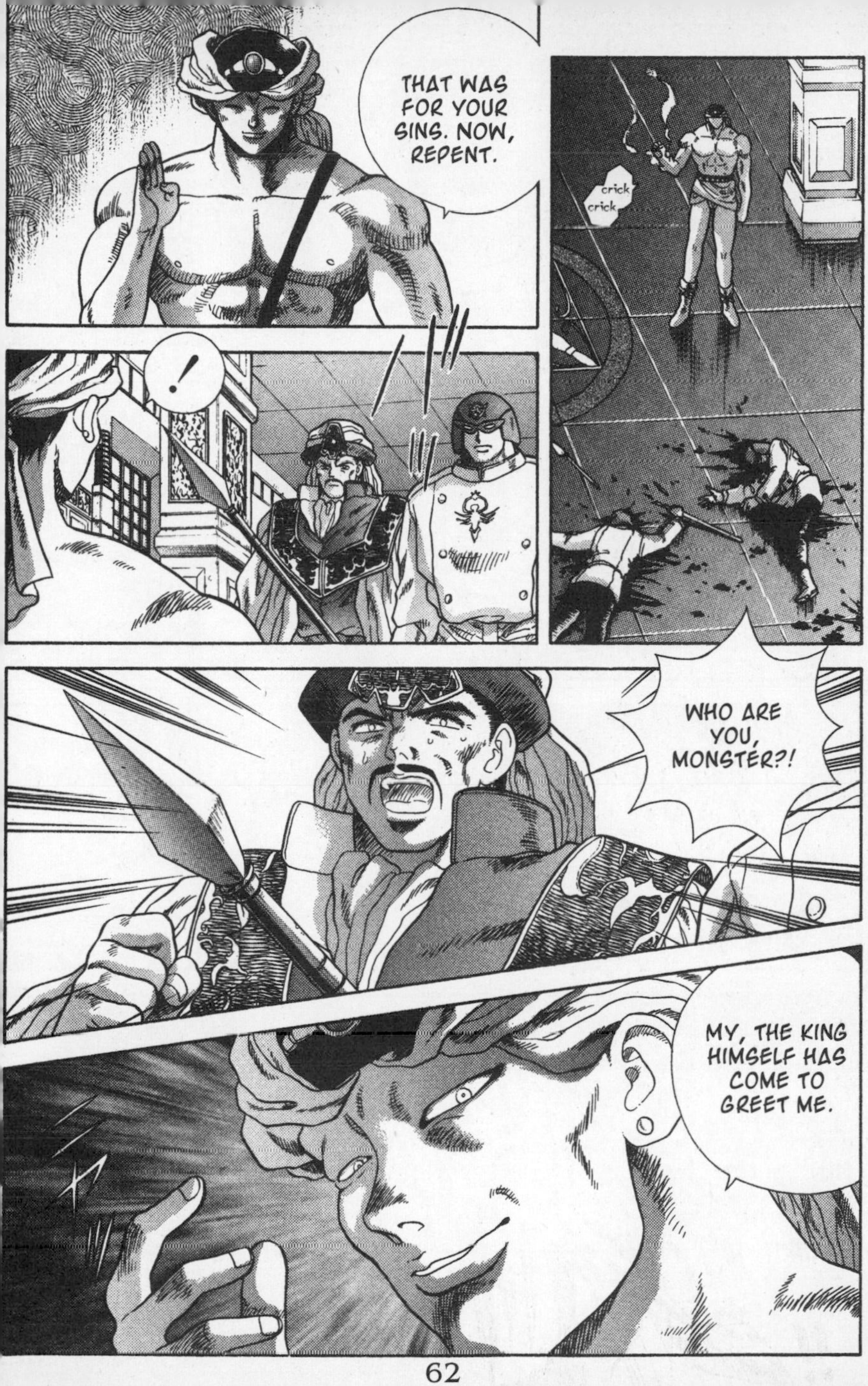
crick
crick
THAT WAS FOR YOUR SINS. NOW, REPENT.
!
WHO ARE YOU, MONSTER?!
MY, THE KING HIMSELF HAS COME TO GREET ME.

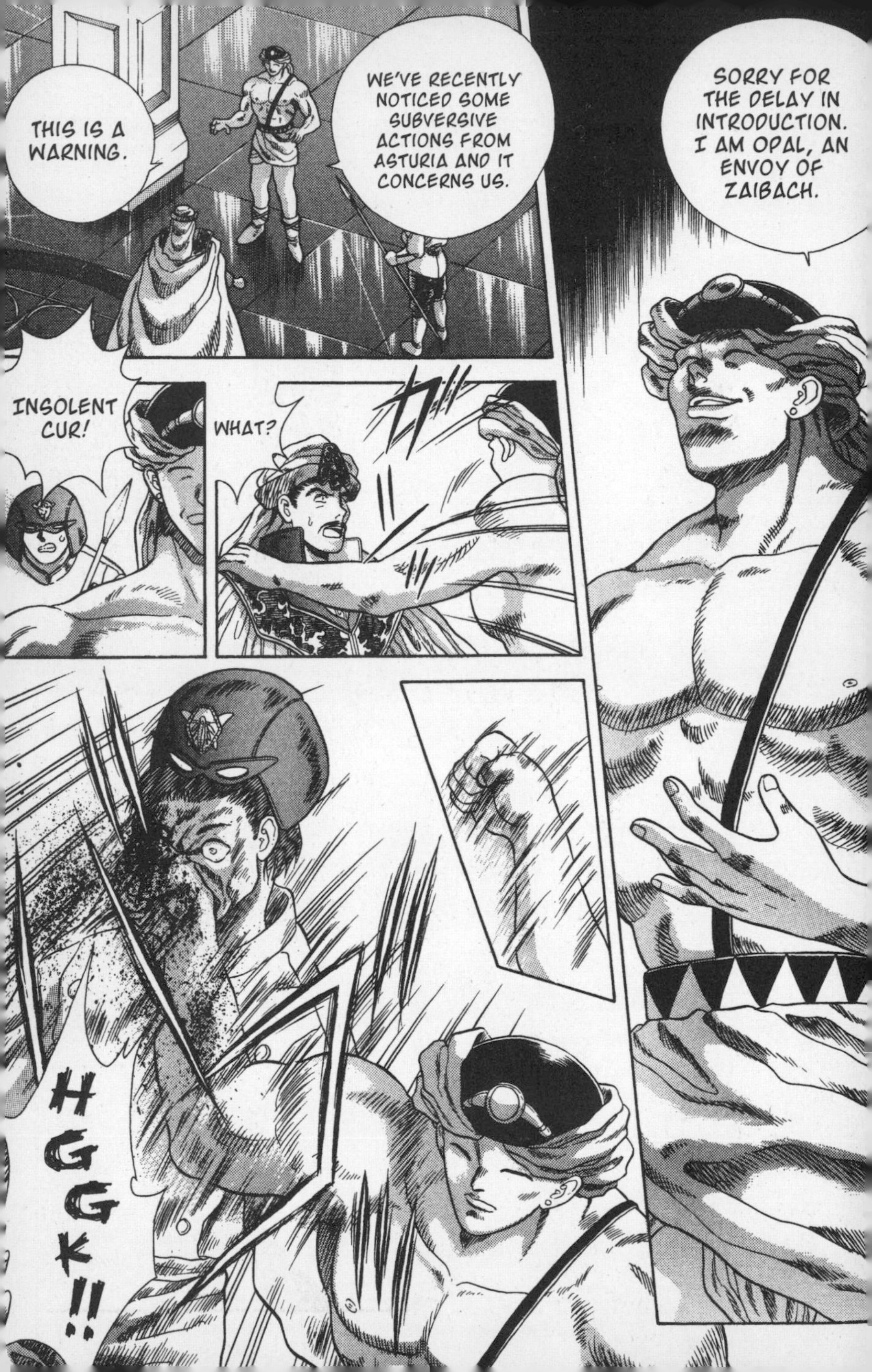
SORRY FOR THE DELAY IN INTRODUCTION. I AM OPAL, AN ENVOY OF ZAIBACH.
WE'VE RECENTLY NOTICED SOME SUBVERSIVE ACTIONS FROM ASTURIA AND IT CONCERNS US.
THIS IS A WARNING.
WHAT?
INSOLENT CUR!
HGGK!!

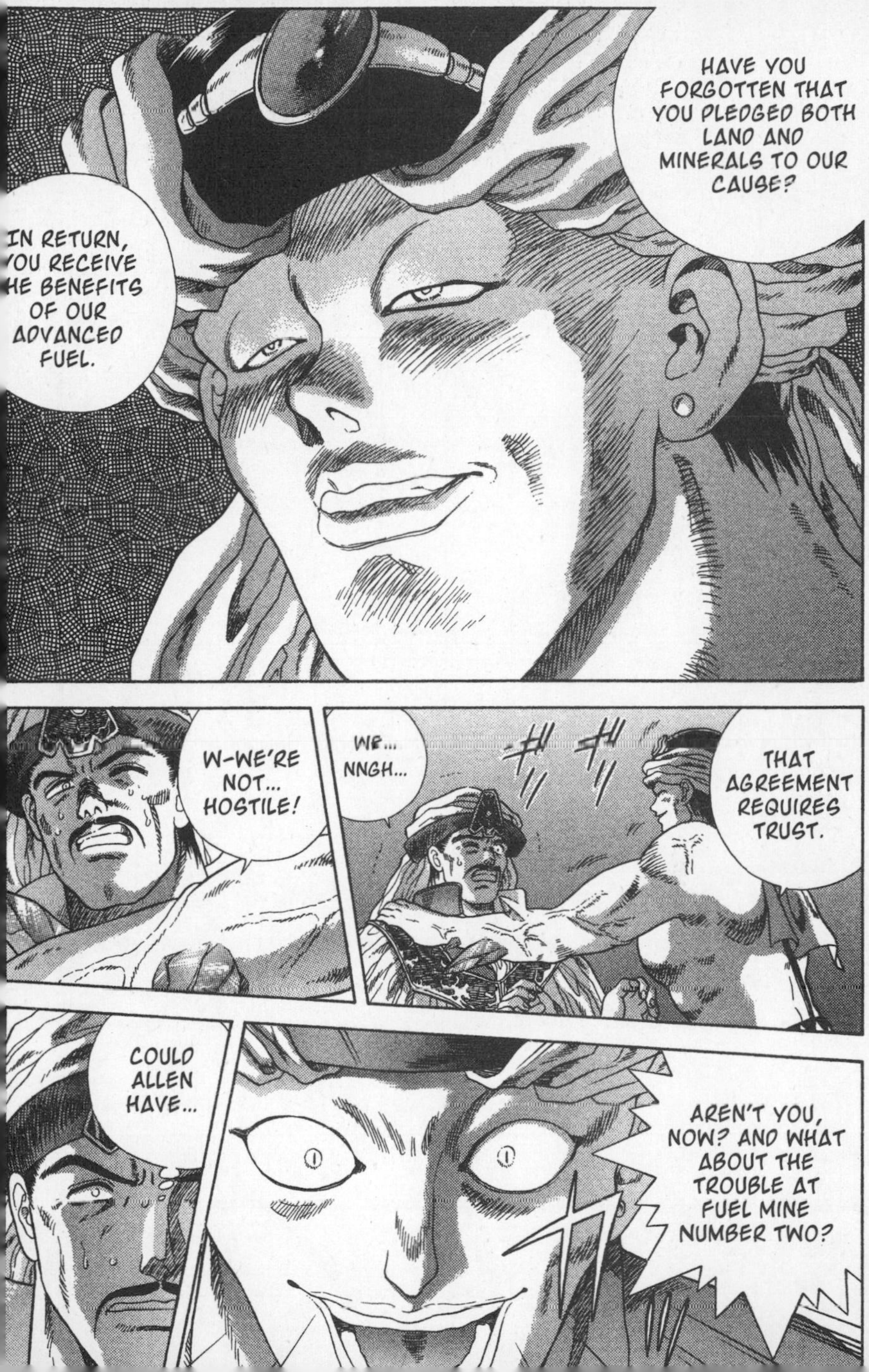
HAVE YOU FORGOTTEN THAT YOU PLEDGED BOTH LAND AND MINERALS TO OUR CAUSE?
IN RETURN, OU RECEIVE HE BENEFITS OF OUR ADVANCED FUEL.
THAT AGREEMENT REQUIRES TRUST.
WE... NNGH...
W-WE'RE NOT... HOSTILE!
AREN'T YOU, NOW? AND WHAT ABOUT THE TROUBLE AT FUEL MINE NUMBER TWO?
COULD ALLEN HAVE...

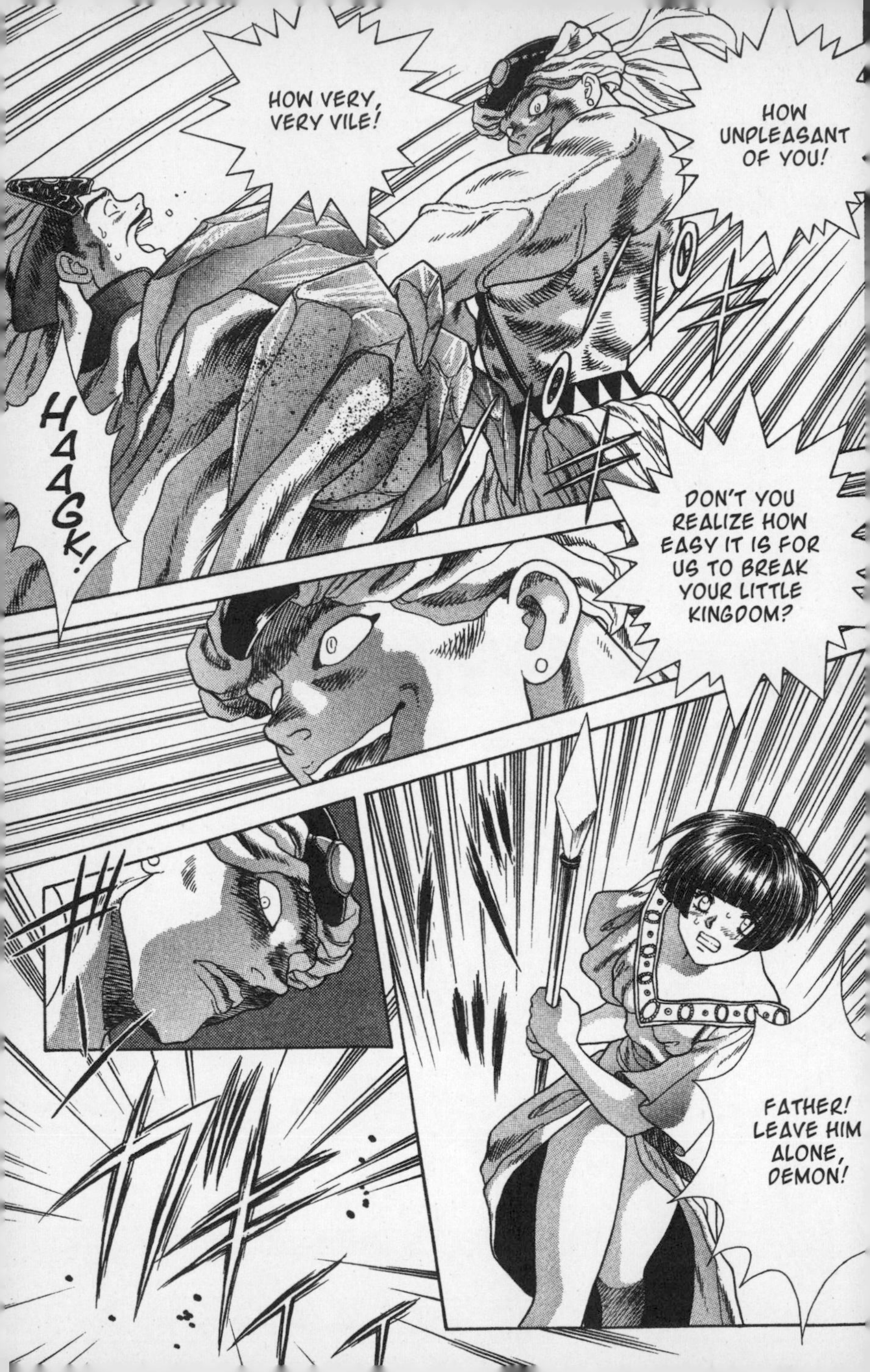
HOW UNPLEASANT OF YOU!
HOW VERY, VERY VILE!
HAAGK!
DON'T YOU REALIZE HOW EASY IT IS FOR US TO BREAK YOUR LITTLE KINGDOM?
FATHER! LEAVE HIM ALONE, DEMON!

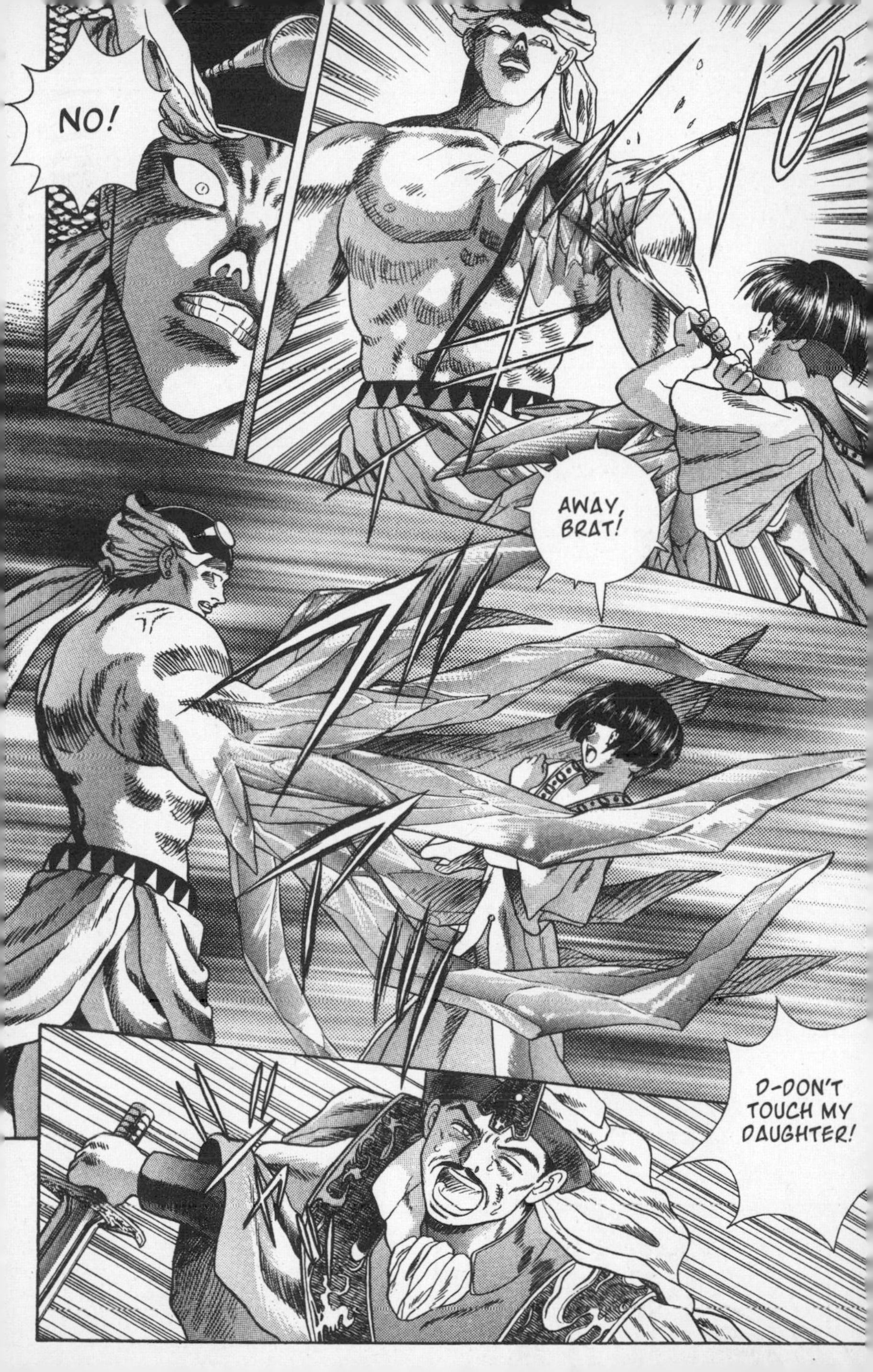
NO!
AWAY, BRAT!
D-DON'T TOUCH MY DAUGHTER!

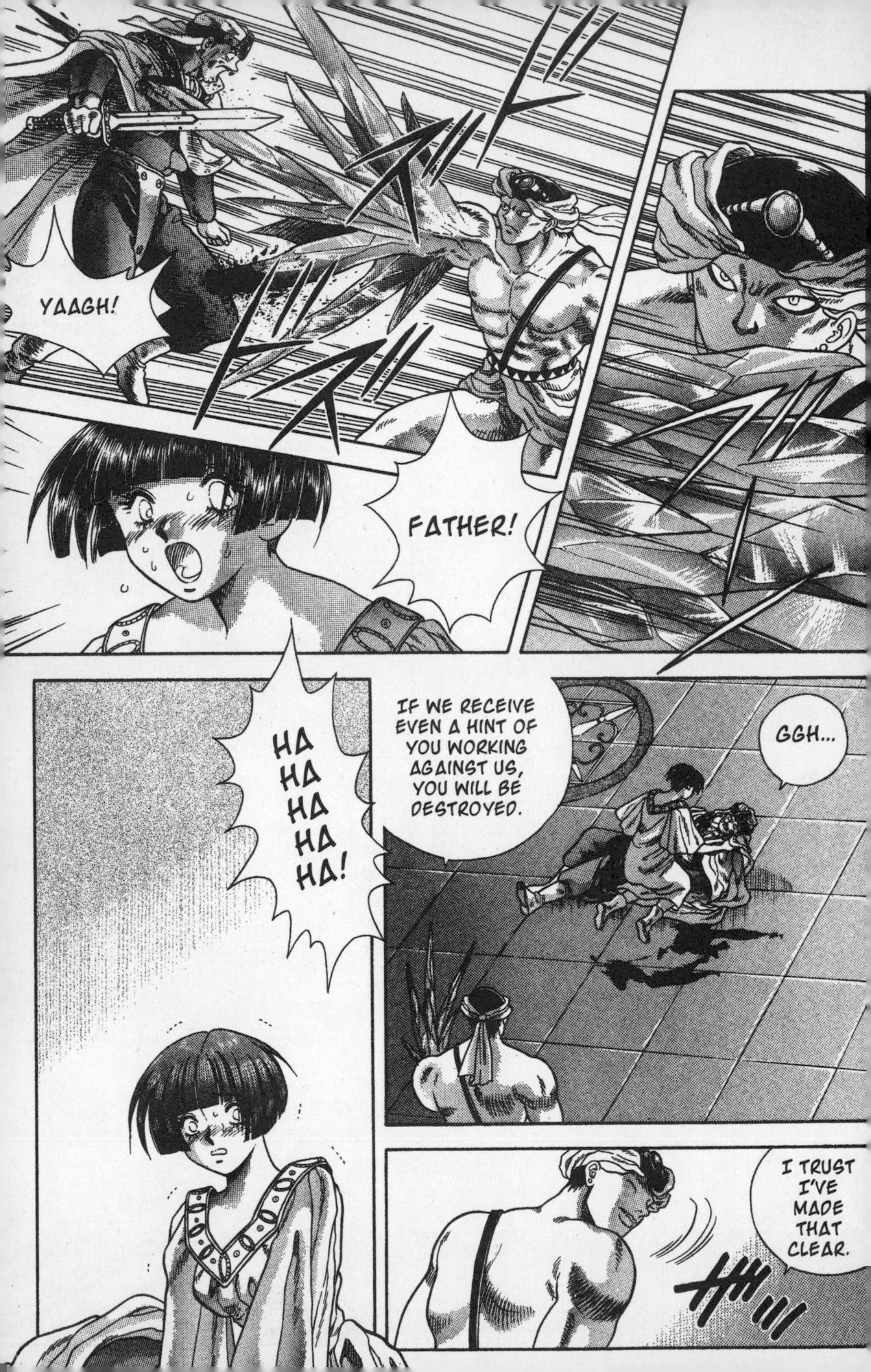
YAAGH!
FATHER!
GGH...
IF WE RECEIVE EVEN A HINT OF YOU WORKING AGAINST US, YOU WILL BE DESTROYED.
I TRUST I'VE MADE THAT CLEAR.
HA HA HA HA HA!

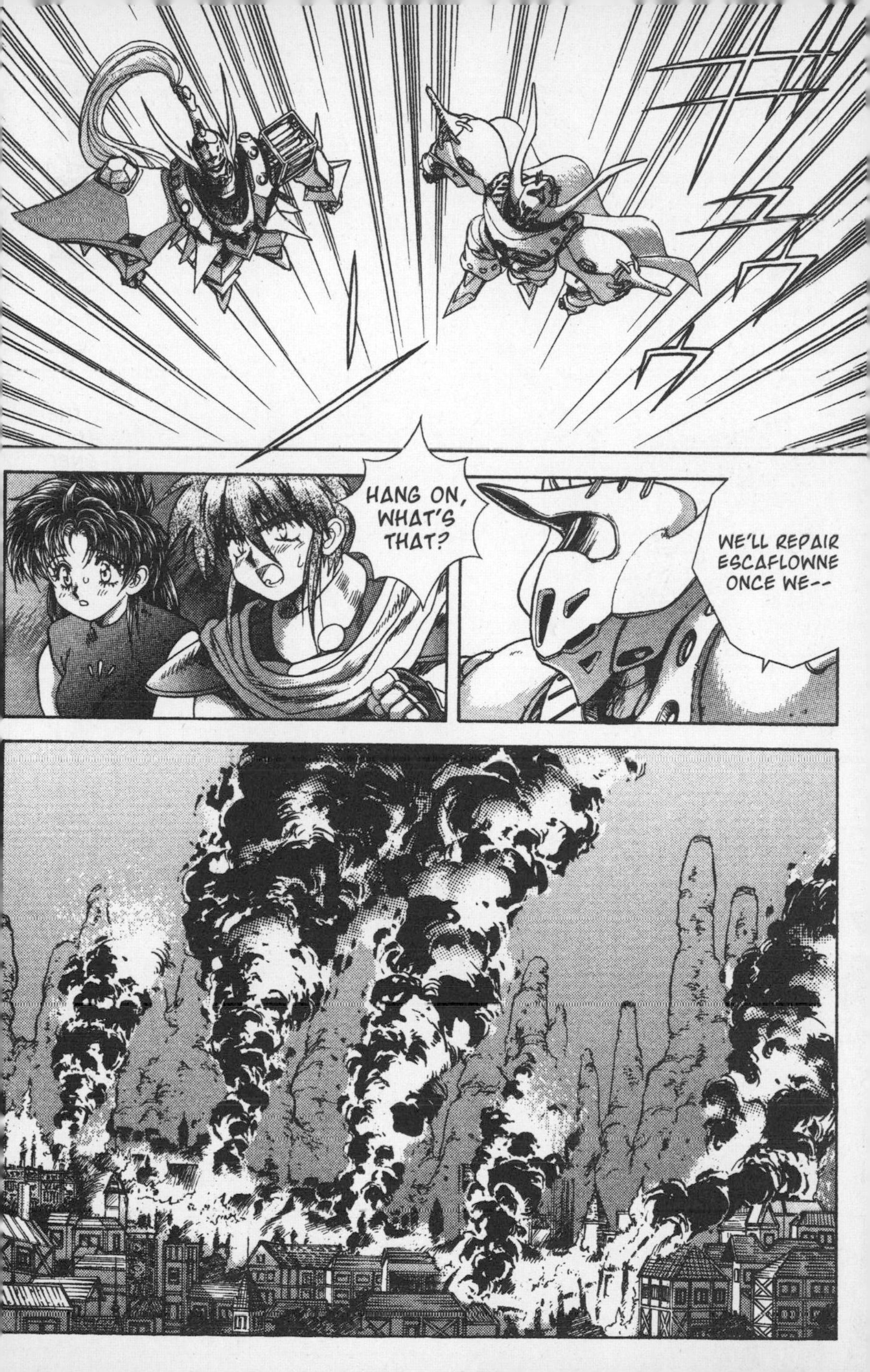
WE'LL REPAIR ESCAFLOWNE ONCE WE--
HANG ON, WHAT'S THAT?

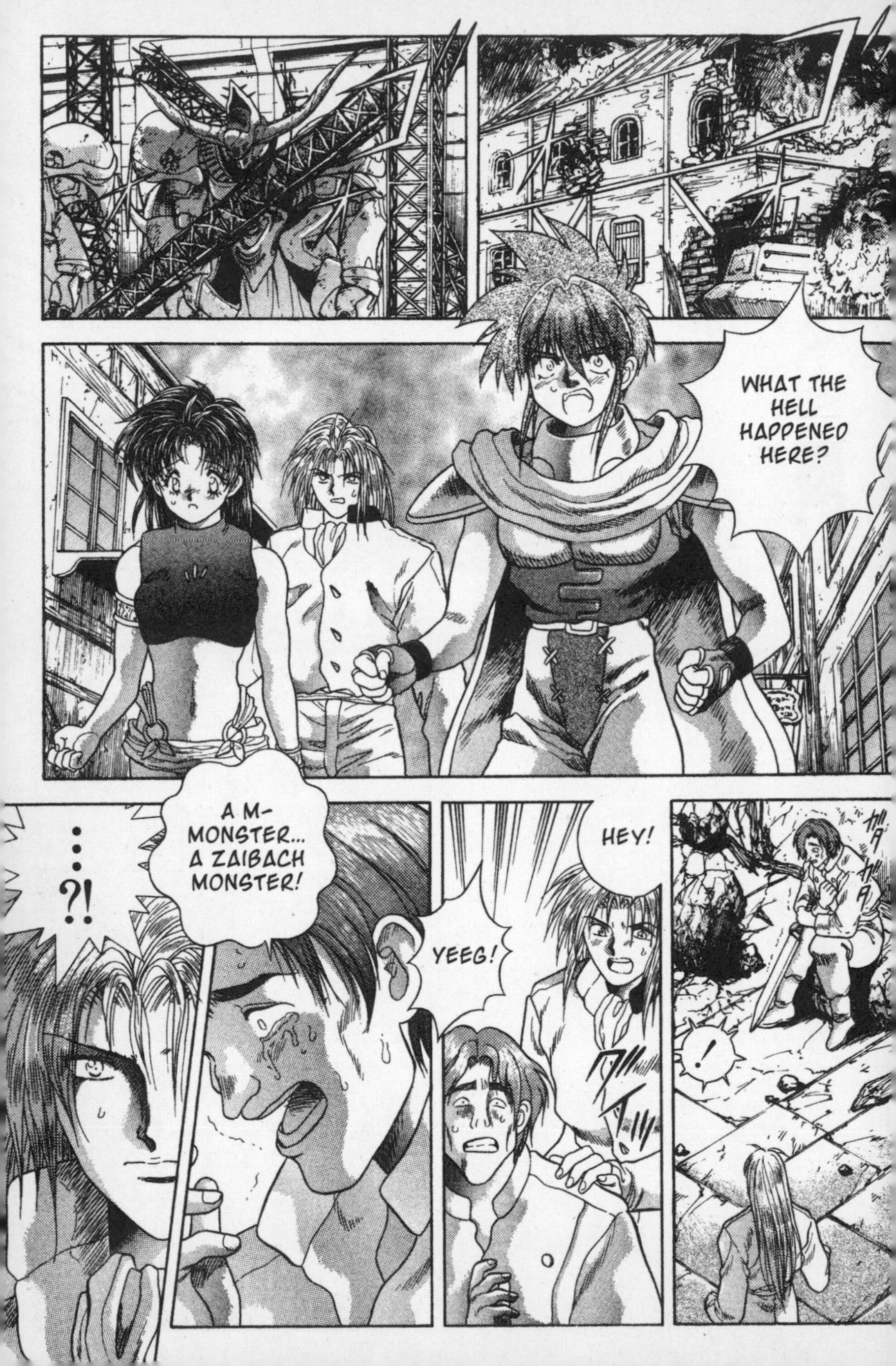
WHAT THE HELL HAPPENED HERE?
!
HEY!
YEEG!
A M-MONSTER... A ZAIBACH MONSTER!
...?!

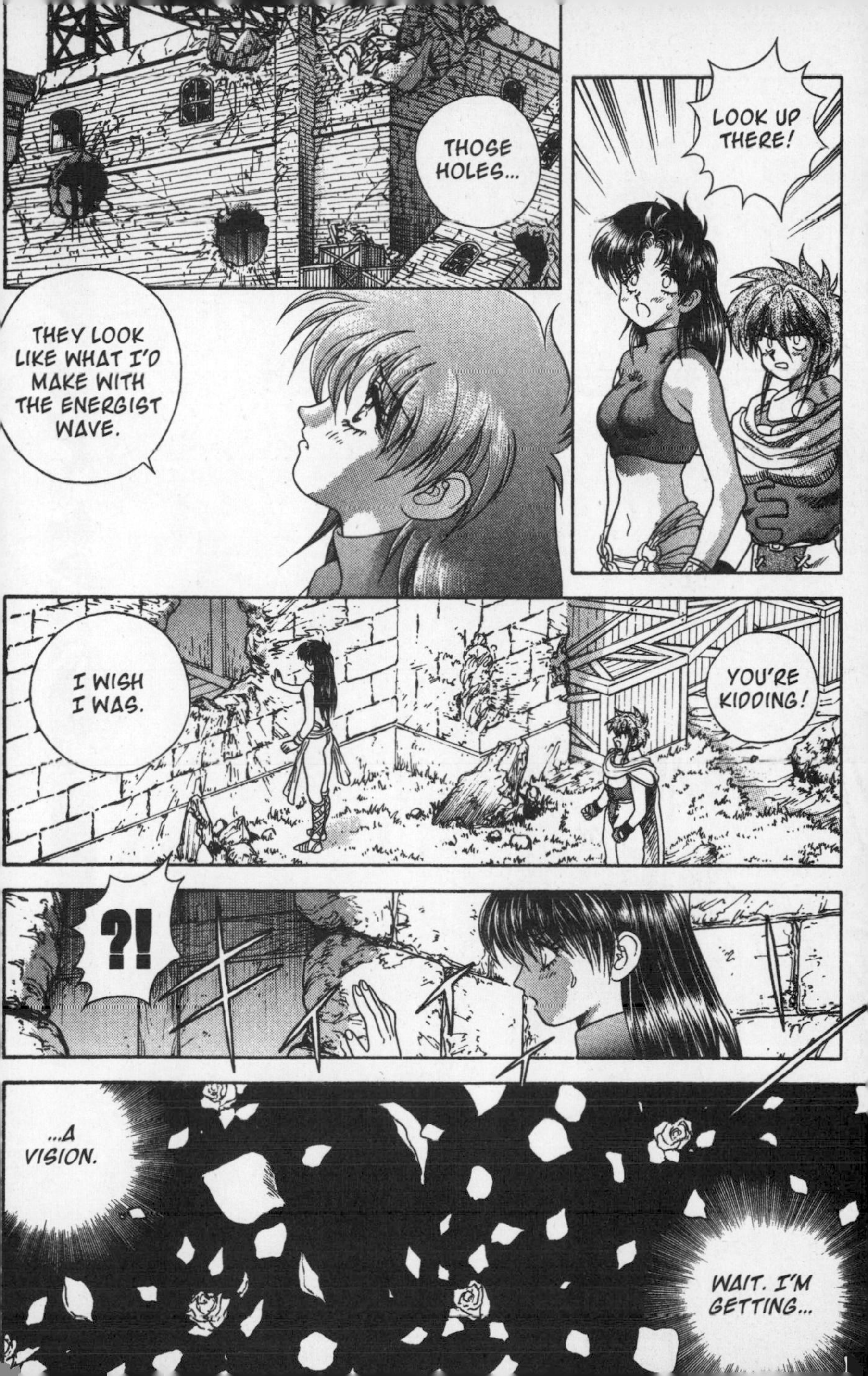
LOOK UP THERE!
THOSE HOLES...
THEY LOOK LIKE WHAT I'D MAKE WITH THE ENERGIST WAVE.
YOU'RE KIDDING!
I WISH I WAS.
?!
WAIT. I'M GETTING...
...A VISION.

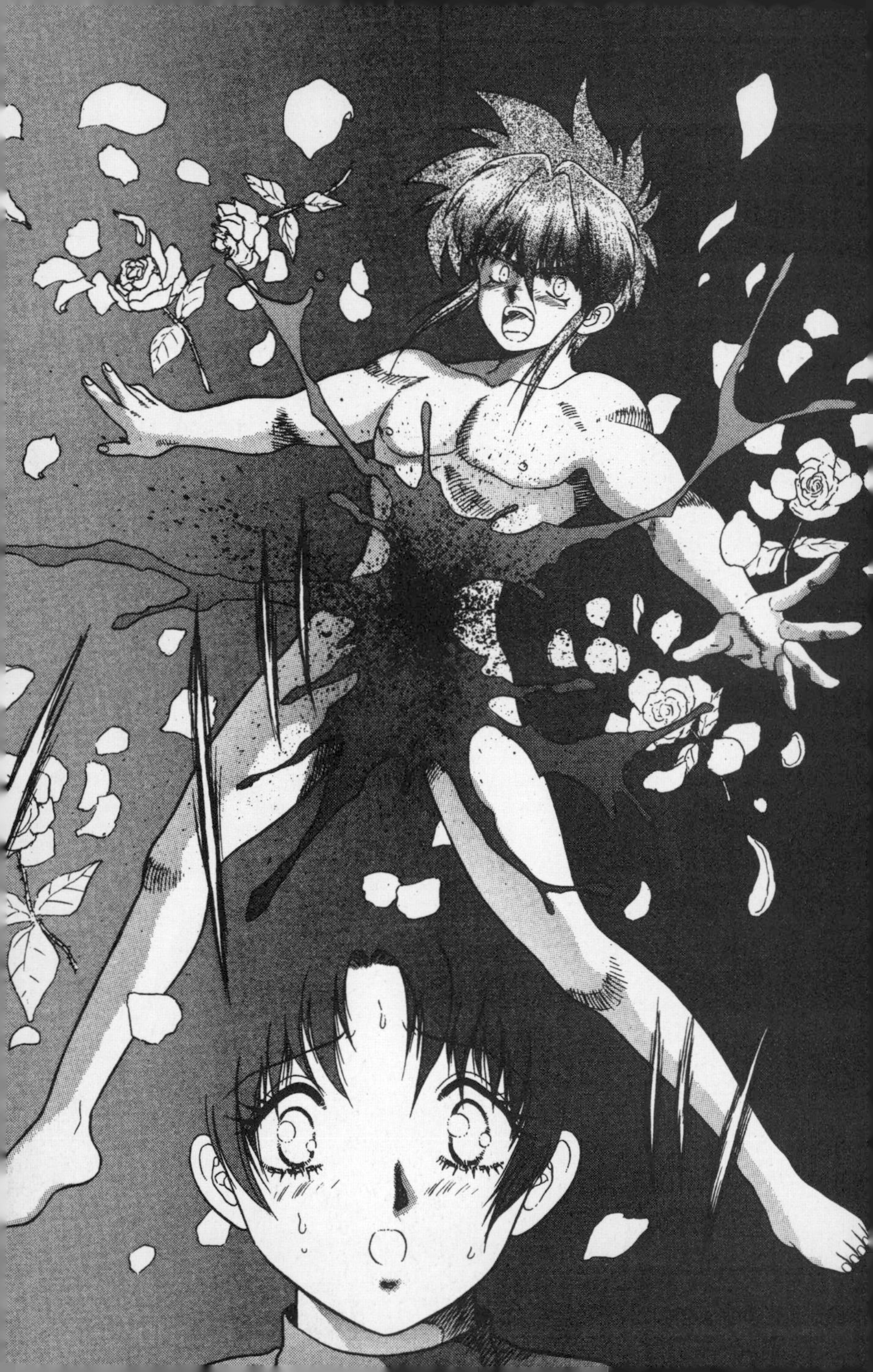

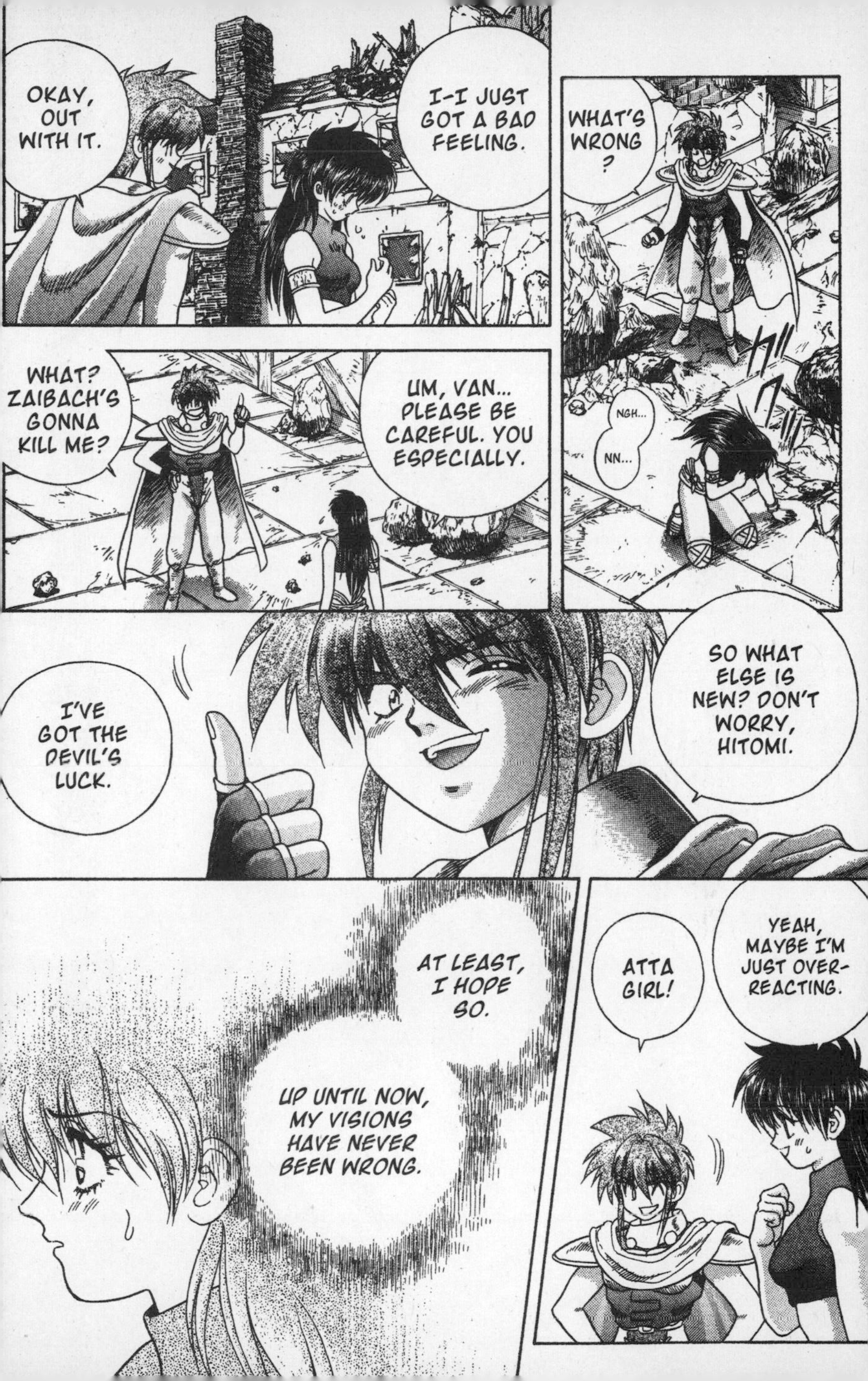
WHAT'S WRONG ?
NGH...
NN...
I-I JUST GOT A BAD FEELING.
OKAY, OUT WITH IT.
UM, VAN... PLEASE BE CAREFUL. YOU ESPECIALLY.
WHAT? ZAIBACH'S GONNA KILL ME?
SO WHAT ELSE IS NEW? DON'T WORRY, HITOMI.
I'VE GOT THE DEVIL'S LUCK.
YEAH, MAYBE I'M JUST OVER-REACTING.
ATTA GIRL!
AT LEAST, I HOPE SO.
UP UNTIL NOW, MY VISIONS HAVE NEVER BEEN WRONG.

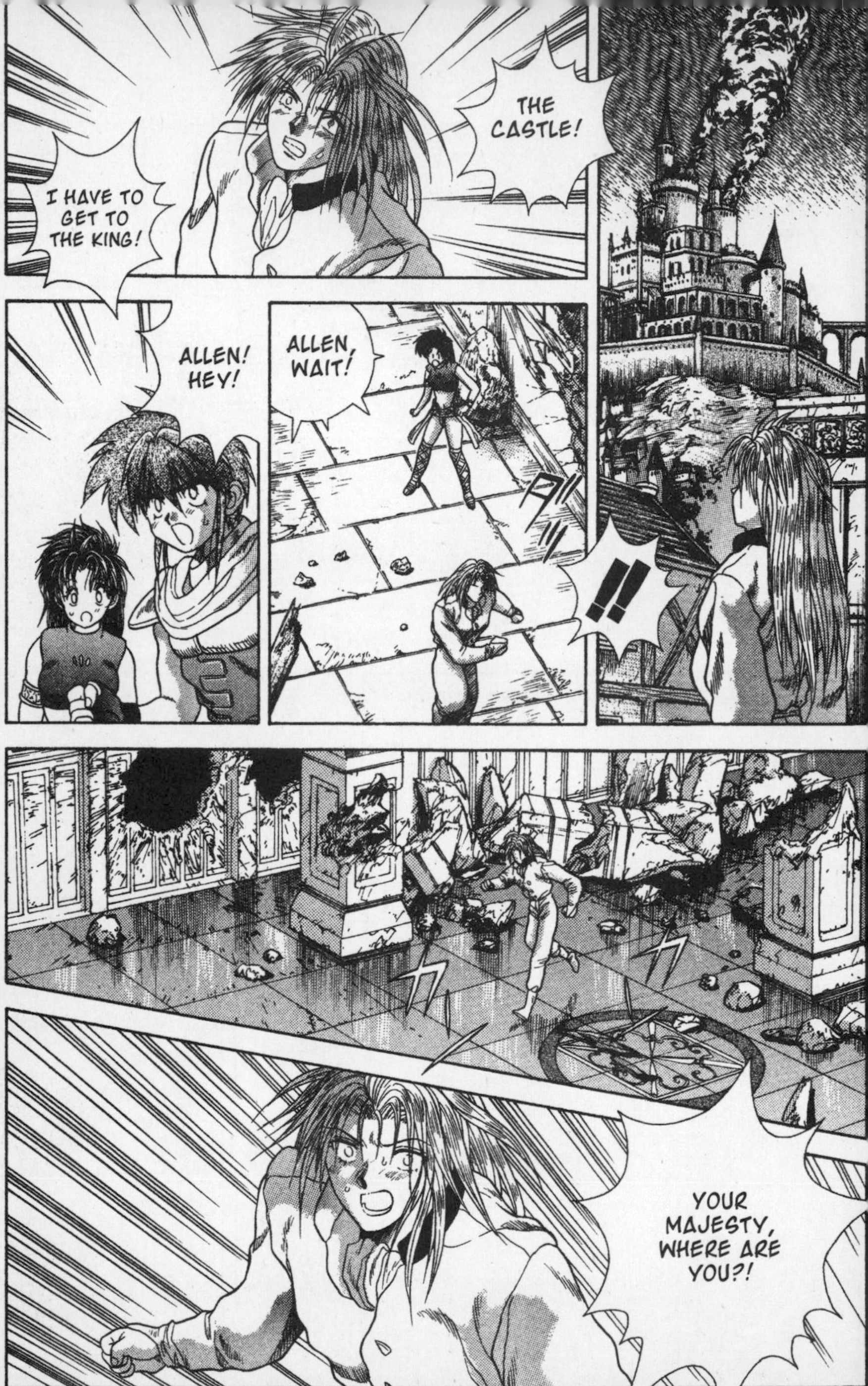
!!
THE CASTLE!
I HAVE TO GET TO THE KING!
ALLEN, WAIT!
ALLEN! HEY!
YOUR MAJESTY, WHERE ARE YOU?!

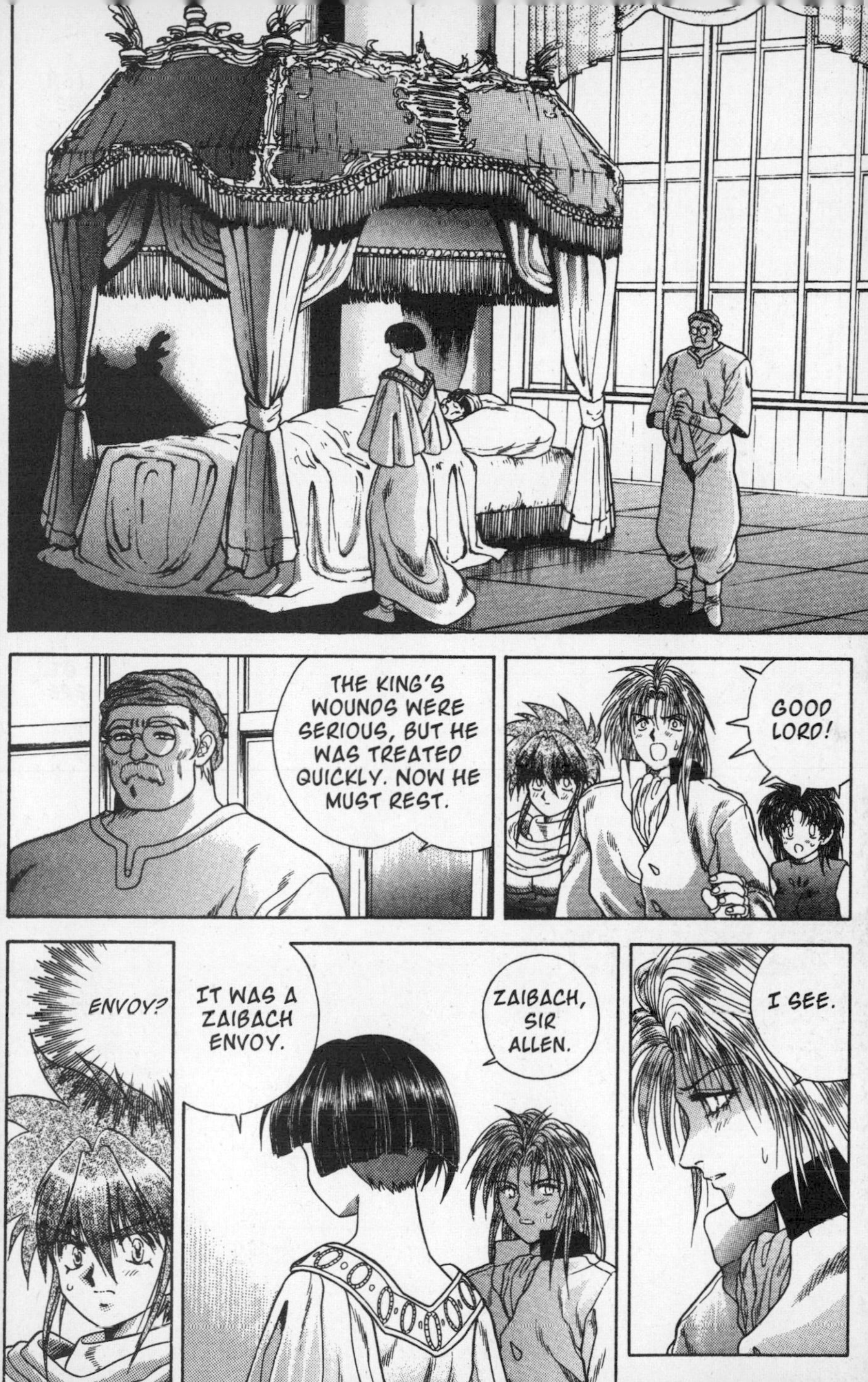
GOOD LORD!
THE KING'S WOUNDS WERE SERIOUS, BUT HE WAS TREATED QUICKLY. NOW HE MUST REST.
I SEE.
ZAIBACH, SIR ALLEN.
IT WAS A ZAIBACH ENVOY.
ENVOY?

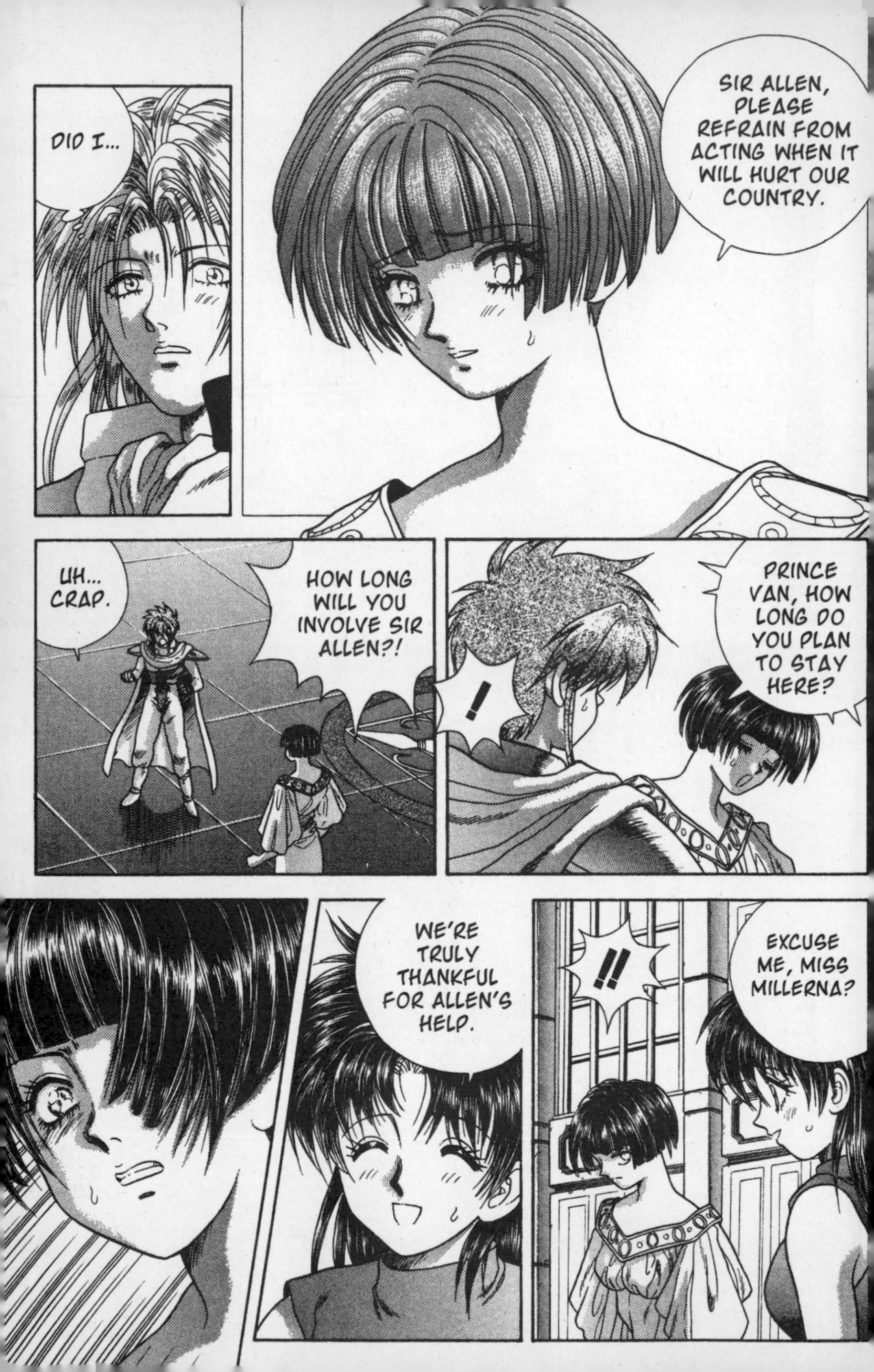

SIR ALLEN, PLEASE REFRAIN FROM ACTING WHEN IT WILL HURT OUR COUNTRY.
DID I...
PRINCE VAN, HOW LONG DO YOU PLAN TO STAY HERE?
!
HOW LONG WILL YOU INVOLVE SIR ALLEN?!
UH... CRAP.
EXCUSE ME, MISS MILLERNA?
!!
WE'RE TRULY THANKFUL FOR ALLEN'S HELP.

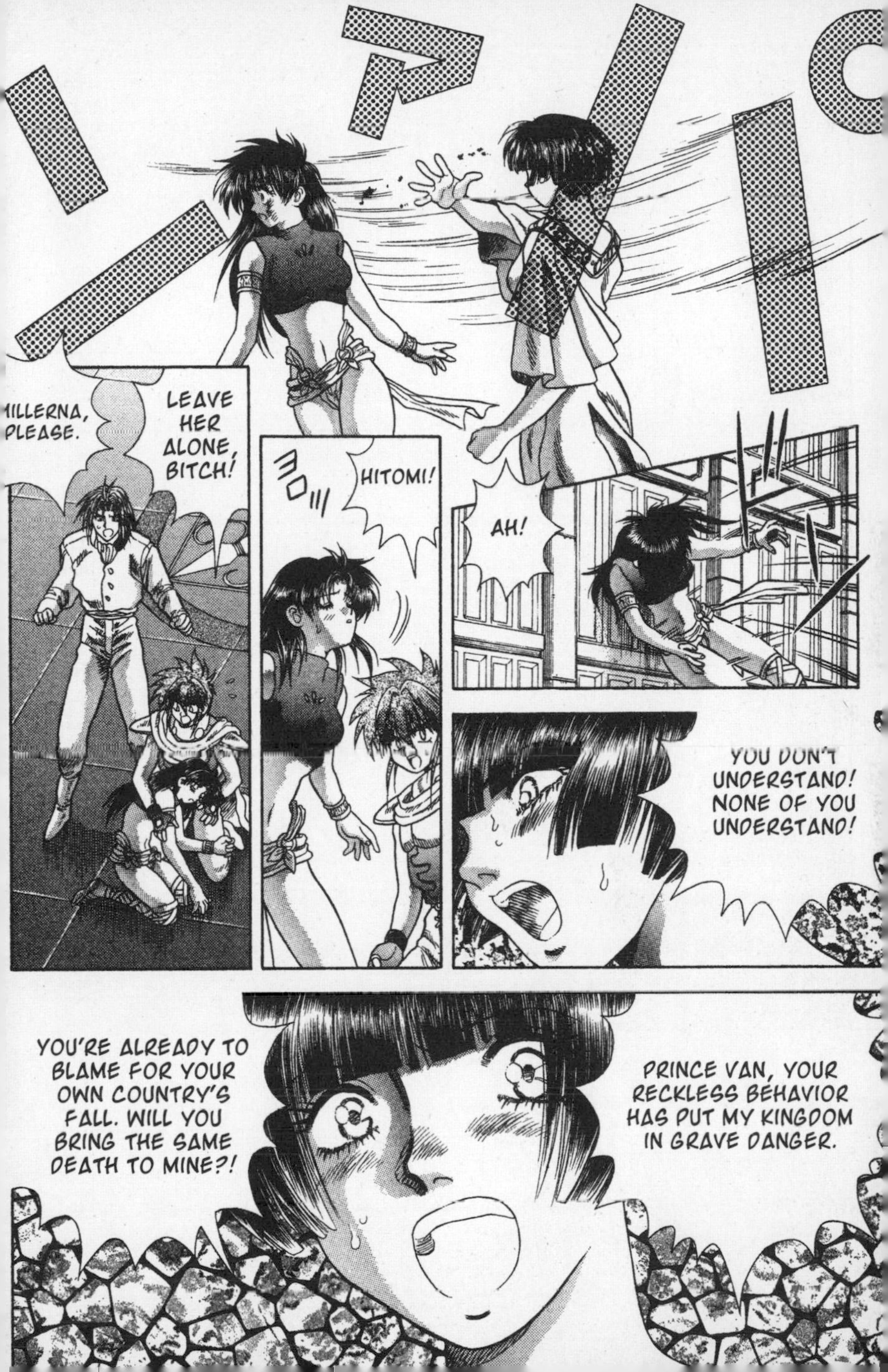
AH!
YOU DON'T UNDERSTAND! NONE OF YOU UNDERSTAND!
HITOMI!
LEAVE HER ALONE, BITCH!
ILLERNA, PLEASE.
PRINCE VAN, YOUR RECKLESS BEHAVIOR HAS PUT MY KINGDOM IN GRAVE DANGER.
YOU'RE ALREADY TO BLAME FOR YOUR OWN COUNTRY'S FALL. WILL YOU BRING THE SAME DEATH TO MINE?!

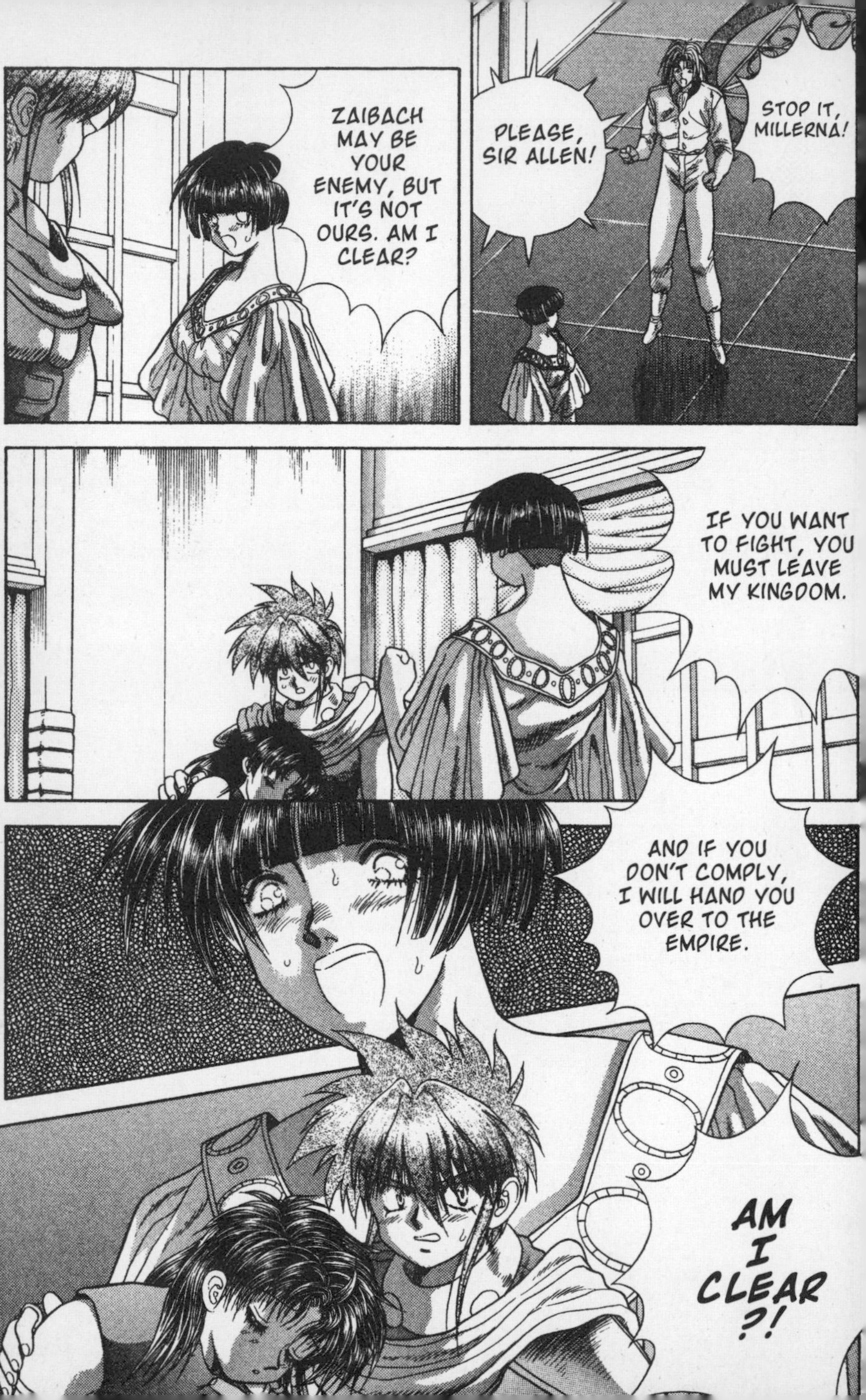
STOP IT, MILLERNA!
PLEASE, SIR ALLEN!
ZAIBACH MAY BE YOUR ENEMY, BUT IT'S NOT OURS. AM I CLEAR?
IF YOU WANT TO FIGHT, YOU MUST LEAVE MY KINGDOM.
AND IF YOU DON'T COMPLY, I WILL HAND YOU OVER TO THE EMPIRE.
AM I CLEAR?!

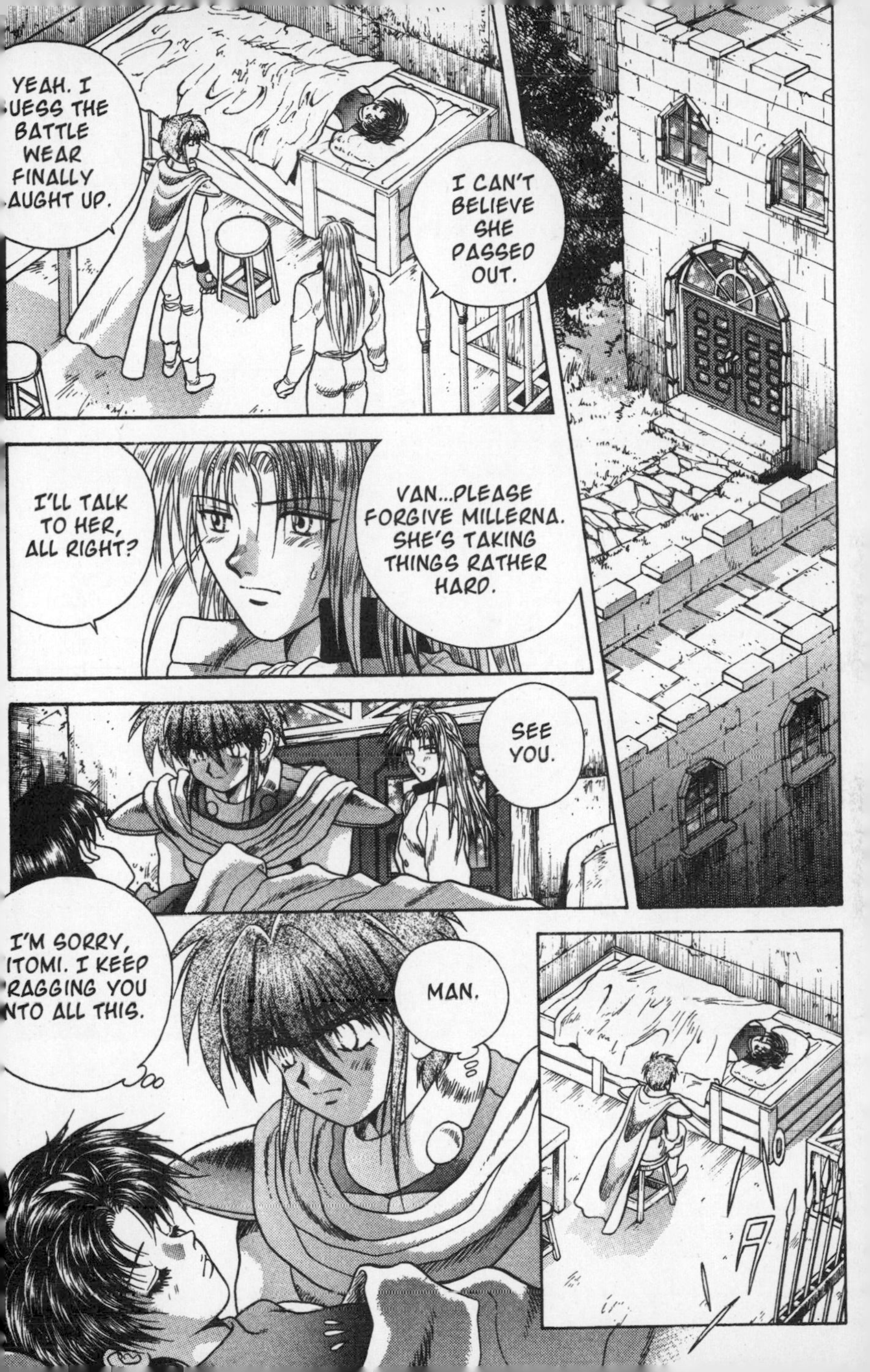
I CAN'T BELIEVE SHE PASSED OUT.
YEAH. I UESS THE BATTLE WEAR FINALLY AUGHT UP.
VAN...PLEASE FORGIVE MILLERNA. SHE'S TAKING THINGS RATHER HARD.
I'LL TALK TO HER, ALL RIGHT?
SEE YOU.
MAN.
I'M SORRY, ITOMI. I KEEP RAGGING YOU NTO ALL THIS.

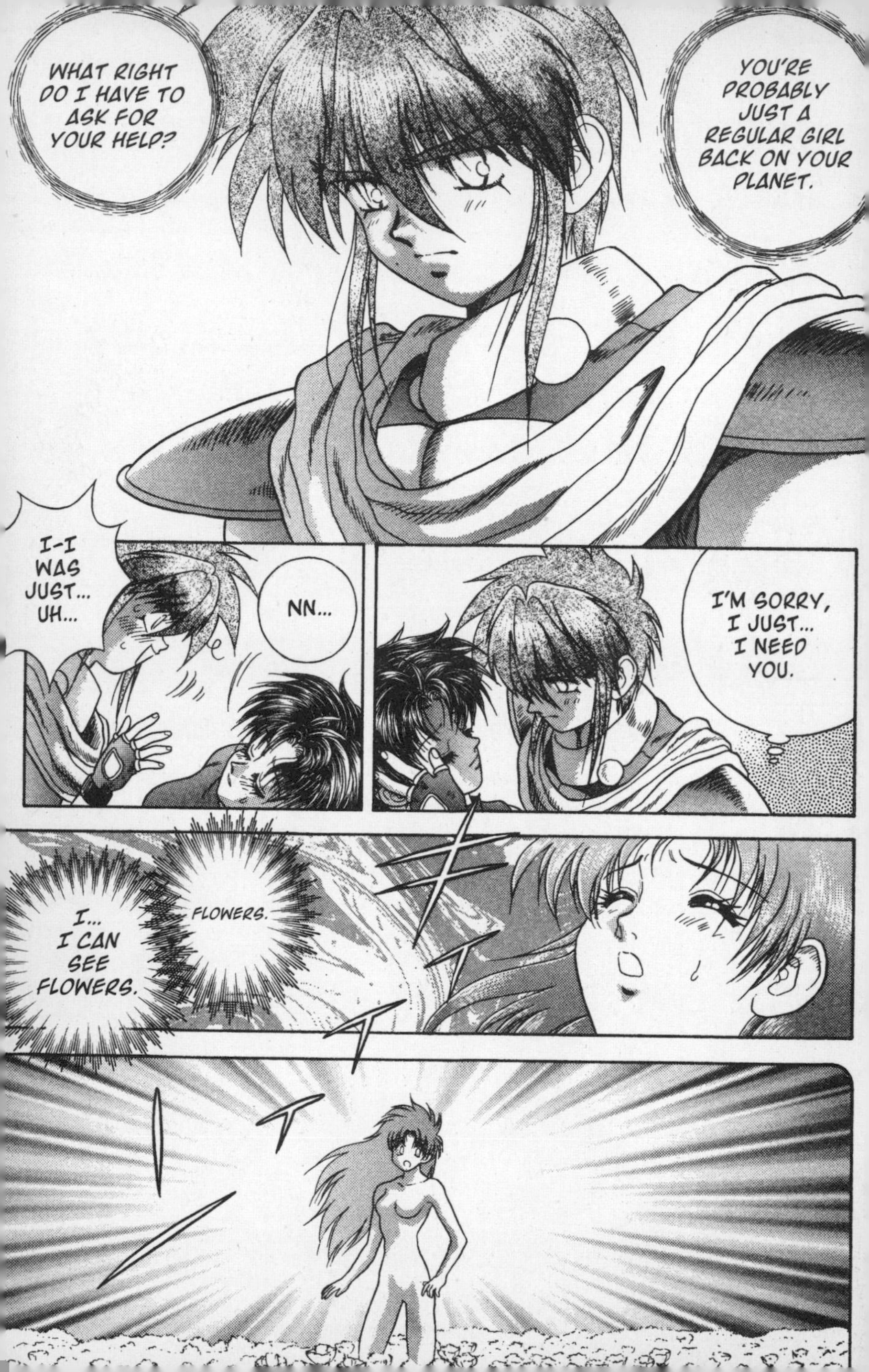
YOU'RE PROBABLY JUST A REGULAR GIRL BACK ON YOUR PLANET.
WHAT RIGHT DO I HAVE TO ASK FOR YOUR HELP?
I'M SORRY, I JUST... I NEED YOU.
I-I WAS JUST... UH...
NN...
FLOWERS.
I... I CAN SEE FLOWERS.

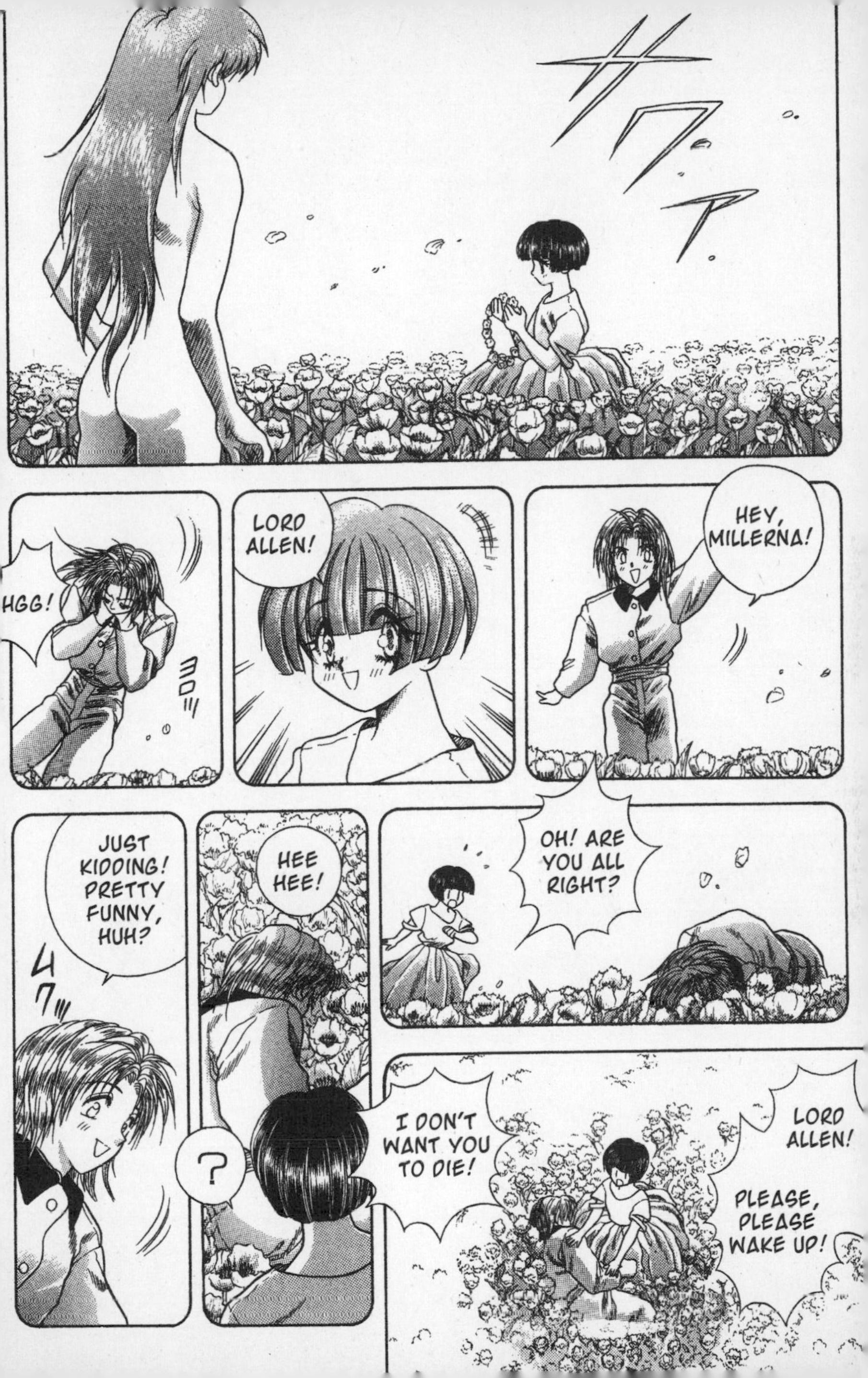
HEY, MILLERNA!
LORD ALLEN!
HGG!
OH! ARE YOU ALL RIGHT?
HEE HEE!
JUST KIDDING! PRETTY FUNNY, HUH?
LORD ALLEN!
PLEASE, PLEASE WAKE UP!
I DON'T WANT YOU TO DIE!
?

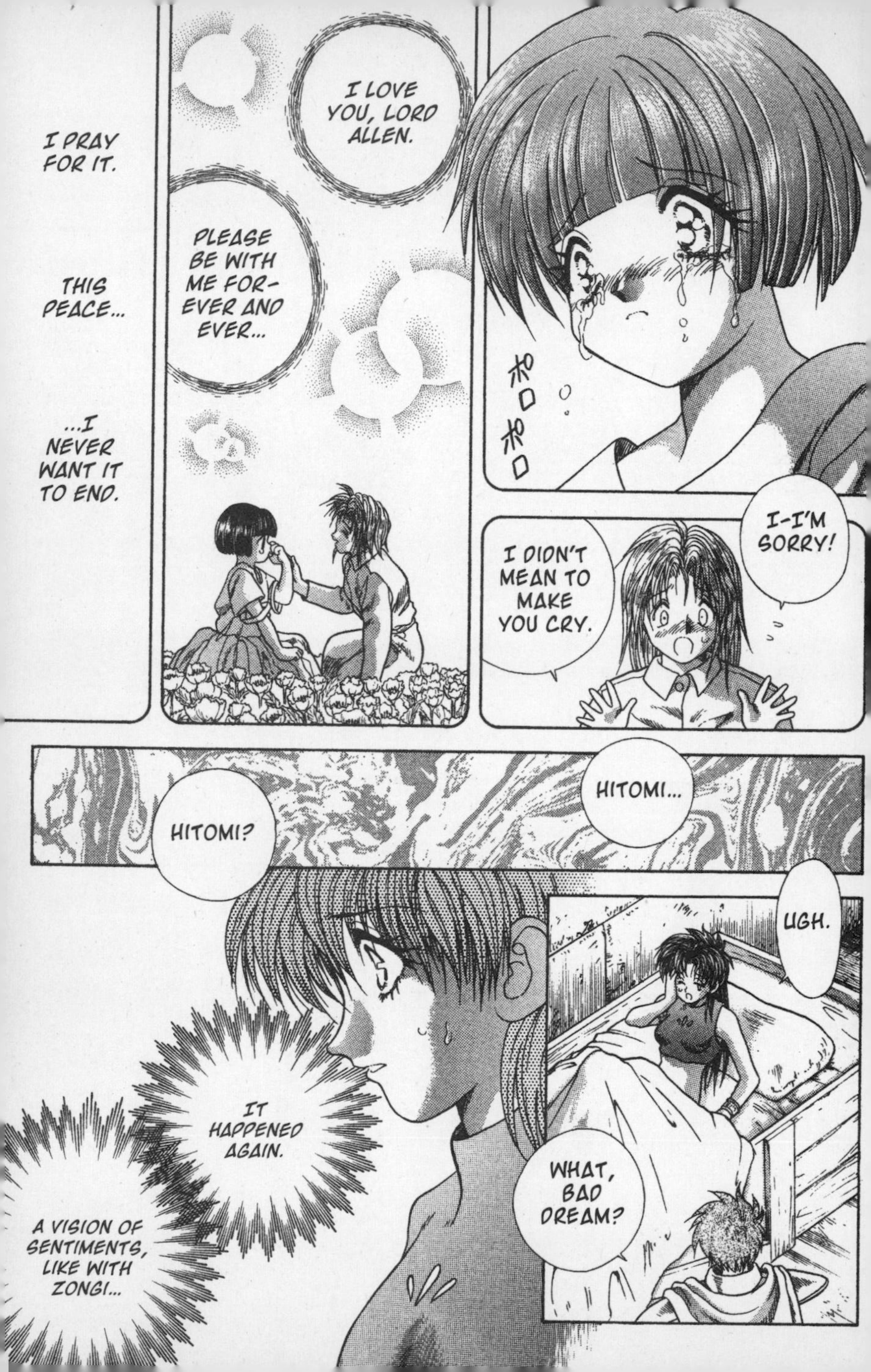
ポロポロ
I-I'M SORRY!
I DIDN'T MEAN TO MAKE YOU CRY.
I LOVE YOU, LORD ALLEN.
PLEASE BE WITH ME FOR-EVER AND EVER...
I PRAY FOR IT.
THIS PEACE...
...I NEVER WANT IT TO END.
HITOMI...
HITOMI?
UGH.
WHAT, BAD DREAM?
IT HAPPENED AGAIN.
A VISION OF SENTIMENTS, LIKE WITH ZONGI...

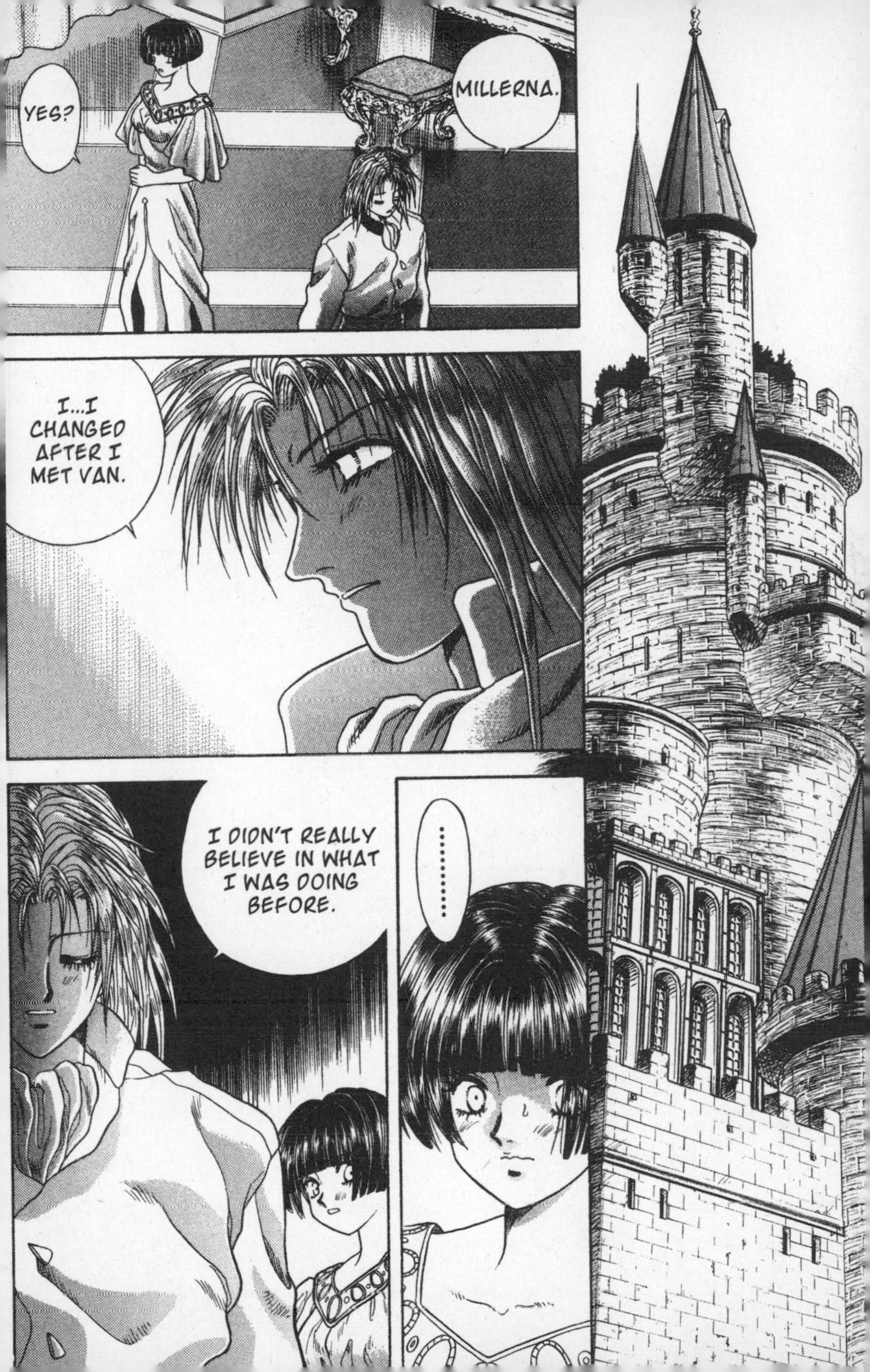
MILLERNA.
YES?
I...I CHANGED AFTER I MET VAN.
......
I DIDN'T REALLY BELIEVE IN WHAT I WAS DOING BEFORE.

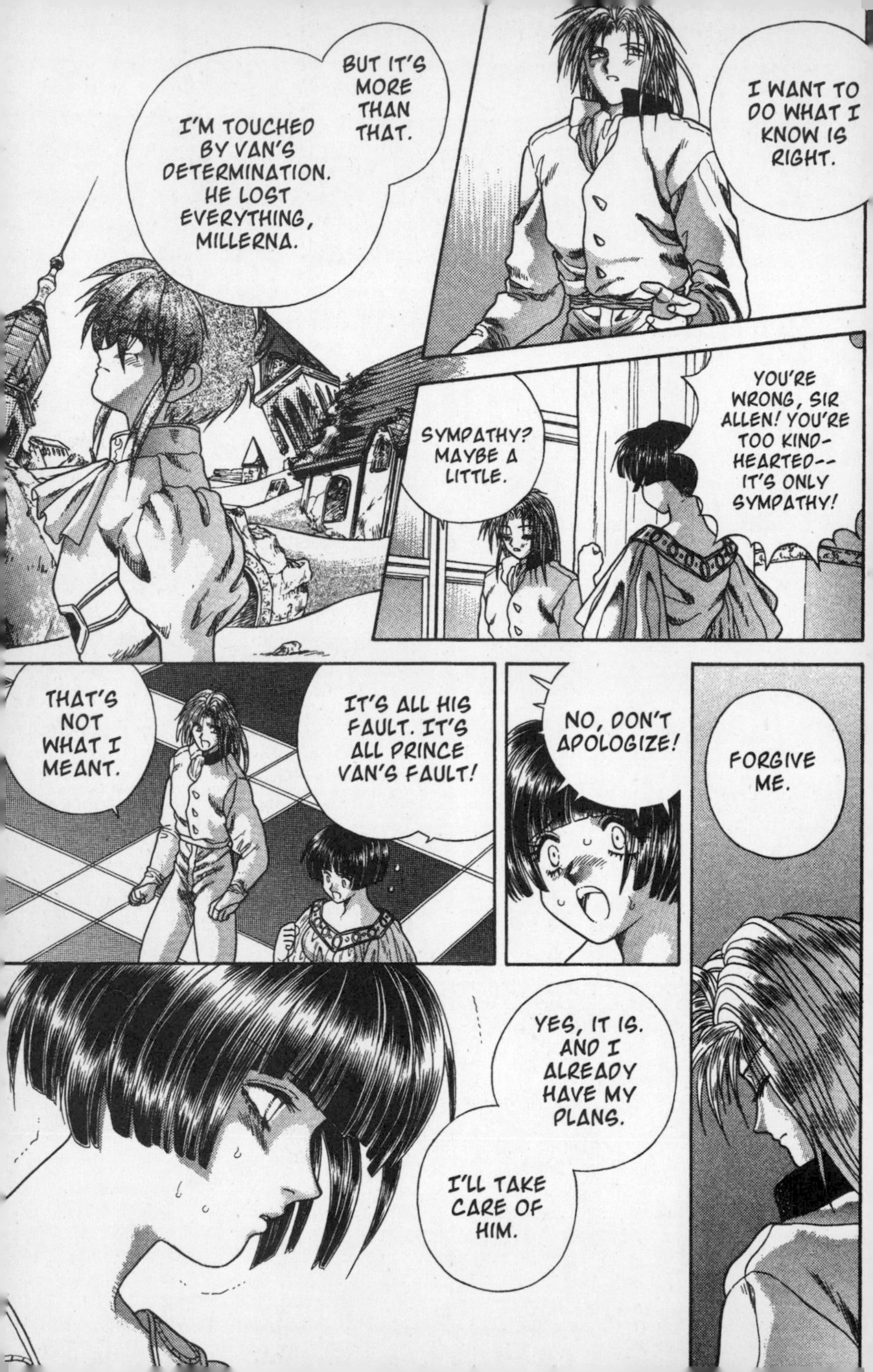
I WANT TO DO WHAT I KNOW IS RIGHT.
YOU'RE WRONG, SIR ALLEN! YOU'RE TOO KIND-HEARTED--IT'S ONLY SYMPATHY!
SYMPATHY? MAYBE A LITTLE.
I'M TOUCHED BY VAN'S DETERMINATION. HE LOST EVERYTHING, MILLERNA.
BUT IT'S MORE THAN THAT.
FORGIVE ME.
NO, DON'T APOLOGIZE!
IT'S ALL HIS FAULT. IT'S ALL PRINCE VAN'S FAULT!
THAT'S NOT WHAT I MEANT.
YES, IT IS. AND I ALREADY HAVE MY PLANS.
I'LL TAKE CARE OF HIM.

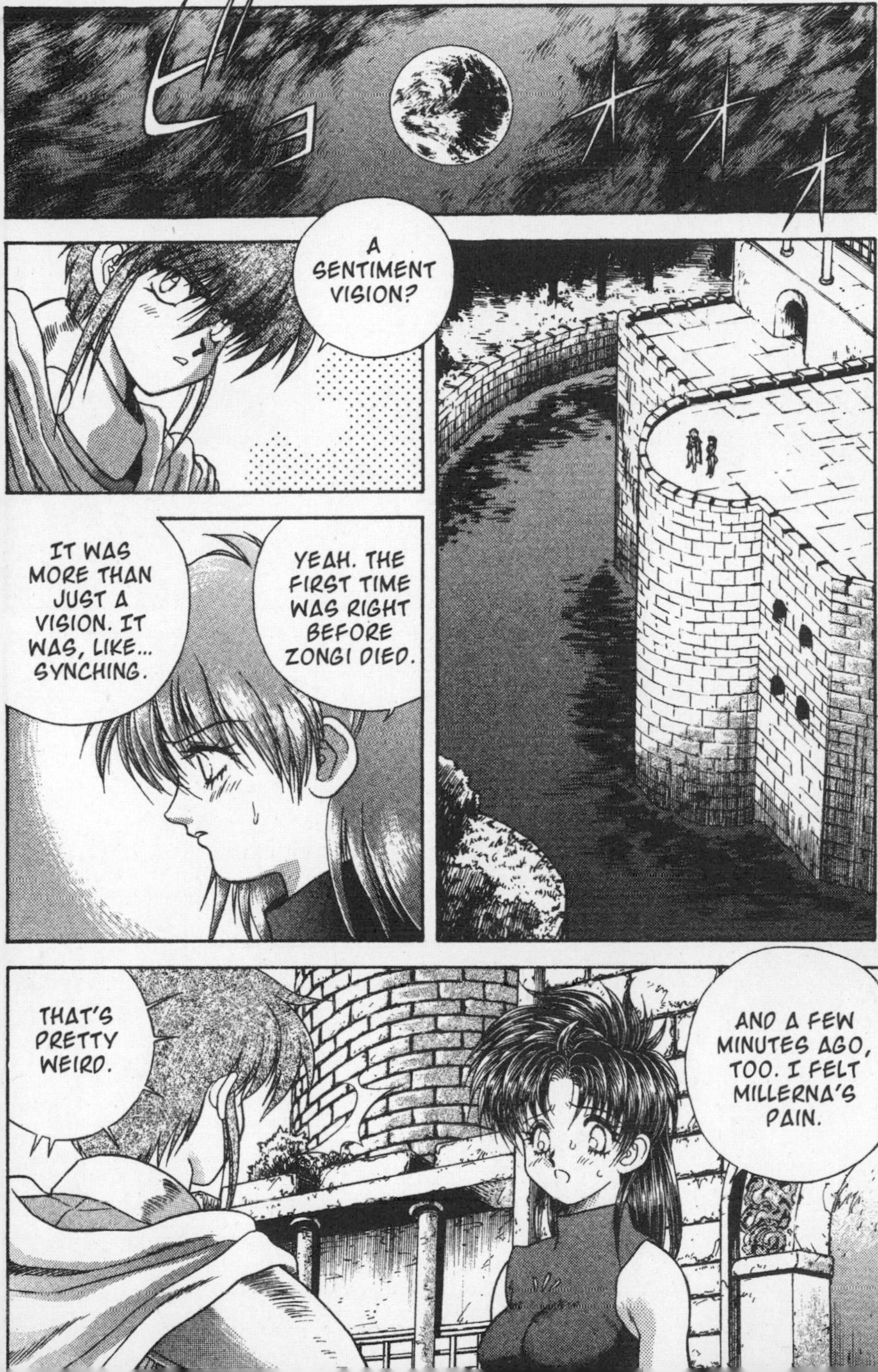
ビュオオオ
A SENTIMENT VISION?
YEAH. THE FIRST TIME WAS RIGHT BEFORE ZONGI DIED.
IT WAS MORE THAN JUST A VISION. IT WAS, LIKE... SYNCHING.
AND A FEW MINUTES AGO, TOO. I FELT MILLERNA'S PAIN.
THAT'S PRETTY WEIRD.

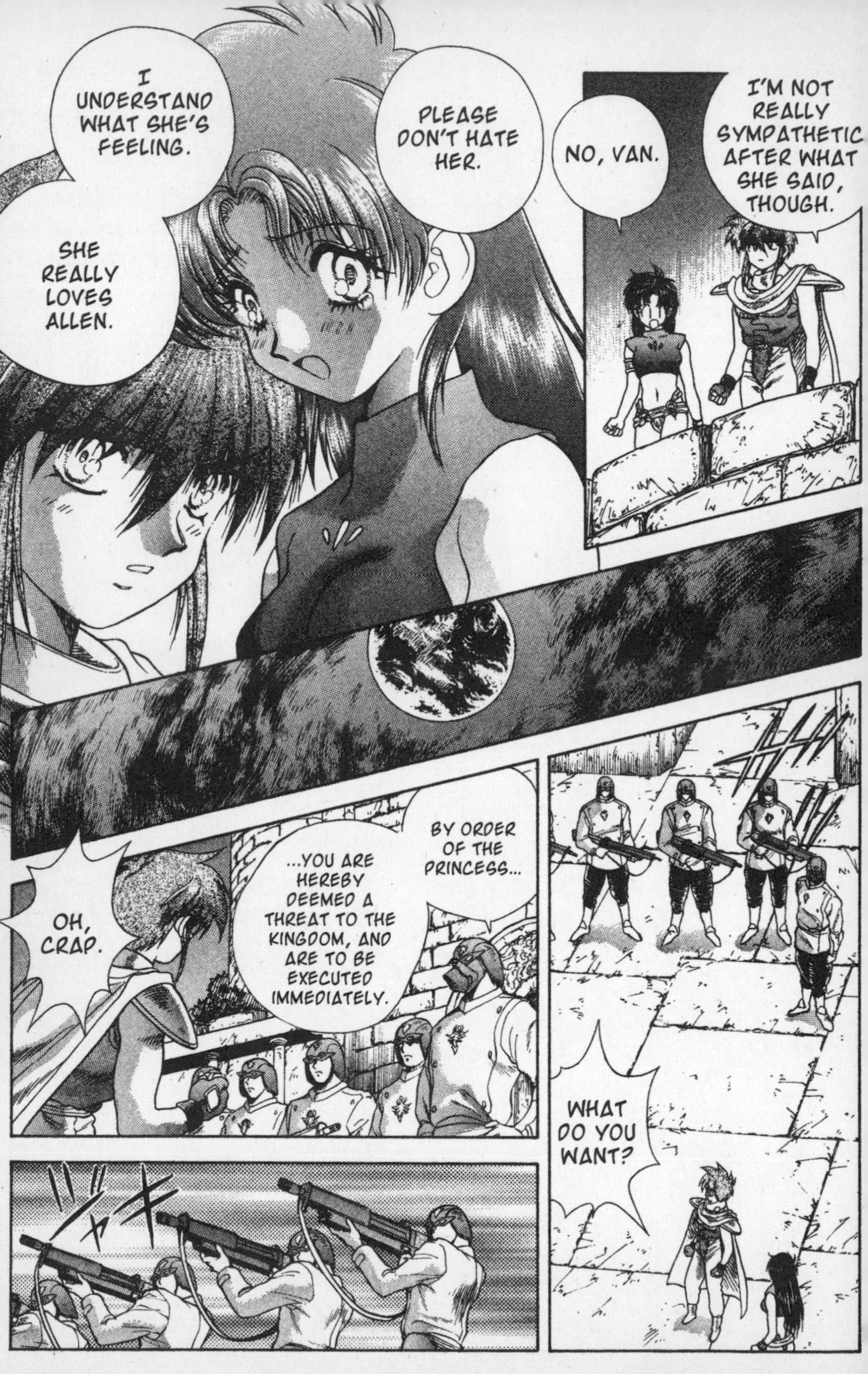
I'M NOT REALLY SYMPATHETIC AFTER WHAT SHE SAID, THOUGH.
NO, VAN.
PLEASE DON'T HATE HER.
I UNDERSTAND WHAT SHE'S FEELING.
SHE REALLY LOVES ALLEN.
WHAT DO YOU WANT?
BY ORDER OF THE PRINCESS...
...YOU ARE HEREBY DEEMED A THREAT TO THE KINGDOM, AND ARE TO BE EXECUTED IMMEDIATELY.
OH, CRAP.

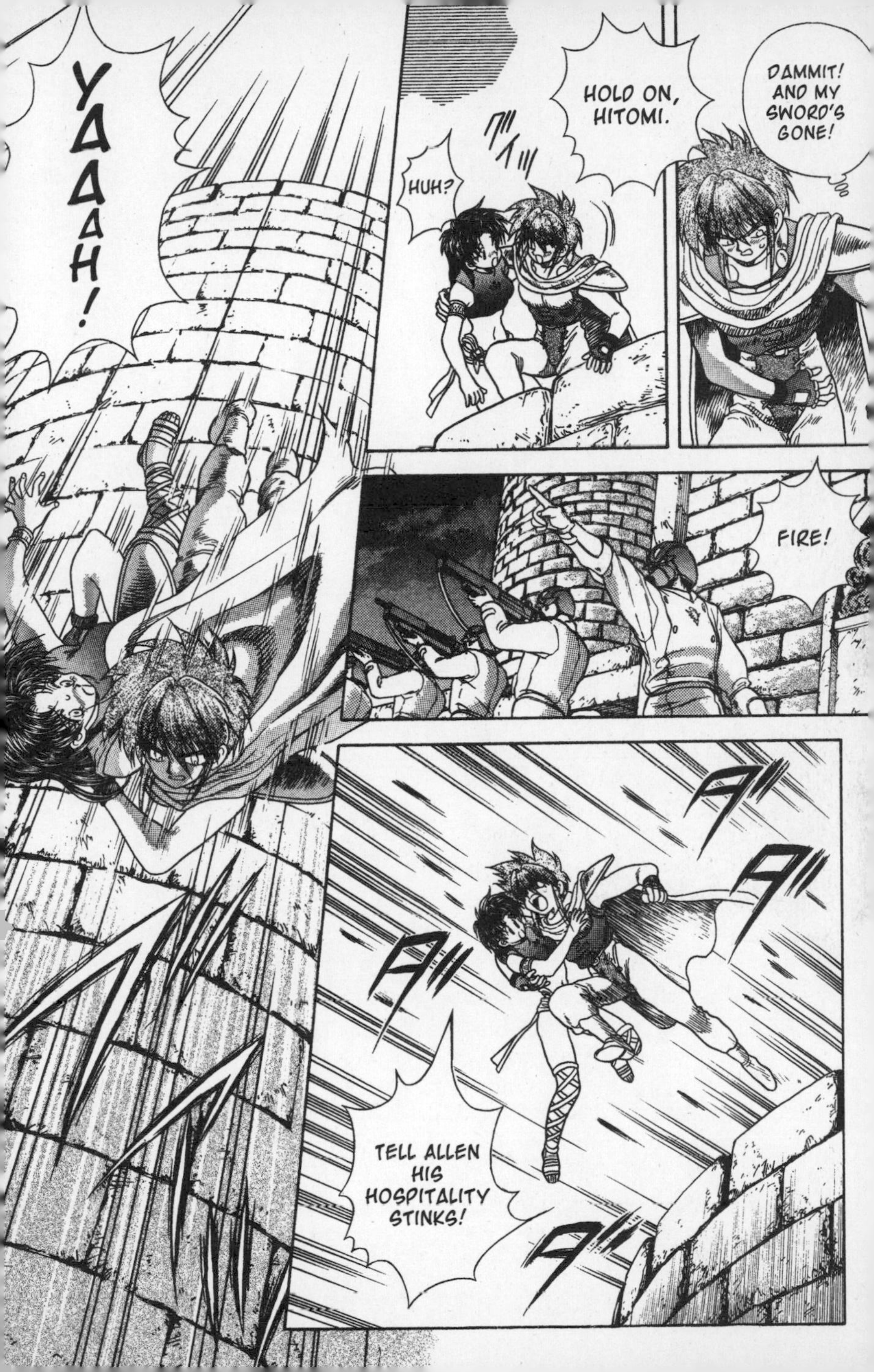
DAMMIT! AND MY SWORD'S GONE!
HOLD ON, HITOMI.
HUH?
FIRE!
TELL ALLEN HIS HOSPITALITY STINKS!
YAAAAH!

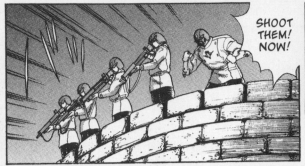

SHOOT THEM! NOW!

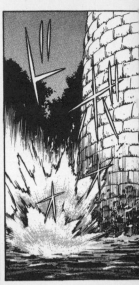

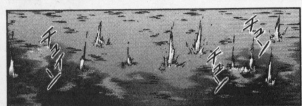

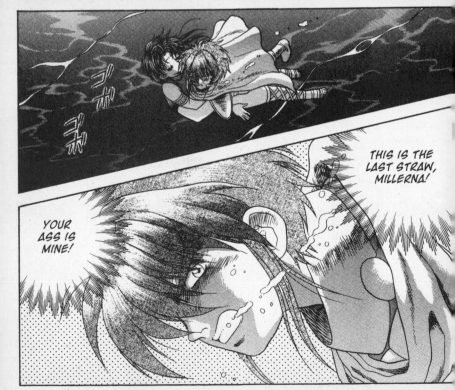

THIS IS THE LAST STRAW, MILLERNA!

YOUR ASS IS MINE!

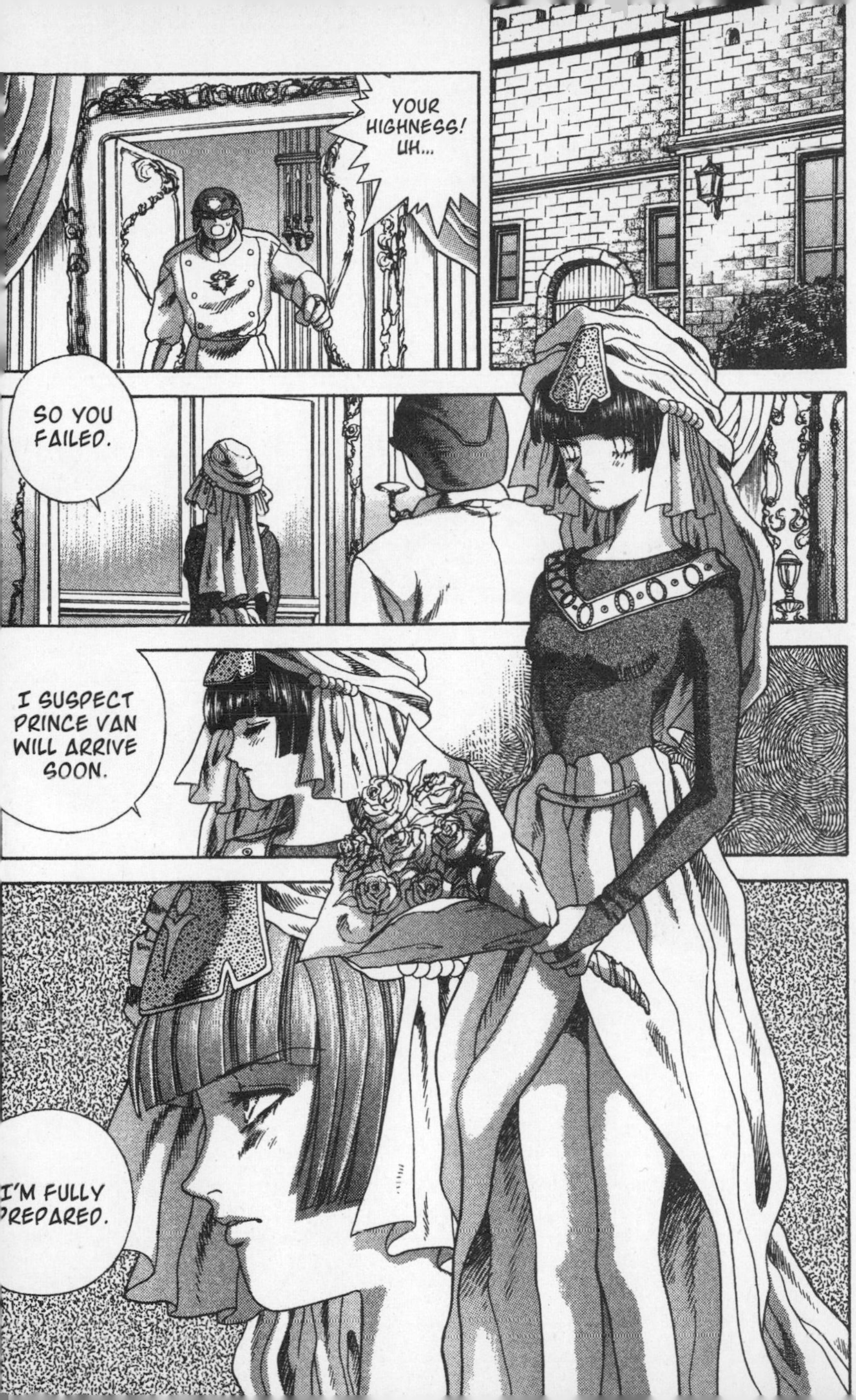
YOUR HIGHNESS! UH...
SO YOU FAILED.
I SUSPECT PRINCE VAN WILL ARRIVE SOON.
I'M FULLY PREPARED.

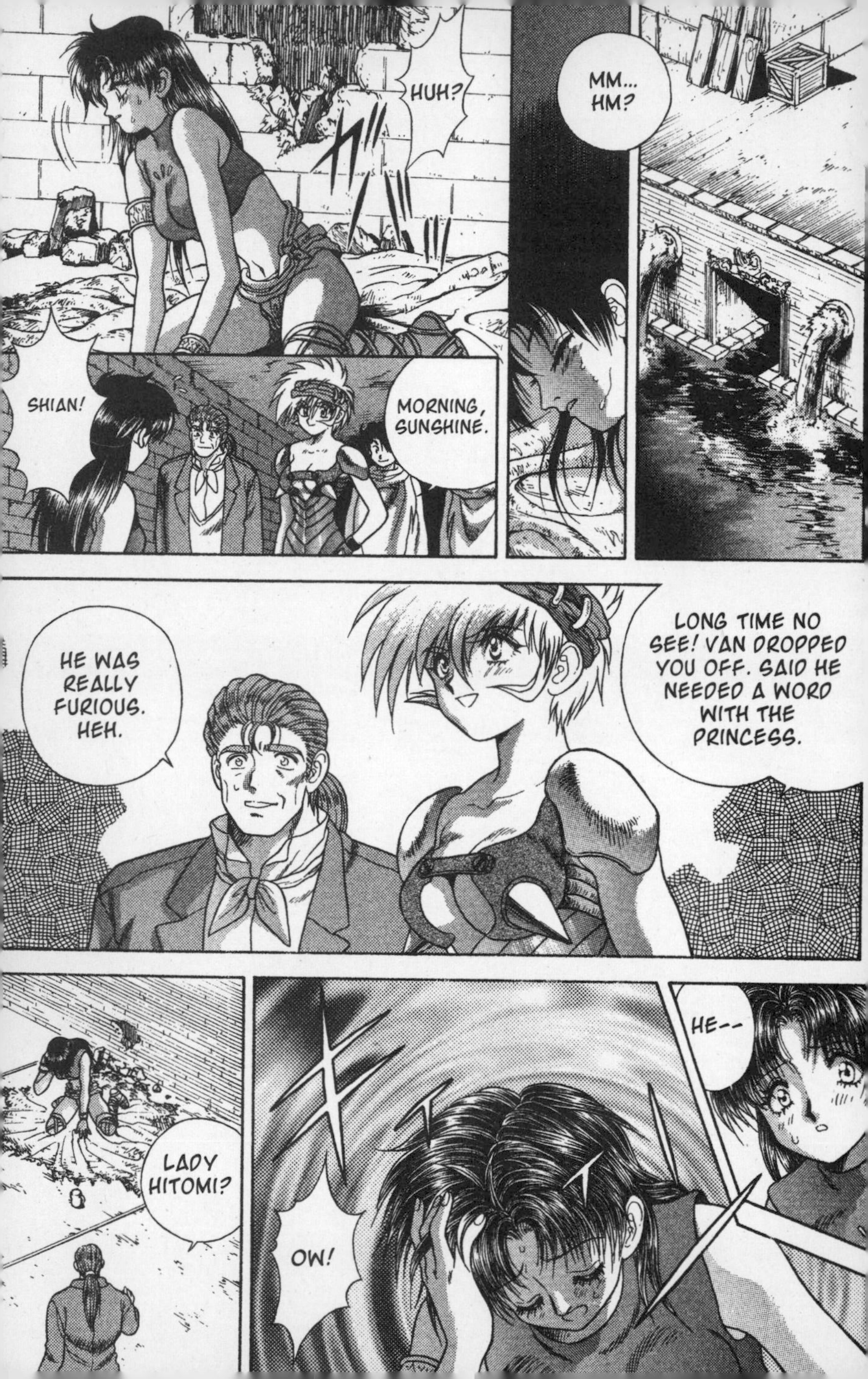
MM... HM?
HUH?
MORNING, SUNSHINE.
SHIAN!
LONG TIME NO SEE! VAN DROPPED YOU OFF. SAID HE NEEDED A WORD WITH THE PRINCESS.
HE WAS REALLY FURIOUS. HEH.
HE--
OW!
LADY HITOMI?

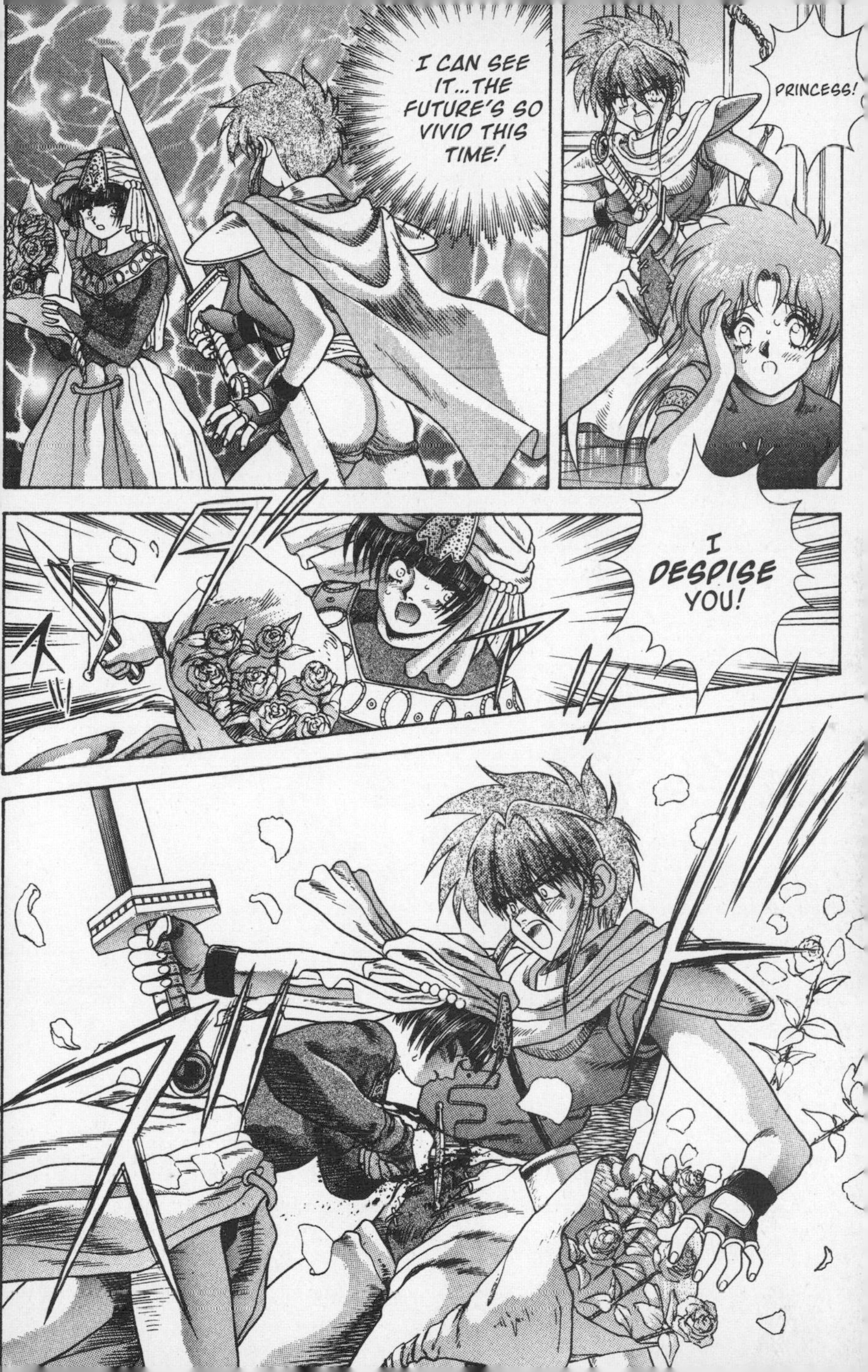
PRINCESS!
I CAN SEE IT...THE FUTURE'S SO VIVID THIS TIME!
I DESPISE YOU!

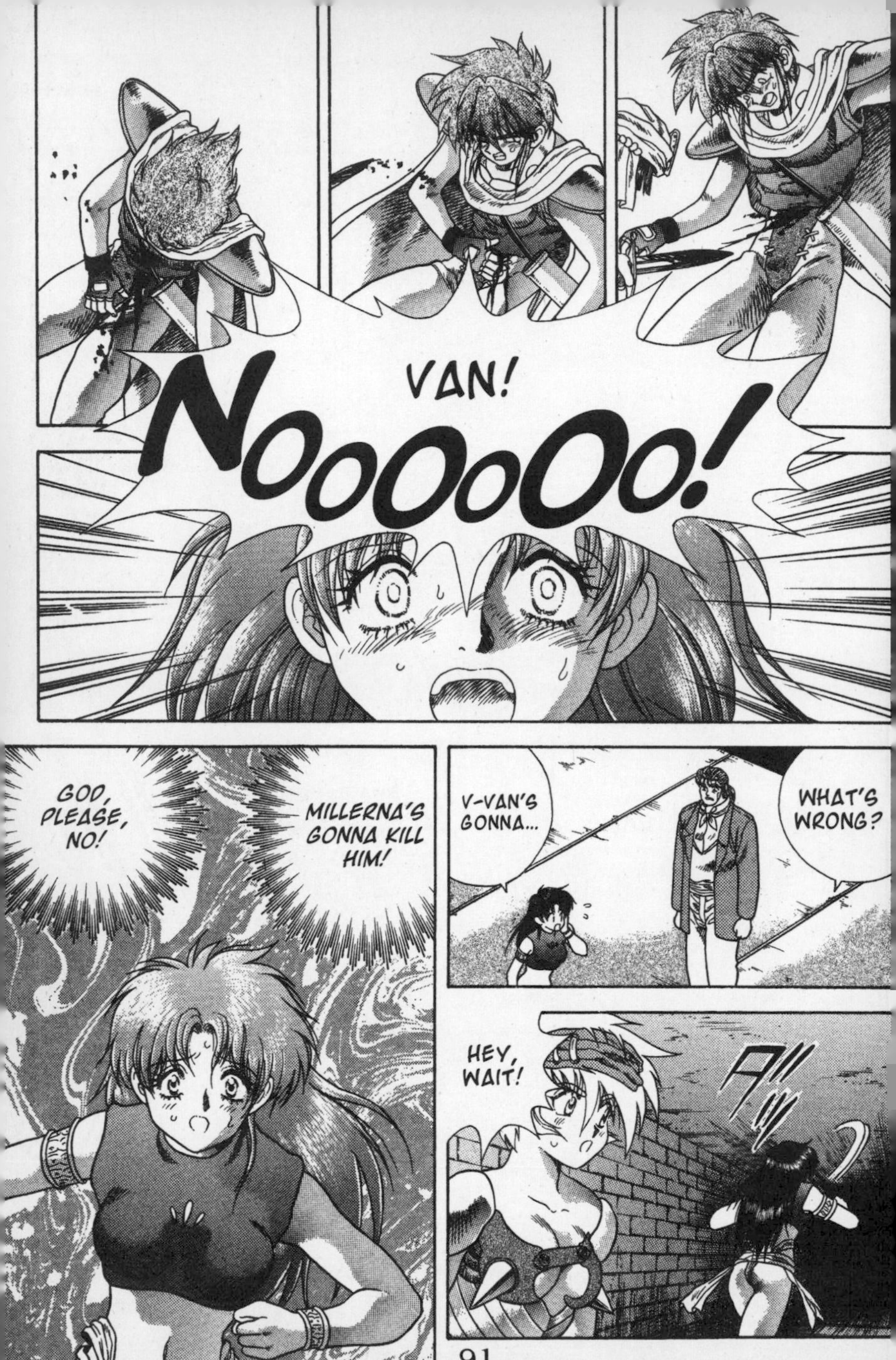
VAN!
NOOOOOO!
WHAT'S WRONG?
V-VAN'S GONNA...
HEY, WAIT!
MILLERNA'S GONNA KILL HIM!
GOD, PLEASE, NO!

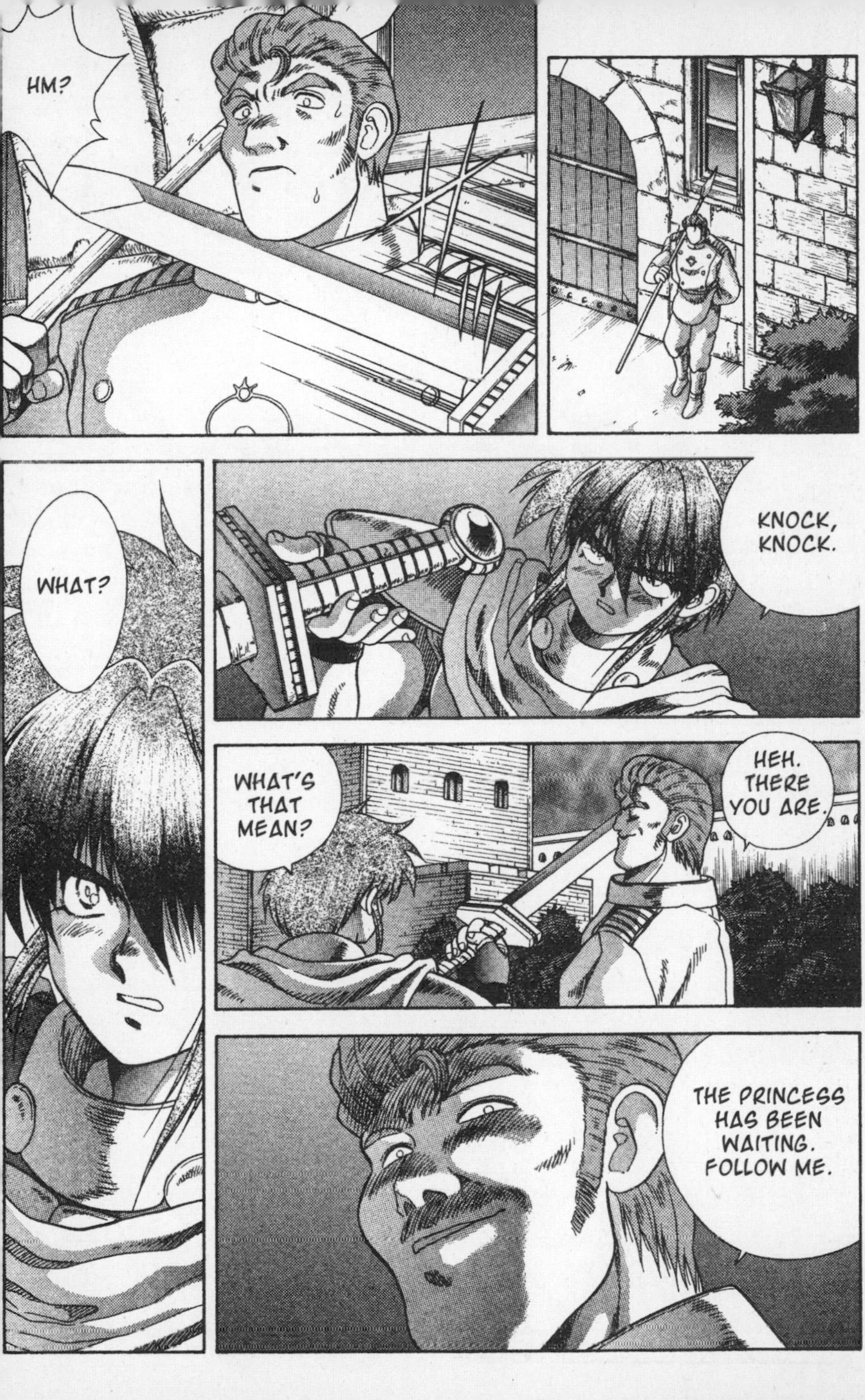
HM?
KNOCK, KNOCK.
HEH. THERE YOU ARE.
WHAT'S THAT MEAN?
THE PRINCESS HAS BEEN WAITING. FOLLOW ME.
WHAT?

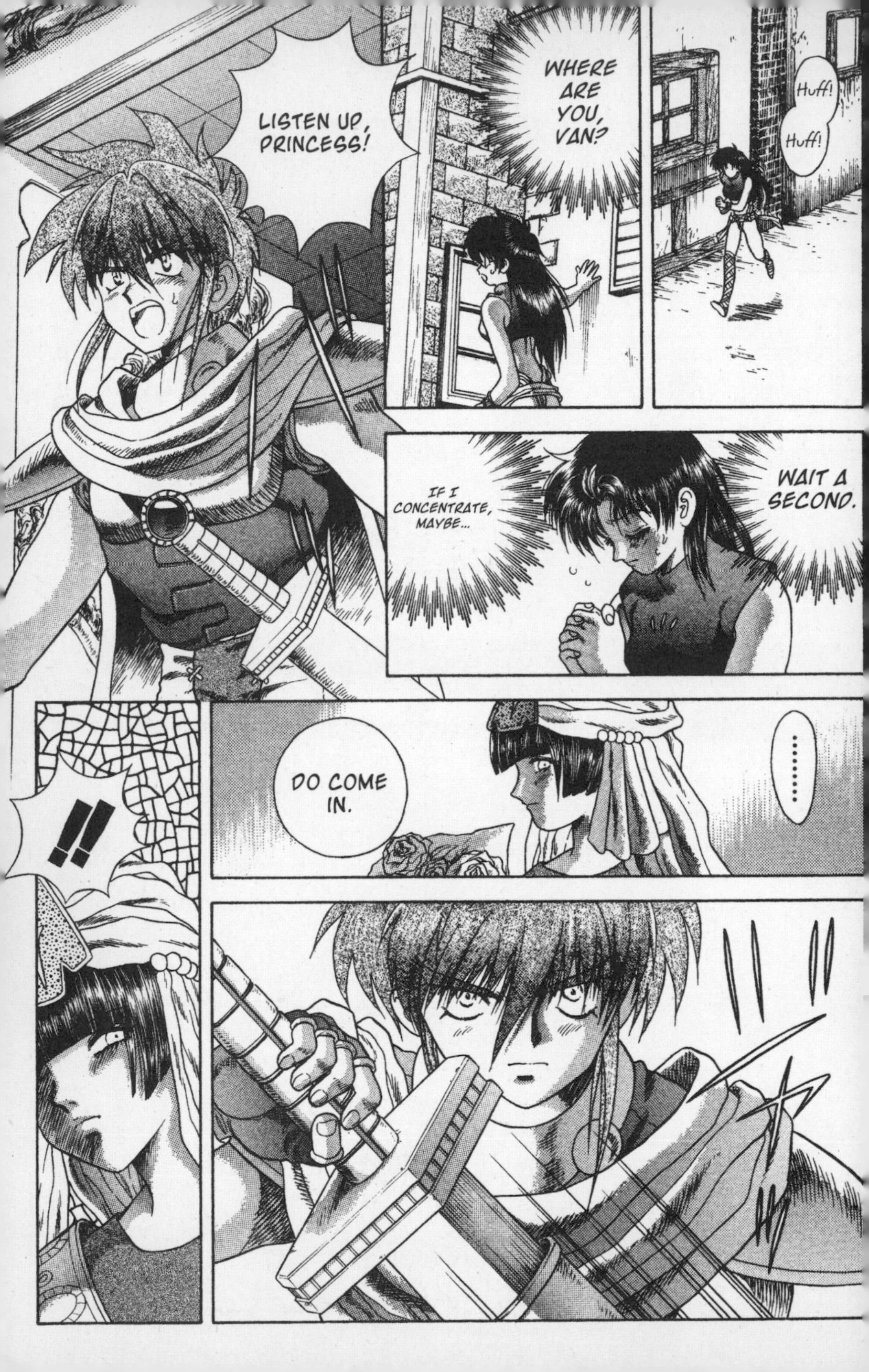
Huff!
Huff!
WHERE ARE YOU, VAN?
WAIT A SECOND.
IF I CONCENTRATE, MAYBE...
LISTEN UP, PRINCESS!
......
DO COME IN.
!!

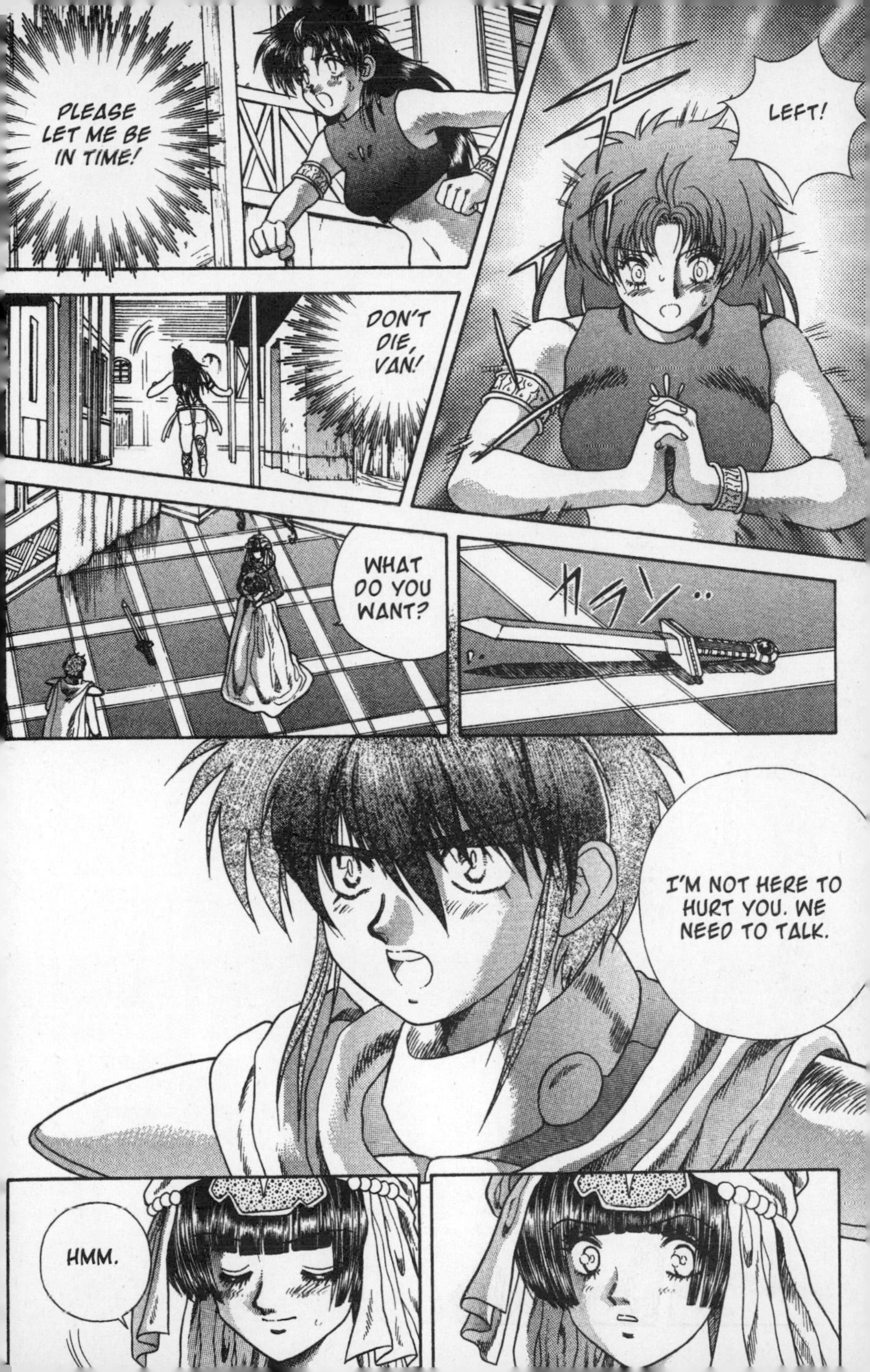
LEFT!
PLEASE LET ME BE IN TIME!
DON'T DIE, VAN!
カラン
WHAT DO YOU WANT?
I'M NOT HERE TO HURT YOU. WE NEED TO TALK.
HMM.

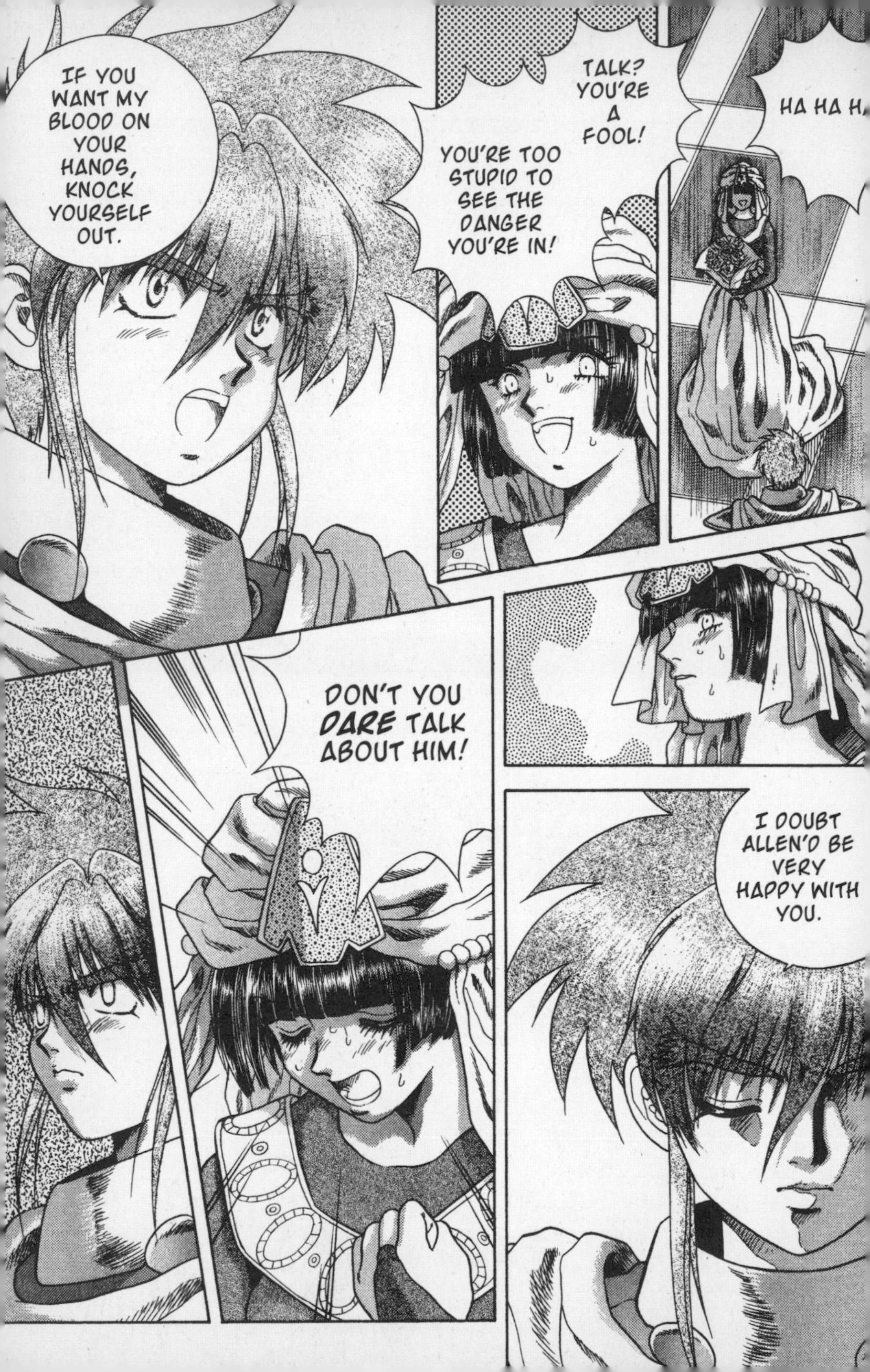
HA HA H,
TALK? YOU'RE A FOOL!
YOU'RE TOO STUPID TO SEE THE DANGER YOU'RE IN!
IF YOU WANT MY BLOOD ON YOUR HANDS, KNOCK YOURSELF OUT.
I DOUBT ALLEN'D BE VERY HAPPY WITH YOU.
DON'T YOU *DARE* TALK ABOUT HIM!

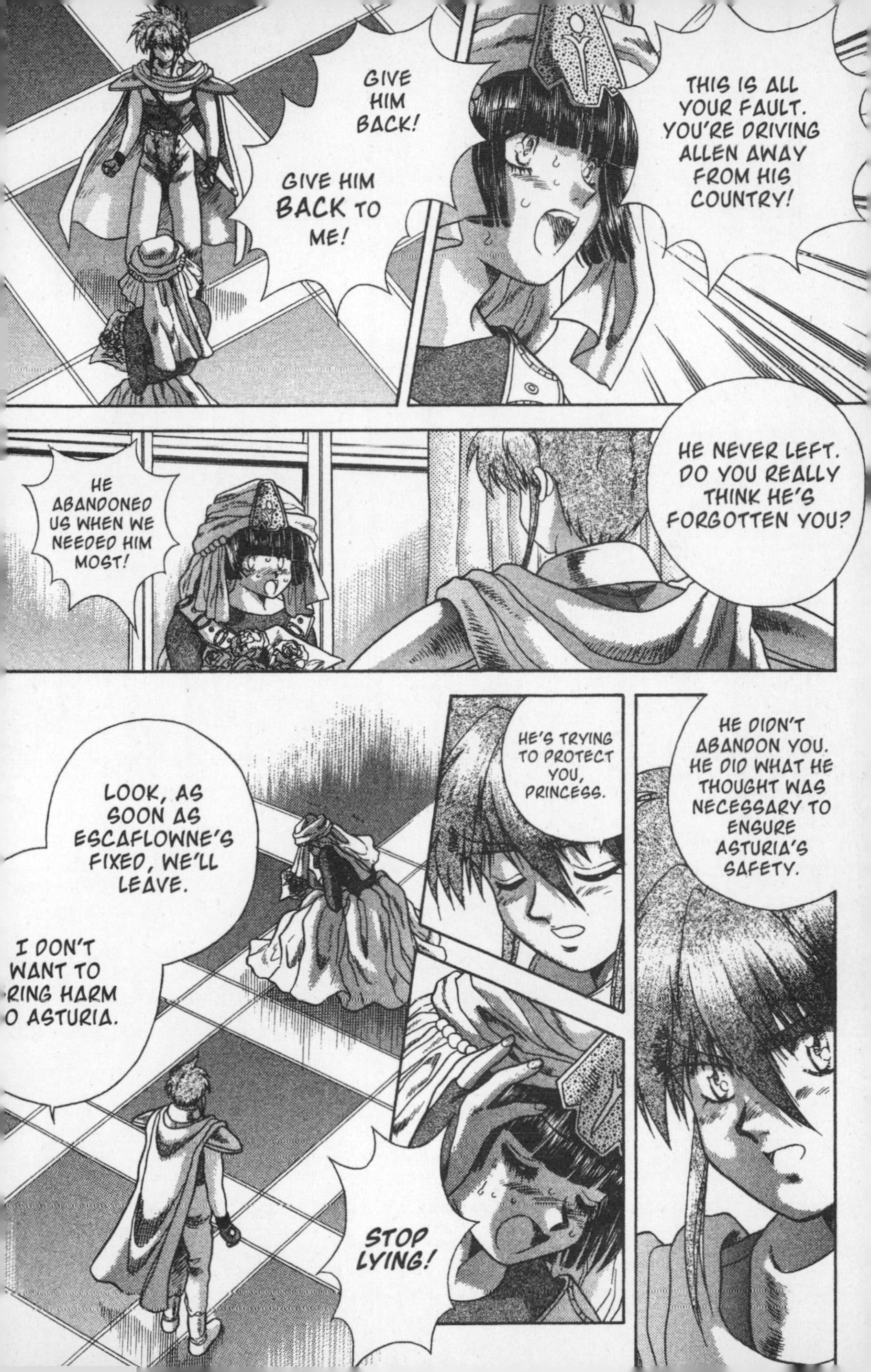
THIS IS ALL YOUR FAULT. YOU'RE DRIVING ALLEN AWAY FROM HIS COUNTRY!
GIVE HIM BACK!
GIVE HIM BACK TO ME!
HE NEVER LEFT. DO YOU REALLY THINK HE'S FORGOTTEN YOU?
HE ABANDONED US WHEN WE NEEDED HIM MOST!
HE DIDN'T ABANDON YOU. HE DID WHAT HE THOUGHT WAS NECESSARY TO ENSURE ASTURIA'S SAFETY.
HE'S TRYING TO PROTECT YOU, PRINCESS.
STOP LYING!
LOOK, AS SOON AS ESCAFLOWNE'S FIXED, WE'LL LEAVE.
I DON'T WANT TO RING HARM O ASTURIA.

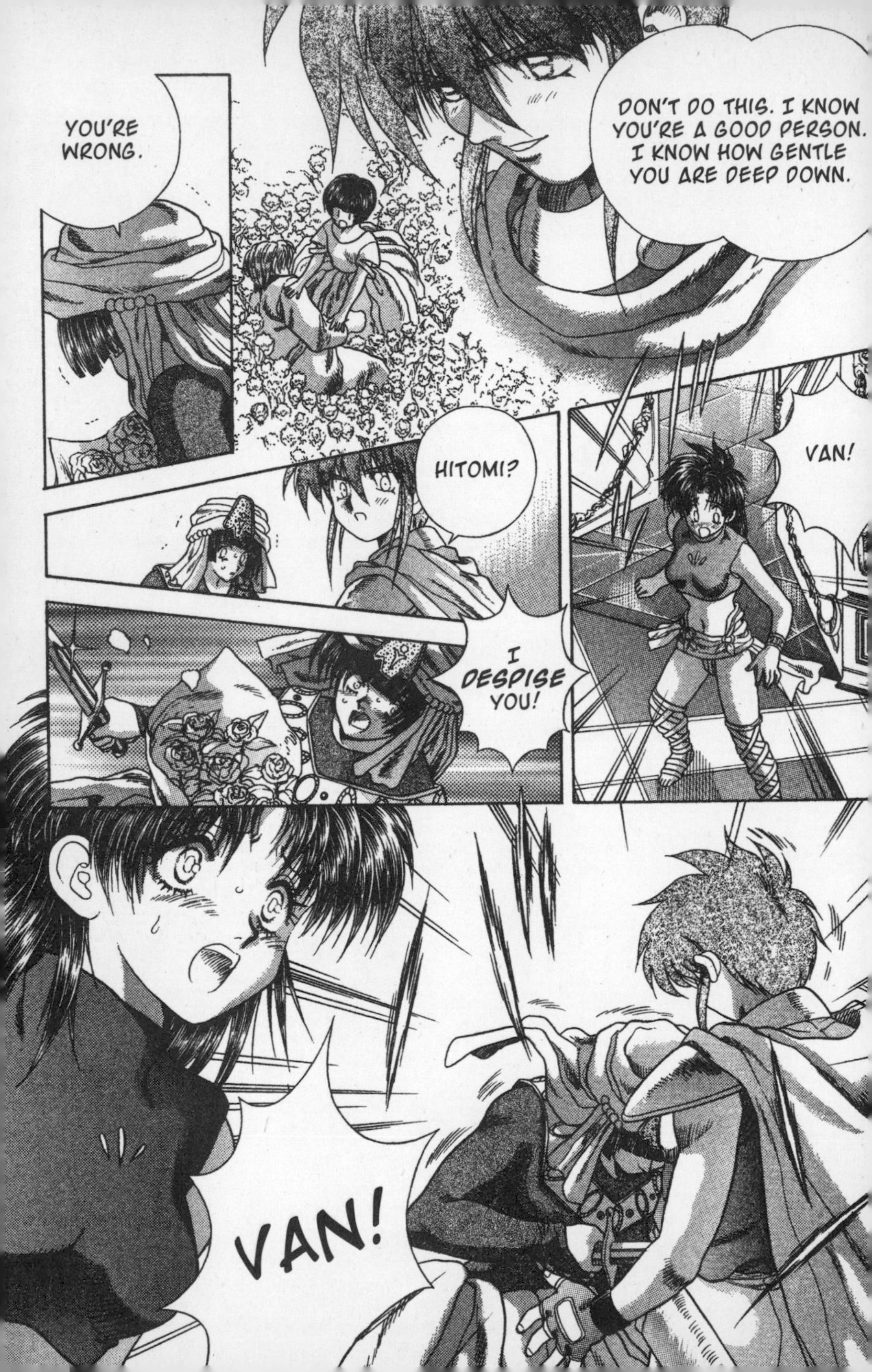
DON'T DO THIS. I KNOW YOU'RE A GOOD PERSON. I KNOW HOW GENTLE YOU ARE DEEP DOWN.
YOU'RE WRONG.
VAN!
HITOMI?
I DESPISE YOU!
VAN!

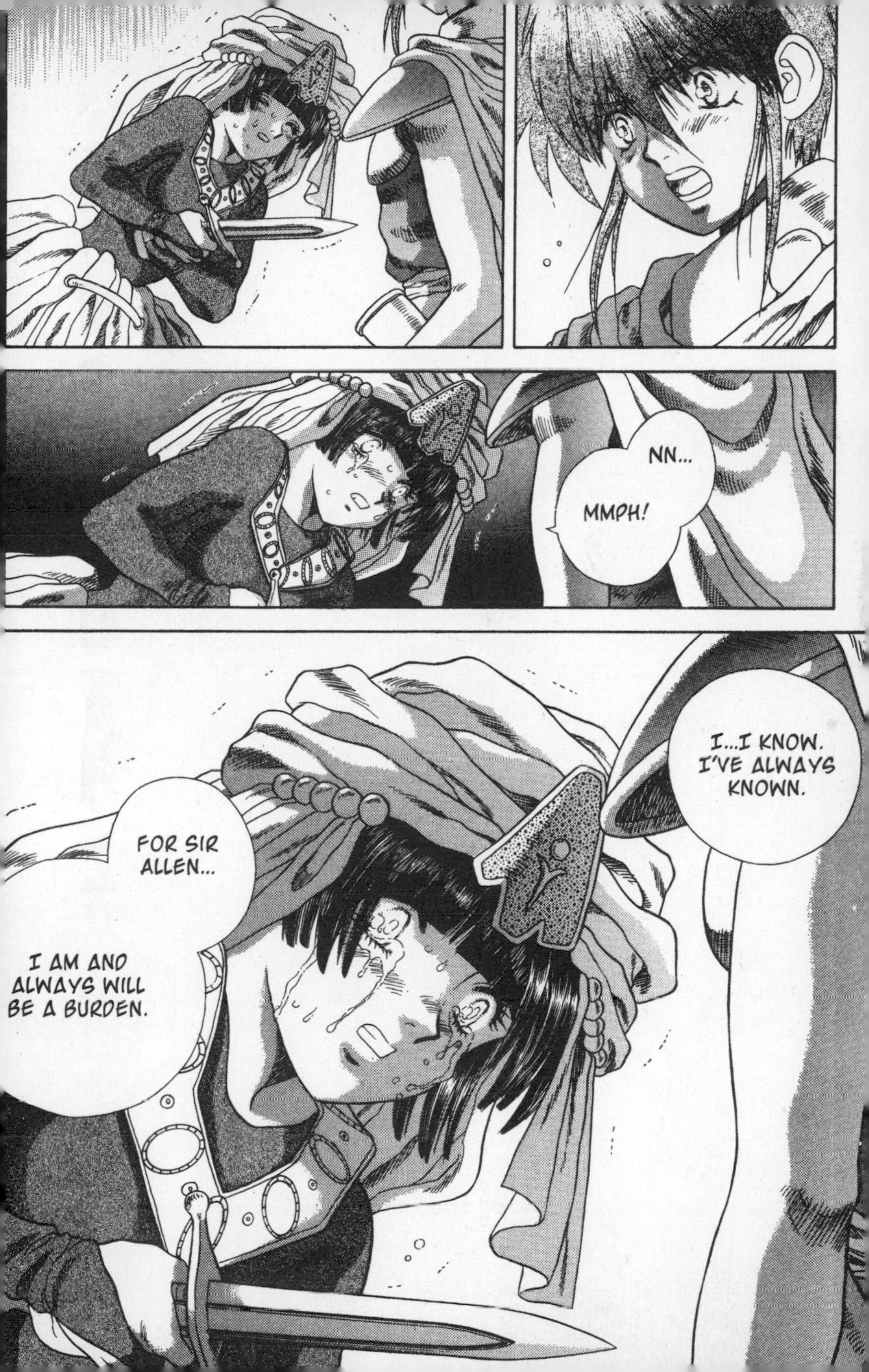
NN...
MMPH!
I...I KNOW. I'VE ALWAYS KNOWN.
FOR SIR ALLEN...
I AM AND ALWAYS WILL BE A BURDEN.

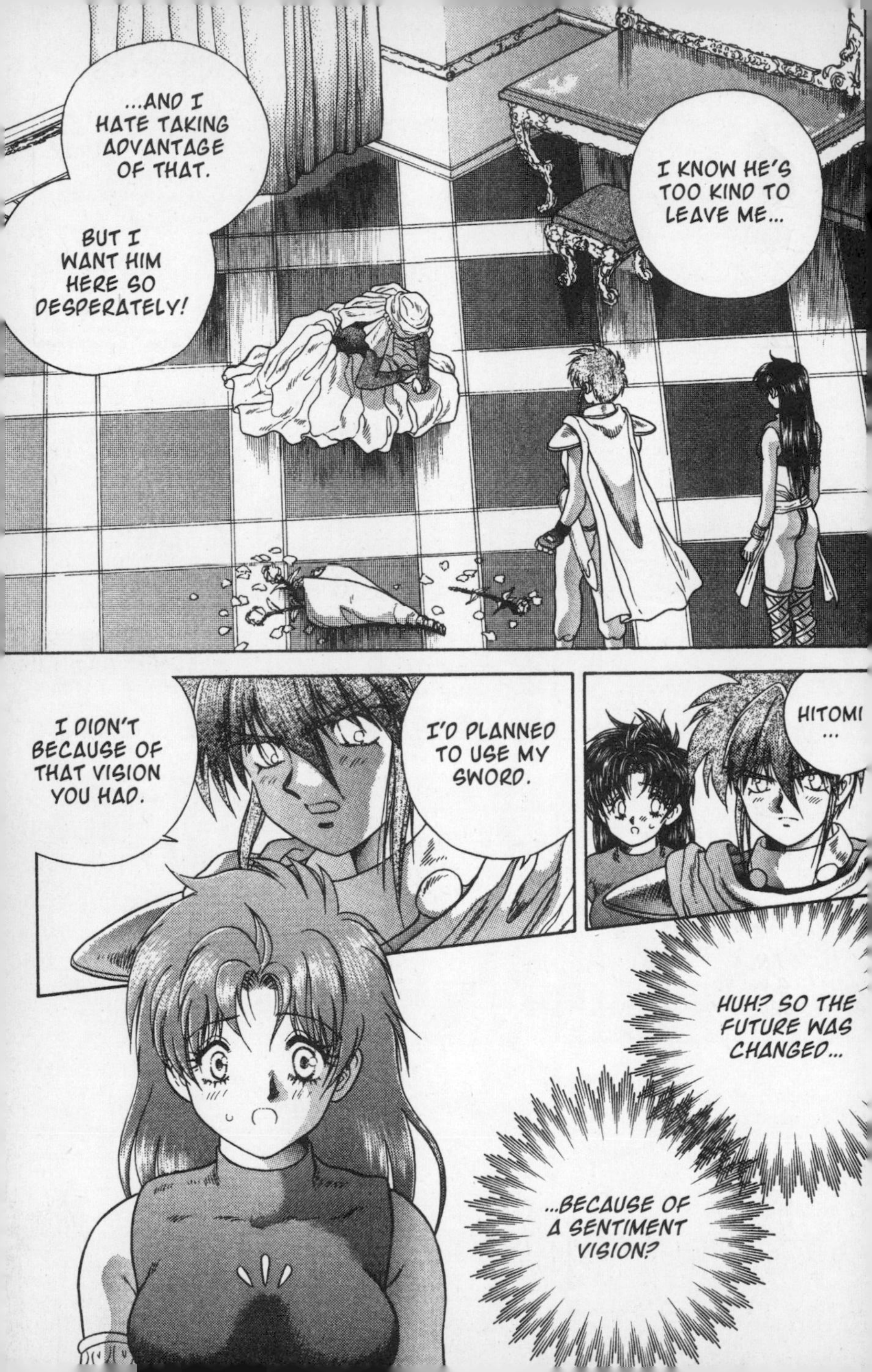
I KNOW HE'S TOO KIND TO LEAVE ME...
...AND I HATE TAKING ADVANTAGE OF THAT.
BUT I WANT HIM HERE SO DESPERATELY!
HITOMI ...
I'D PLANNED TO USE MY SWORD.
I DIDN'T BECAUSE OF THAT VISION YOU HAD.
HUH? SO THE FUTURE WAS CHANGED...
...BECAUSE OF A SENTIMENT VISION?

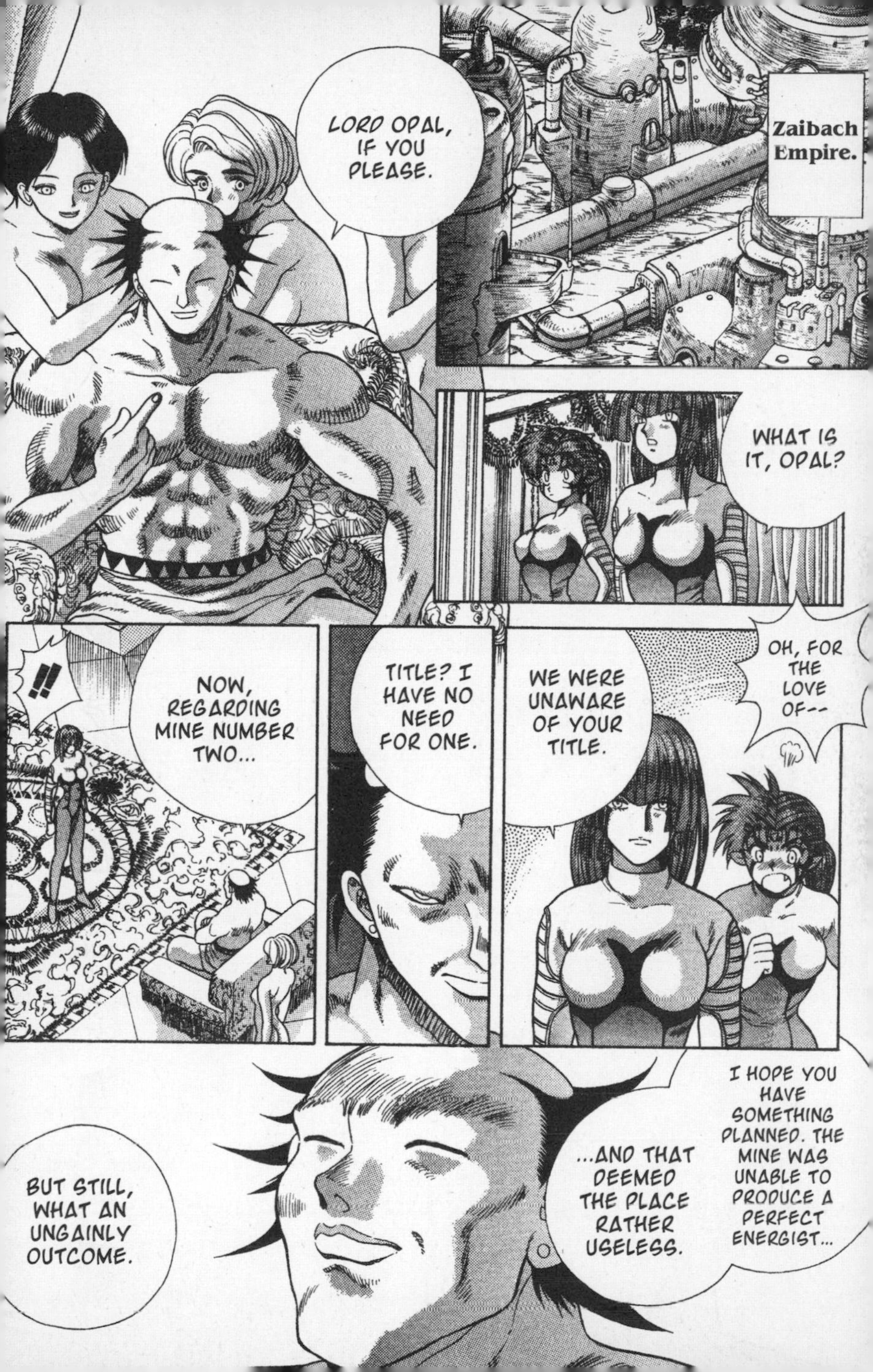

Zaibach Empire.
WHAT IS IT, OPAL?
LORD OPAL, IF YOU PLEASE.
OH, FOR THE LOVE OF--
WE WERE UNAWARE OF YOUR TITLE.
TITLE? I HAVE NO NEED FOR ONE.
NOW, REGARDING MINE NUMBER TWO...
!!
I HOPE YOU HAVE SOMETHING PLANNED. THE MINE WAS UNABLE TO PRODUCE A PERFECT ENERGIST...
...AND THAT DEEMED THE PLACE RATHER USELESS.
BUT STILL, WHAT AN UNGAINLY OUTCOME.

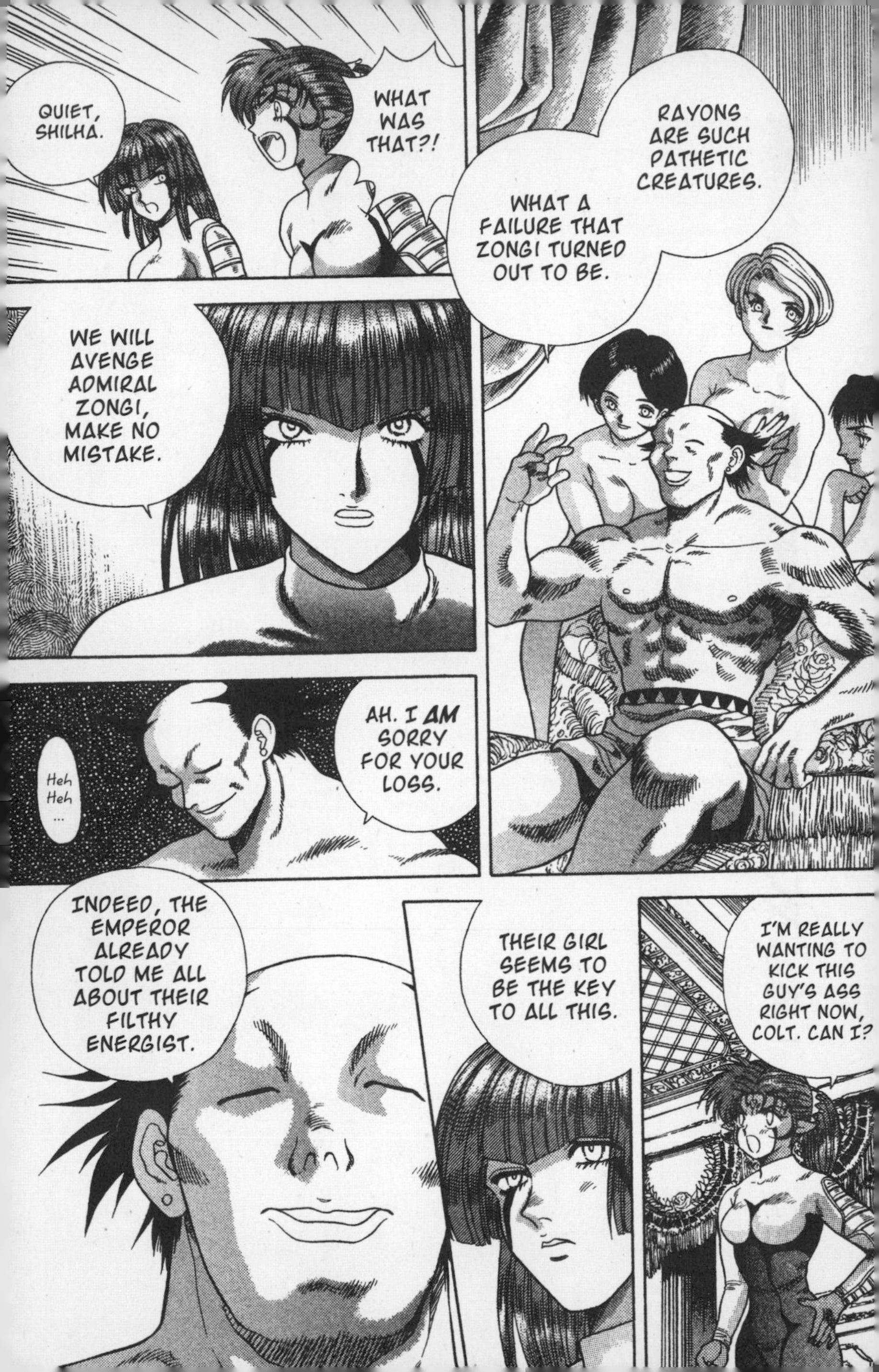
RAYONS ARE SUCH PATHETIC CREATURES.
WHAT A FAILURE THAT ZONGI TURNED OUT TO BE.
WHAT WAS THAT?!
QUIET, SHILHA.
WE WILL AVENGE ADMIRAL ZONGI, MAKE NO MISTAKE.
AH. I *AM* SORRY FOR YOUR LOSS.
Heh Heh ...
I'M REALLY WANTING TO KICK THIS GUY'S ASS RIGHT NOW, COLT. CAN I?
THEIR GIRL SEEMS TO BE THE KEY TO ALL THIS.
INDEED, THE EMPEROR ALREADY TOLD ME ALL ABOUT THEIR FILTHY ENERGIST.

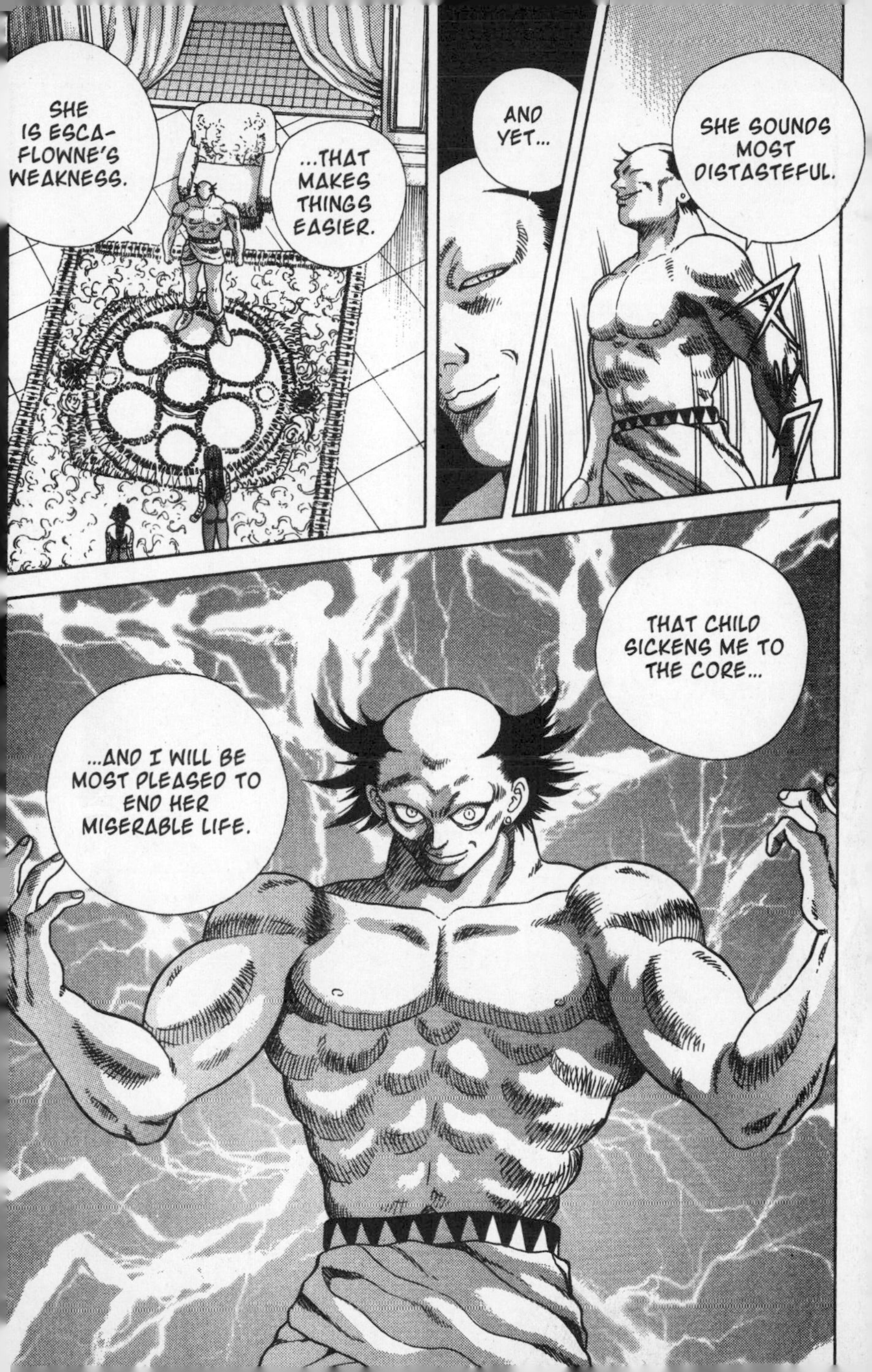

SHE SOUNDS MOST DISTASTEFUL.
AND YET...
...THAT MAKES THINGS EASIER.
SHE IS ESCA-FLOWNE'S WEAKNESS.
THAT CHILD SICKENS ME TO THE CORE...
...AND I WILL BE MOST PLEASED TO END HER MISERABLE LIFE.

VISION 21: RENEGADE?!

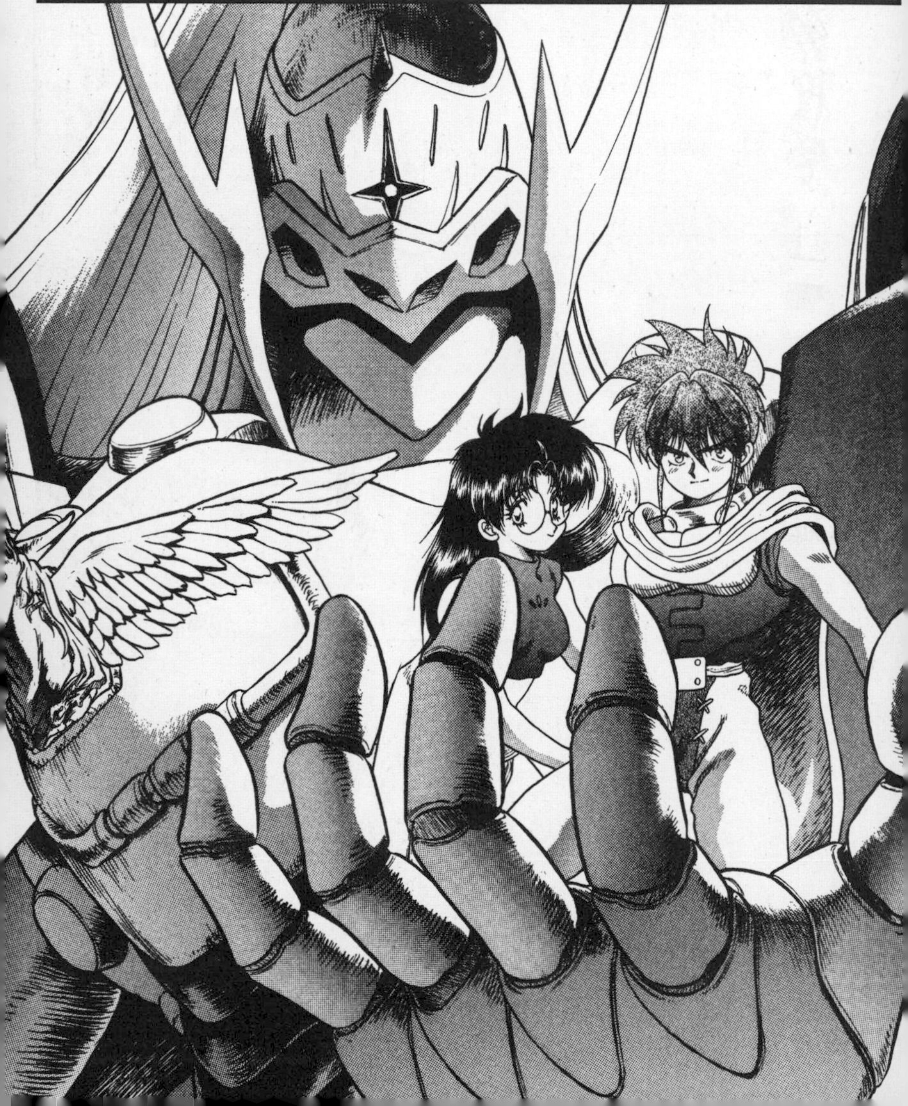

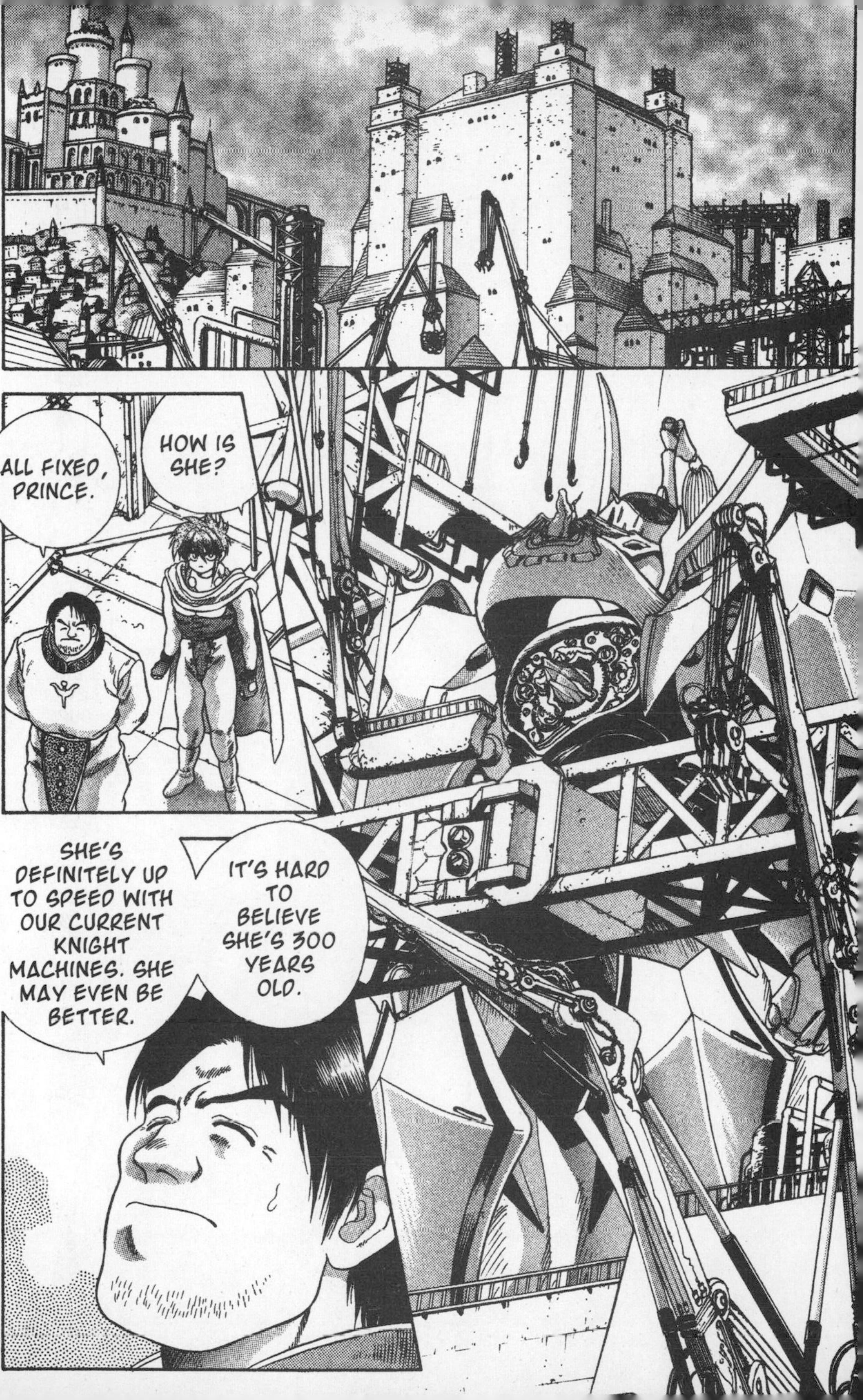
HOW IS SHE?
ALL FIXED, PRINCE.
IT'S HARD TO BELIEVE SHE'S 300 YEARS OLD.
SHE'S DEFINITELY UP TO SPEED WITH OUR CURRENT KNIGHT MACHINES. SHE MAY EVEN BE BETTER.

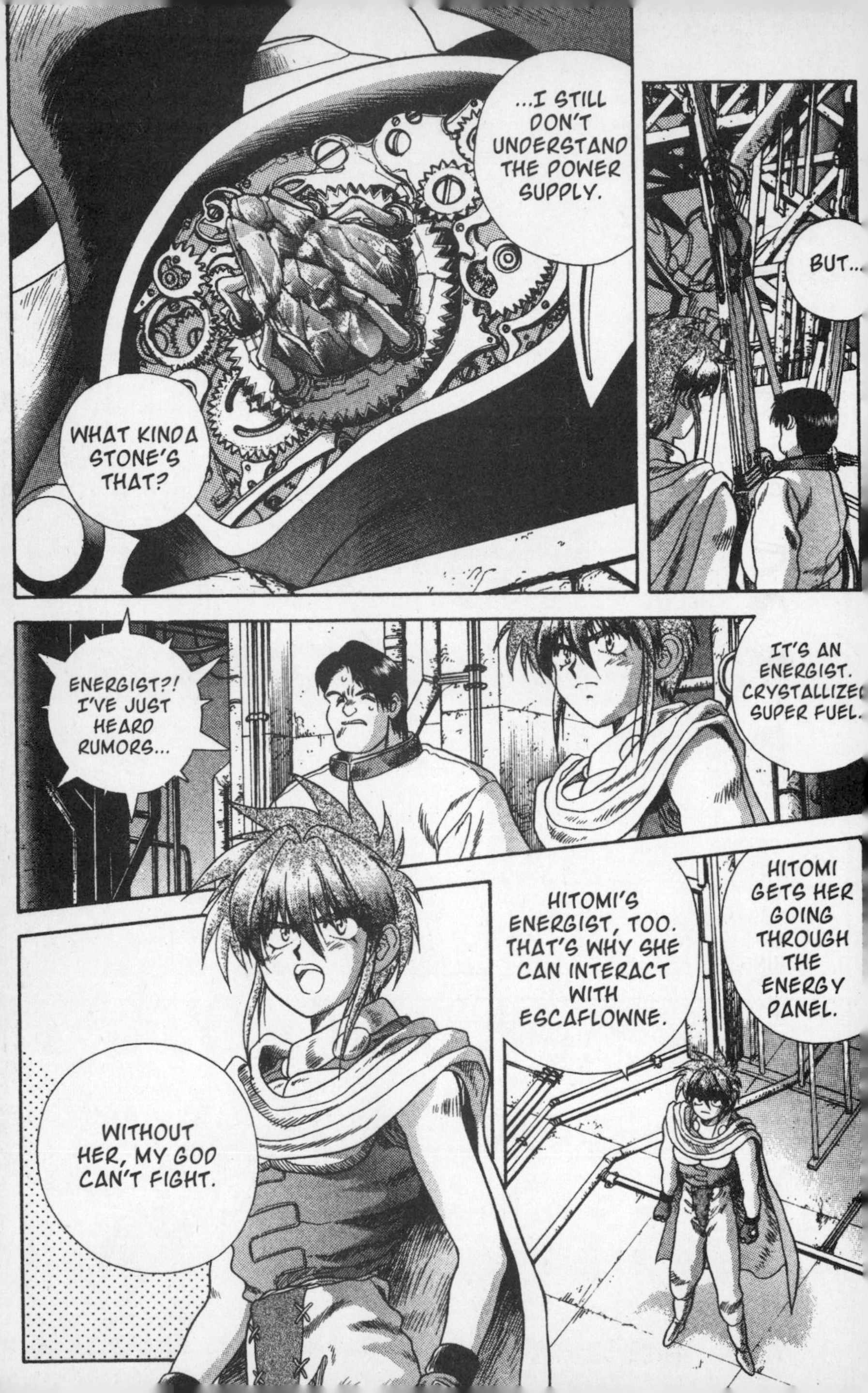
BUT...
...I STILL DON'T UNDERSTAND THE POWER SUPPLY.
WHAT KINDA STONE'S THAT?
IT'S AN ENERGIST. CRYSTALLIZE SUPER FUEL.
ENERGIST?! I'VE JUST HEARD RUMORS...
HITOMI GETS HER GOING THROUGH THE ENERGY PANEL.
HITOMI'S ENERGIST, TOO. THAT'S WHY SHE CAN INTERACT WITH ESCAFLOWNE.
WITHOUT HER, MY GOD CAN'T FIGHT.

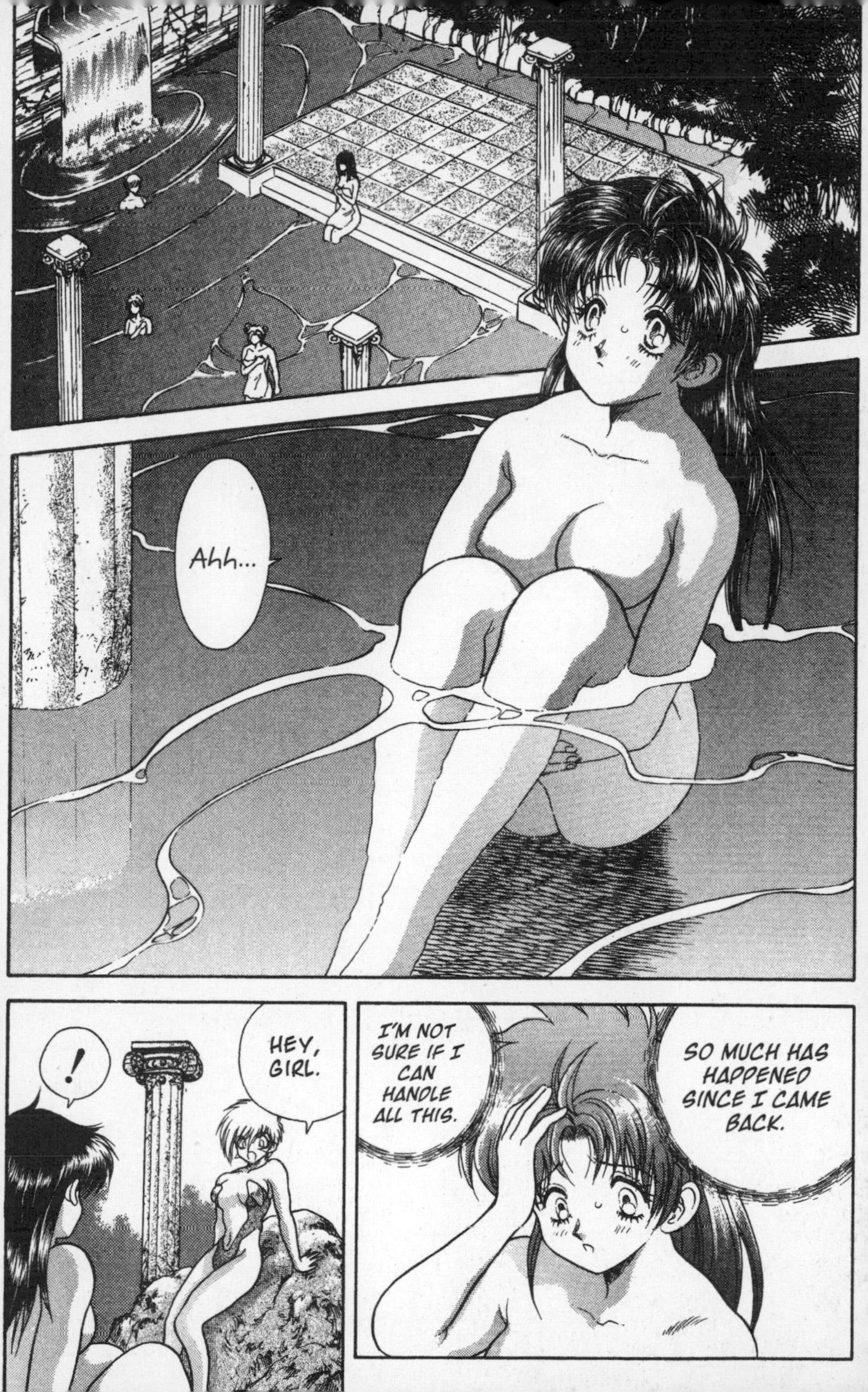
Ahh...
SO MUCH HAS HAPPENED SINCE I CAME BACK.
I'M NOT SURE IF I CAN HANDLE ALL THIS.
HEY, GIRL.
!

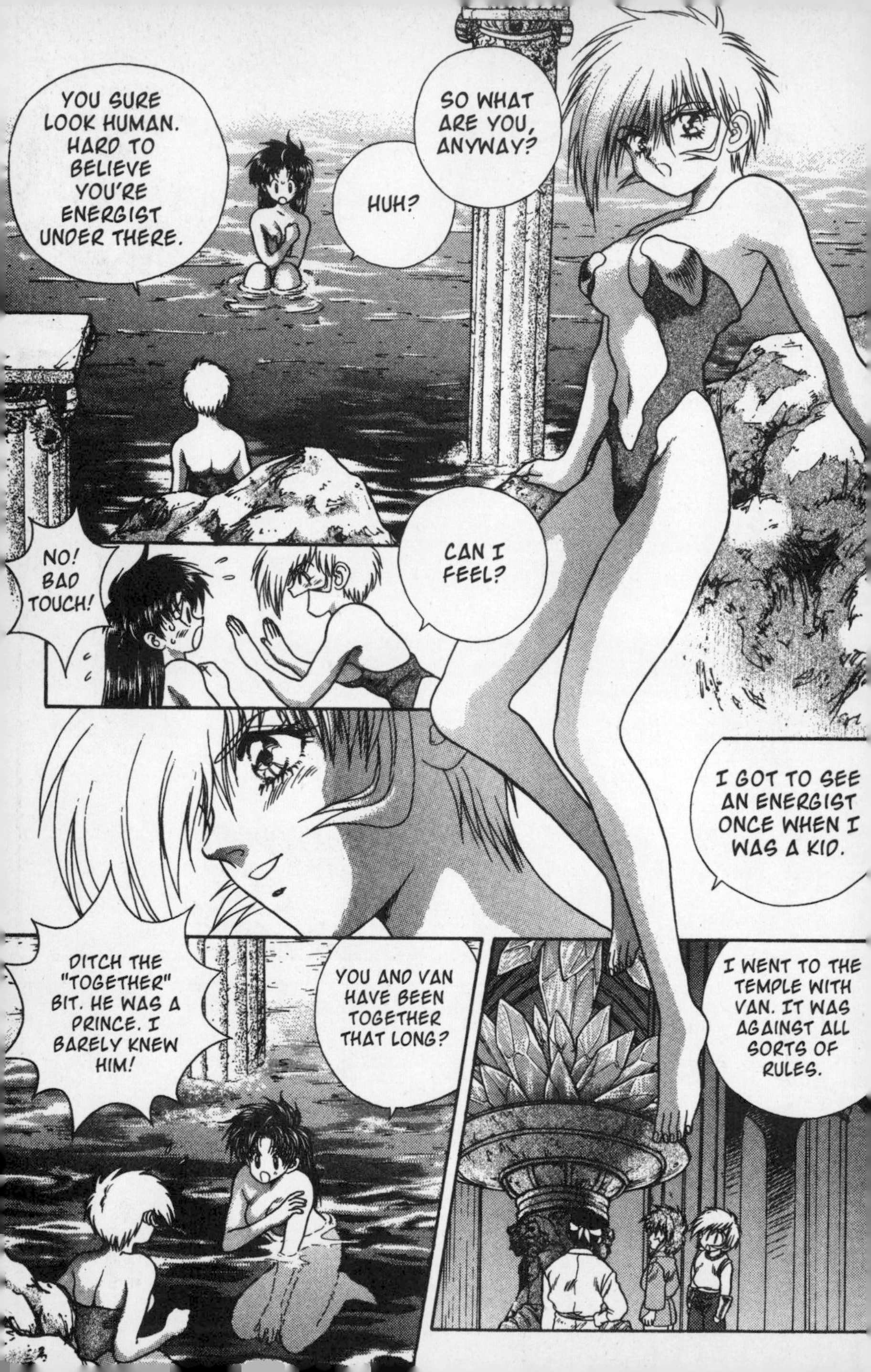
SO WHAT ARE YOU, ANYWAY?
HUH?
YOU SURE LOOK HUMAN. HARD TO BELIEVE YOU'RE ENERGIST UNDER THERE.
CAN I FEEL?
NO! BAD TOUCH!
I GOT TO SEE AN ENERGIST ONCE WHEN I WAS A KID.
I WENT TO THE TEMPLE WITH VAN. IT WAS AGAINST ALL SORTS OF RULES.
YOU AND VAN HAVE BEEN TOGETHER THAT LONG?
DITCH THE "TOGETHER" BIT. HE WAS A PRINCE. I BARELY KNEW HIM!

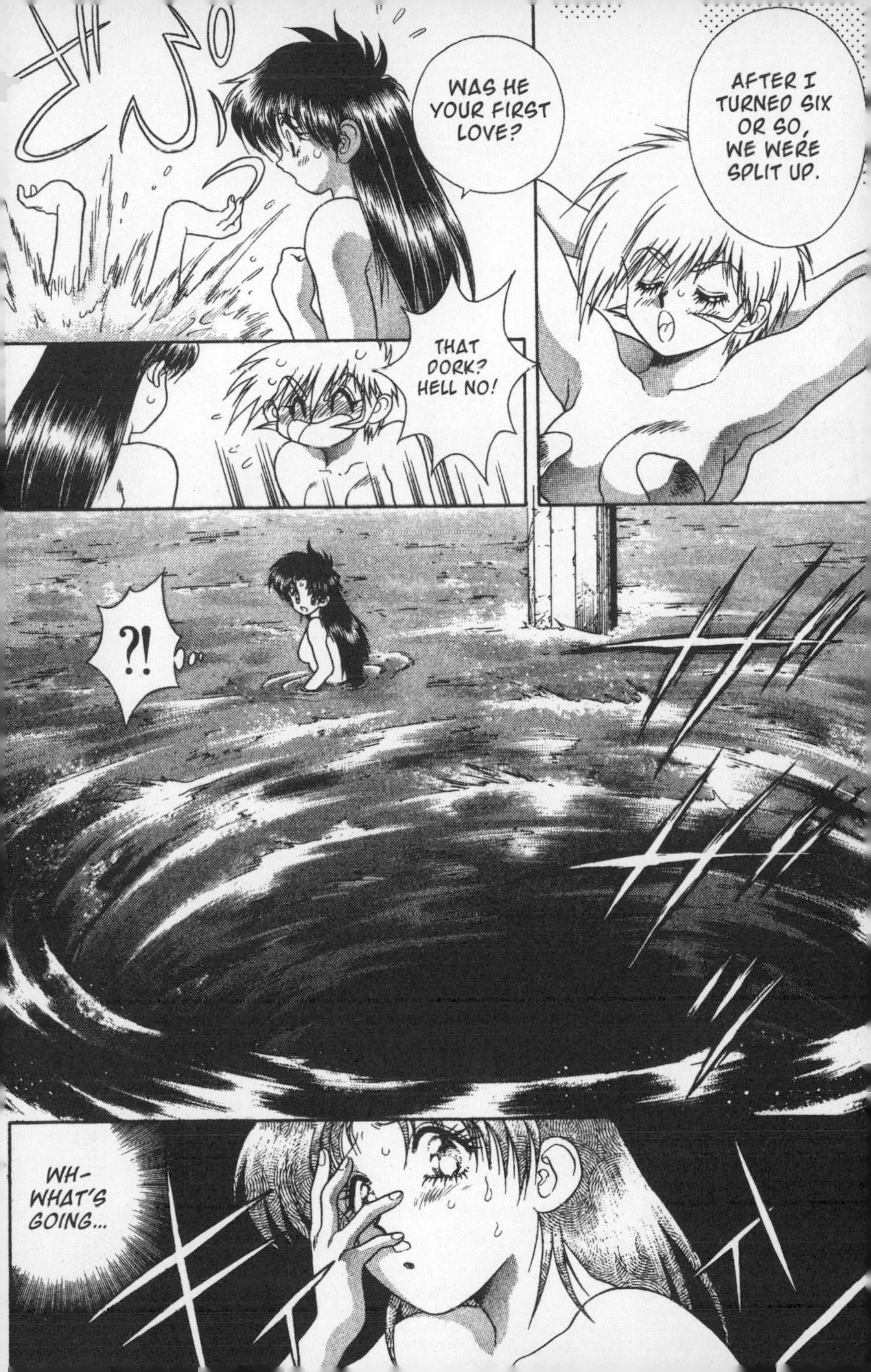
AFTER I TURNED SIX OR SO, WE WERE SPLIT UP.
WAS HE YOUR FIRST LOVE?
THAT DORK? HELL NO!
?!
WH- WHAT'S GOING...

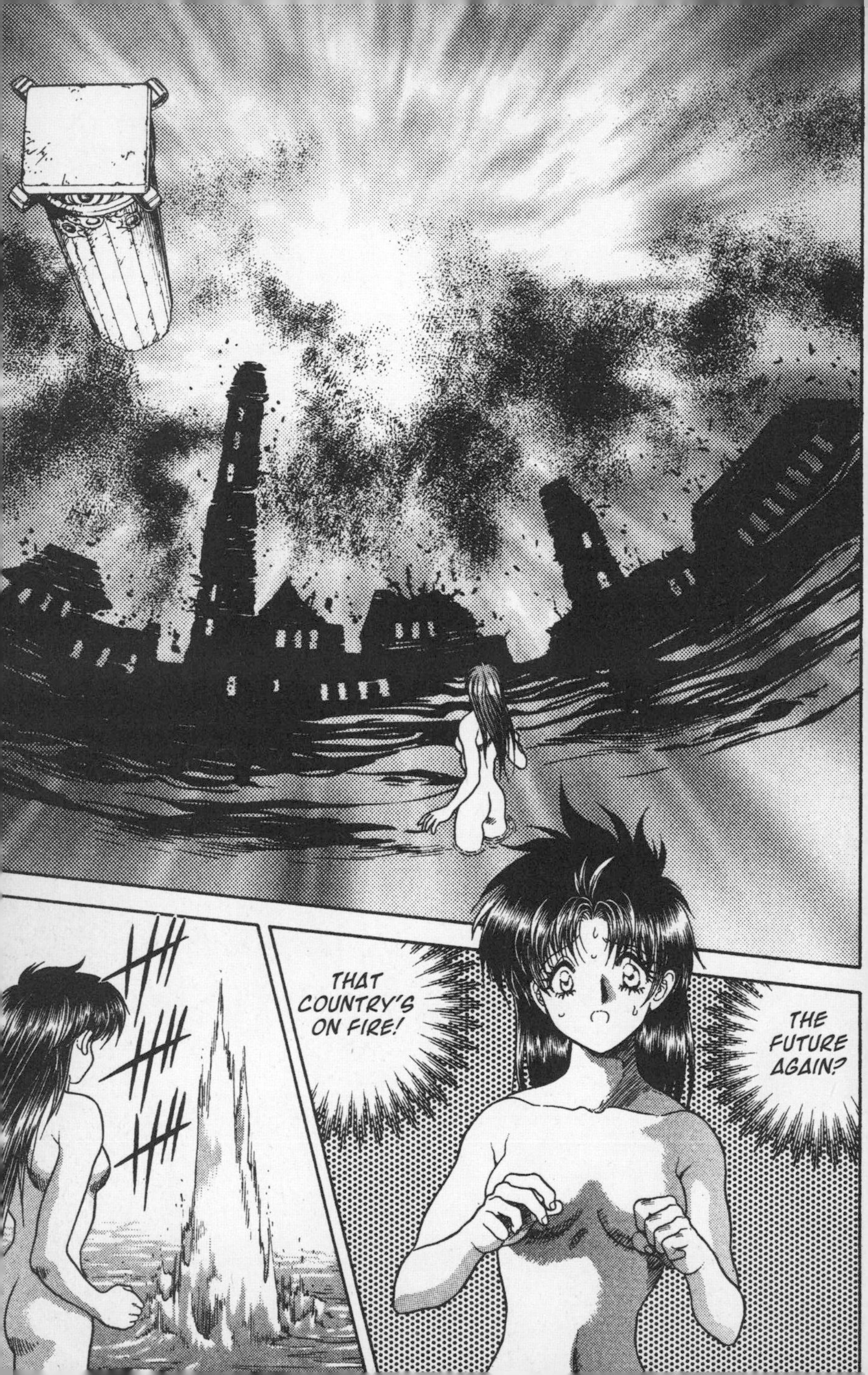
THE FUTURE AGAIN?
THAT COUNTRY'S ON FIRE!

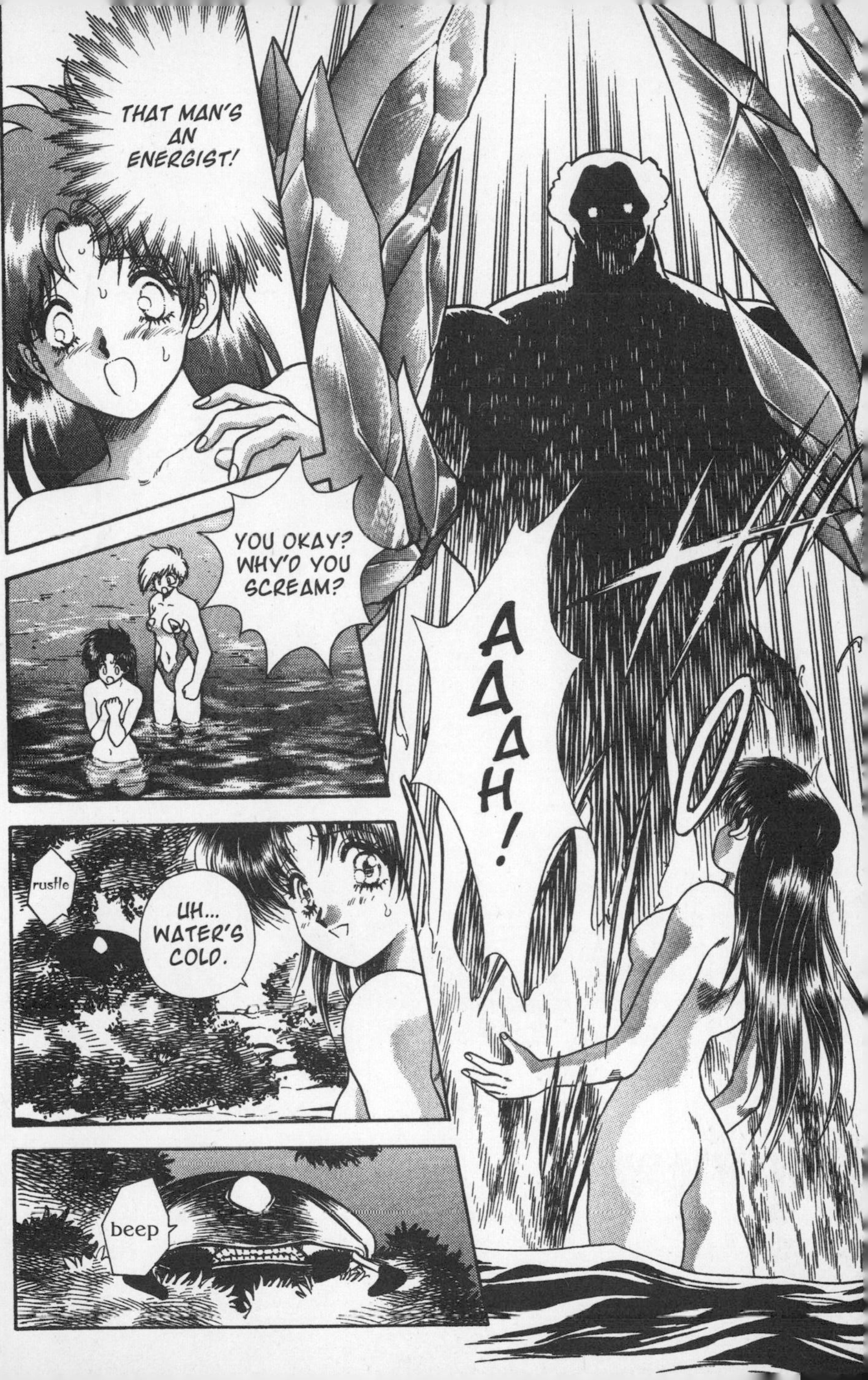
AAAH!
THAT MAN'S AN ENERGIST!
YOU OKAY? WHY'D YOU SCREAM?
UH... WATER'S COLD.
rustle
beep

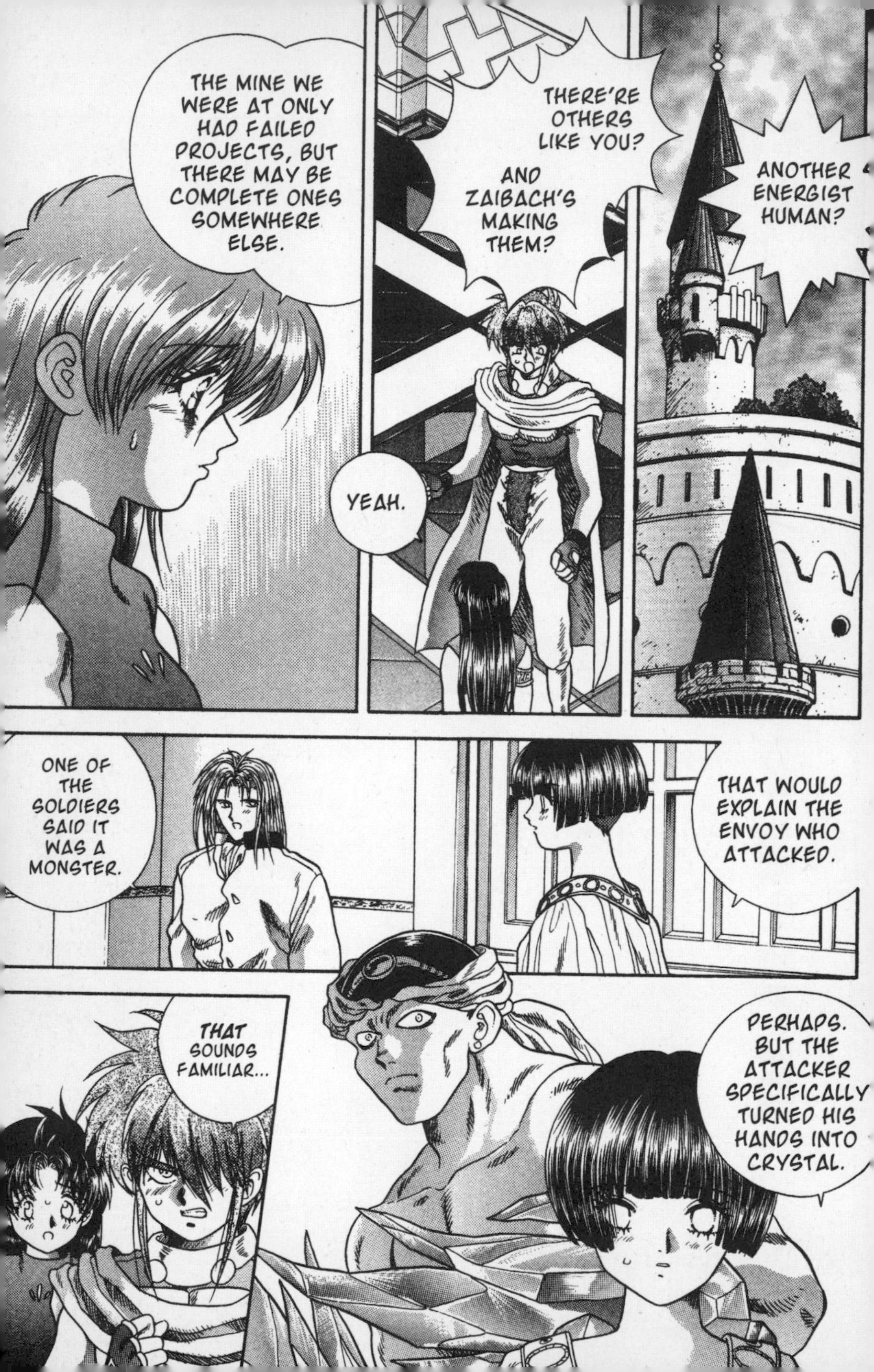
ANOTHER ENERGIST HUMAN?
THERE'RE OTHERS LIKE YOU?
AND ZAIBACH'S MAKING THEM?
YEAH.
THE MINE WE WERE AT ONLY HAD FAILED PROJECTS, BUT THERE MAY BE COMPLETE ONES SOMEWHERE ELSE.
THAT WOULD EXPLAIN THE ENVOY WHO ATTACKED.
ONE OF THE SOLDIERS SAID IT WAS A MONSTER.
PERHAPS. BUT THE ATTACKER SPECIFICALLY TURNED HIS HANDS INTO CRYSTAL.
THAT SOUNDS FAMILIAR...

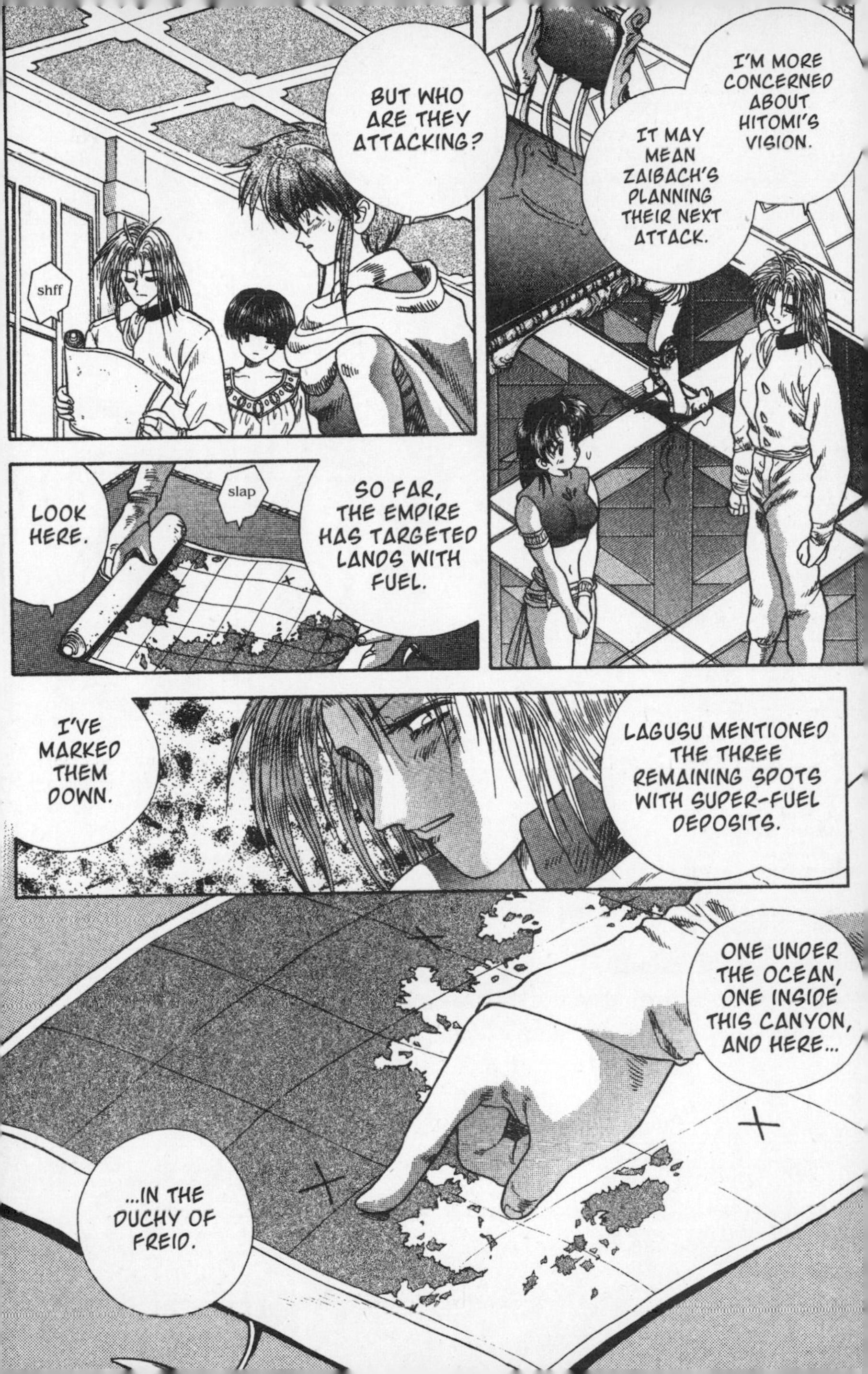
I'M MORE CONCERNED ABOUT HITOMI'S VISION.
IT MAY MEAN ZAIBACH'S PLANNING THEIR NEXT ATTACK.
BUT WHO ARE THEY ATTACKING?
shff
SO FAR, THE EMPIRE HAS TARGETED LANDS WITH FUEL.
slap
LOOK HERE.
LAGUSU MENTIONED THE THREE REMAINING SPOTS WITH SUPER-FUEL DEPOSITS.
I'VE MARKED THEM DOWN.
ONE UNDER THE OCEAN, ONE INSIDE THIS CANYON, AND HERE...
...IN THE DUCHY OF FREID.

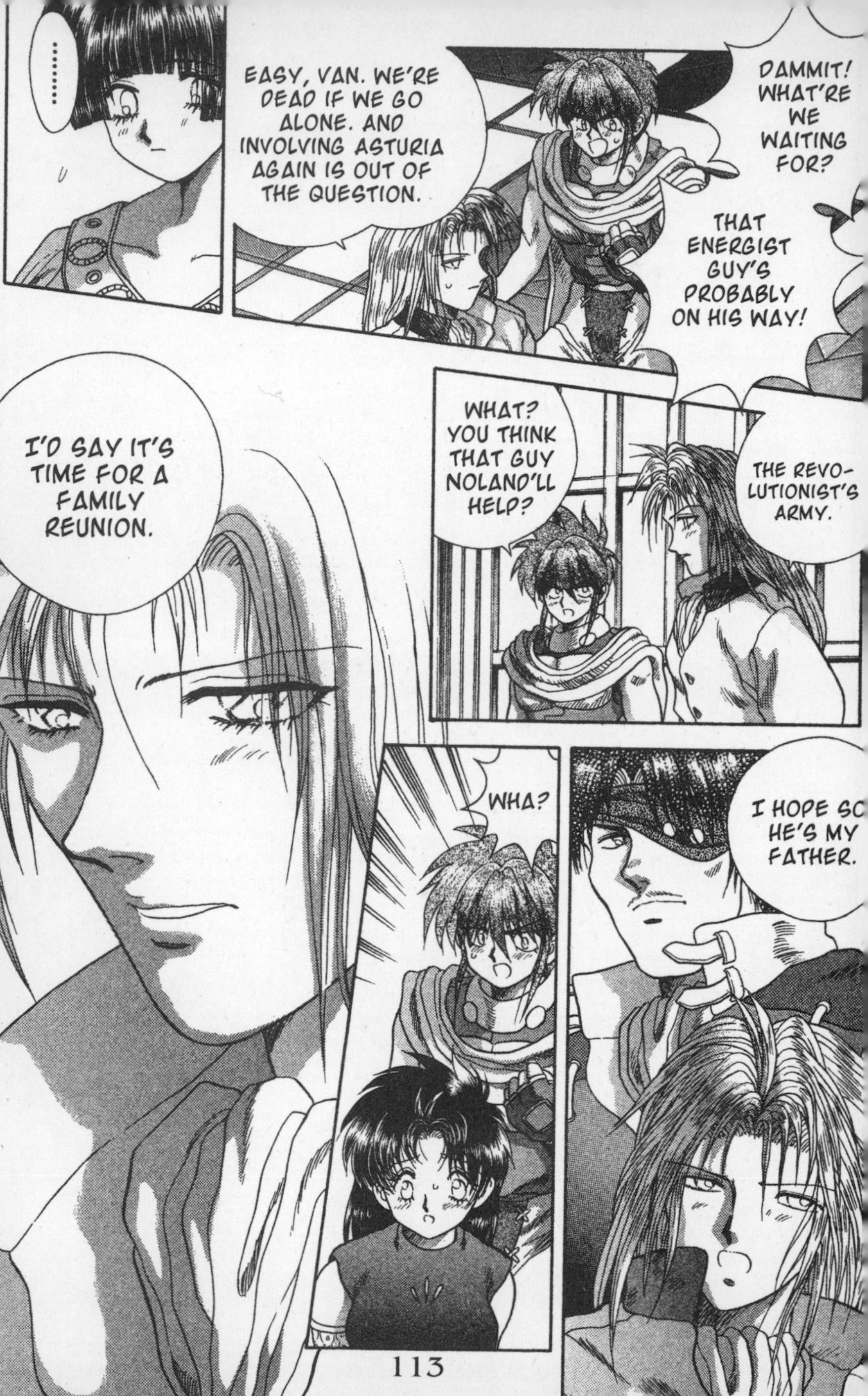
DAMMIT! WHAT'RE WE WAITING FOR?
THAT ENERGIST GUY'S PROBABLY ON HIS WAY!
EASY, VAN. WE'RE DEAD IF WE GO ALONE. AND INVOLVING ASTURIA AGAIN IS OUT OF THE QUESTION.
......
THE REVO-LUTIONIST'S ARMY.
WHAT? YOU THINK THAT GUY NOLAND'LL HELP?
I HOPE SO HE'S MY FATHER.
WHA?
I'D SAY IT'S TIME FOR A FAMILY REUNION.

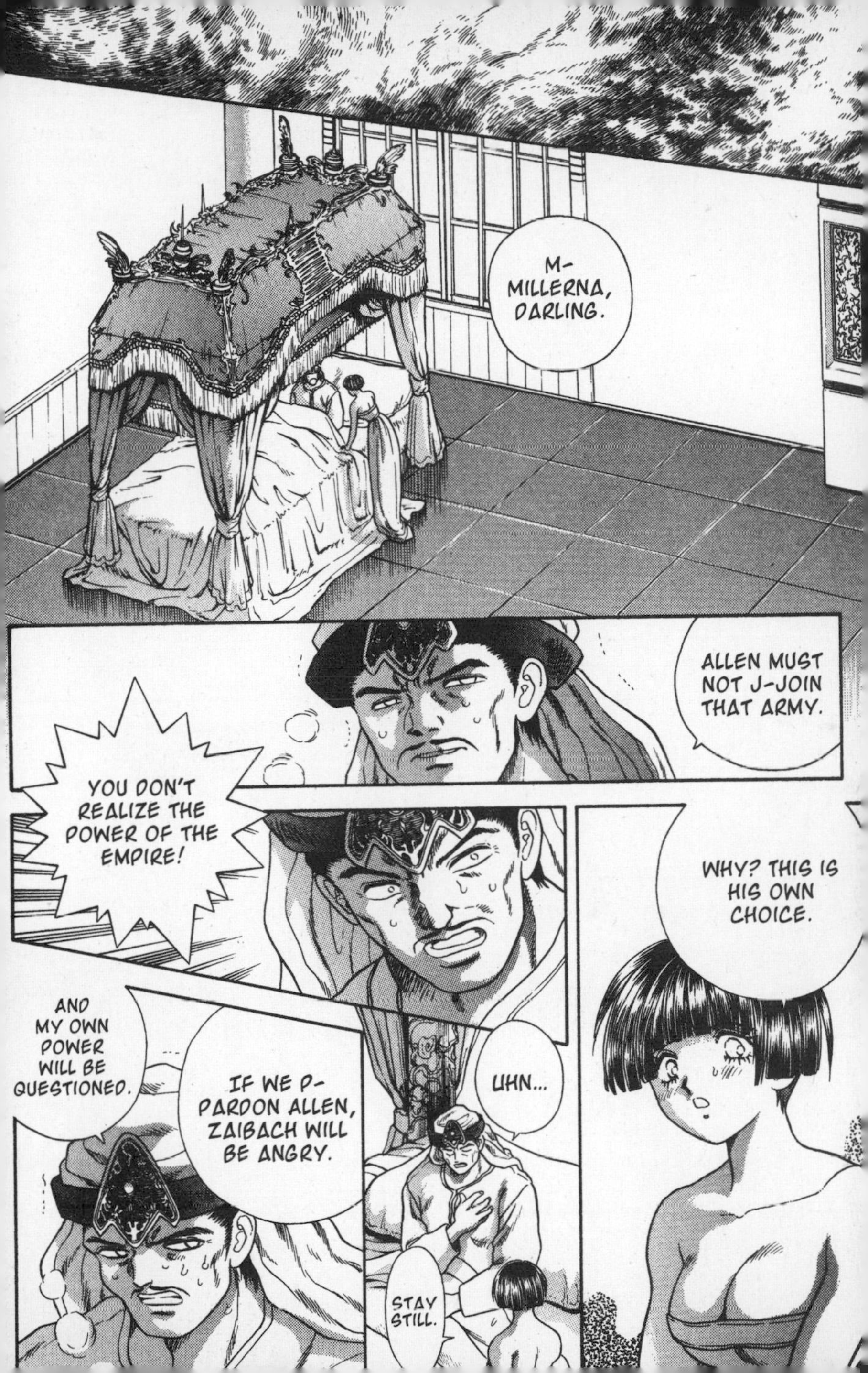
M- MILLERNA, DARLING.
ALLEN MUST NOT J-JOIN THAT ARMY.
WHY? THIS IS HIS OWN CHOICE.
YOU DON'T REALIZE THE POWER OF THE EMPIRE!
UHN...
STAY STILL.
IF WE P-PARDON ALLEN, ZAIBACH WILL BE ANGRY.
AND MY OWN POWER WILL BE QUESTIONED.

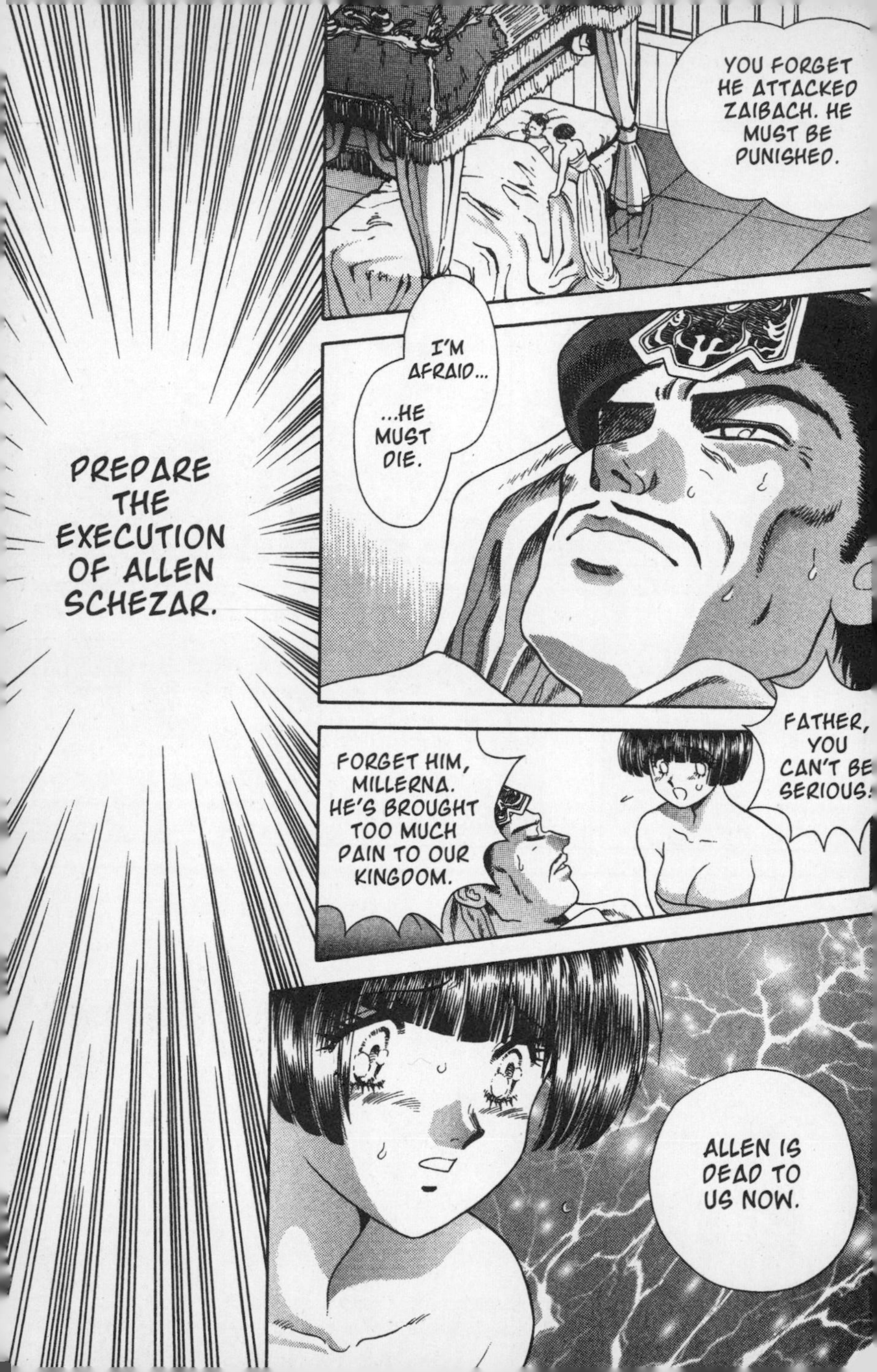
YOU FORGET HE ATTACKED ZAIBACH. HE MUST BE PUNISHED.
I'M AFRAID...
...HE MUST DIE.
FATHER, YOU CAN'T BE SERIOUS!
FORGET HIM, MILLERNA. HE'S BROUGHT TOO MUCH PAIN TO OUR KINGDOM.
ALLEN IS DEAD TO US NOW.
PREPARE THE EXECUTION OF ALLEN SCHEZAR.

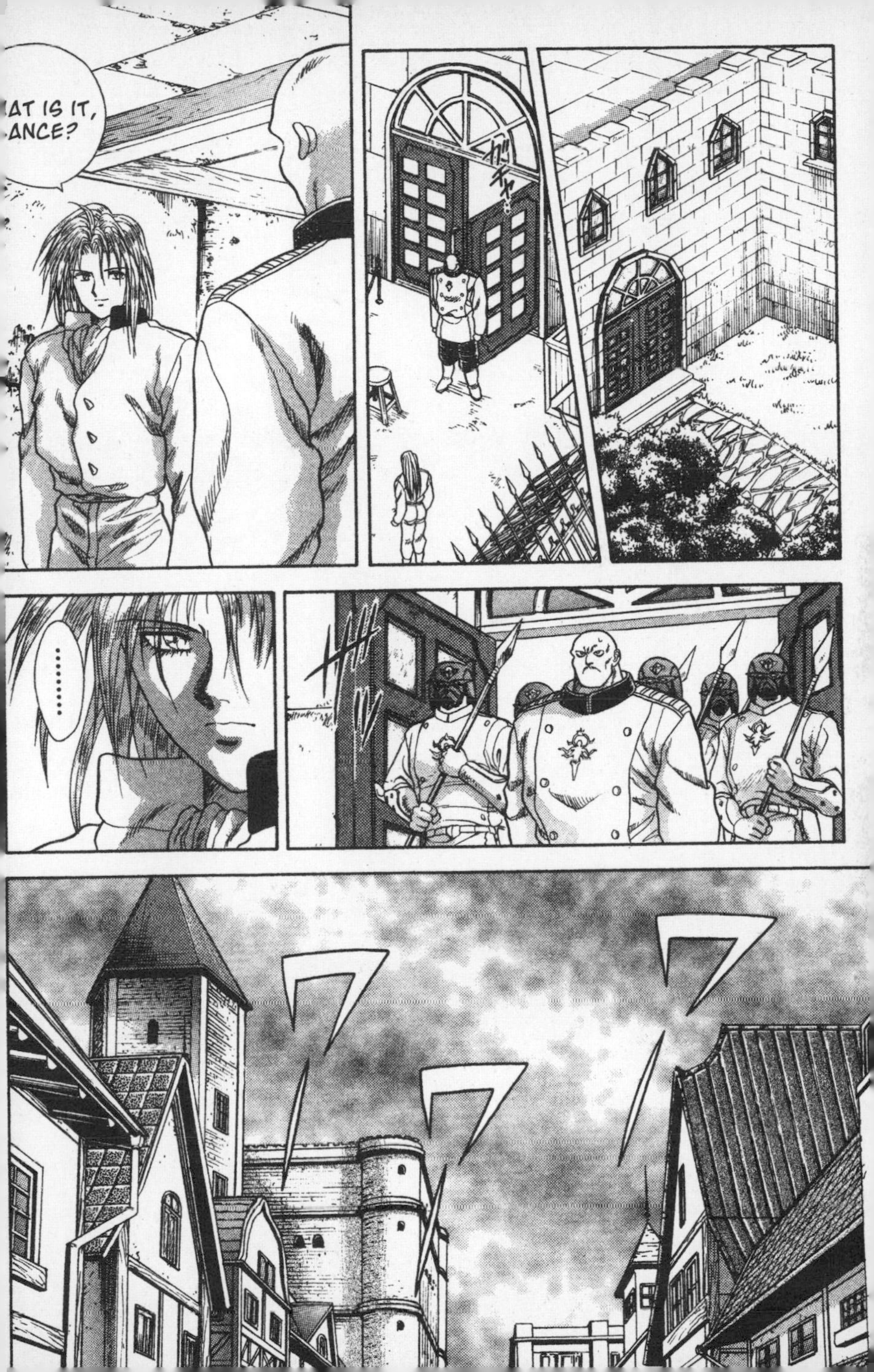
ガチャ…
AT IS IT, ANCE?
……
ワ
ワ
ワ

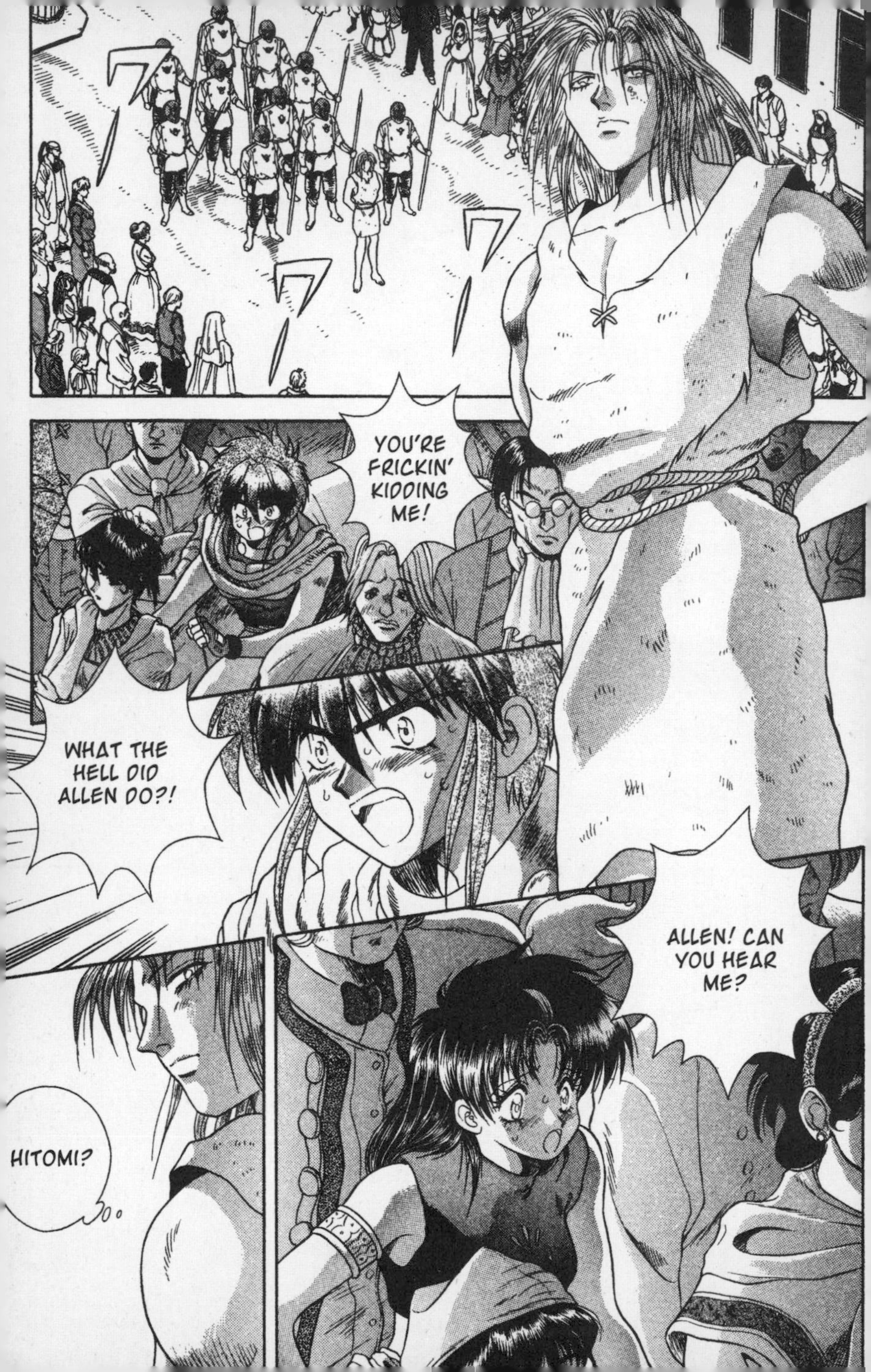
YOU'RE FRICKIN' KIDDING ME!
WHAT THE HELL DID ALLEN DO?!
ALLEN! CAN YOU HEAR ME?
HITOMI?

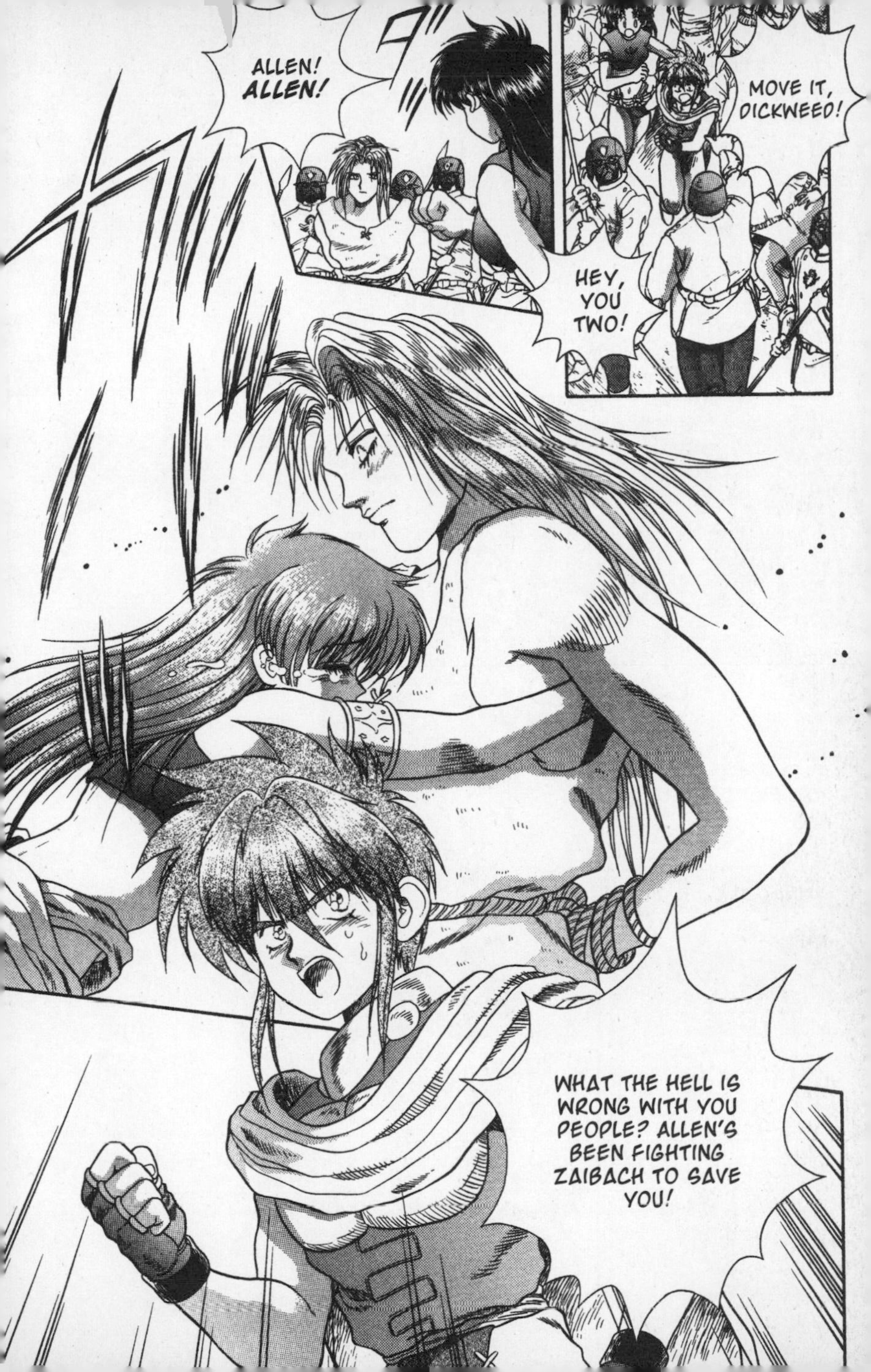
MOVE IT, DICKWEED!
HEY, YOU TWO!
ALLEN! ALLEN!
WHAT THE HELL IS WRONG WITH YOU PEOPLE? ALLEN'S BEEN FIGHTING ZAIBACH TO SAVE YOU!

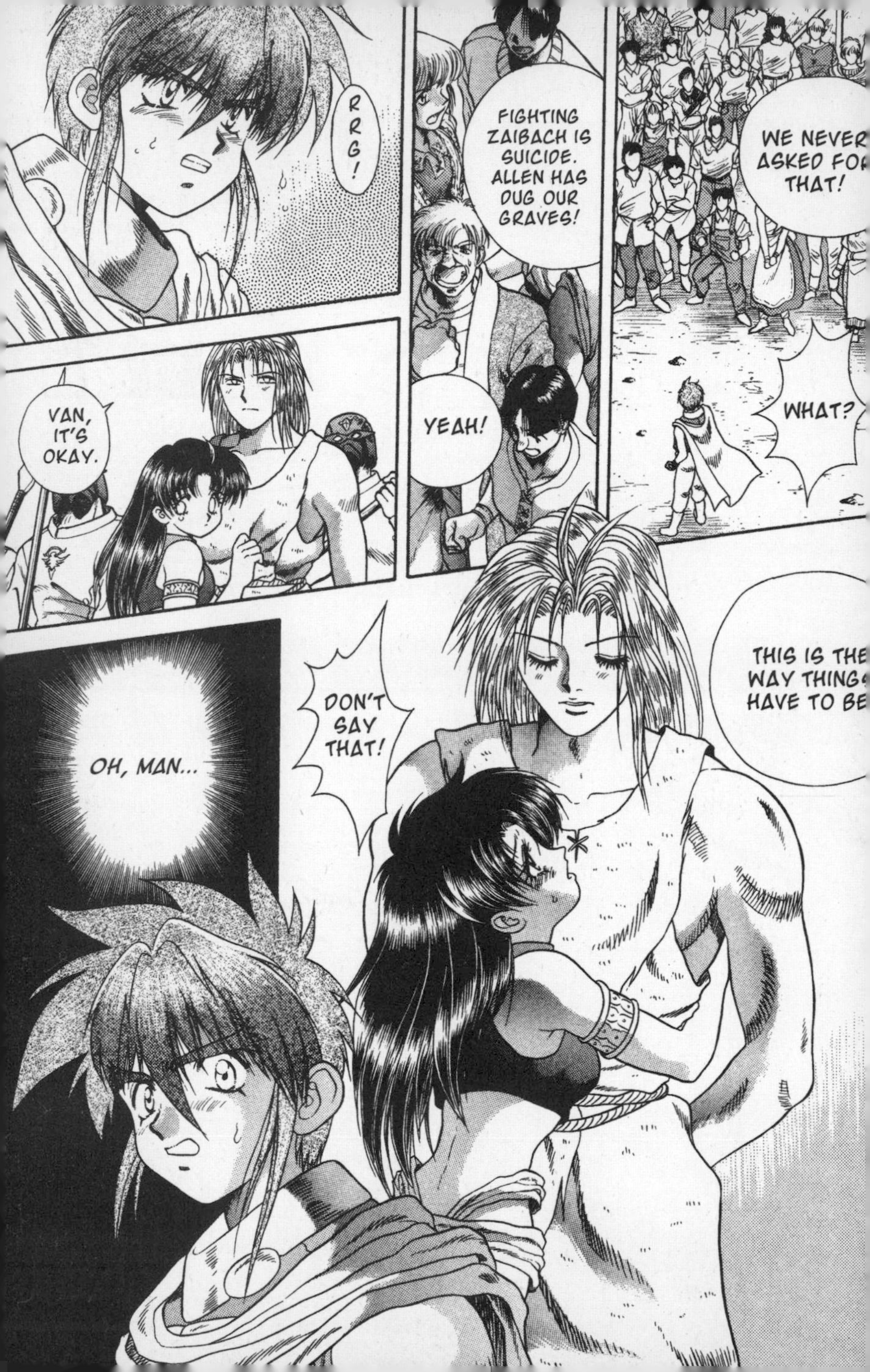
WE NEVER ASKED FOR THAT!
WHAT?
FIGHTING ZAIBACH IS SUICIDE. ALLEN HAS DUG OUR GRAVES!
YEAH!
RRG!
VAN, IT'S OKAY.
THIS IS THE WAY THINGS HAVE TO BE
DON'T SAY THAT!
OH, MAN...

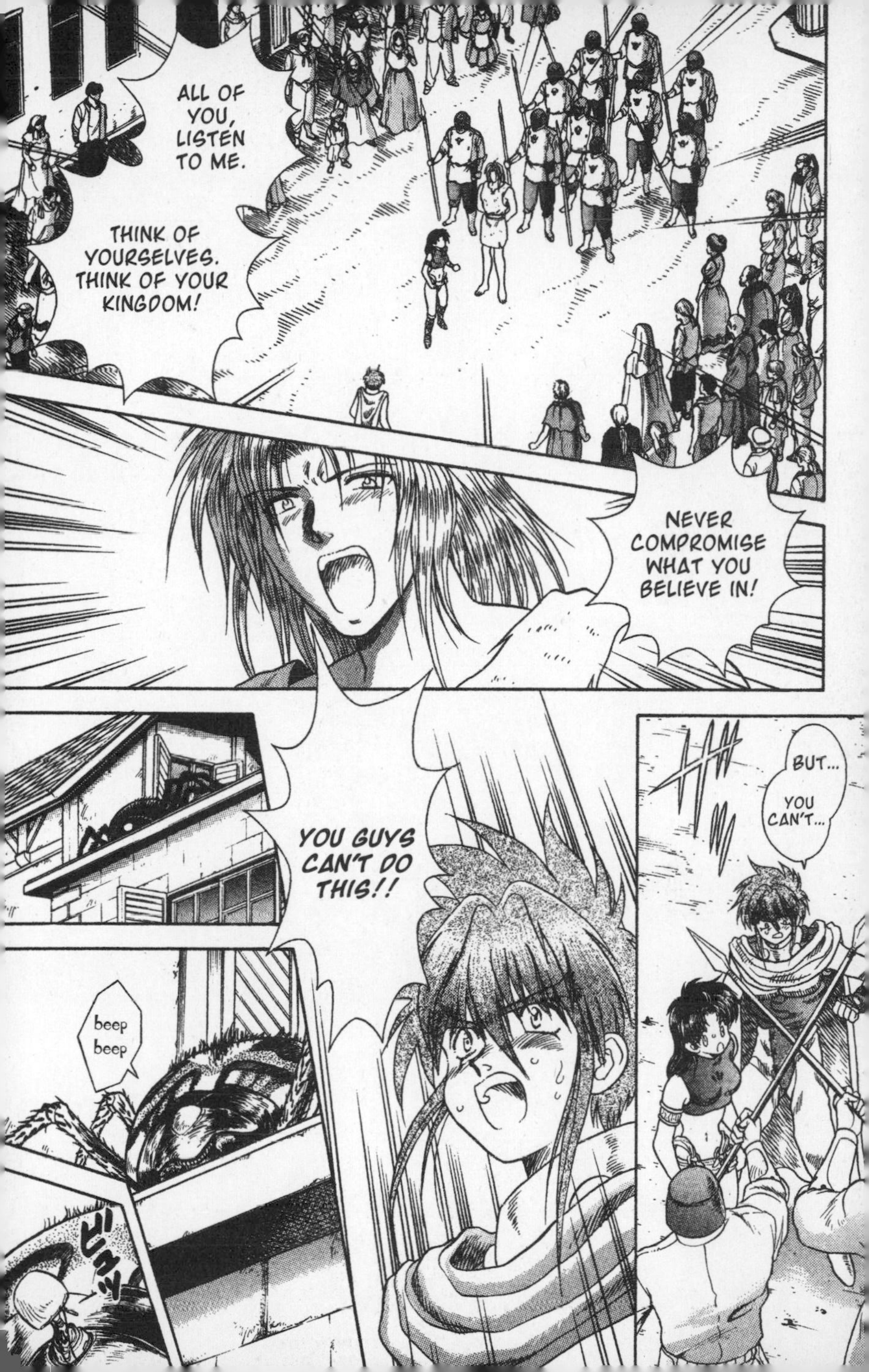
ALL OF YOU, LISTEN TO ME.
THINK OF YOURSELVES. THINK OF YOUR KINGDOM!
NEVER COMPROMISE WHAT YOU BELIEVE IN!
BUT... YOU CAN'T...
YOU GUYS CAN'T DO THIS!!
beep beep
ビクッ

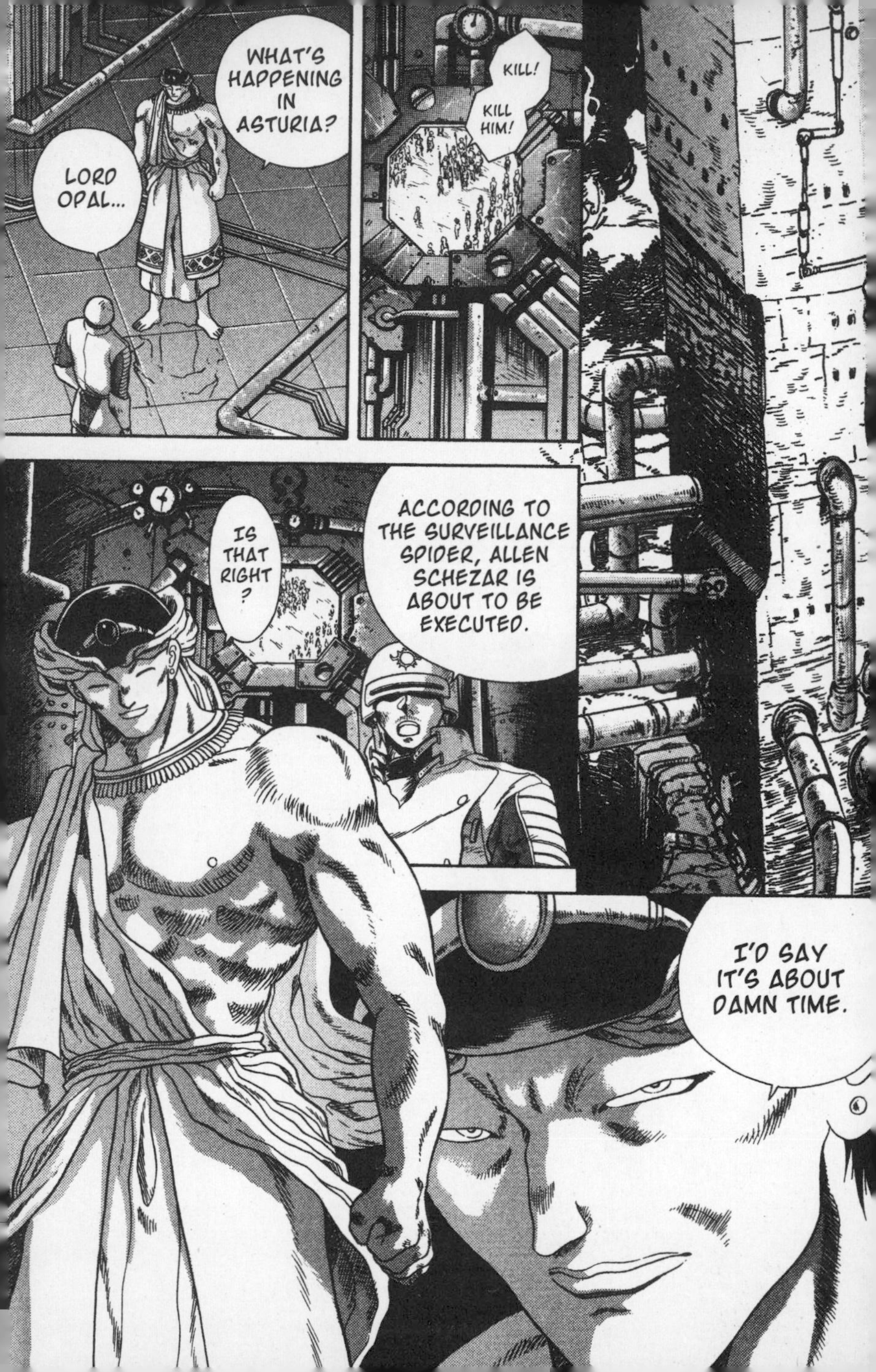
KILL!
KILL HIM!
WHAT'S HAPPENING IN ASTURIA?
LORD OPAL...
ACCORDING TO THE SURVEILLANCE SPIDER, ALLEN SCHEZAR IS ABOUT TO BE EXECUTED.
IS THAT RIGHT?
I'D SAY IT'S ABOUT DAMN TIME.

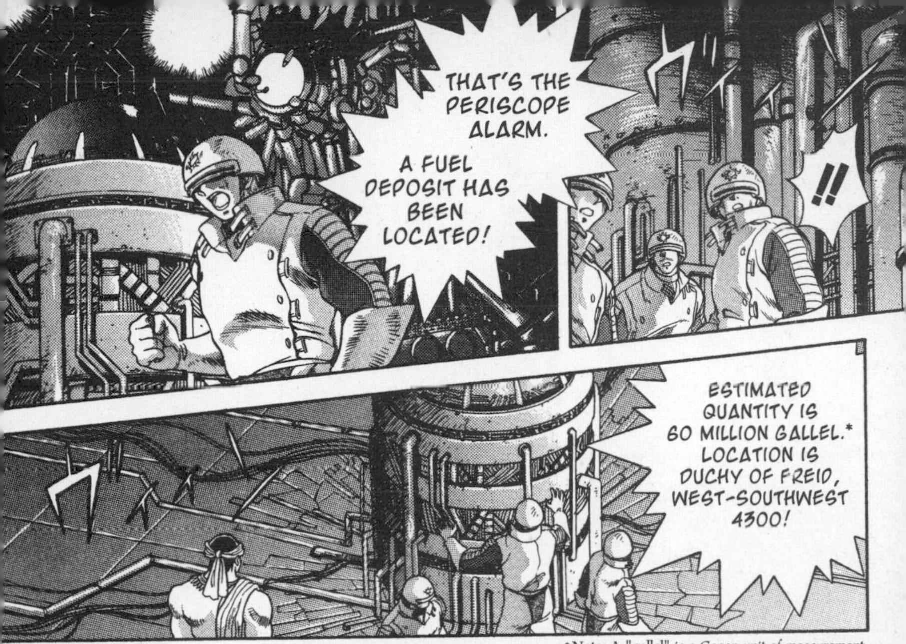
!!
THAT'S THE PERISCOPE ALARM.
A FUEL DEPOSIT HAS BEEN LOCATED!
ESTIMATED QUANTITY IS 60 MILLION GALLEL.* LOCATION IS DUCHY OF FREID, WEST-SOUTHWEST 4300!

*Note: A "gallel" is a Gaean unit of measurement.

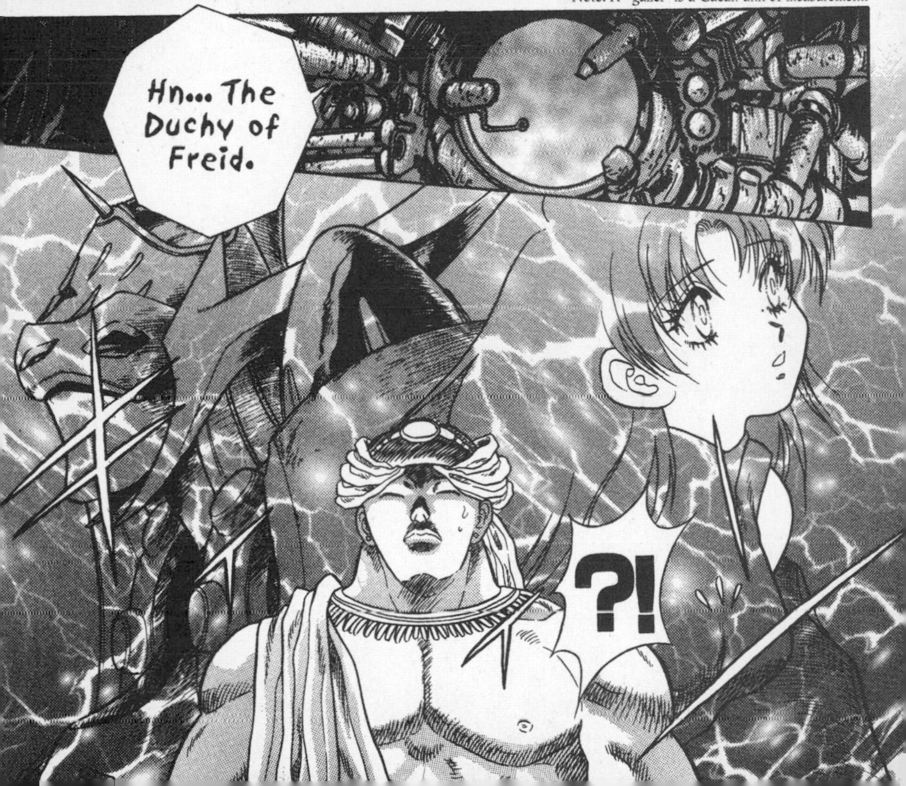
Hn... The Duchy of Freid.
?!

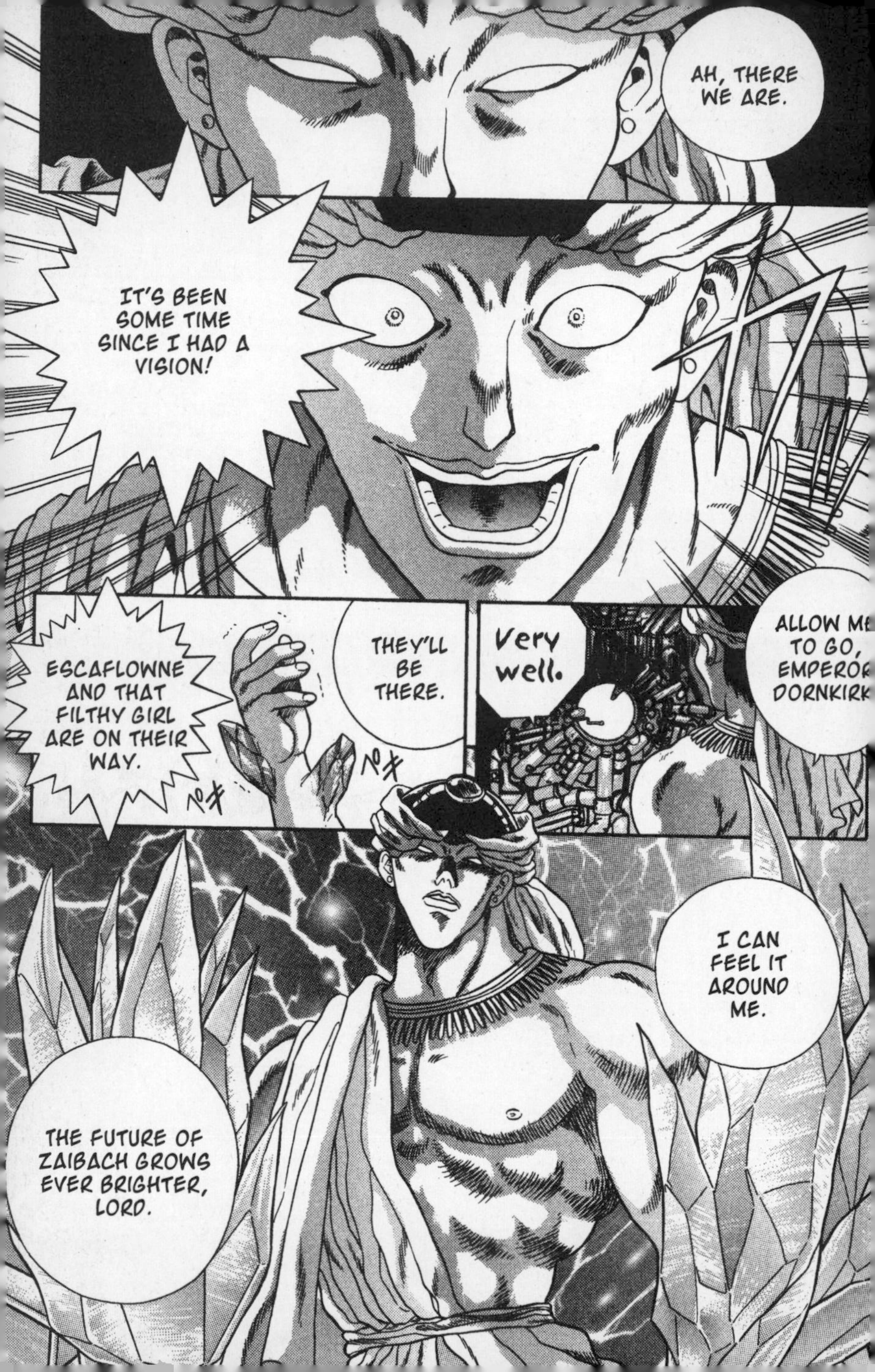
AH, THERE WE ARE.
IT'S BEEN SOME TIME SINCE I HAD A VISION!
ALLOW ME TO GO, EMPEROR DORNKIRK
Very well.
THEY'LL BE THERE.
ペキ
ESCAFLOWNE AND THAT FILTHY GIRL ARE ON THEIR WAY.
ペキ
I CAN FEEL IT AROUND ME.
THE FUTURE OF ZAIBACH GROWS EVER BRIGHTER, LORD.

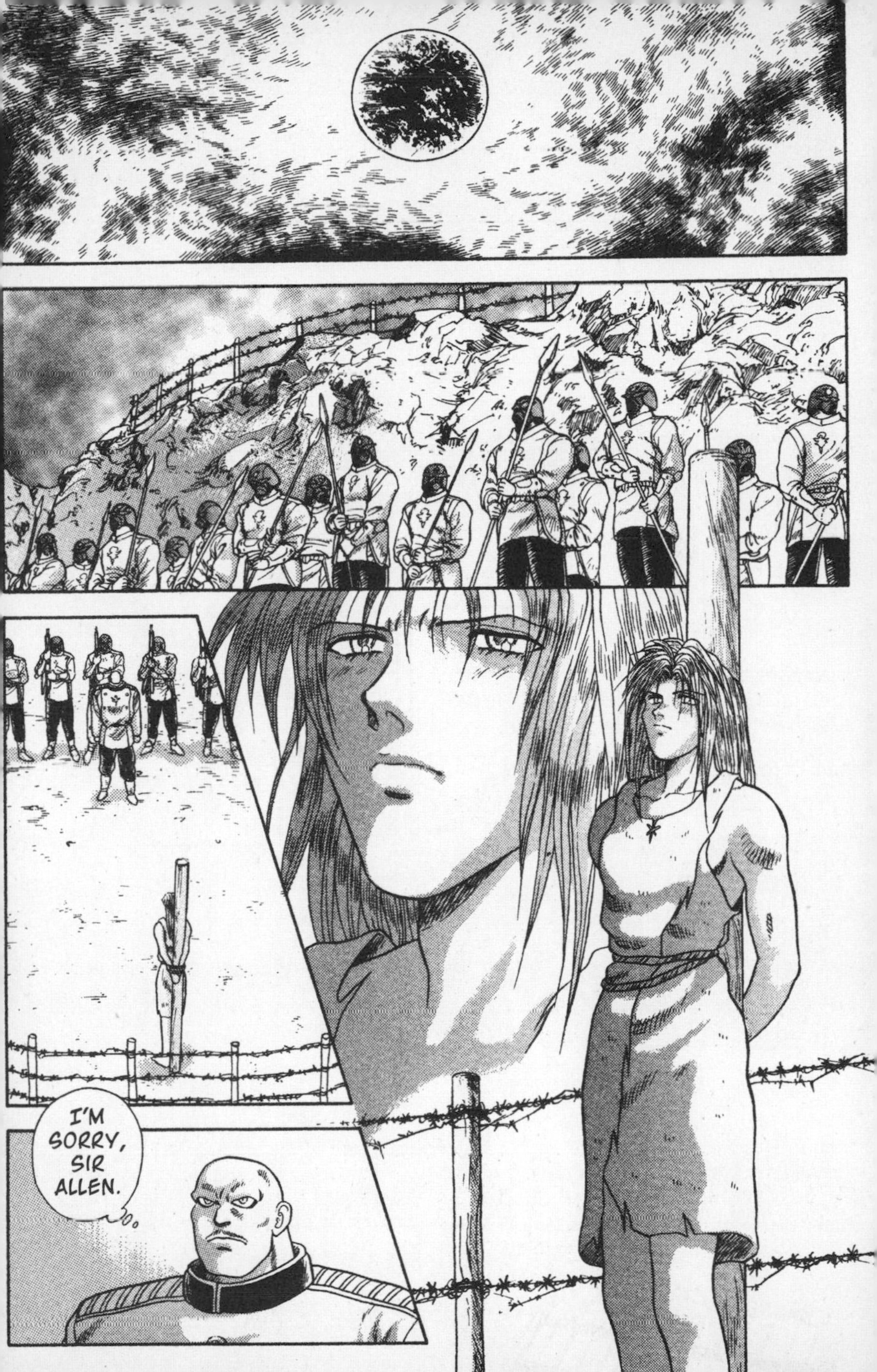
I'M SORRY, SIR ALLEN.

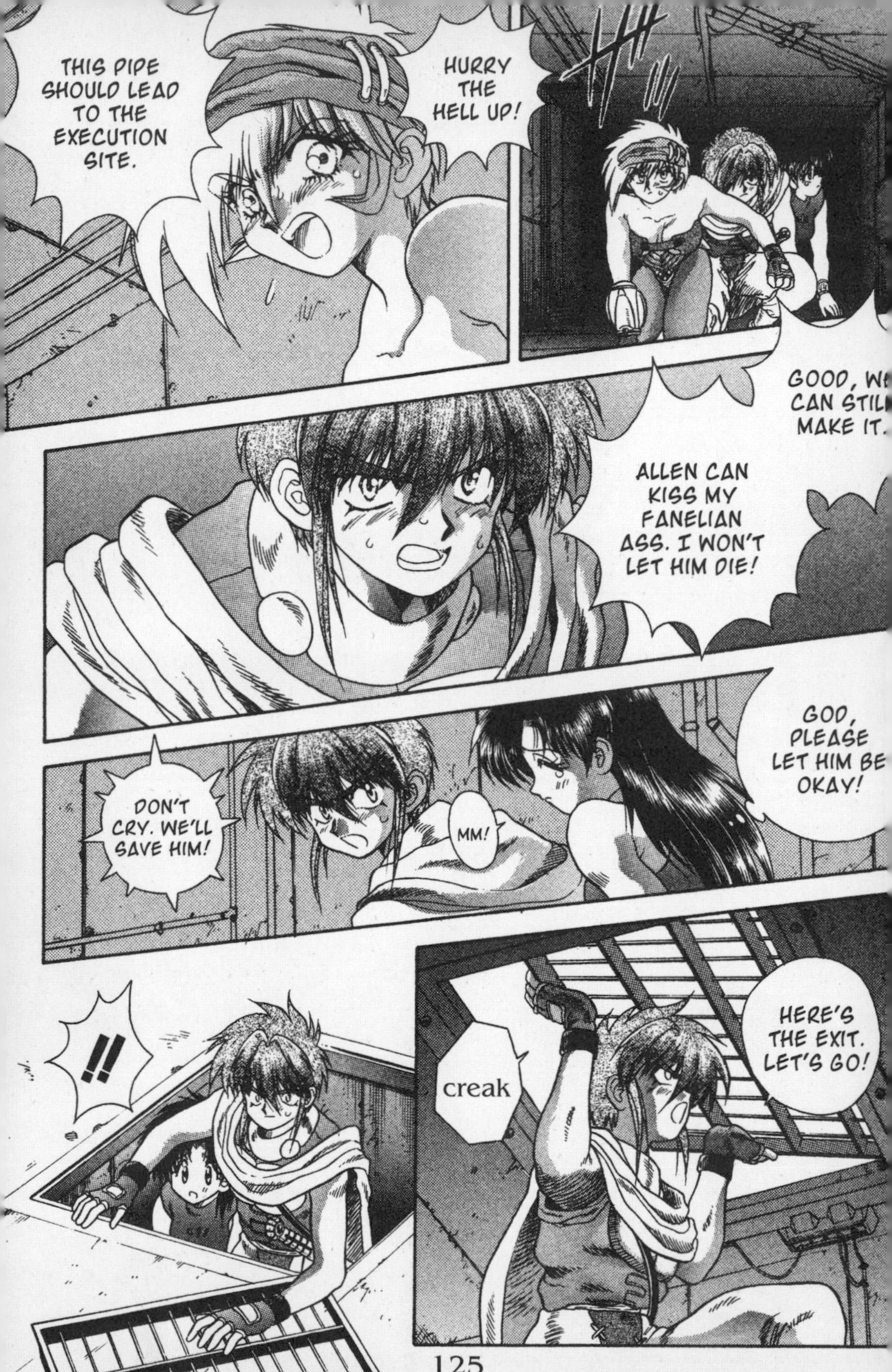
GOOD, WE CAN STILL MAKE IT.
HURRY THE HELL UP!
THIS PIPE SHOULD LEAD TO THE EXECUTION SITE.
ALLEN CAN KISS MY FANELIAN ASS. I WON'T LET HIM DIE!
GOD, PLEASE LET HIM BE OKAY!
MM!
DON'T CRY. WE'LL SAVE HIM!
HERE'S THE EXIT. LET'S GO!
creak
!!

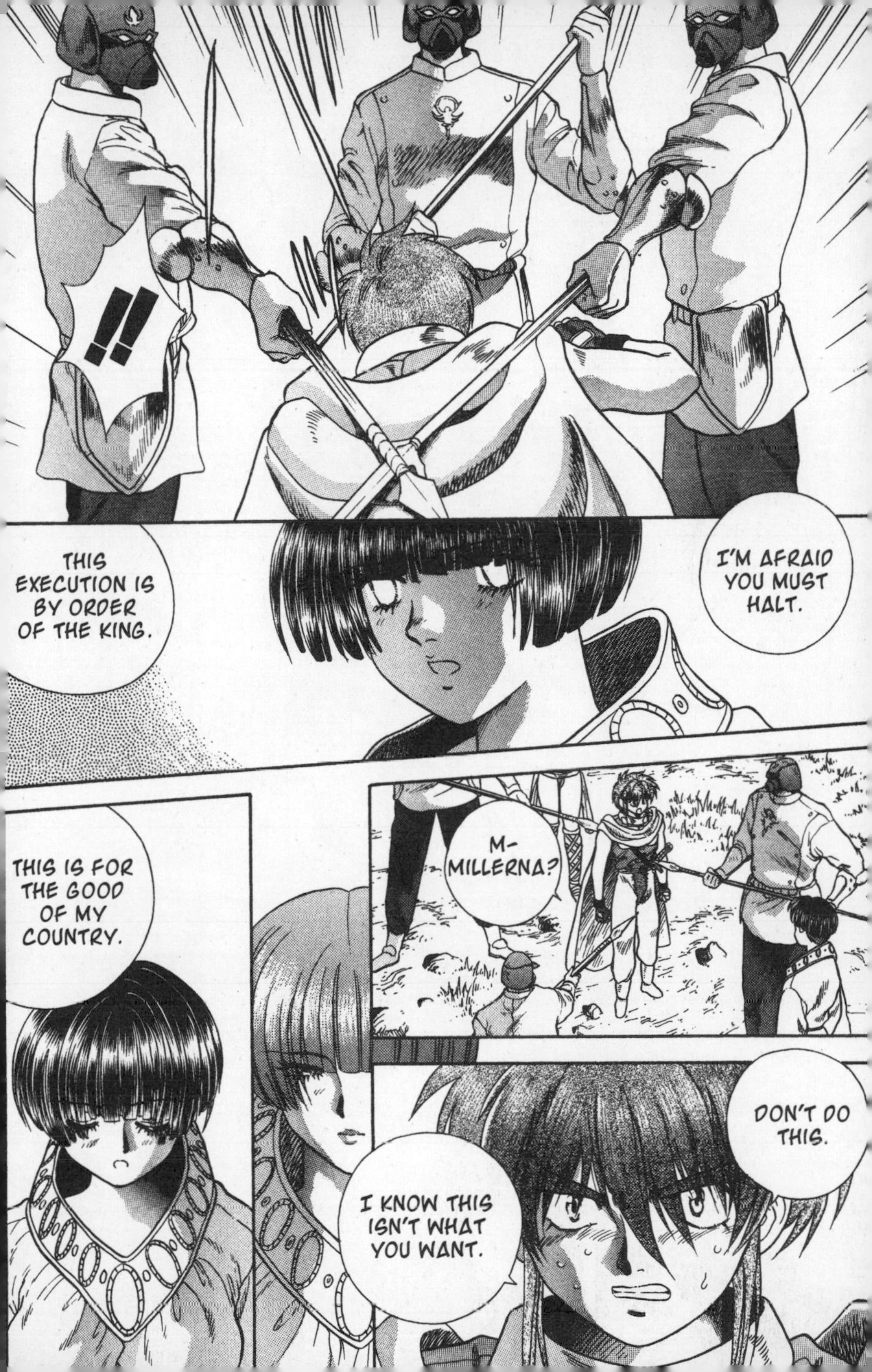
!!
I'M AFRAID YOU MUST HALT.
THIS EXECUTION IS BY ORDER OF THE KING.
M-MILLERNA?
DON'T DO THIS.
I KNOW THIS ISN'T WHAT YOU WANT.
THIS IS FOR THE GOOD OF MY COUNTRY.

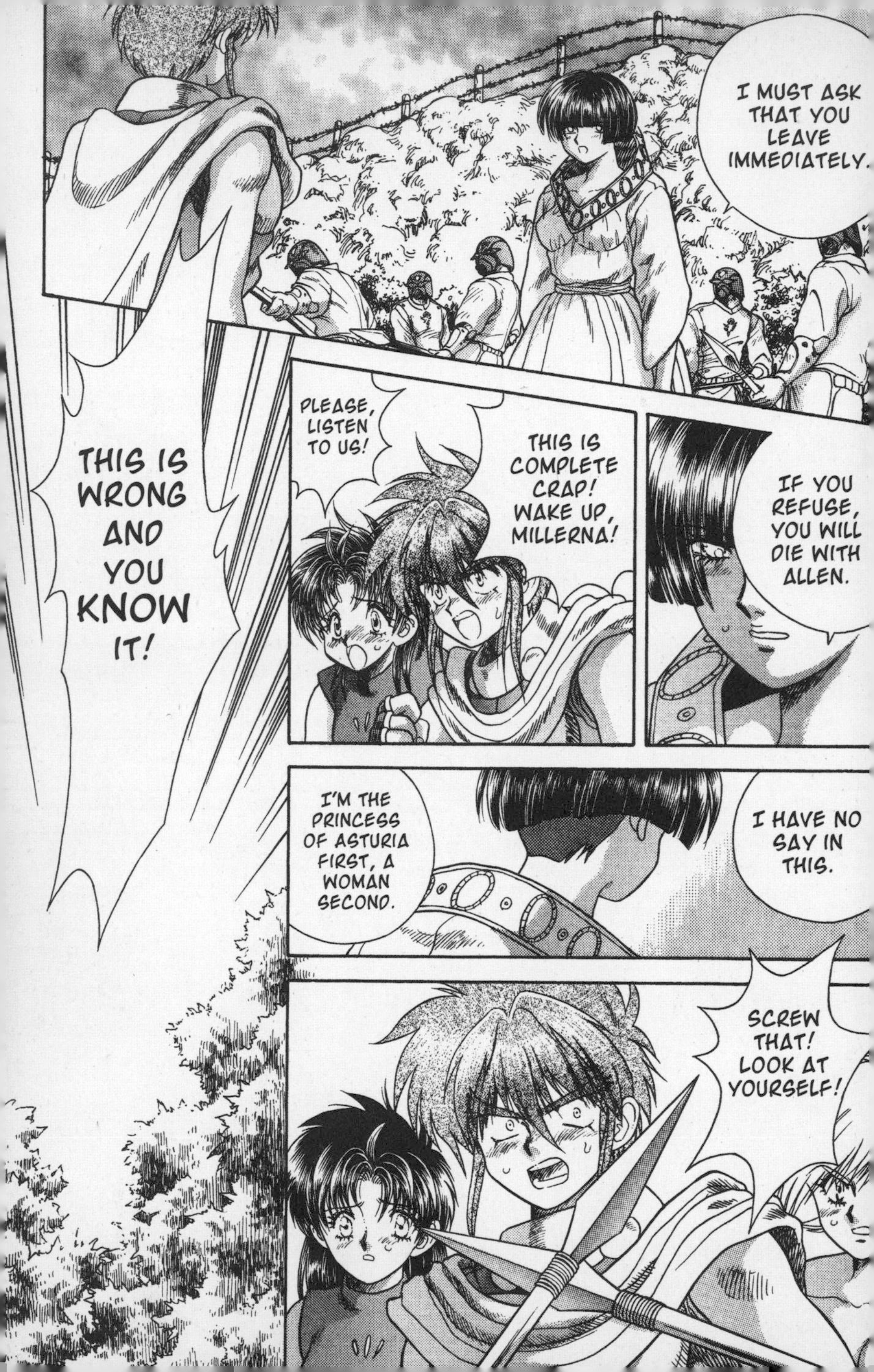
I MUST ASK THAT YOU LEAVE IMMEDIATELY.
IF YOU REFUSE, YOU WILL DIE WITH ALLEN.
PLEASE, LISTEN TO US!
THIS IS COMPLETE CRAP! WAKE UP, MILLERNA!
I HAVE NO SAY IN THIS.
I'M THE PRINCESS OF ASTURIA FIRST, A WOMAN SECOND.
SCREW THAT! LOOK AT YOURSELF!
THIS IS WRONG AND YOU KNOW IT!

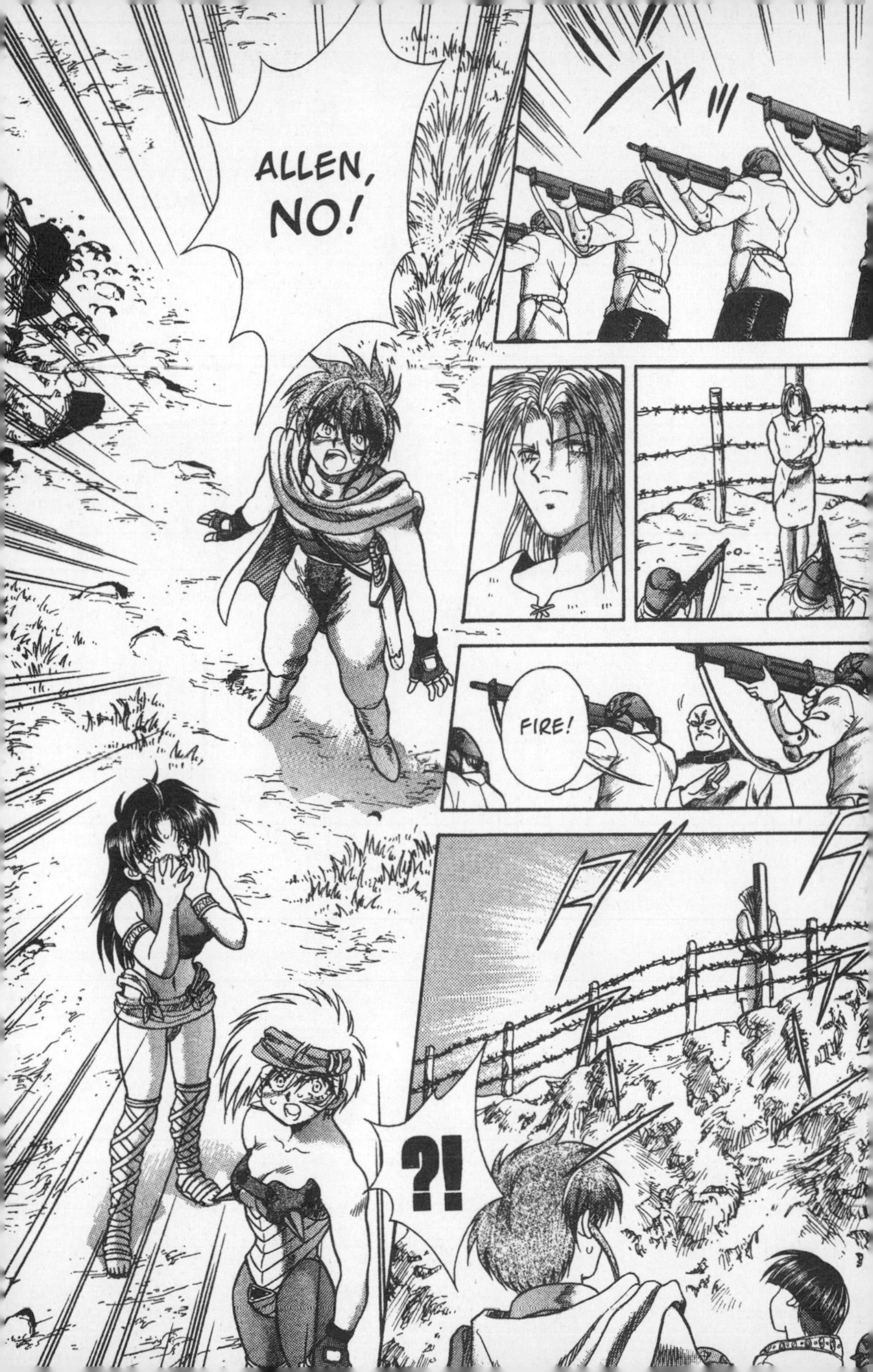
FIRE!
ALLEN,
NO!
?!

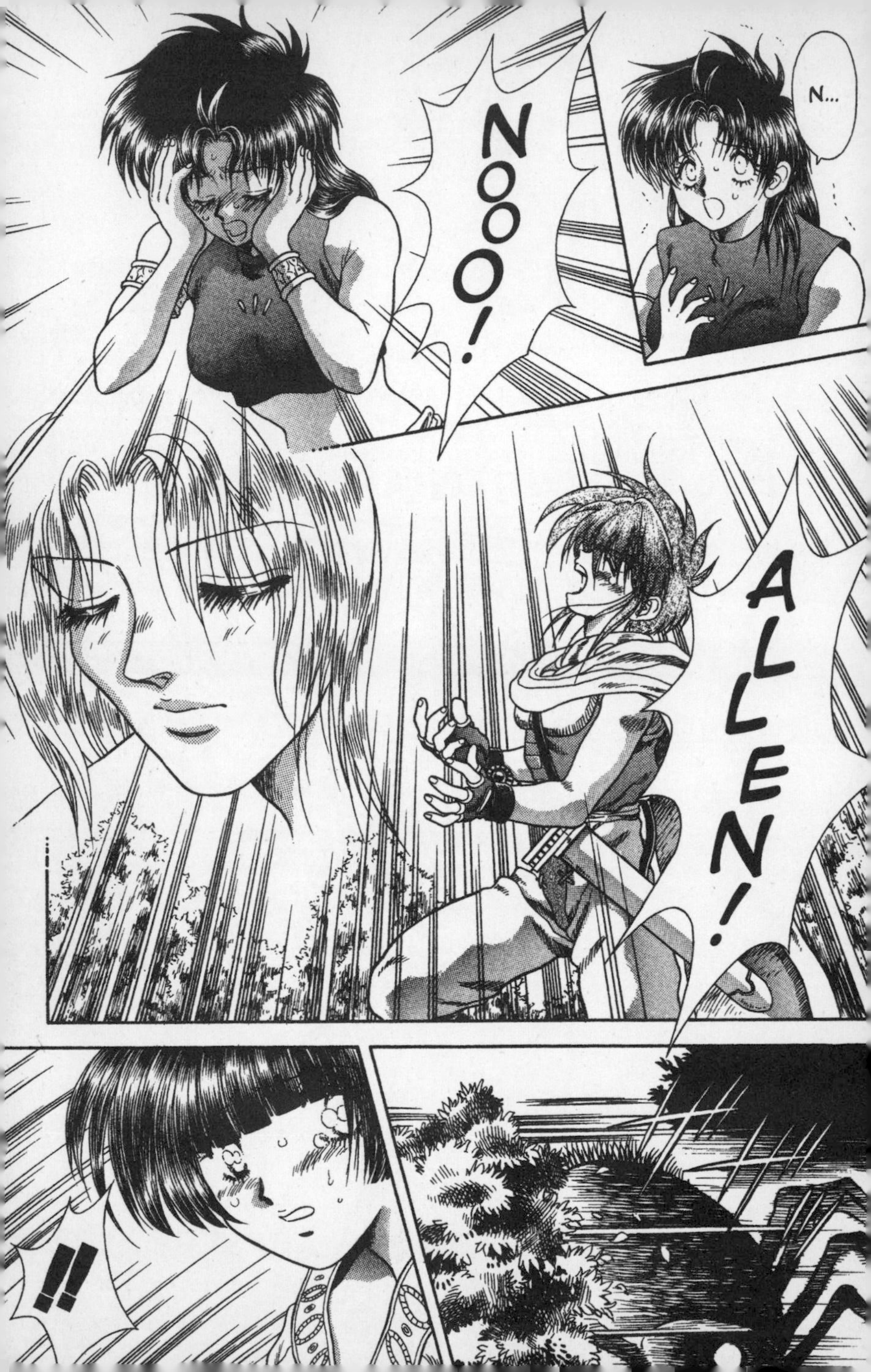
N...
NOOO!
ALLEN!
!!

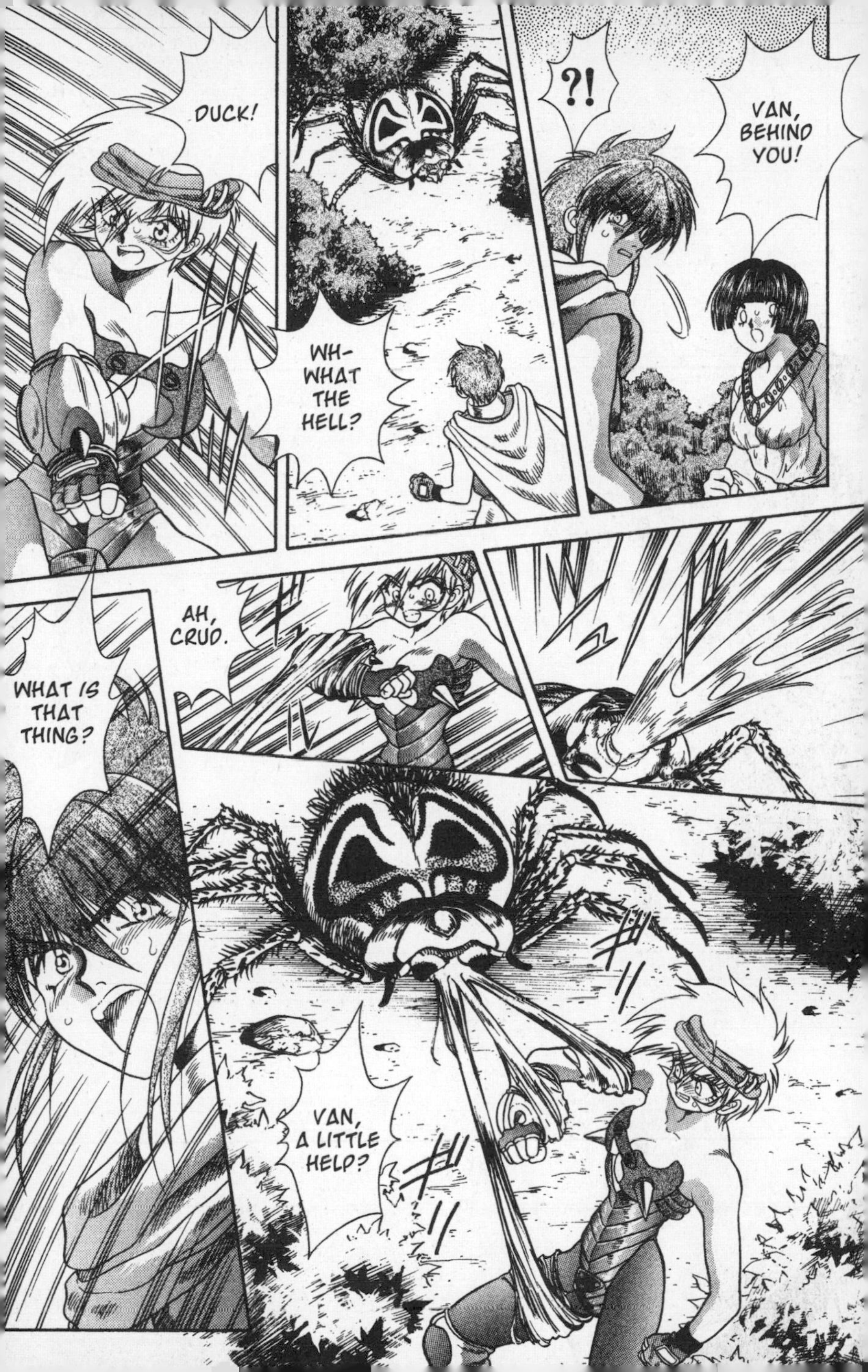
VAN, BEHIND YOU!
?!
WH- WHAT THE HELL?
DUCK!
AH, CRUD.
VAN, A LITTLE HELP?
WHAT IS THAT THING?

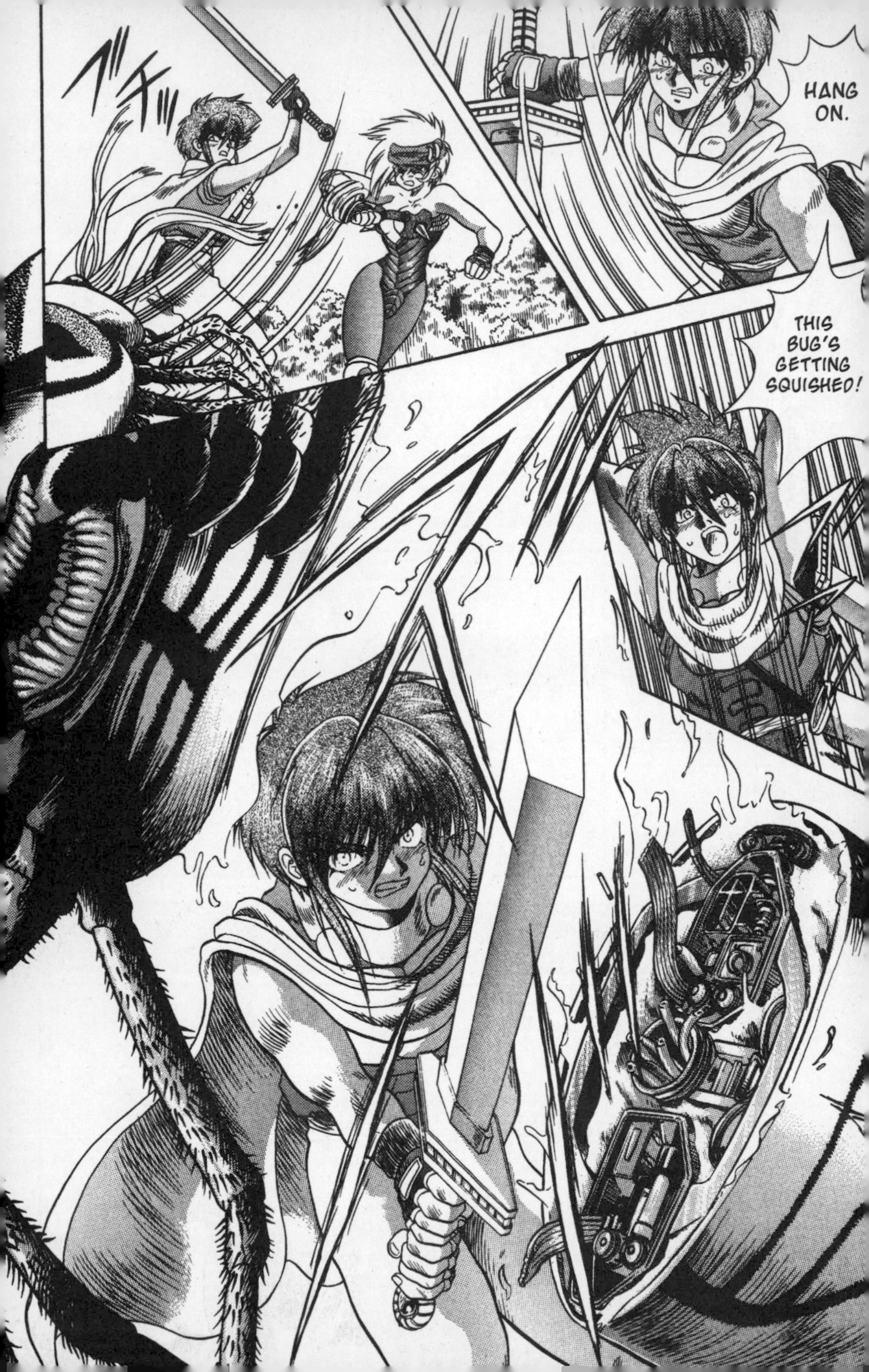
HANG ON.
THIS BUG'S GETTING SQUISHED!

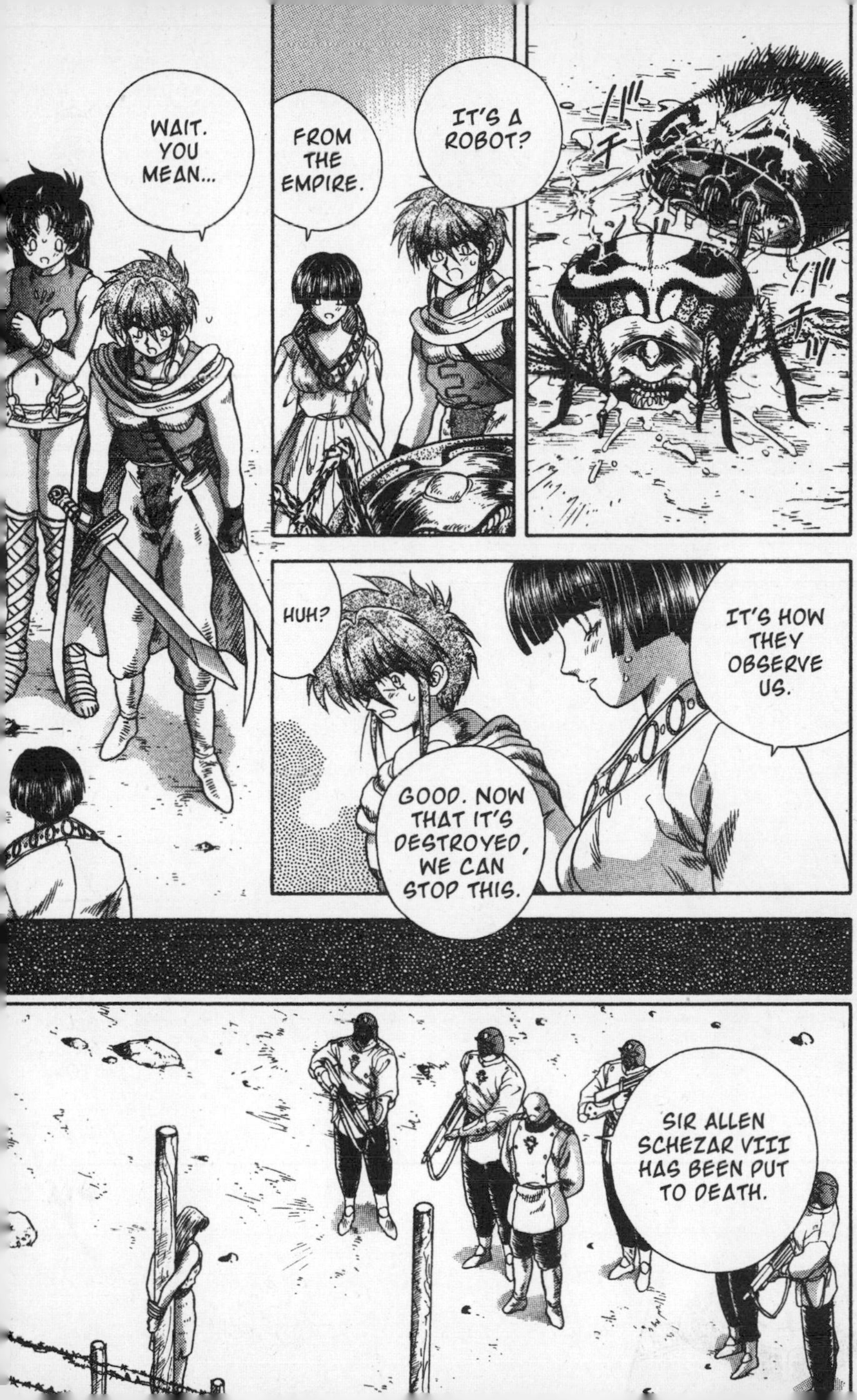
IT'S A ROBOT?
FROM THE EMPIRE.
IT'S HOW THEY OBSERVE US.
HUH?
GOOD. NOW THAT IT'S DESTROYED, WE CAN STOP THIS.
WAIT. YOU MEAN...
SIR ALLEN SCHEZAR VIII HAS BEEN PUT TO DEATH.

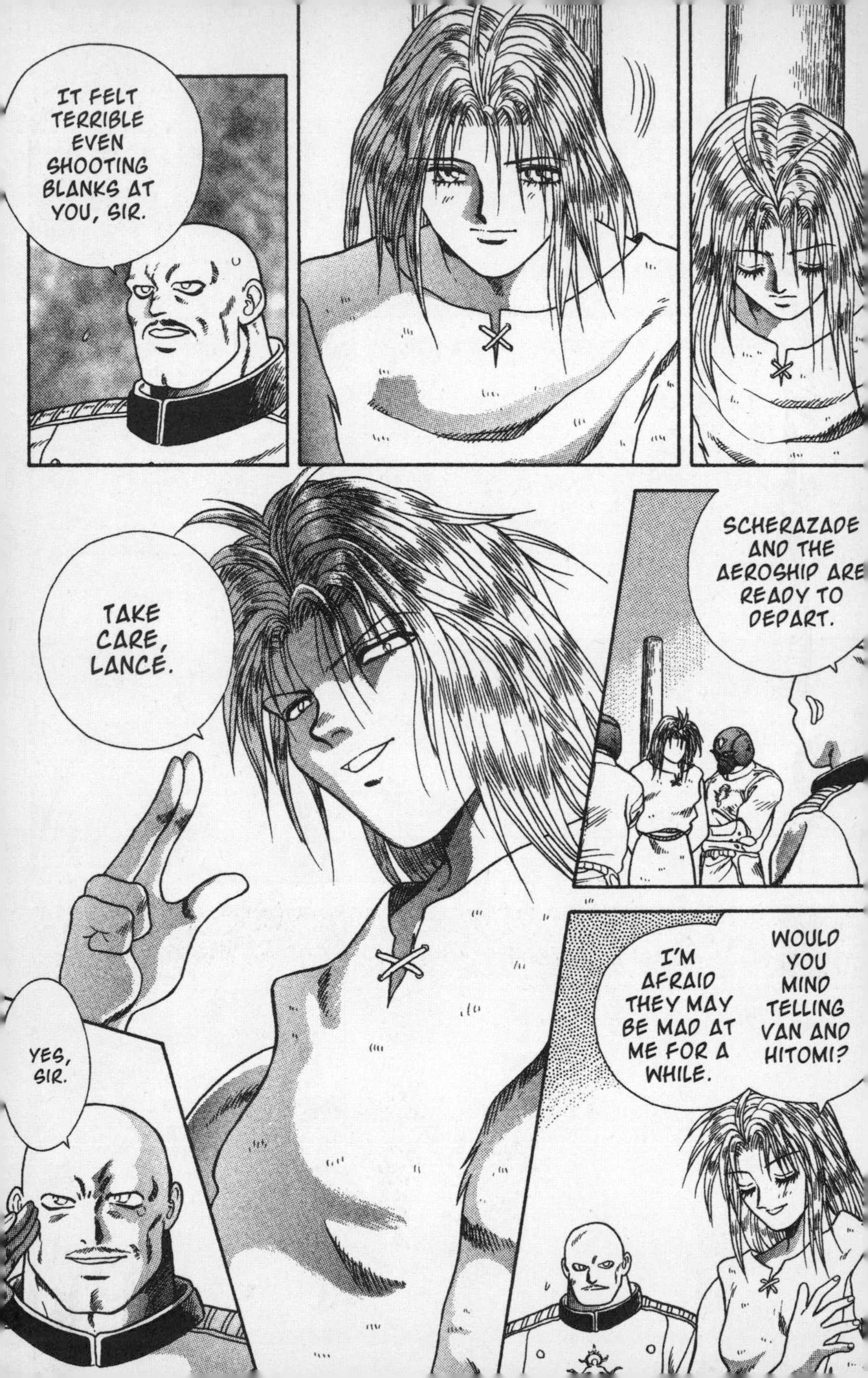
IT FELT TERRIBLE EVEN SHOOTING BLANKS AT YOU, SIR.
SCHERAZADE AND THE AEROSHIP ARE READY TO DEPART.
WOULD YOU MIND TELLING VAN AND HITOMI?
I'M AFRAID THEY MAY BE MAD AT ME FOR A WHILE.
TAKE CARE, LANCE.
YES, SIR.

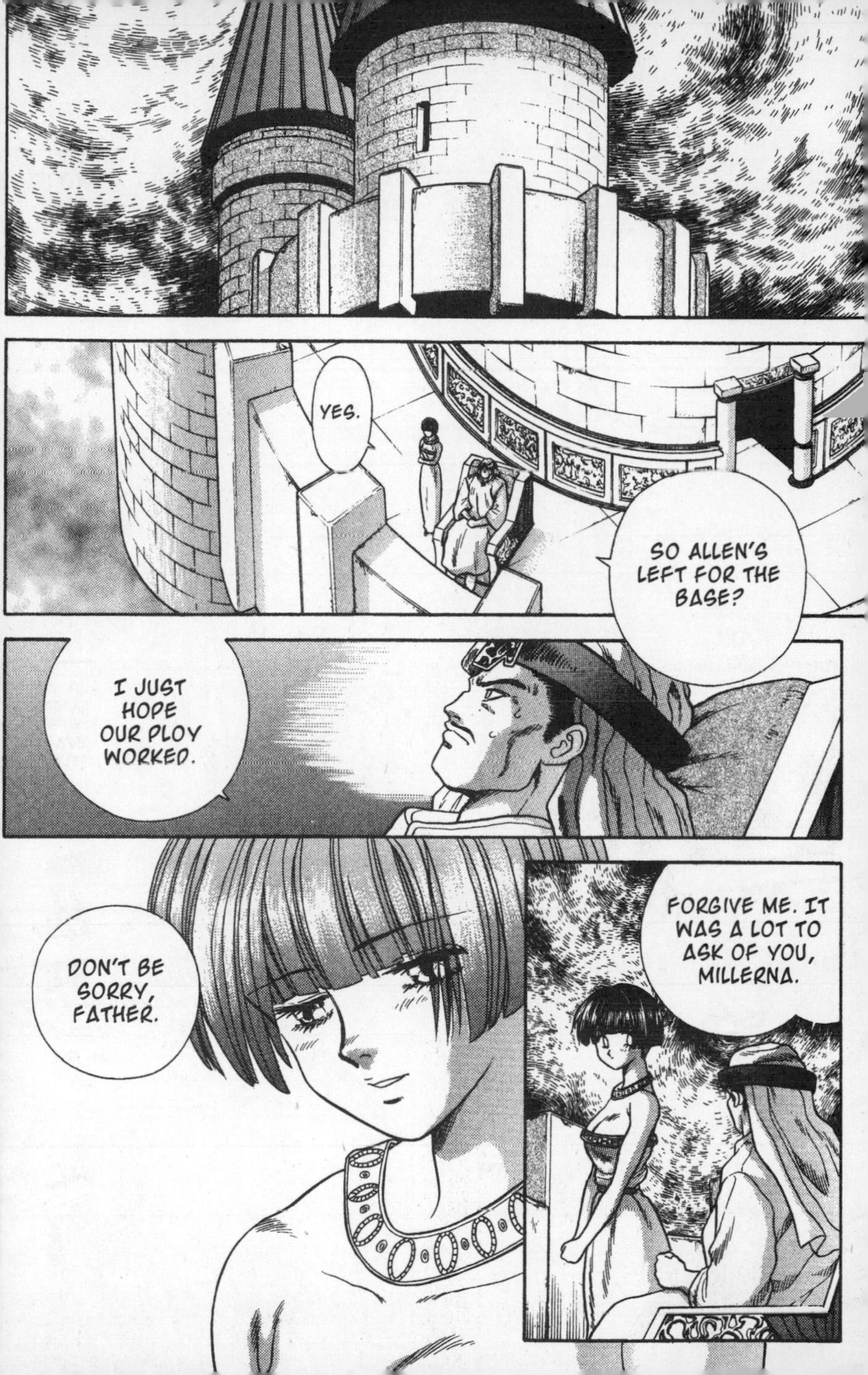
SO ALLEN'S LEFT FOR THE BASE?
YES.
I JUST HOPE OUR PLOY WORKED.
FORGIVE ME. IT WAS A LOT TO ASK OF YOU, MILLERNA.
DON'T BE SORRY, FATHER.

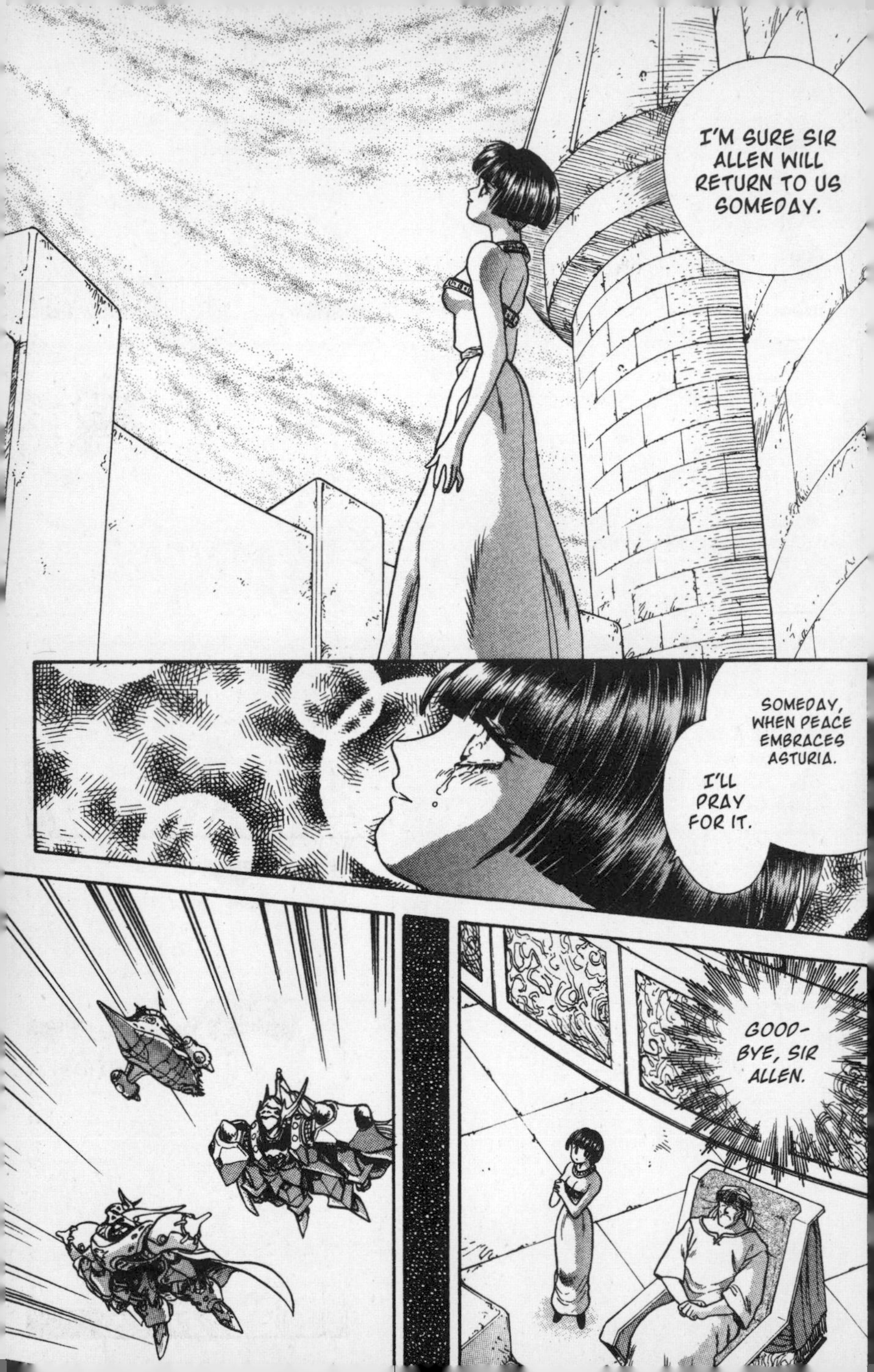
I'M SURE SIR ALLEN WILL RETURN TO US SOMEDAY.
SOMEDAY, WHEN PEACE EMBRACES ASTURIA.
I'LL PRAY FOR IT.
GOOD-BYE, SIR ALLEN.

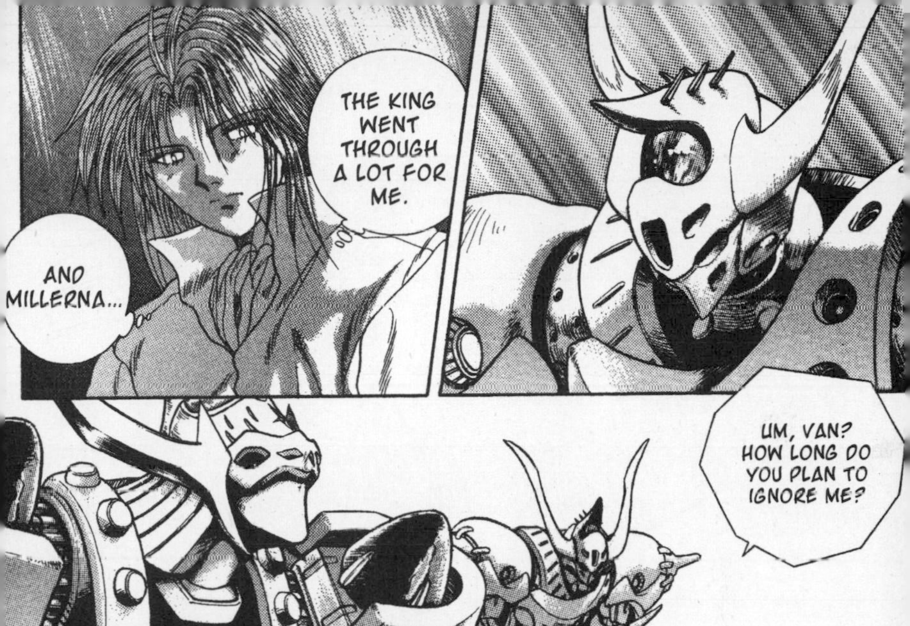
THE KING WENT THROUGH A LOT FOR ME.
AND MILLERNA...
UM, VAN? HOW LONG DO YOU PLAN TO IGNORE ME?
SCREW YOU IN THE EAR, DICK! I HOPE YOU CHOKE ON A KNIFE!
THAT'S RIGHT! LYING LIKE THAT'LL GET ENMA* TO PULL YOUR TONGUE CLEAN OUT!

*Enma: A fabled Japanese demon known to pull out the tongues of liars.

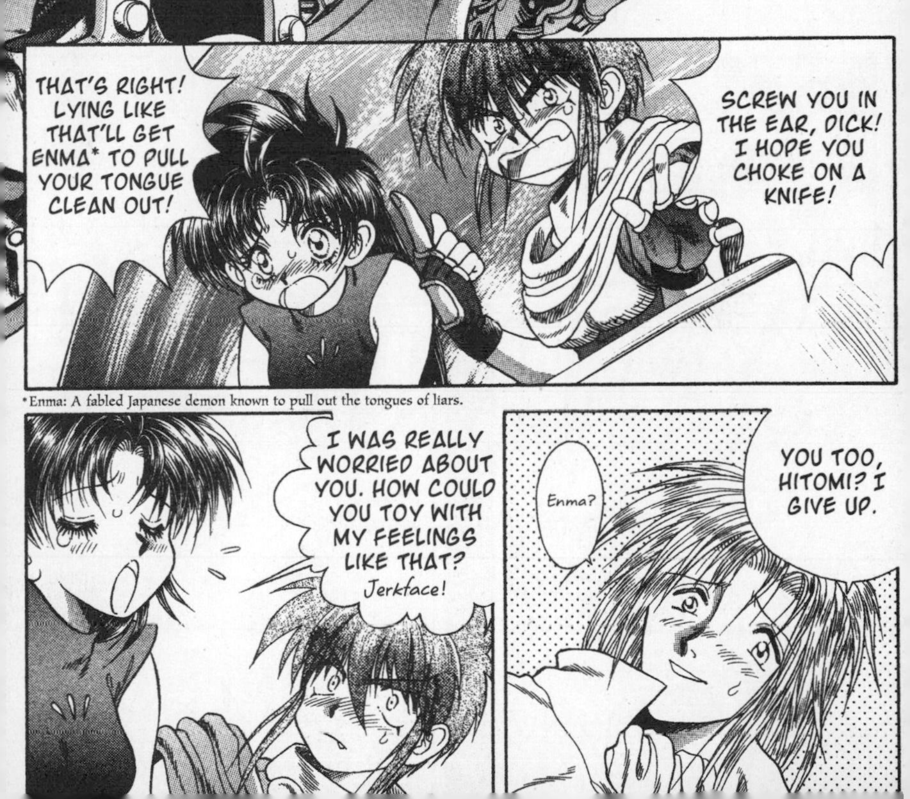
YOU TOO, HITOMI? I GIVE UP.
Enma?
I WAS REALLY WORRIED ABOUT YOU. HOW COULD YOU TOY WITH MY FEELINGS LIKE THAT?
Jerkface!

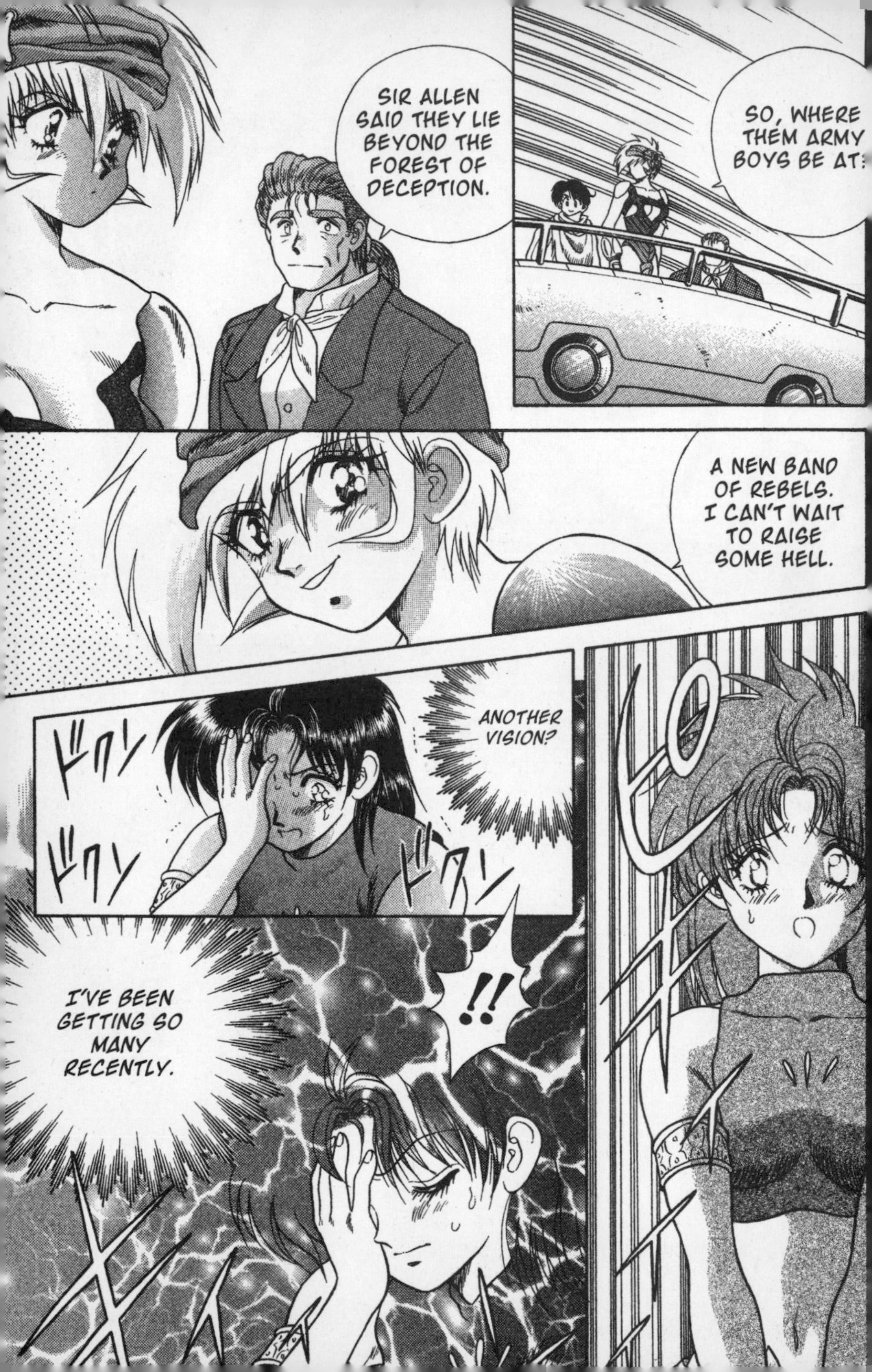
SO, WHERE THEM ARMY BOYS BE AT?
SIR ALLEN SAID THEY LIE BEYOND THE FOREST OF DECEPTION.
A NEW BAND OF REBELS. I CAN'T WAIT TO RAISE SOME HELL.
ANOTHER VISION?
ドクン
ドクン
ドクン
!!
I'VE BEEN GETTING SO MANY RECENTLY.

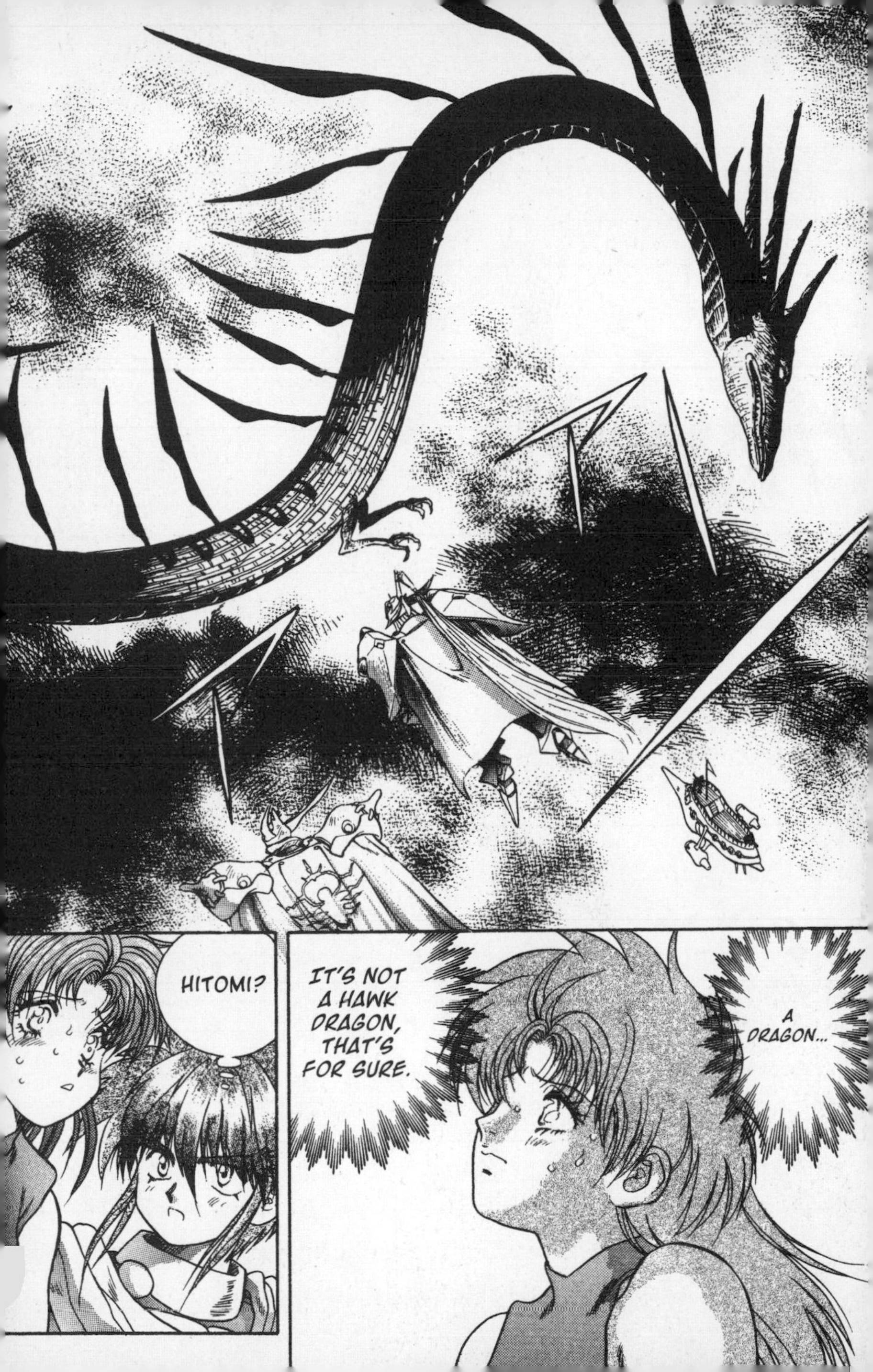
A DRAGON...
IT'S NOT A HAWK DRAGON, THAT'S FOR SURE.
HITOMI?

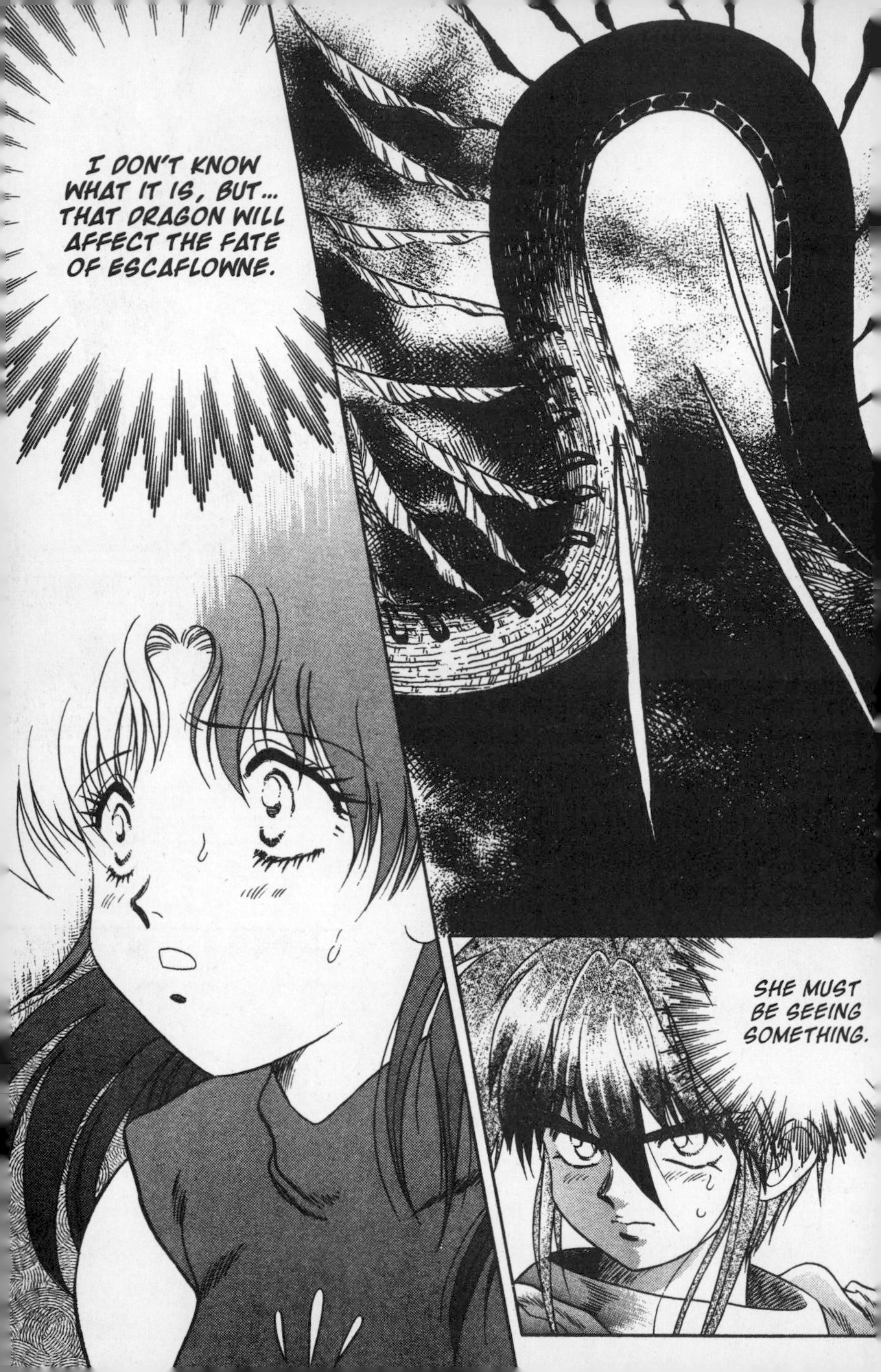
I DON'T KNOW WHAT IT IS, BUT... THAT DRAGON WILL AFFECT THE FATE OF ESCAFLOWNE.
SHE MUST BE SEEING SOMETHING.

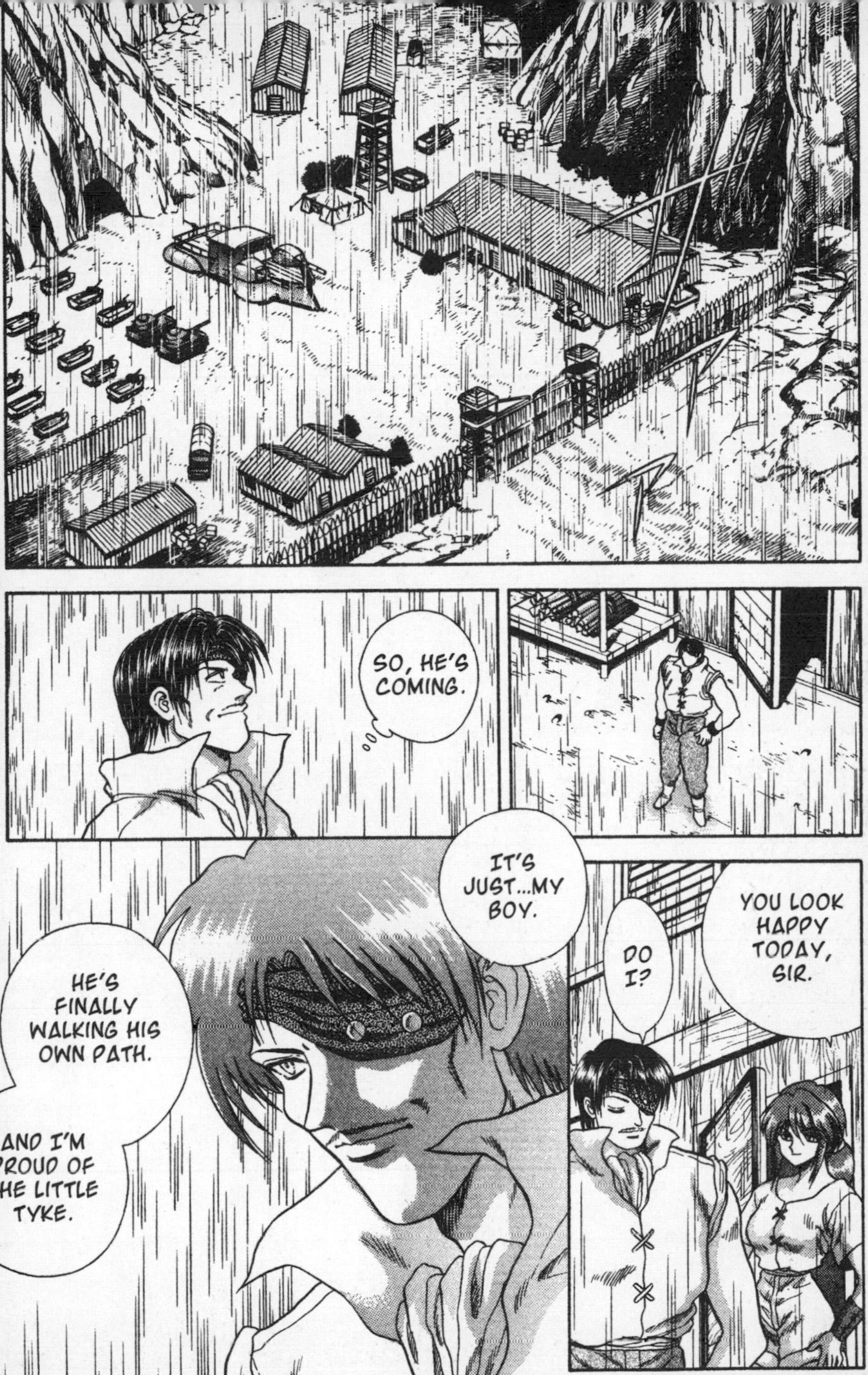
SO, HE'S COMING.
YOU LOOK HAPPY TODAY, SIR.
DO I?
IT'S JUST...MY BOY.
HE'S FINALLY WALKING HIS OWN PATH.
AND I'M ROUD OF HE LITTLE TYKE.

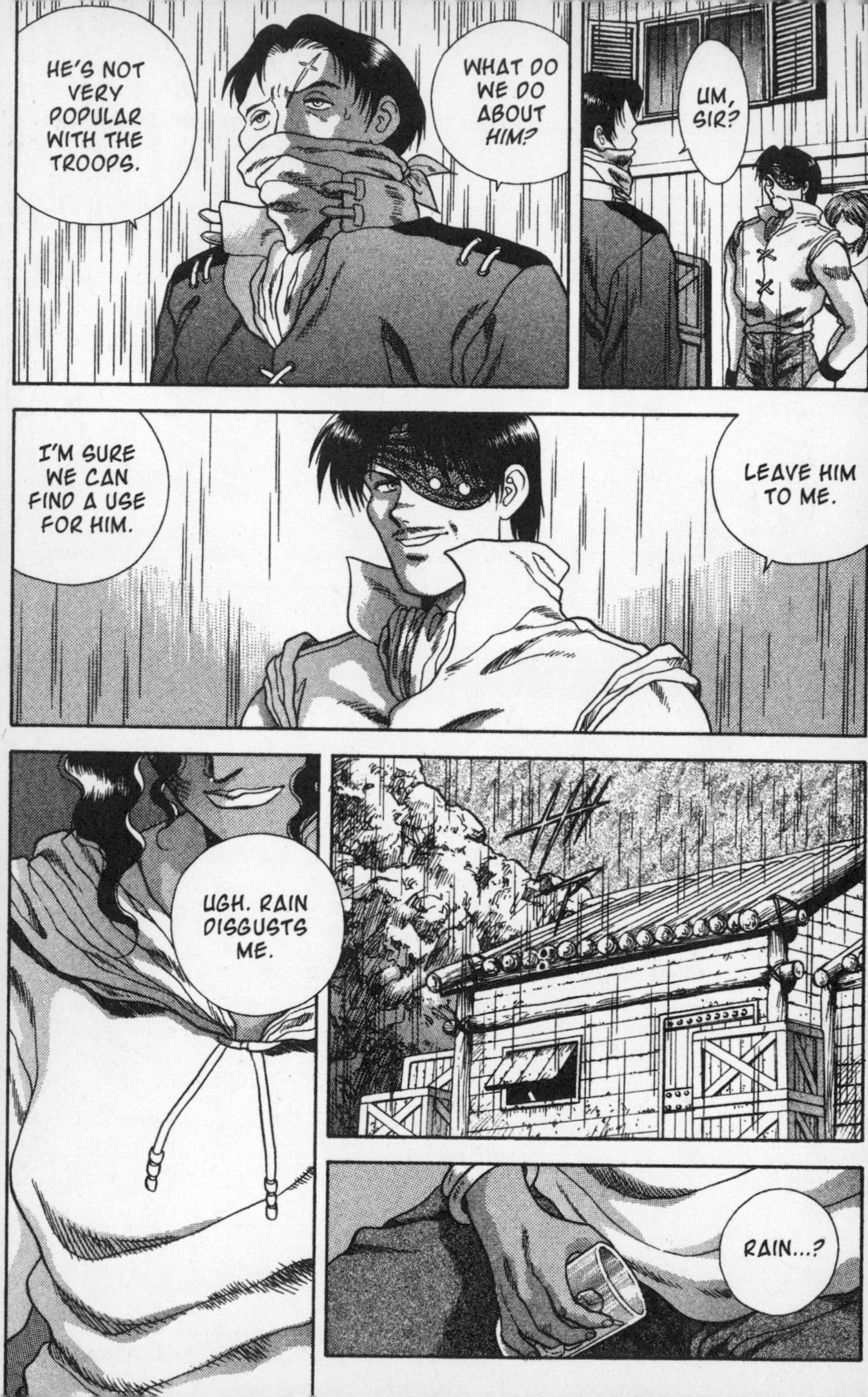
UM, SIR?
WHAT DO WE DO ABOUT HIM?
HE'S NOT VERY POPULAR WITH THE TROOPS.
LEAVE HIM TO ME.
I'M SURE WE CAN FIND A USE FOR HIM.
RAIN...?
UGH. RAIN DISGUSTS ME.

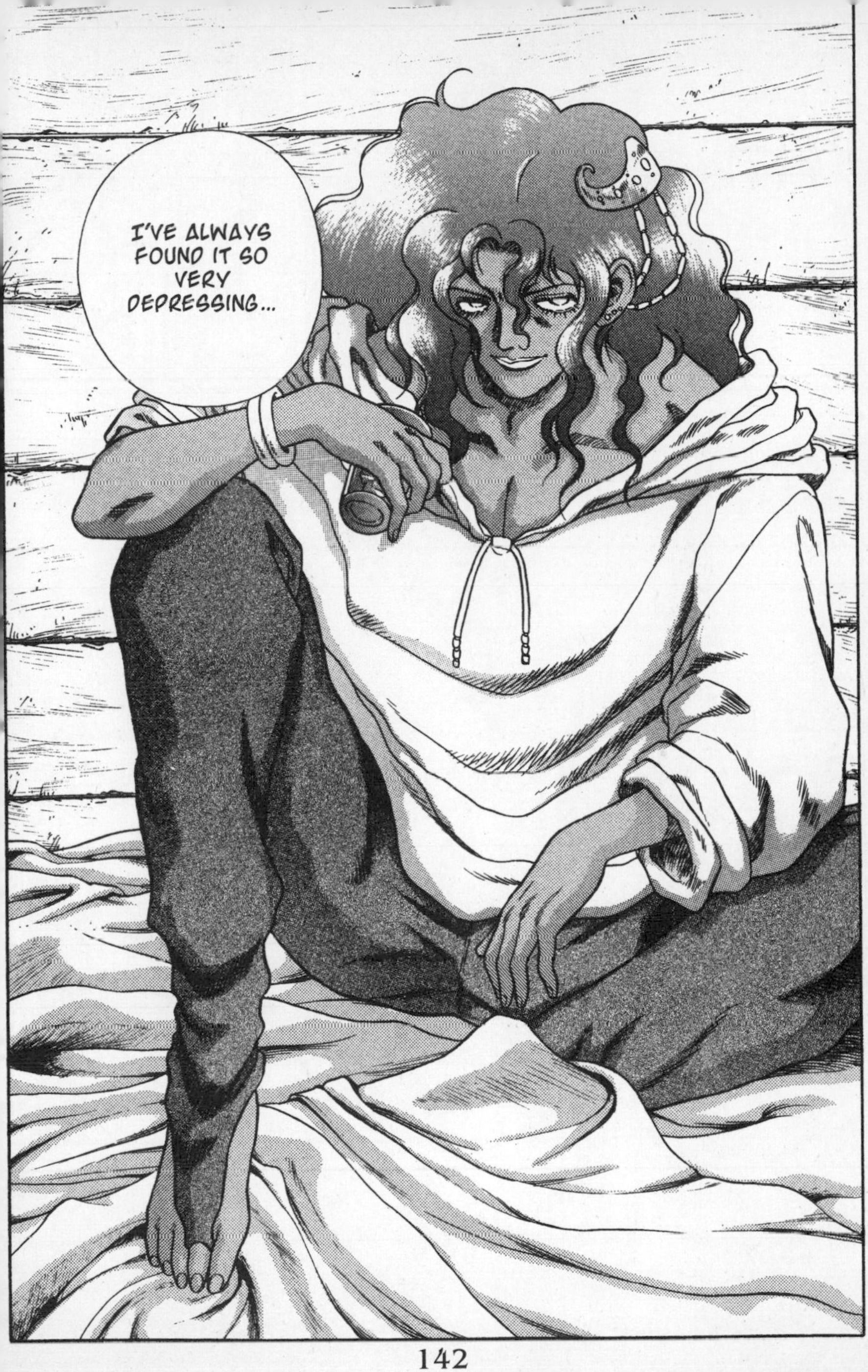
I'VE ALWAYS FOUND IT SO VERY DEPRESSING...

VISION 22:
THE REVOLUTIONIST'S ARMY

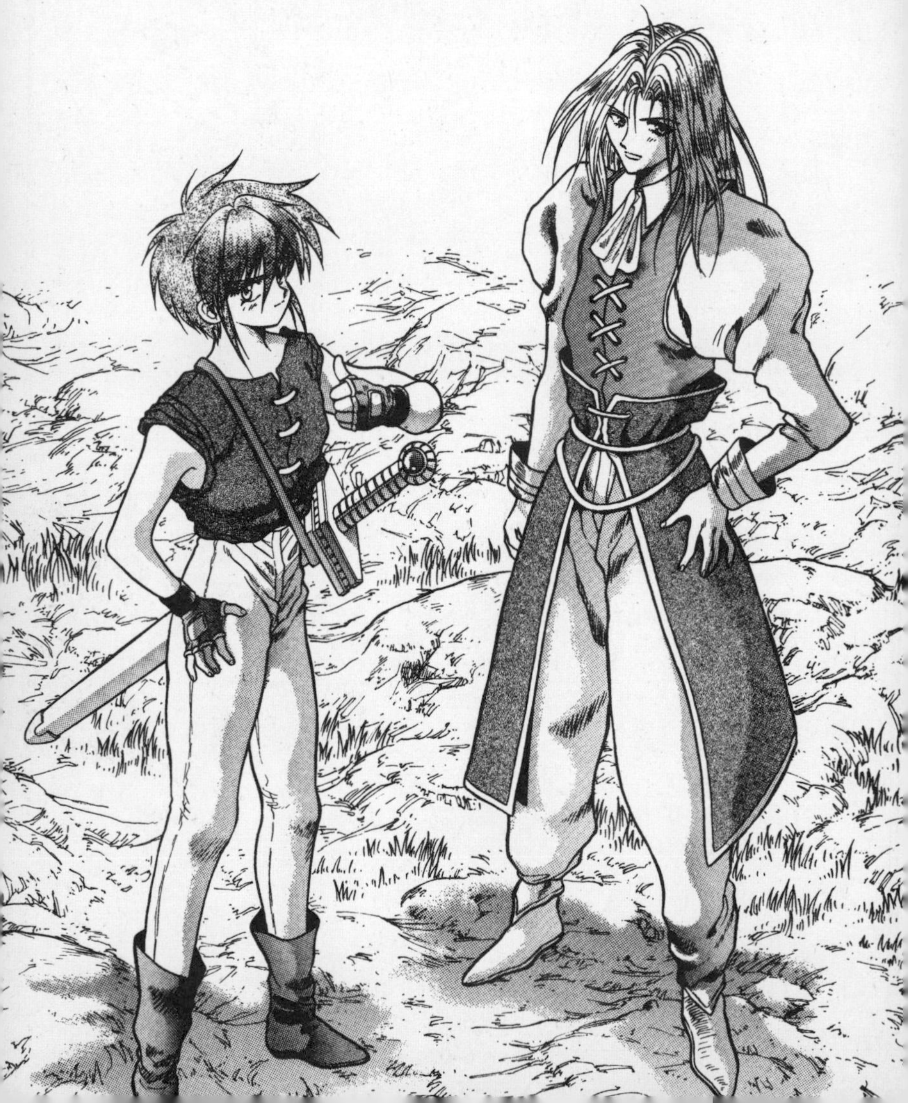

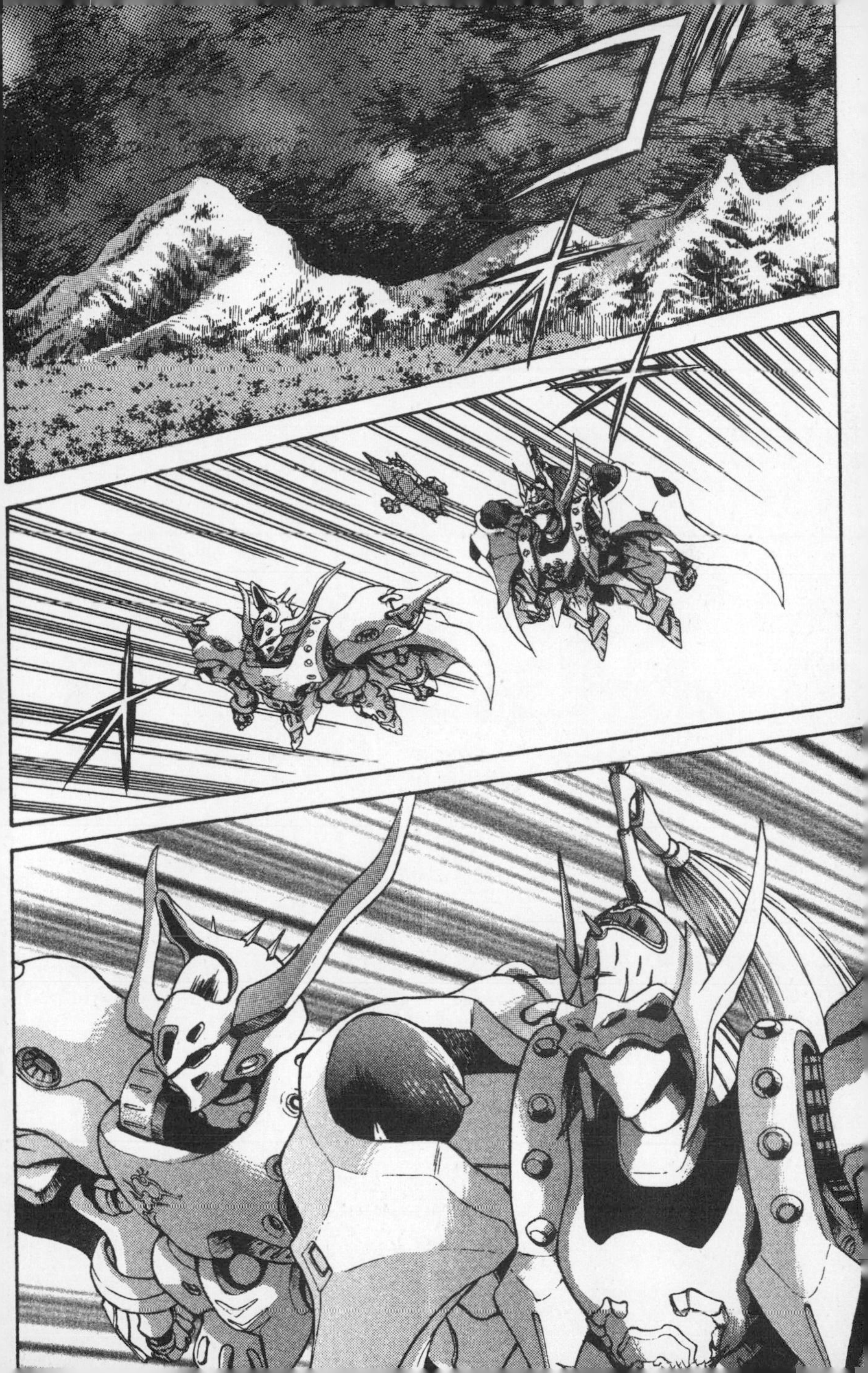

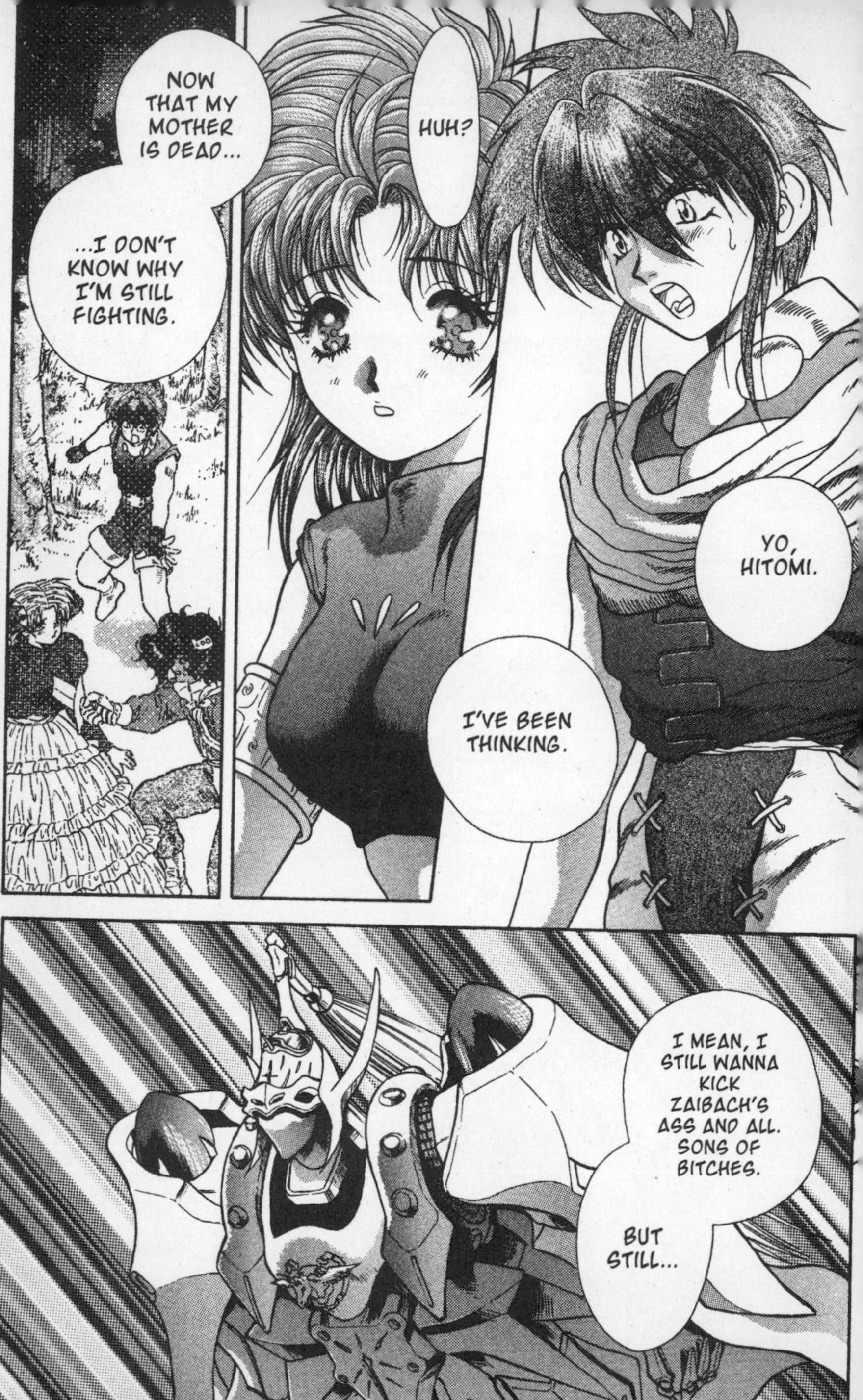
YO, HITOMI.
I'VE BEEN THINKING.
HUH?
NOW THAT MY MOTHER IS DEAD...
...I DON'T KNOW WHY I'M STILL FIGHTING.
I MEAN, I STILL WANNA KICK ZAIBACH'S ASS AND ALL. SONS OF BITCHES.
BUT STILL...

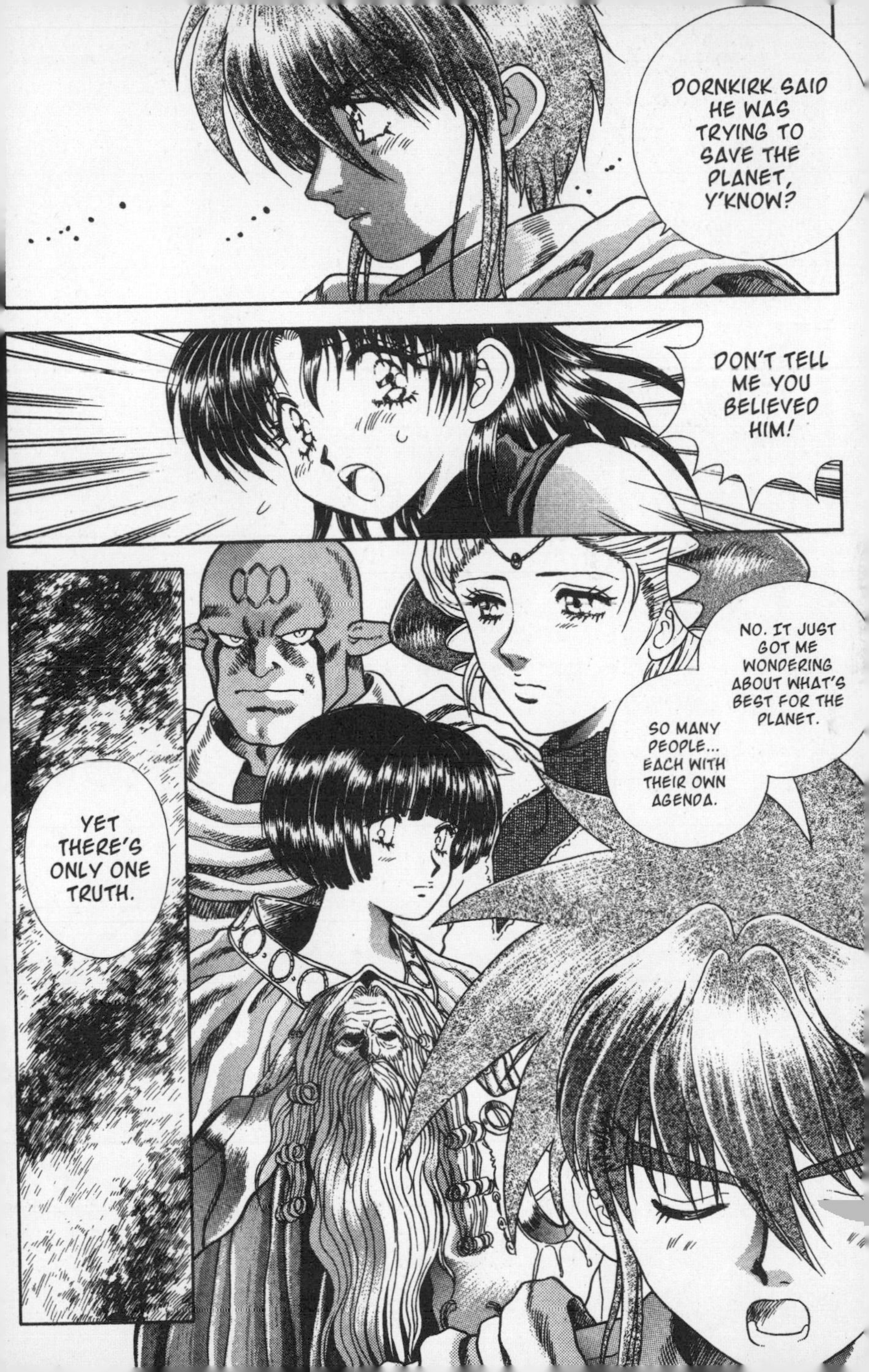
DORNKIRK SAID HE WAS TRYING TO SAVE THE PLANET, Y'KNOW?
DON'T TELL ME YOU BELIEVED HIM!
NO. IT JUST GOT ME WONDERING ABOUT WHAT'S BEST FOR THE PLANET.
SO MANY PEOPLE... EACH WITH THEIR OWN AGENDA.
YET THERE'S ONLY ONE TRUTH.

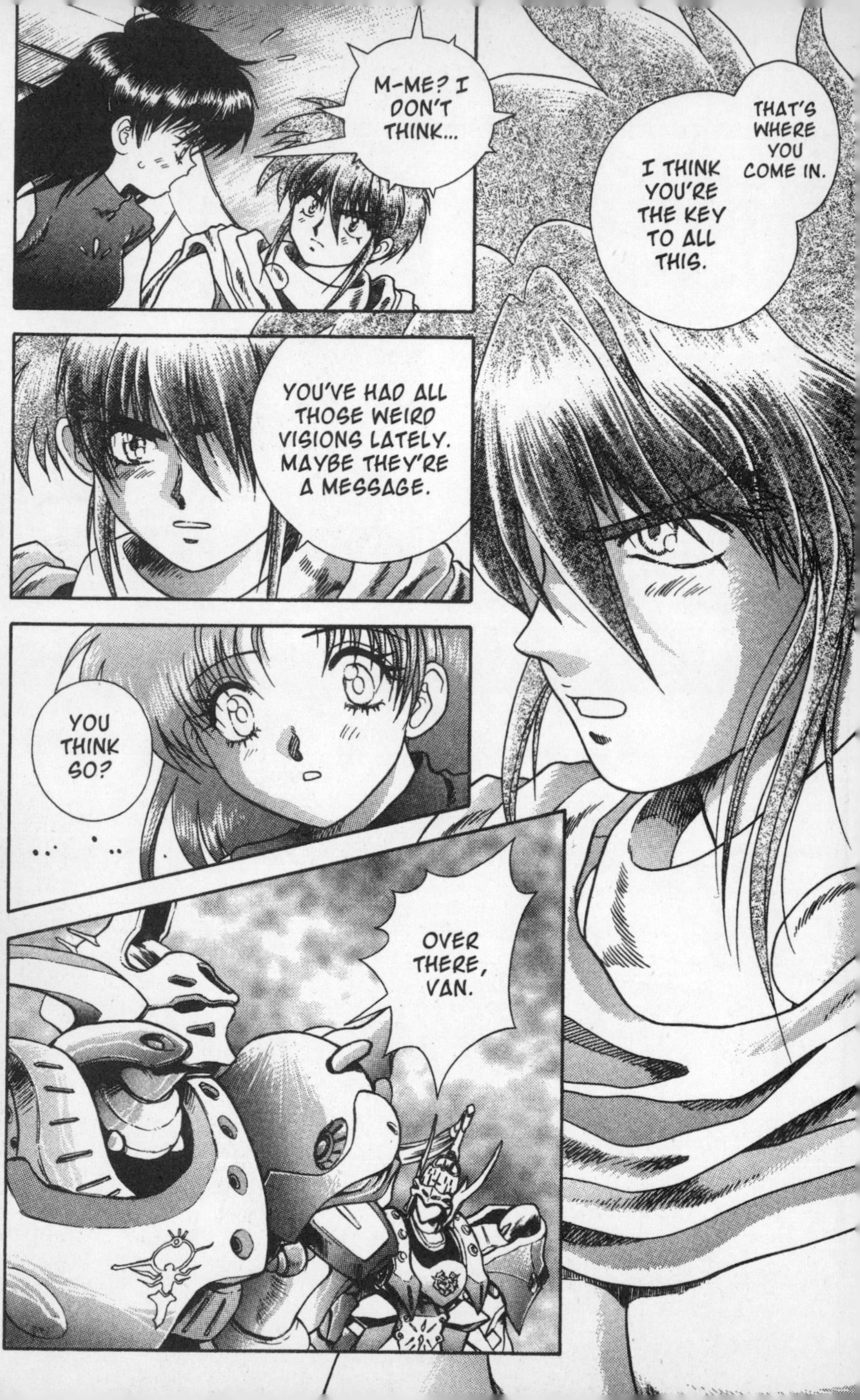
THAT'S WHERE YOU COME IN.
I THINK YOU'RE THE KEY TO ALL THIS.
M-ME? I DON'T THINK...
YOU'VE HAD ALL THOSE WEIRD VISIONS LATELY. MAYBE THEY'RE A MESSAGE.
YOU THINK SO?
...
OVER THERE, VAN.

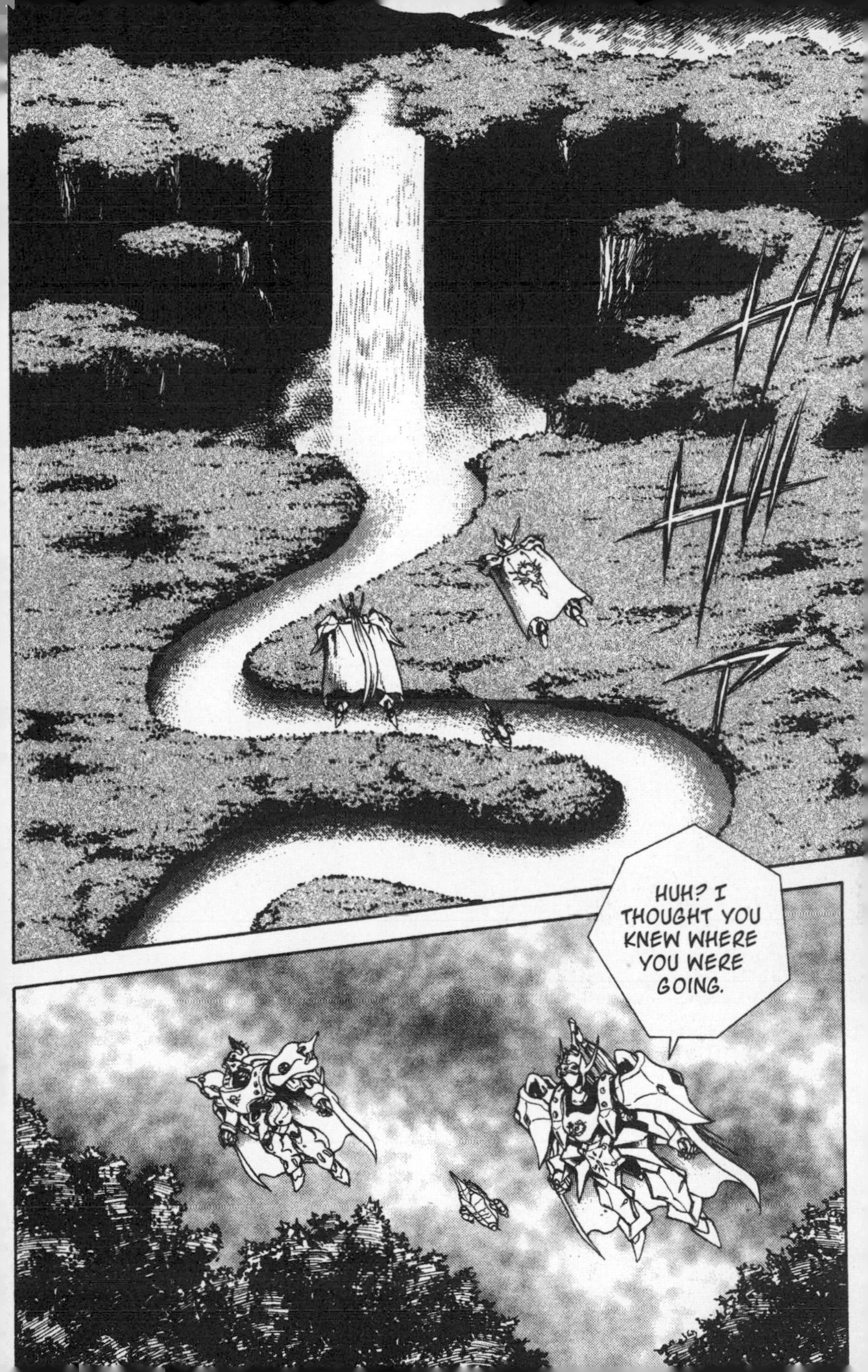
HUH? I THOUGHT YOU KNEW WHERE YOU WERE GOING.

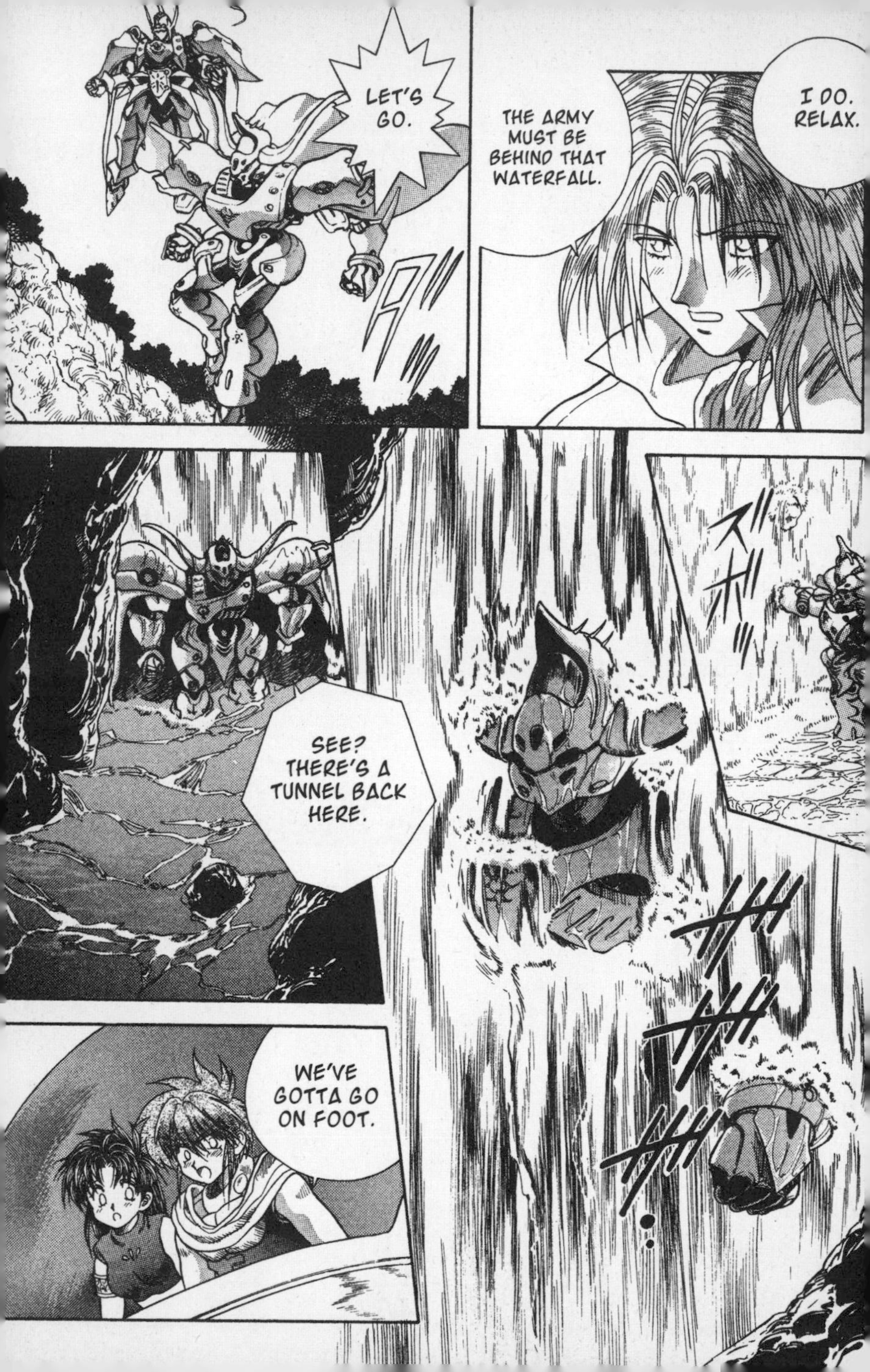
I DO. RELAX.
THE ARMY MUST BE BEHIND THAT WATERFALL.
LET'S GO.
SEE? THERE'S A TUNNEL BACK HERE.
WE'VE GOTTA GO ON FOOT.

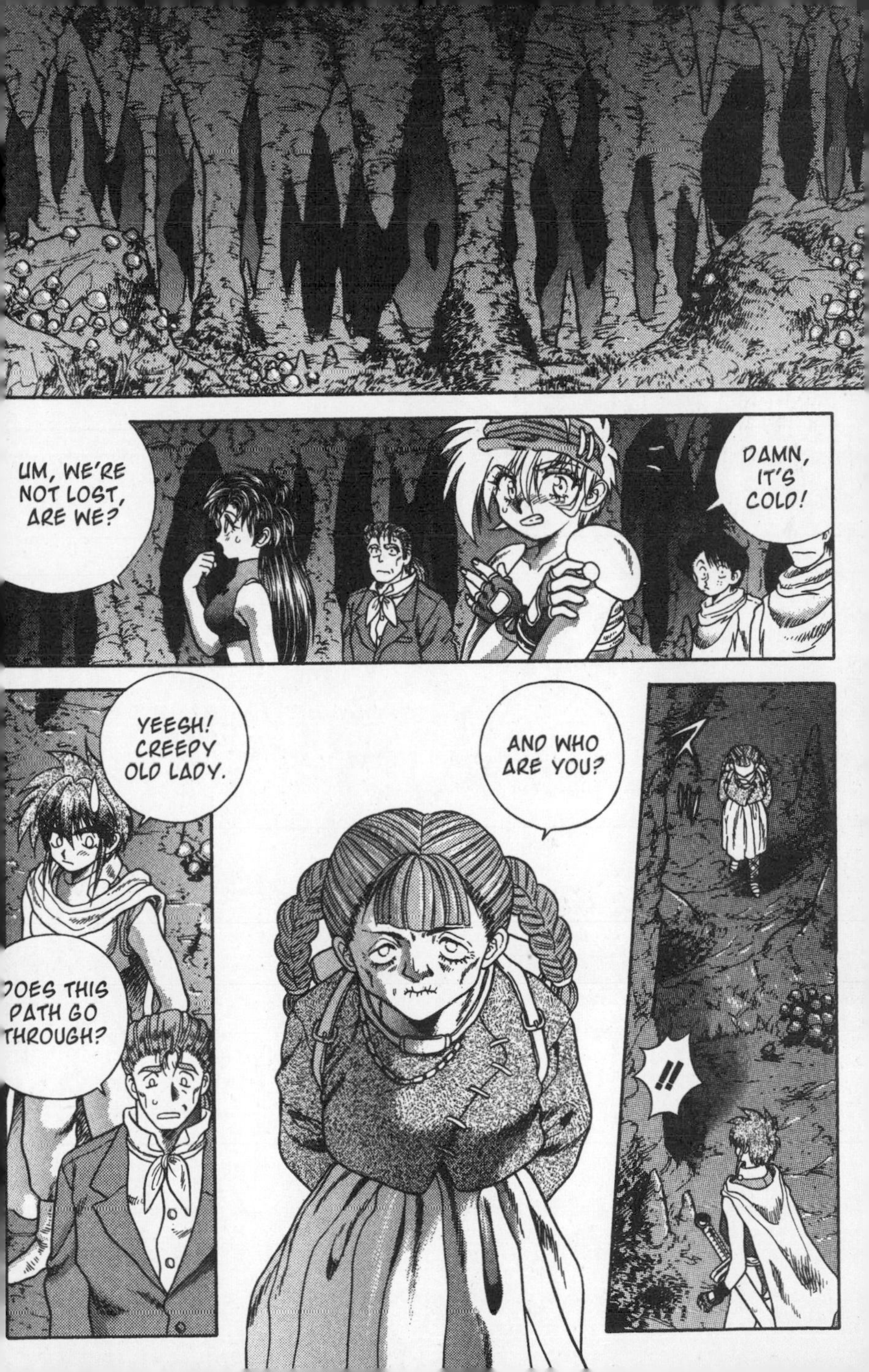
DAMN, IT'S COLD!
UM, WE'RE NOT LOST, ARE WE?
!!
AND WHO ARE YOU?
YEESH! CREEPY OLD LADY.
DOES THIS PATH GO THROUGH?

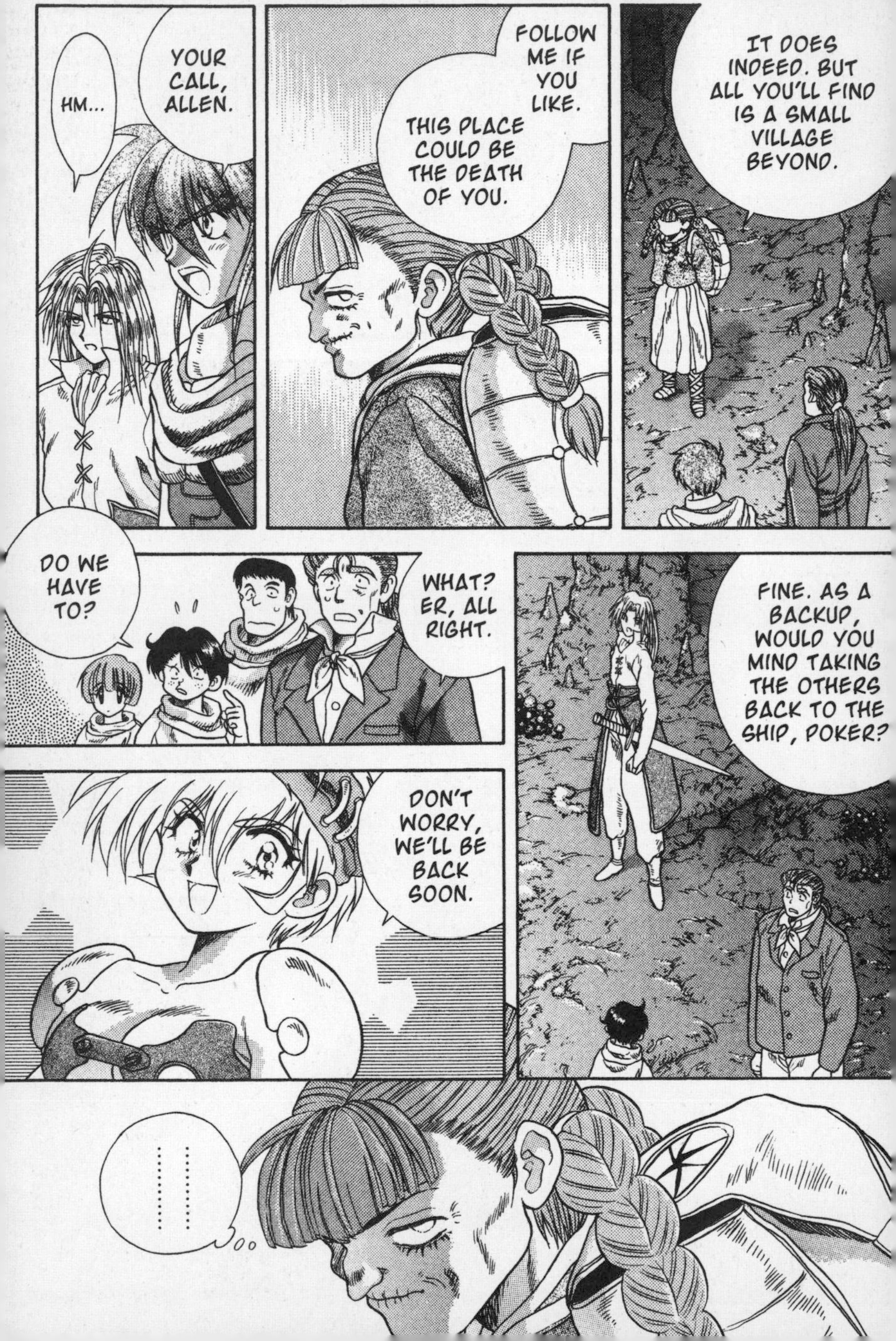
IT DOES INDEED. BUT ALL YOU'LL FIND IS A SMALL VILLAGE BEYOND.
FOLLOW ME IF YOU LIKE.
THIS PLACE COULD BE THE DEATH OF YOU.
YOUR CALL, ALLEN.
HM...
FINE. AS A BACKUP, WOULD YOU MIND TAKING THE OTHERS BACK TO THE SHIP, POKER?
WHAT? ER, ALL RIGHT.
DO WE HAVE TO?
DON'T WORRY, WE'LL BE BACK SOON.
......

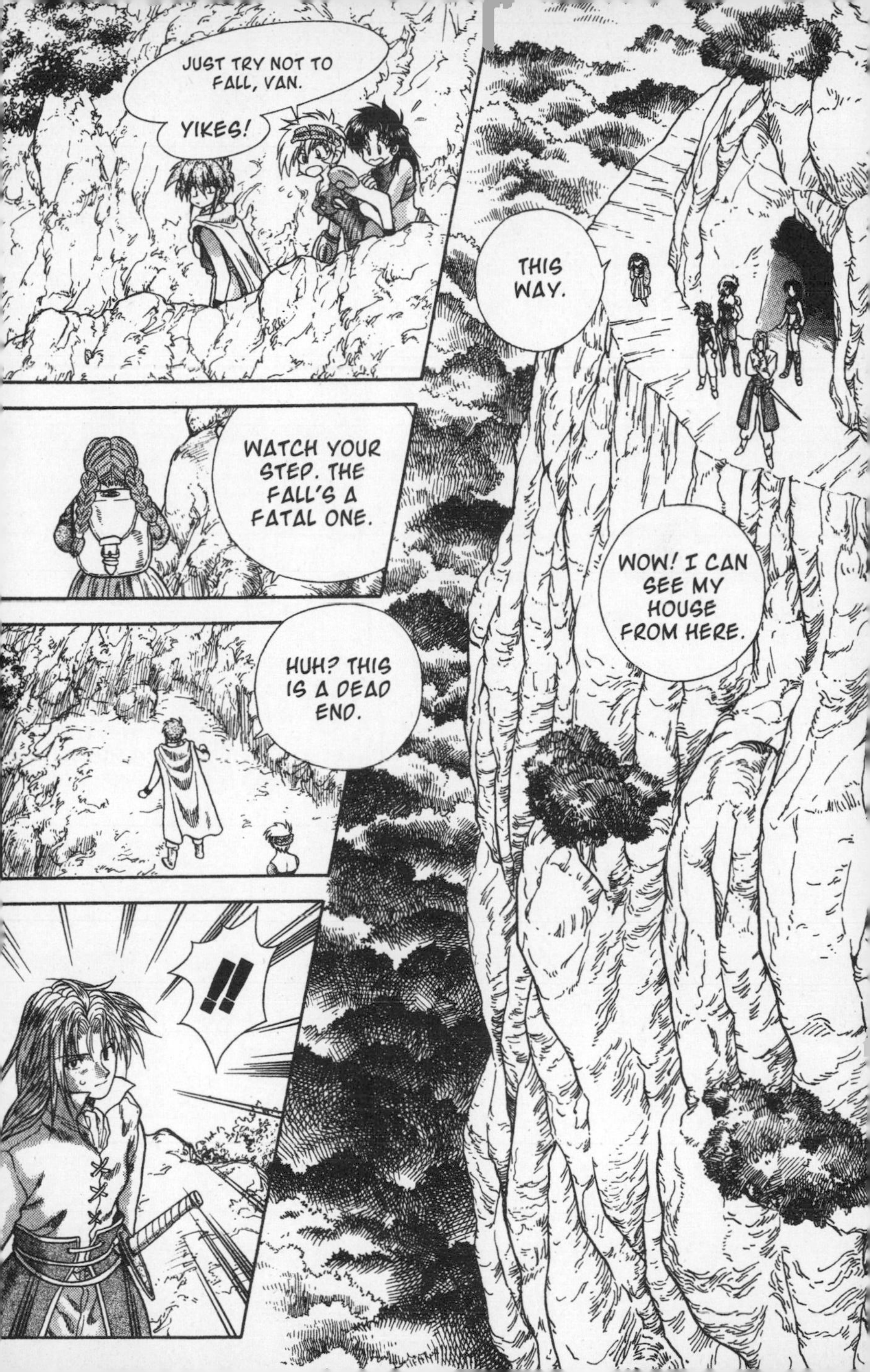
THIS WAY.
WOW! I CAN SEE MY HOUSE FROM HERE.
JUST TRY NOT TO FALL, VAN.
YIKES!
WATCH YOUR STEP. THE FALL'S A FATAL ONE.
HUH? THIS IS A DEAD END.
!!

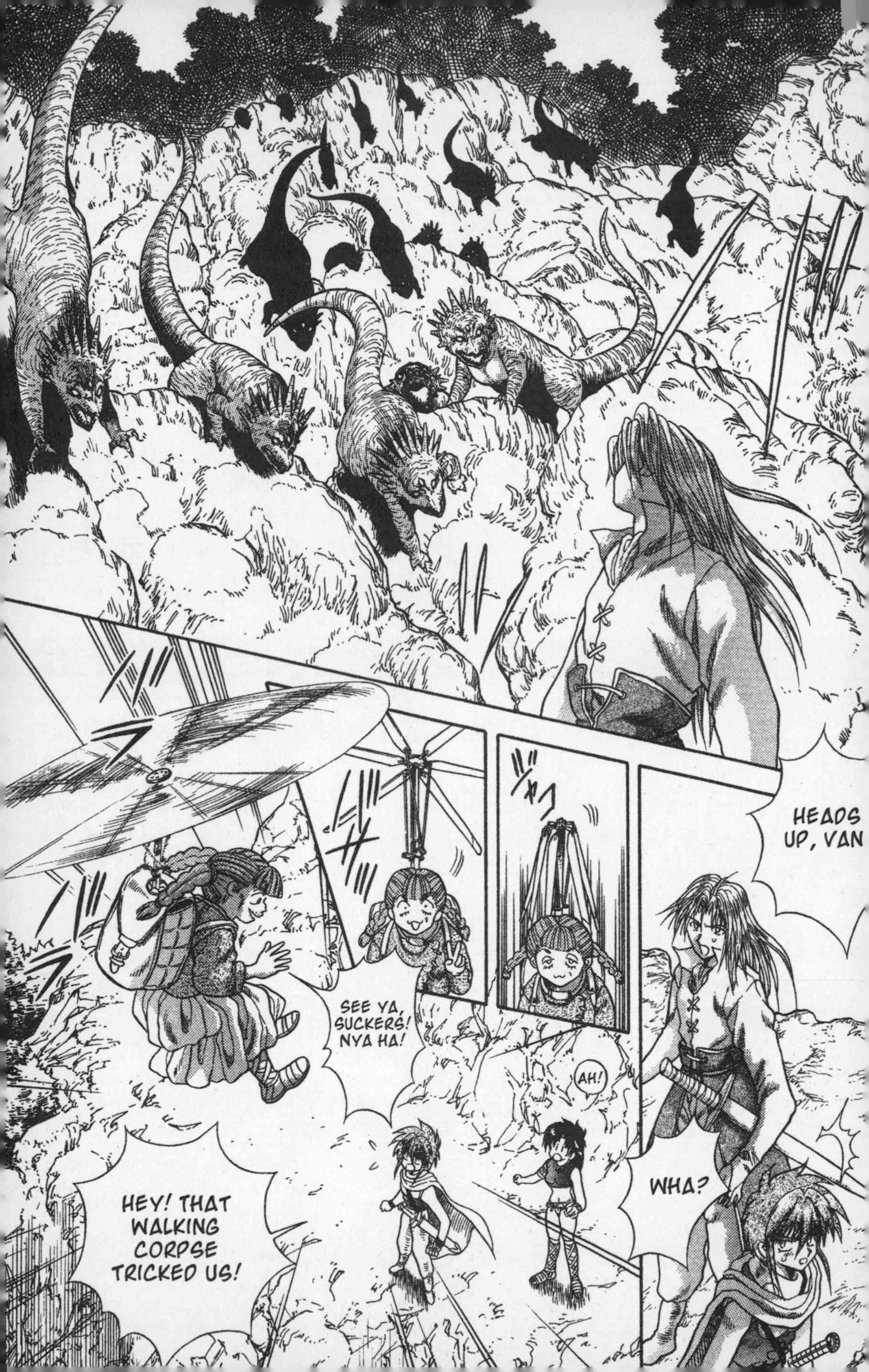
HEADS UP, VAN
WHA?
SEE YA, SUCKERS! NYA HA!
AH!
HEY! THAT WALKING CORPSE TRICKED US!

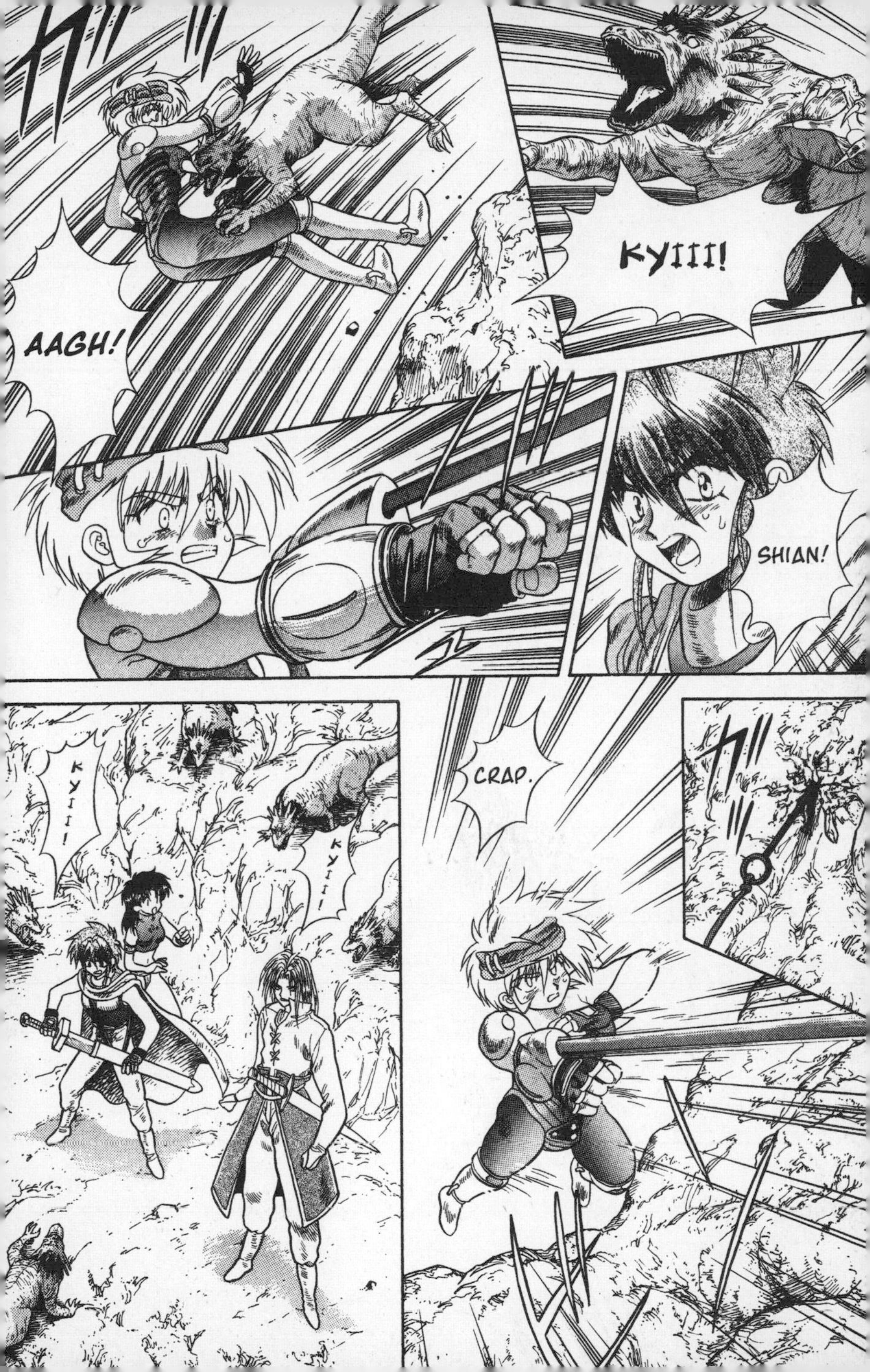
KYIII!
AAGH!
SHIAN!
CRAP.
KYIII!
KYIII!

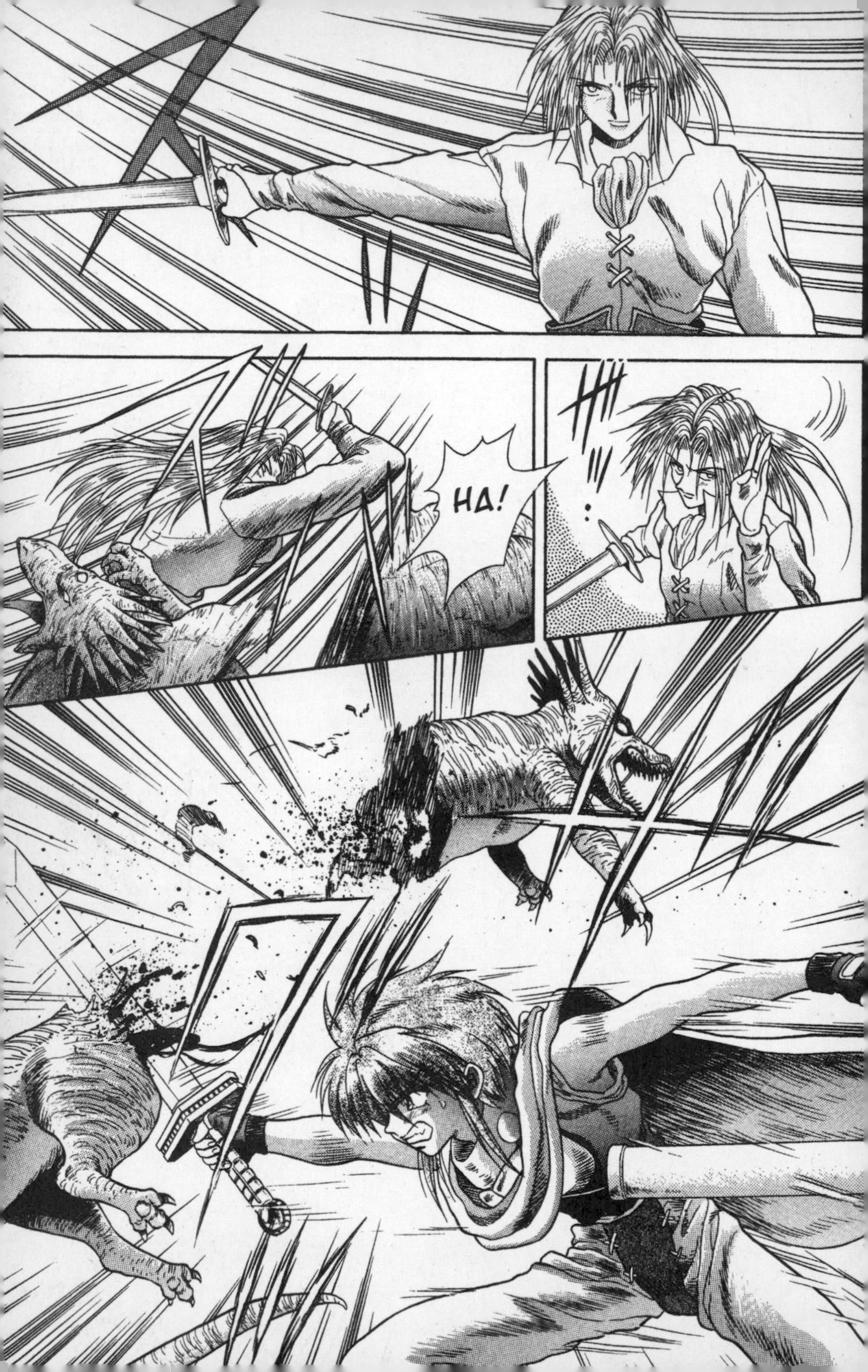
HA!

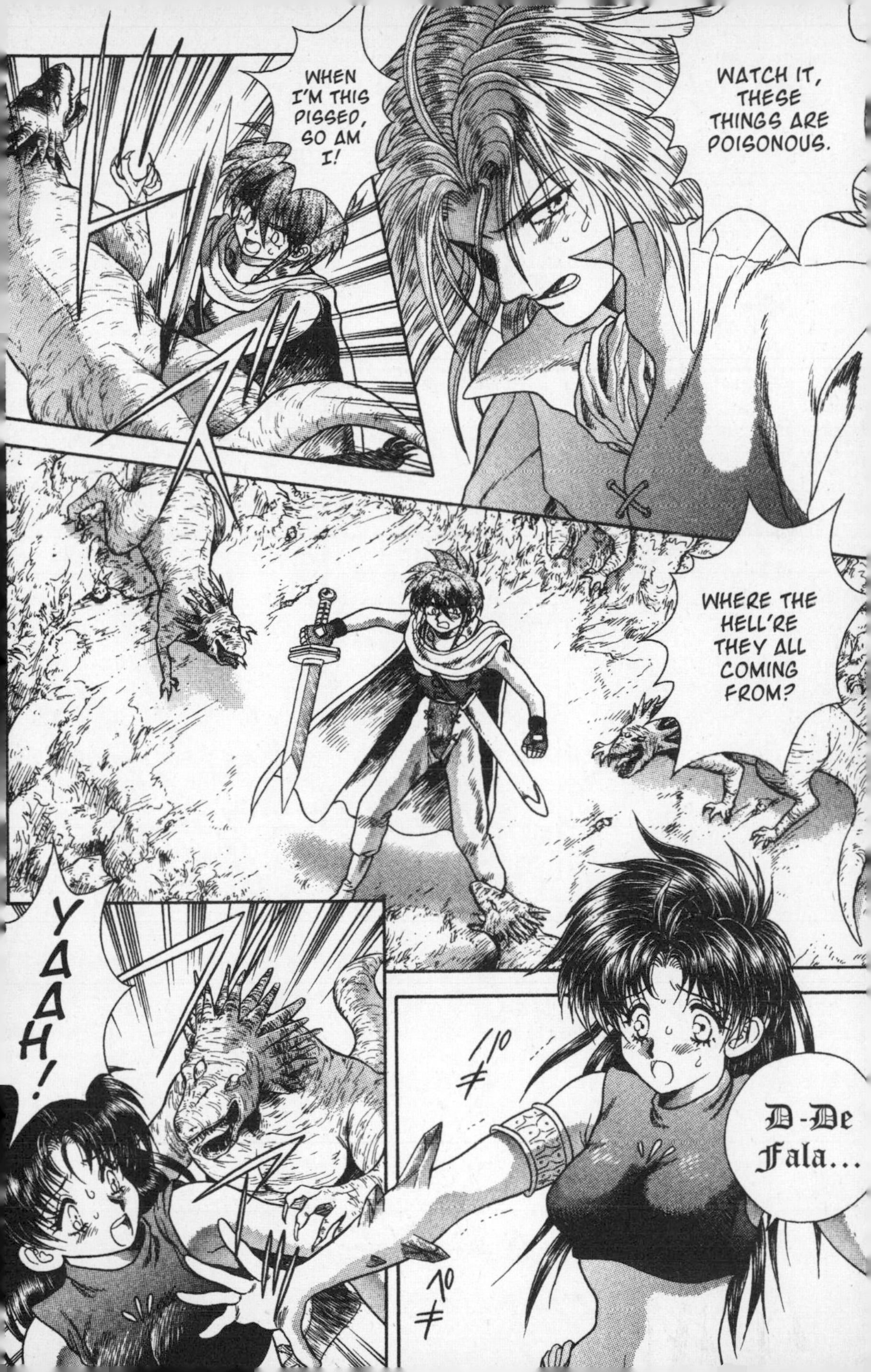
WATCH IT, THESE THINGS ARE POISONOUS.
WHEN I'M THIS PISSED, SO AM I!
WHERE THE HELL'RE THEY ALL COMING FROM?
D-De Fala...
YAAAH!

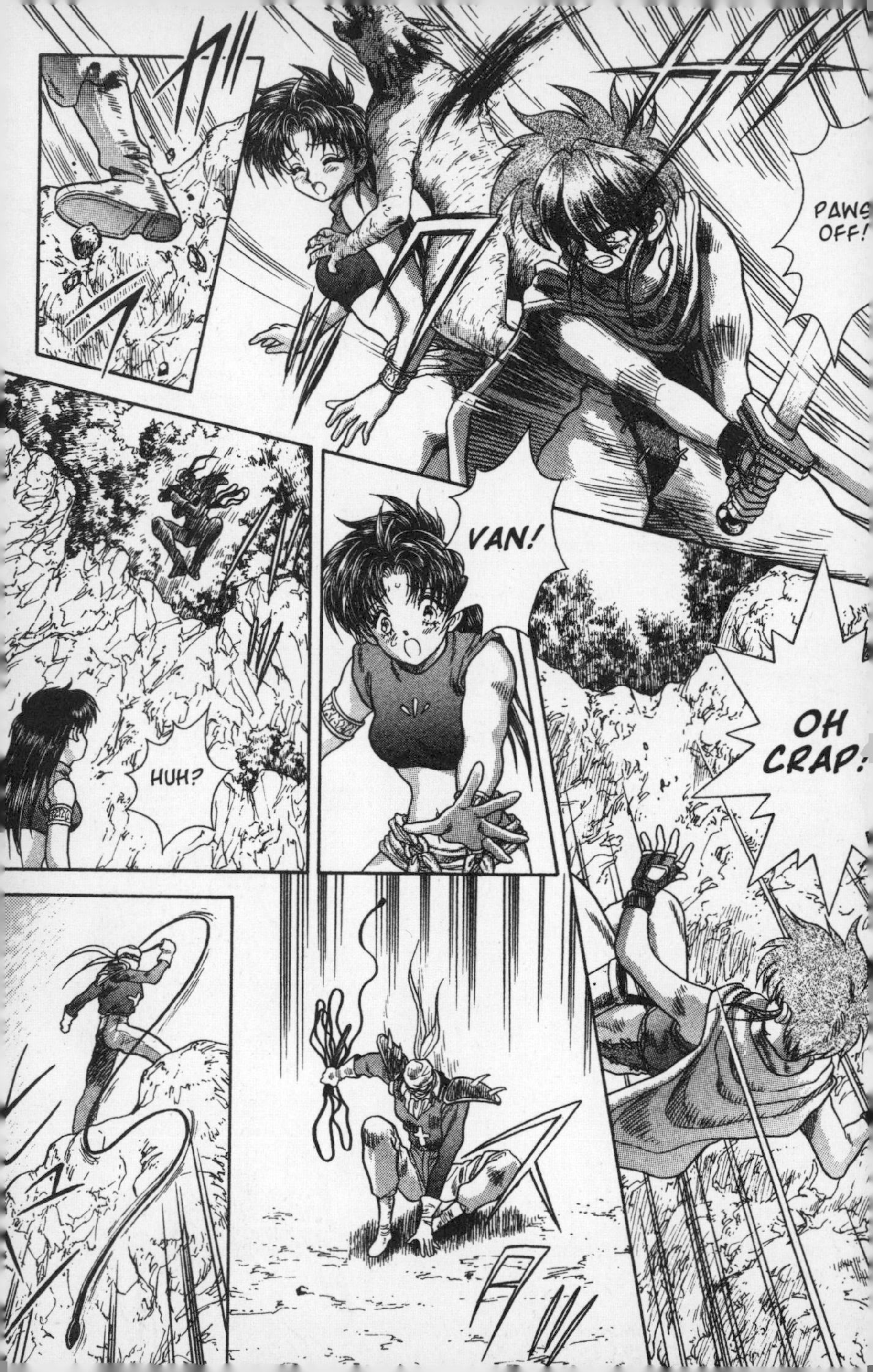
PAWS OFF!
OH CRAP!
VAN!
HUH?

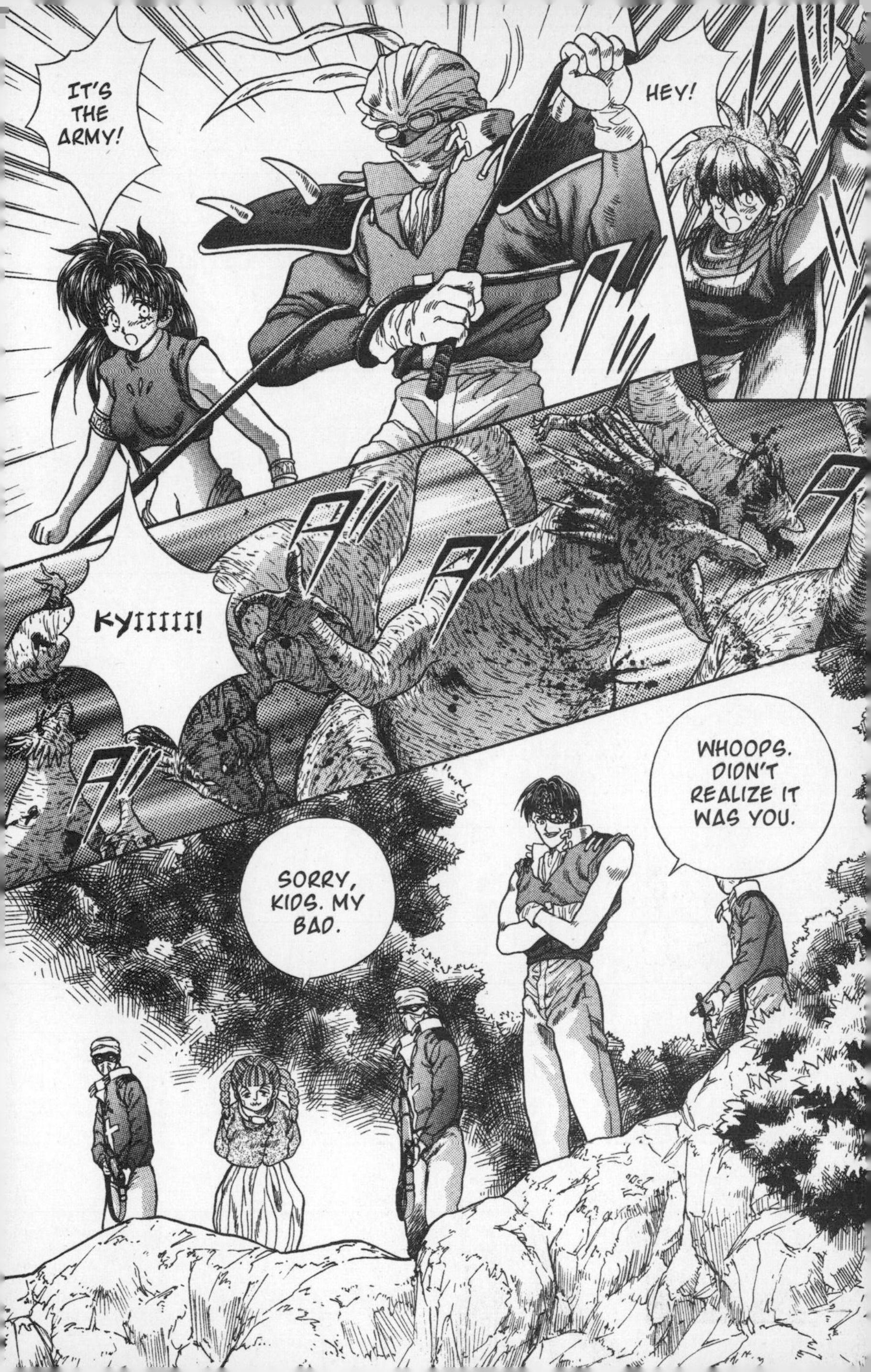
HEY!
IT'S THE ARMY!
KYIIIIII!
WHOOPS. DIDN'T REALIZE IT WAS YOU.
SORRY, KIDS. MY BAD.

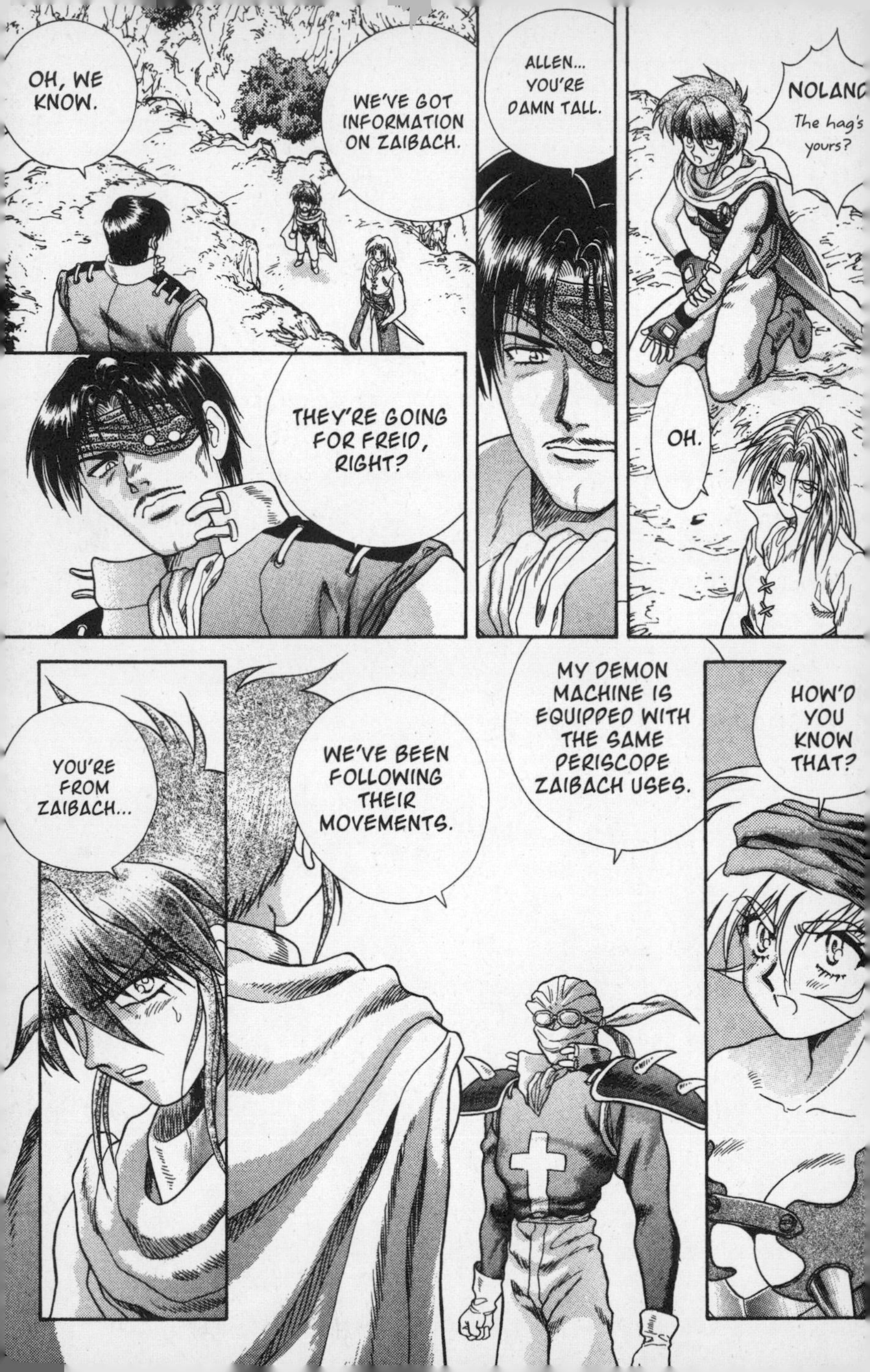
NOLAN
The hag's yours?
OH.
ALLEN... YOU'RE DAMN TALL.
WE'VE GOT INFORMATION ON ZAIBACH.
OH, WE KNOW.
THEY'RE GOING FOR FREID, RIGHT?
HOW'D YOU KNOW THAT?
MY DEMON MACHINE IS EQUIPPED WITH THE SAME PERISCOPE ZAIBACH USES.
WE'VE BEEN FOLLOWING THEIR MOVEMENTS.
YOU'RE FROM ZAIBACH...

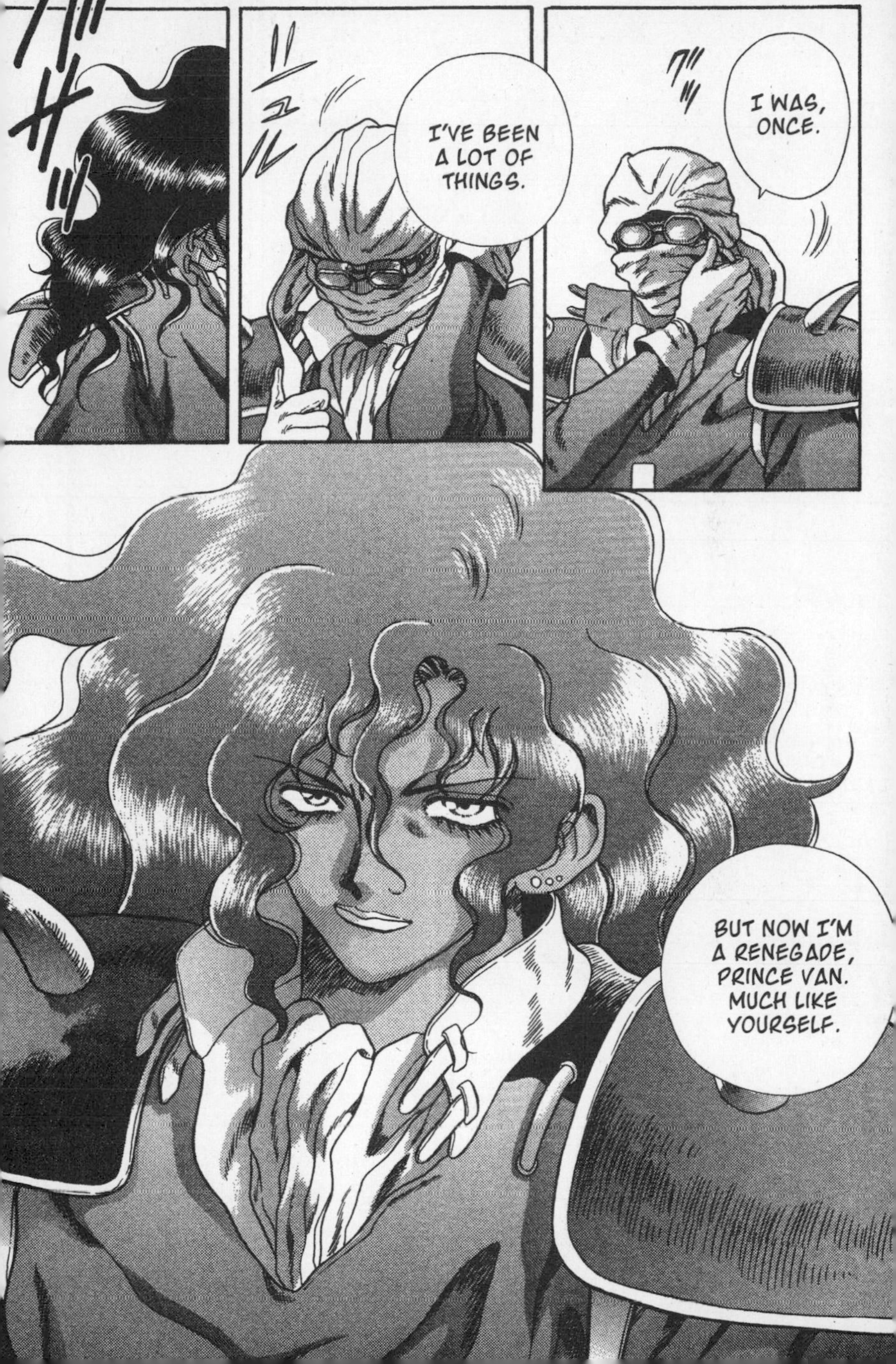
I WAS, ONCE.
I'VE BEEN A LOT OF THINGS.
BUT NOW I'M A RENEGADE, PRINCE VAN. MUCH LIKE YOURSELF.

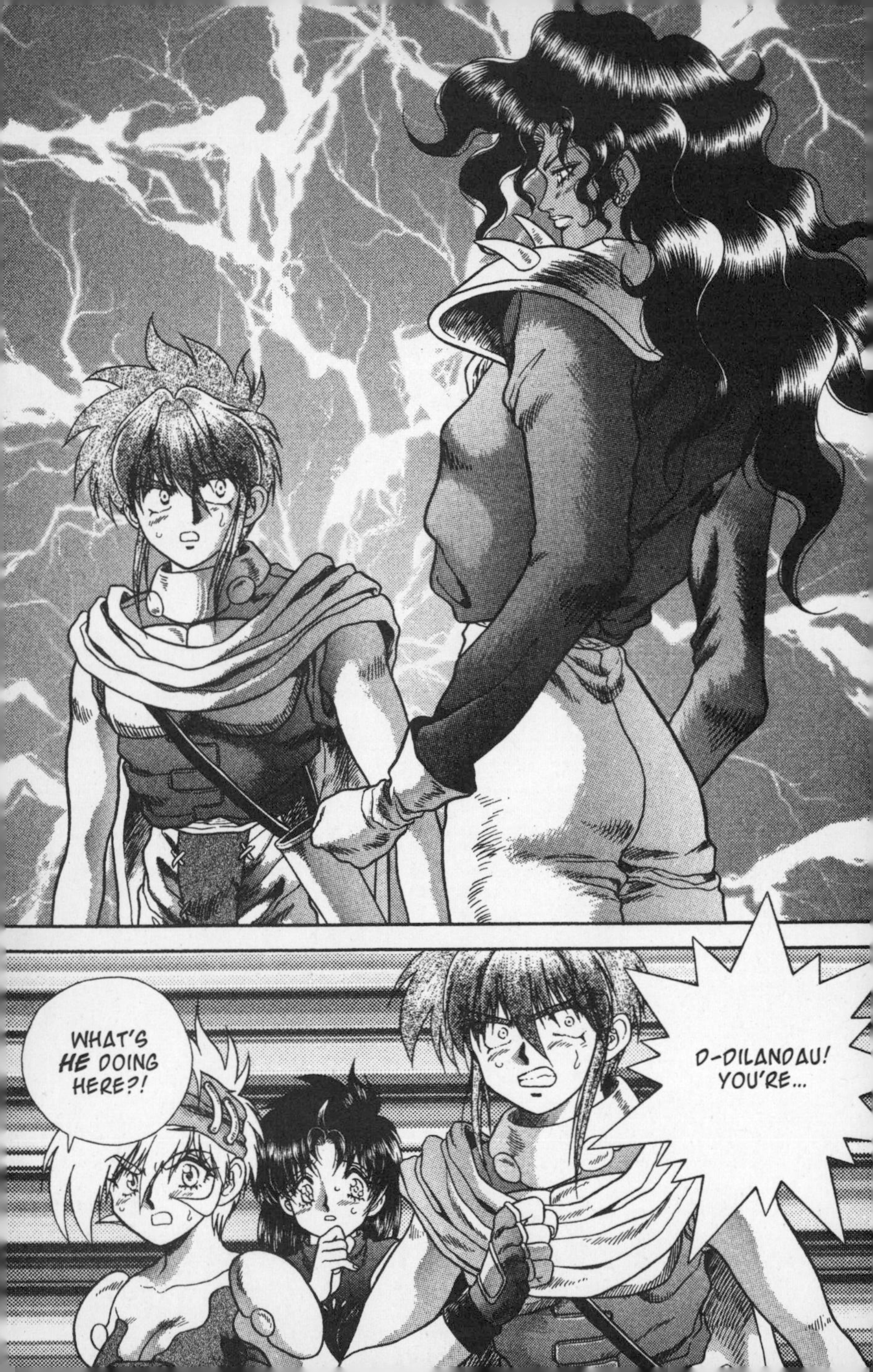
D-DILANDAU! YOU'RE...
WHAT'S HE DOING HERE?!

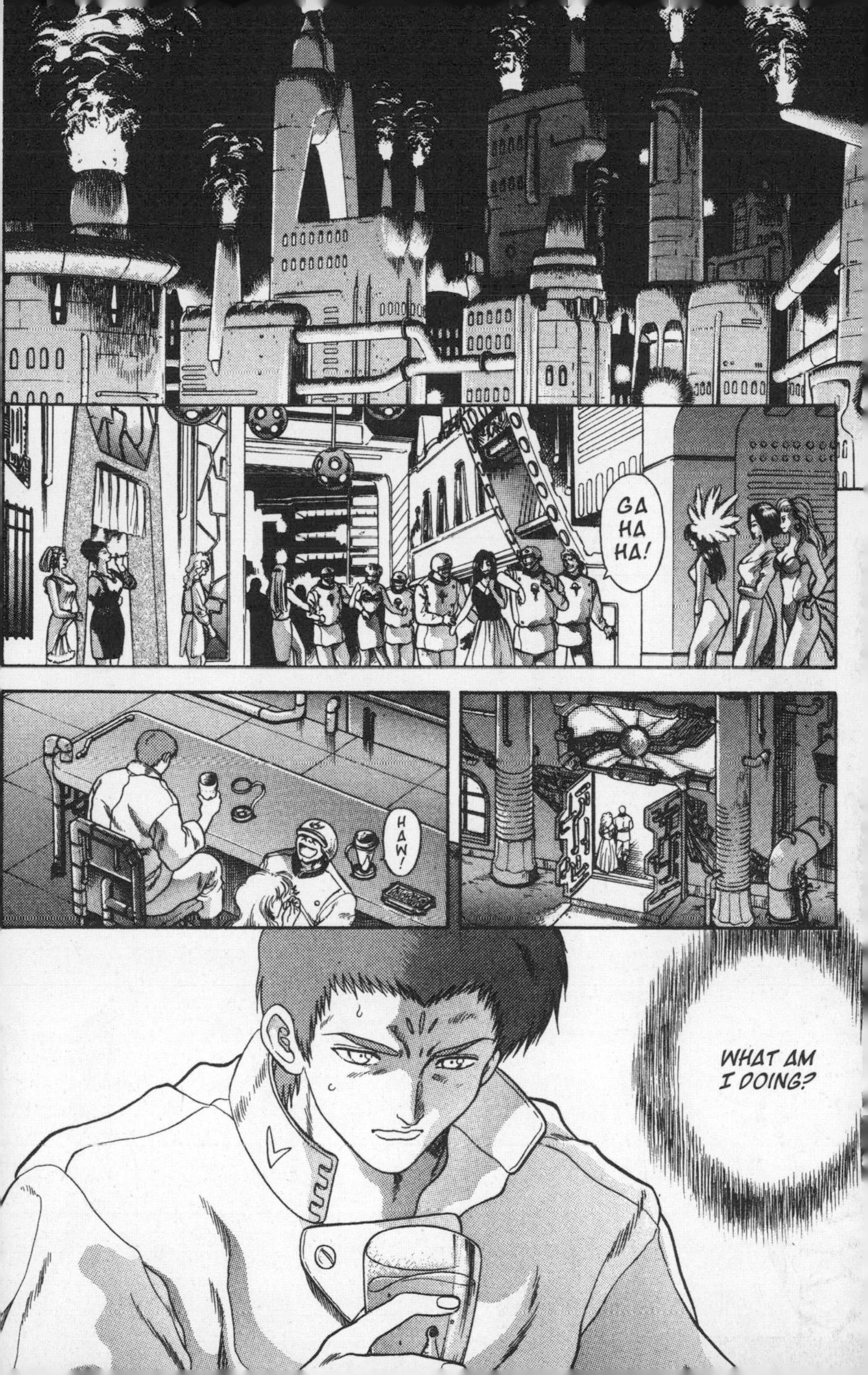
GA HA HA!
HAW!
WHAT AM I DOING?

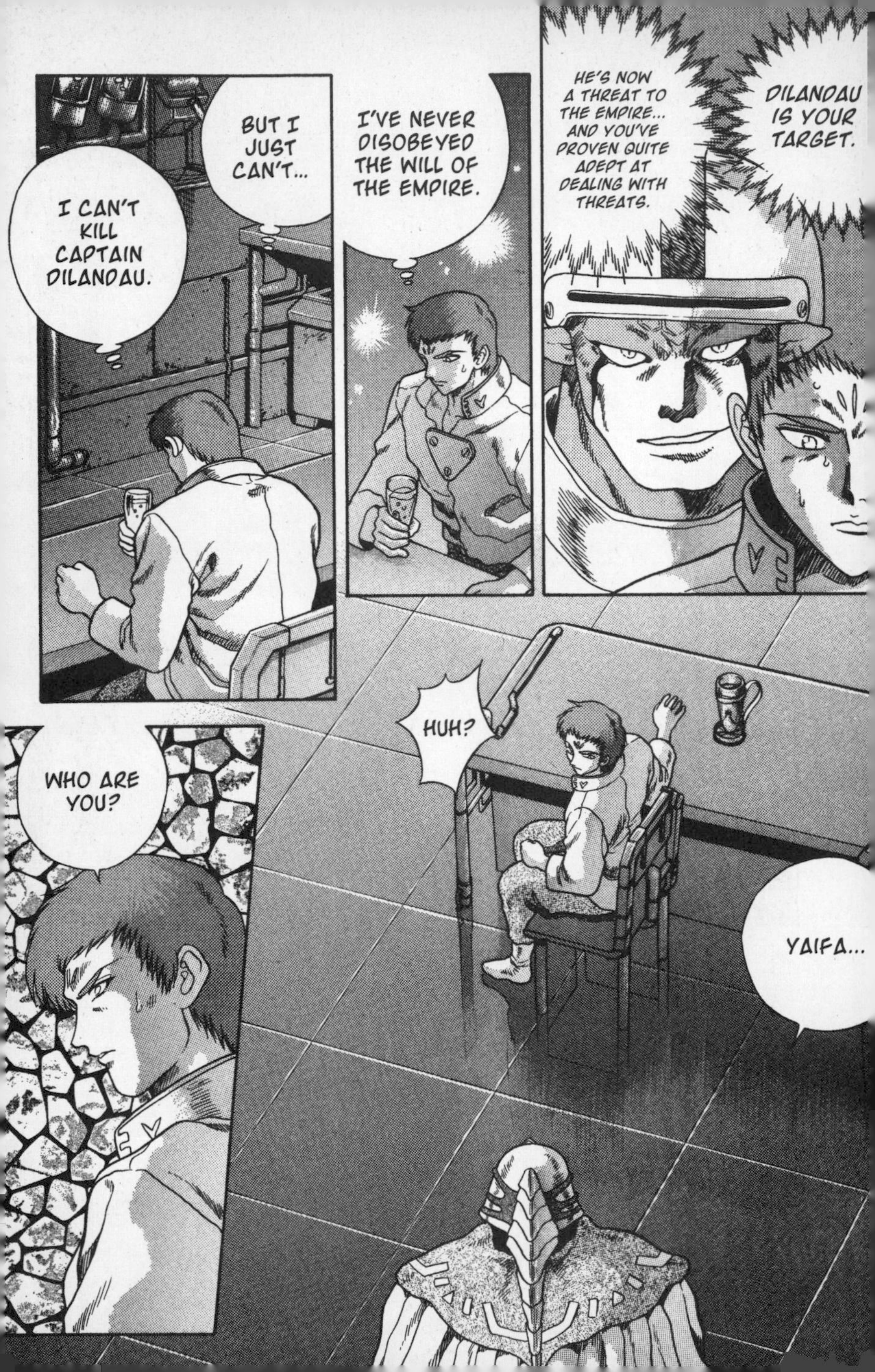
DILANDAU IS YOUR TARGET.
HE'S NOW A THREAT TO THE EMPIRE... AND YOU'VE PROVEN QUITE ADEPT AT DEALING WITH THREATS.
I'VE NEVER DISOBEYED THE WILL OF THE EMPIRE.
BUT I JUST CAN'T...
I CAN'T KILL CAPTAIN DILANDAU.
HUH?
YAIFA...
WHO ARE YOU?

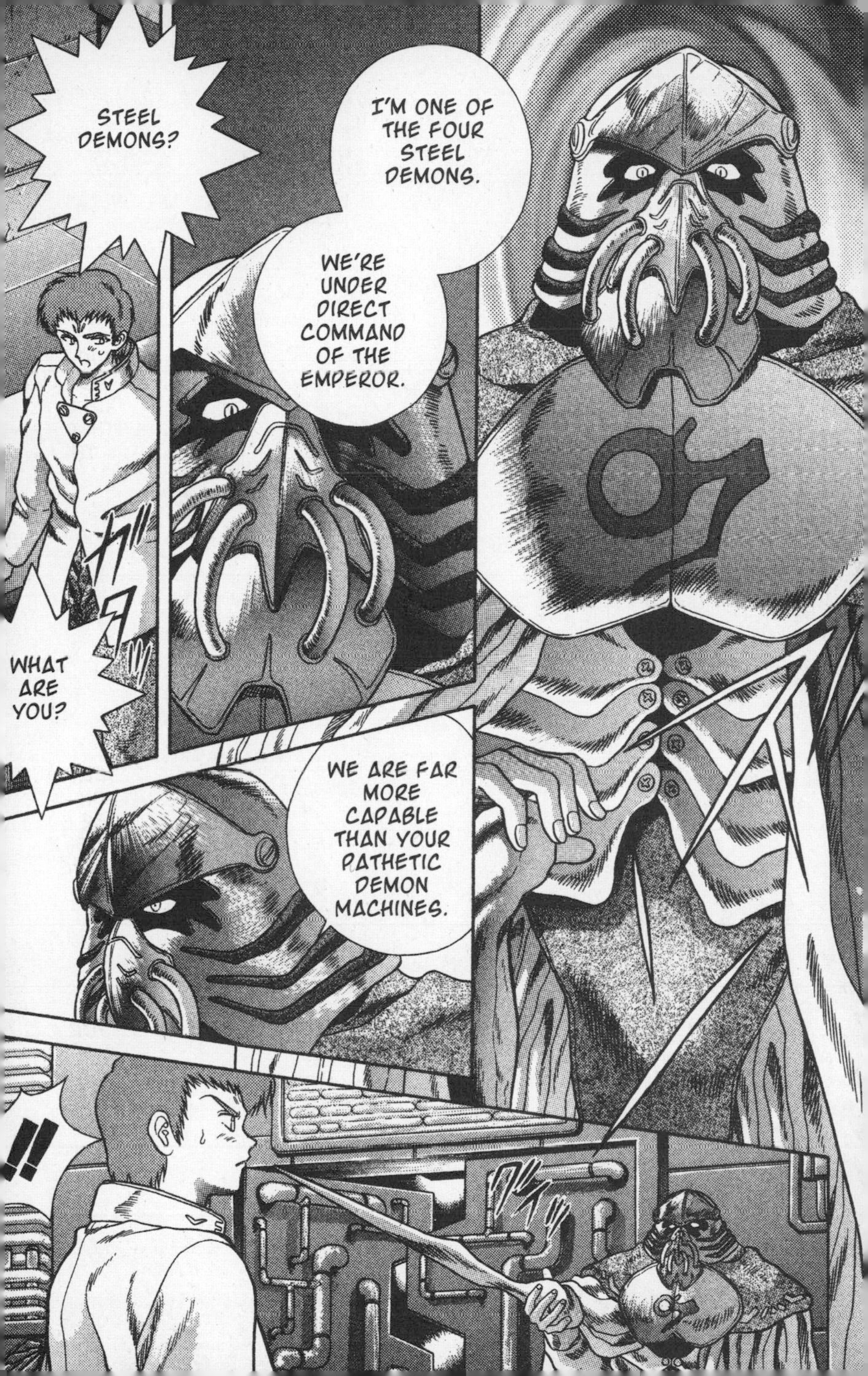
I'M ONE OF THE FOUR STEEL DEMONS.
WE'RE UNDER DIRECT COMMAND OF THE EMPEROR.
STEEL DEMONS?
WHAT ARE YOU?
WE ARE FAR MORE CAPABLE THAN YOUR PATHETIC DEMON MACHINES.
!!

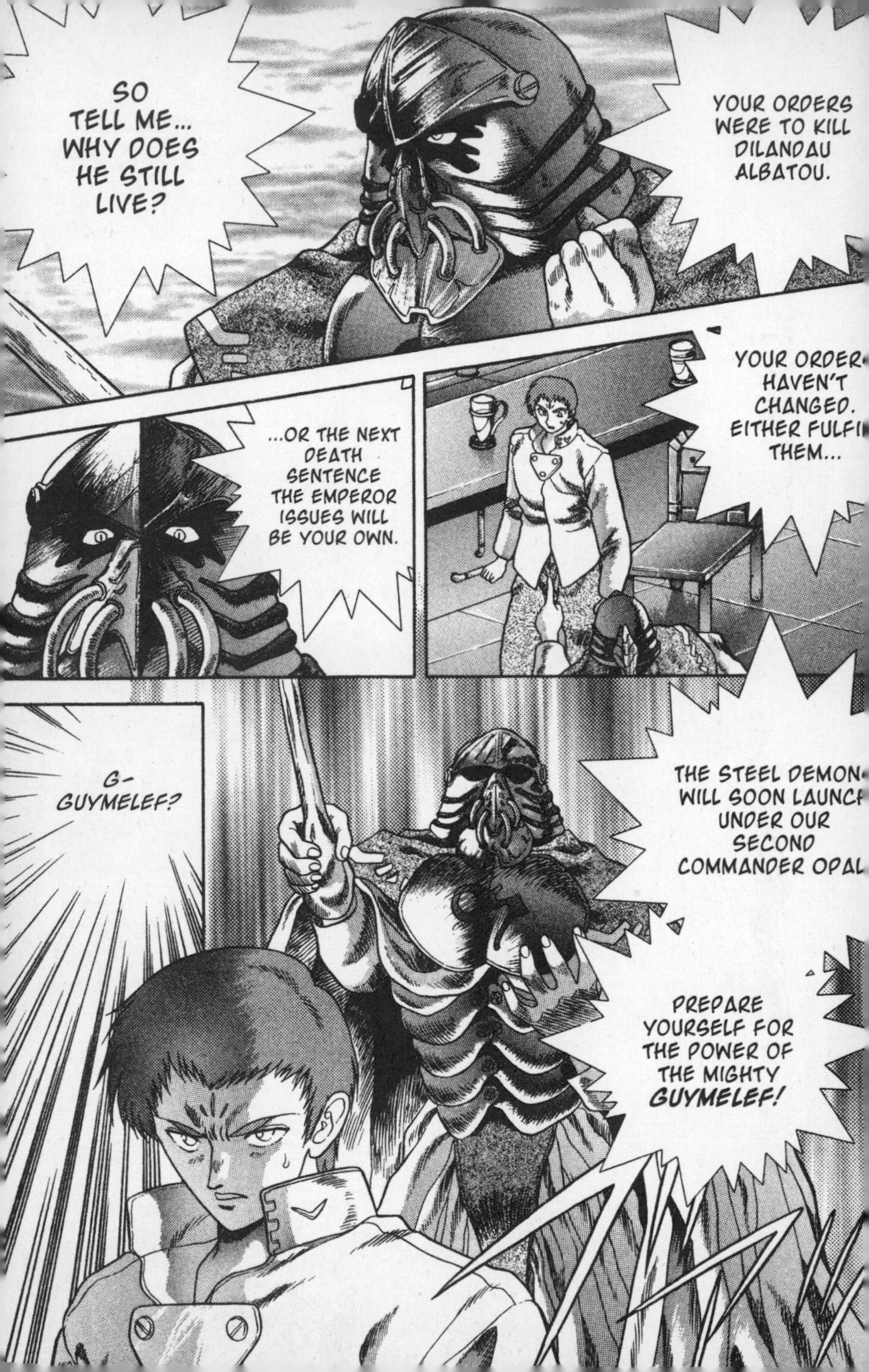
YOUR ORDERS WERE TO KILL DILANDAU ALBATOU.
SO TELL ME... WHY DOES HE STILL LIVE?
YOUR ORDER HAVEN'T CHANGED. EITHER FULFI THEM...
...OR THE NEXT DEATH SENTENCE THE EMPEROR ISSUES WILL BE YOUR OWN.
THE STEEL DEMON WILL SOON LAUNC UNDER OUR SECOND COMMANDER OPAL
PREPARE YOURSELF FOR THE POWER OF THE MIGHTY *GUYMELEF!*
G- GUYMELEF?

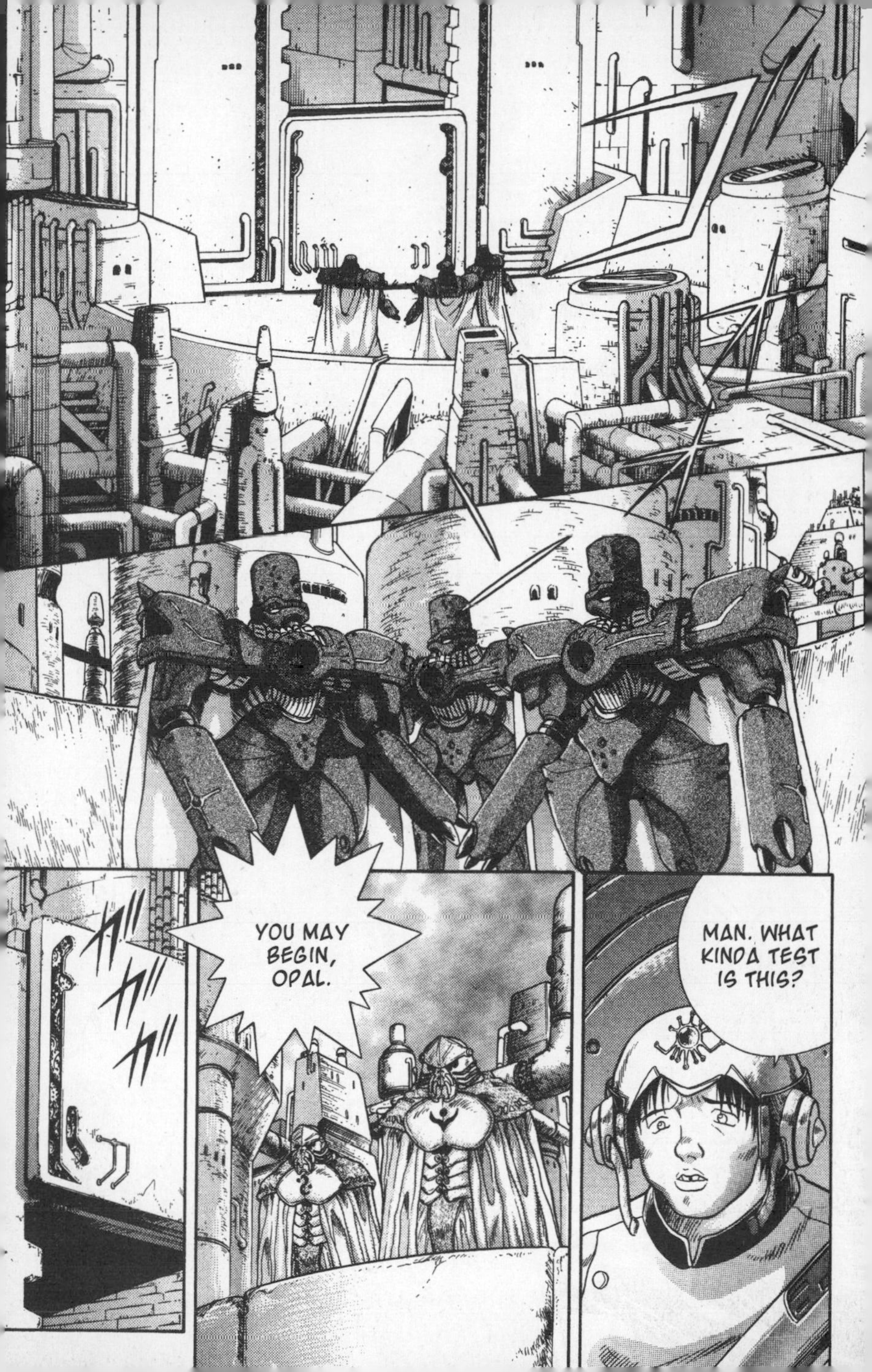
MAN. WHAT KINDA TEST IS THIS?
YOU MAY BEGIN, OPAL.
ガ ガ ガ

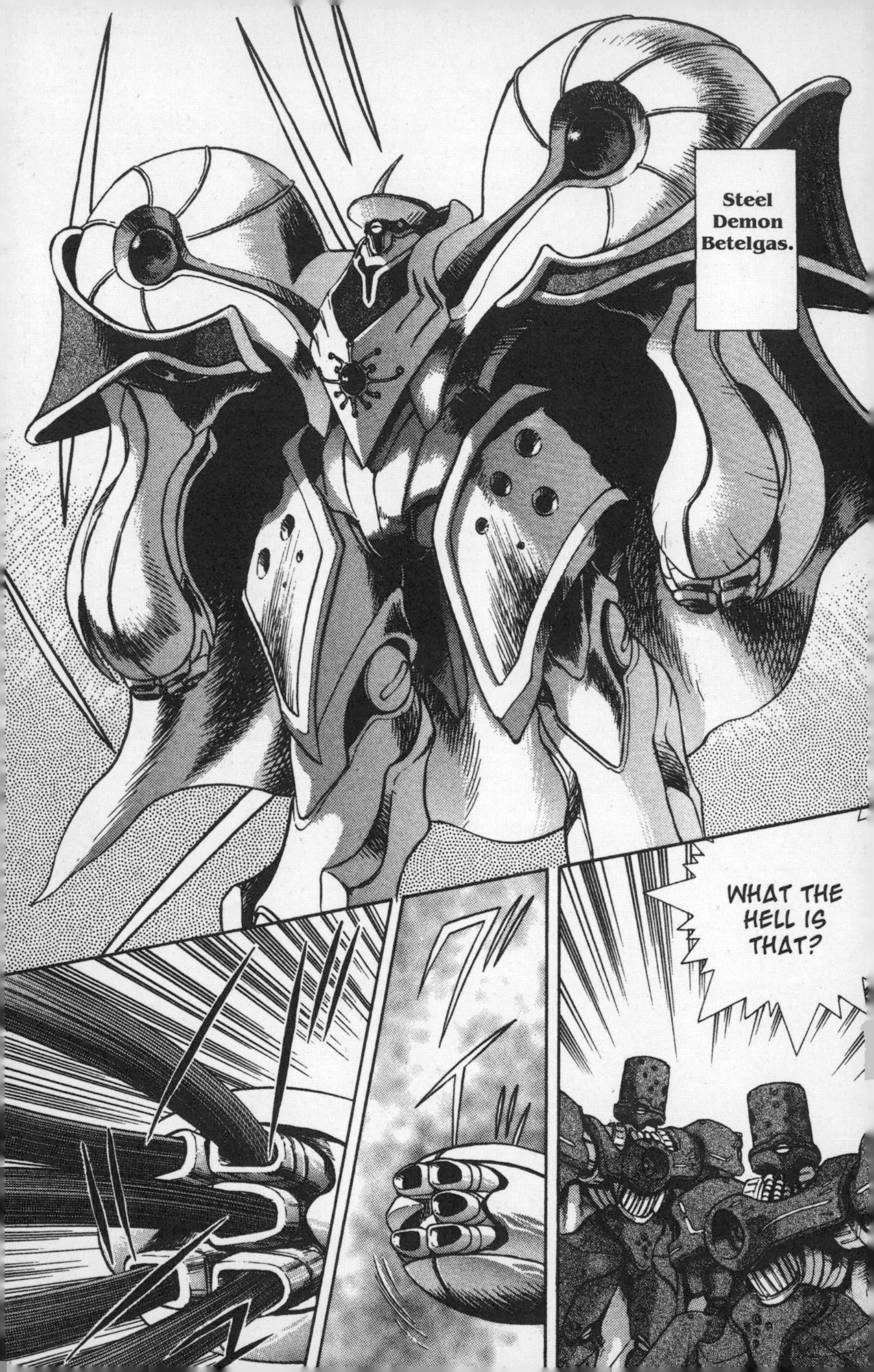
Steel Demon Betelgas.
WHAT THE HELL IS THAT?

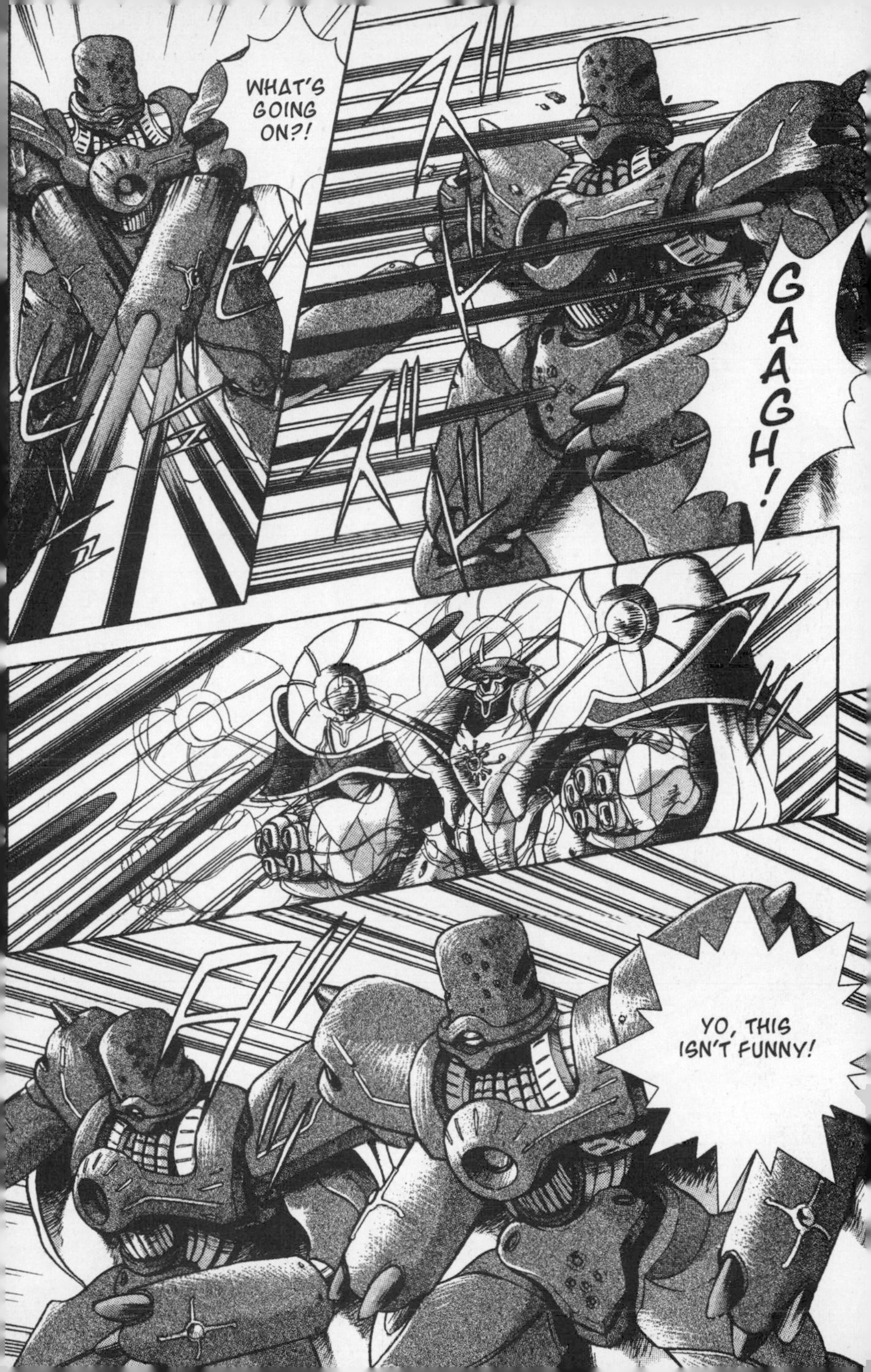
GAAGH!
WHAT'S GOING ON?!
YO, THIS ISN'T FUNNY!

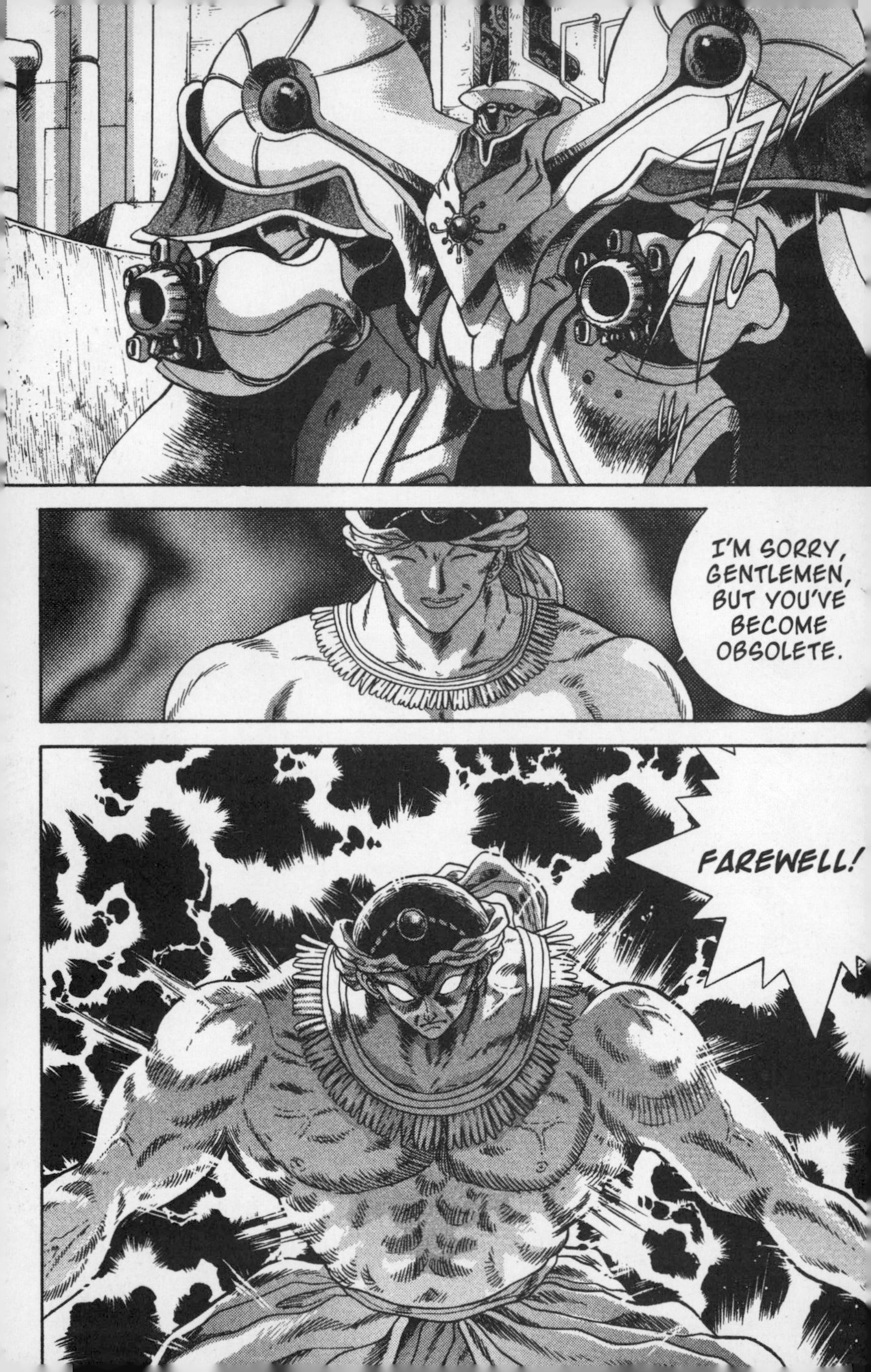
I'M SORRY, GENTLEMEN, BUT YOU'VE BECOME OBSOLETE.
FAREWELL!

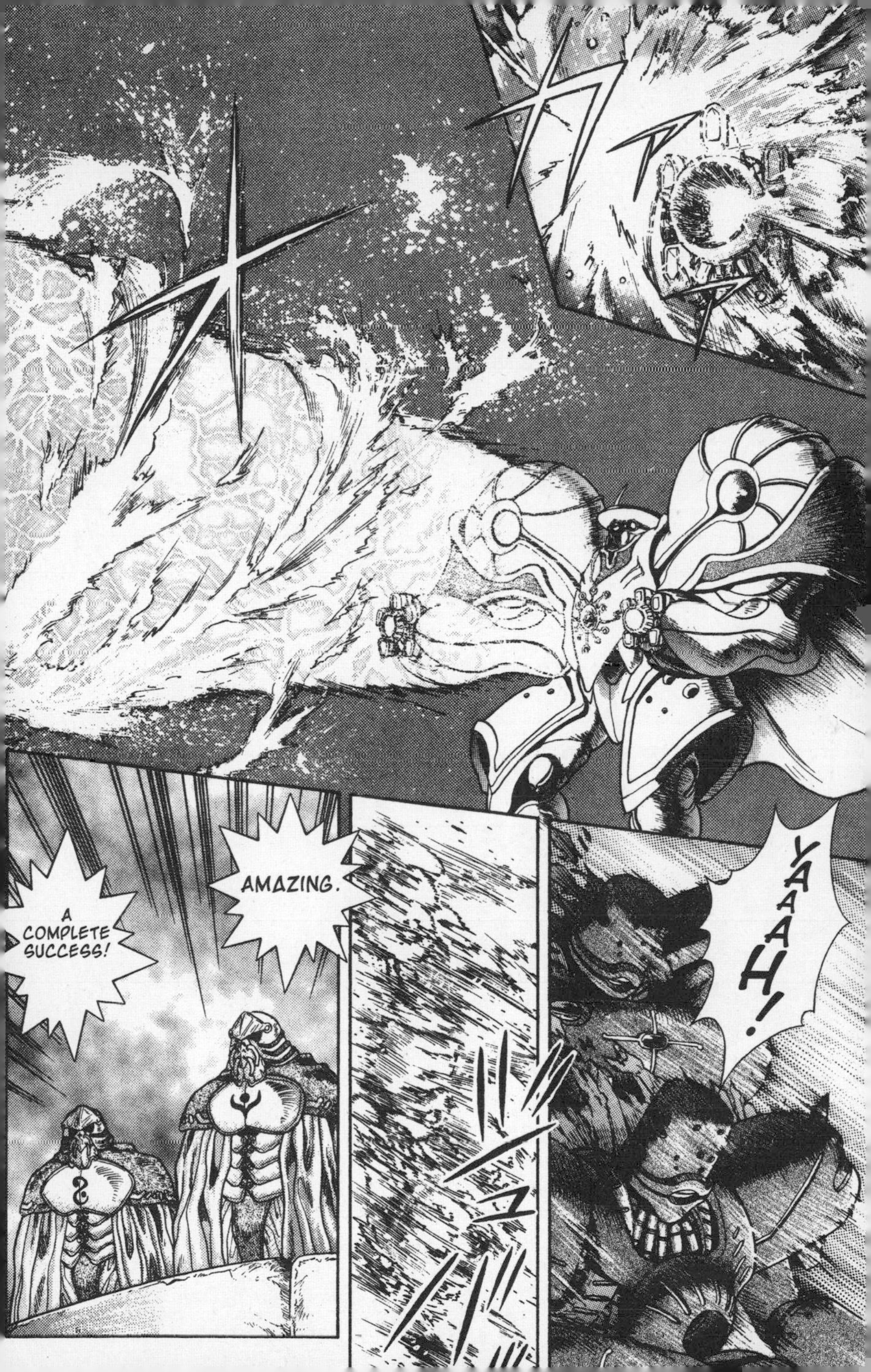
YAAAAH!
AMAZING.
A COMPLETE SUCCESS!

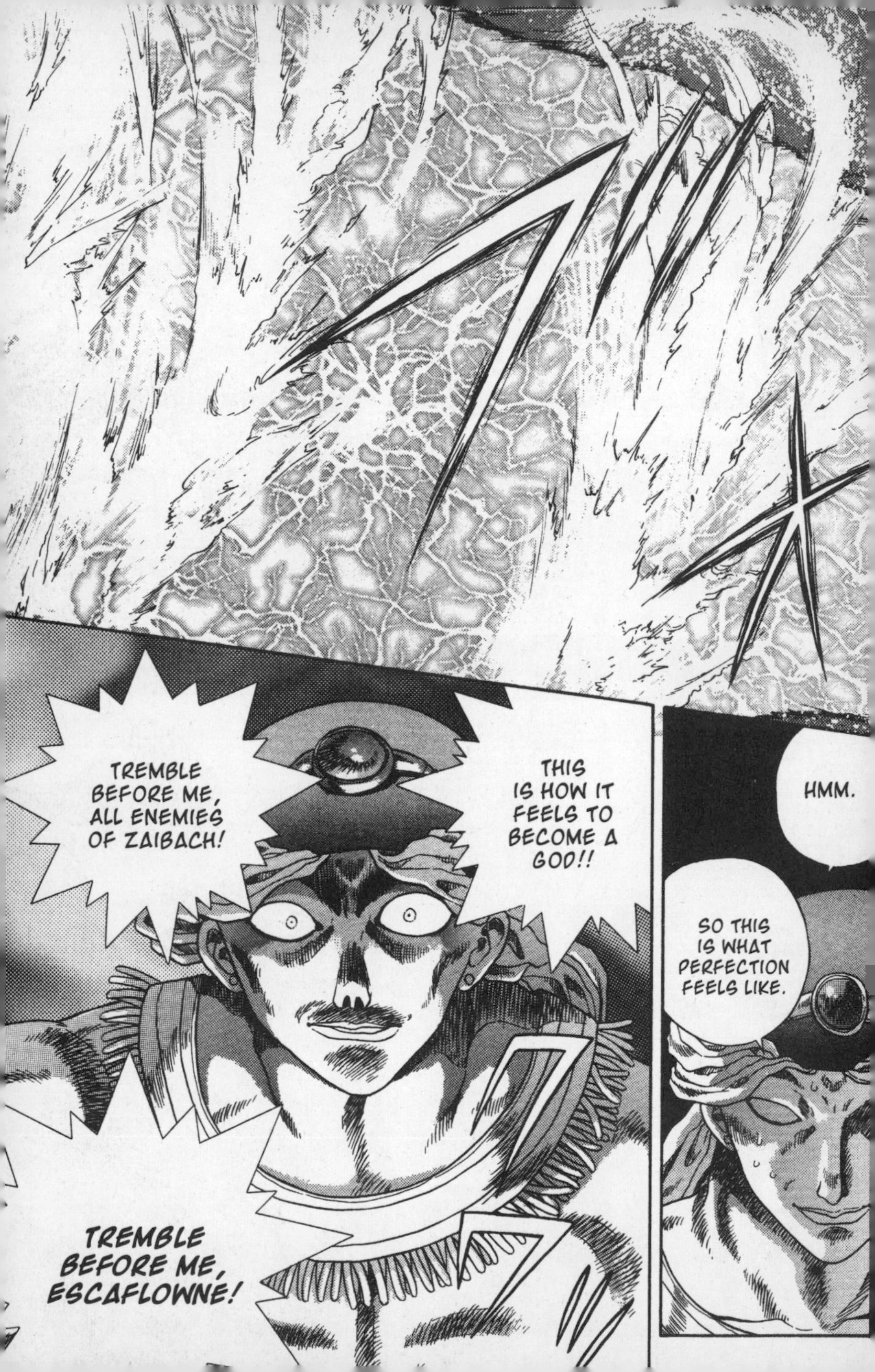
HMM.
SO THIS IS WHAT PERFECTION FEELS LIKE.
THIS IS HOW IT FEELS TO BECOME A GOD!!
TREMBLE BEFORE ME, ALL ENEMIES OF ZAIBACH!
TREMBLE BEFORE ME, ESCAFLOWNE!

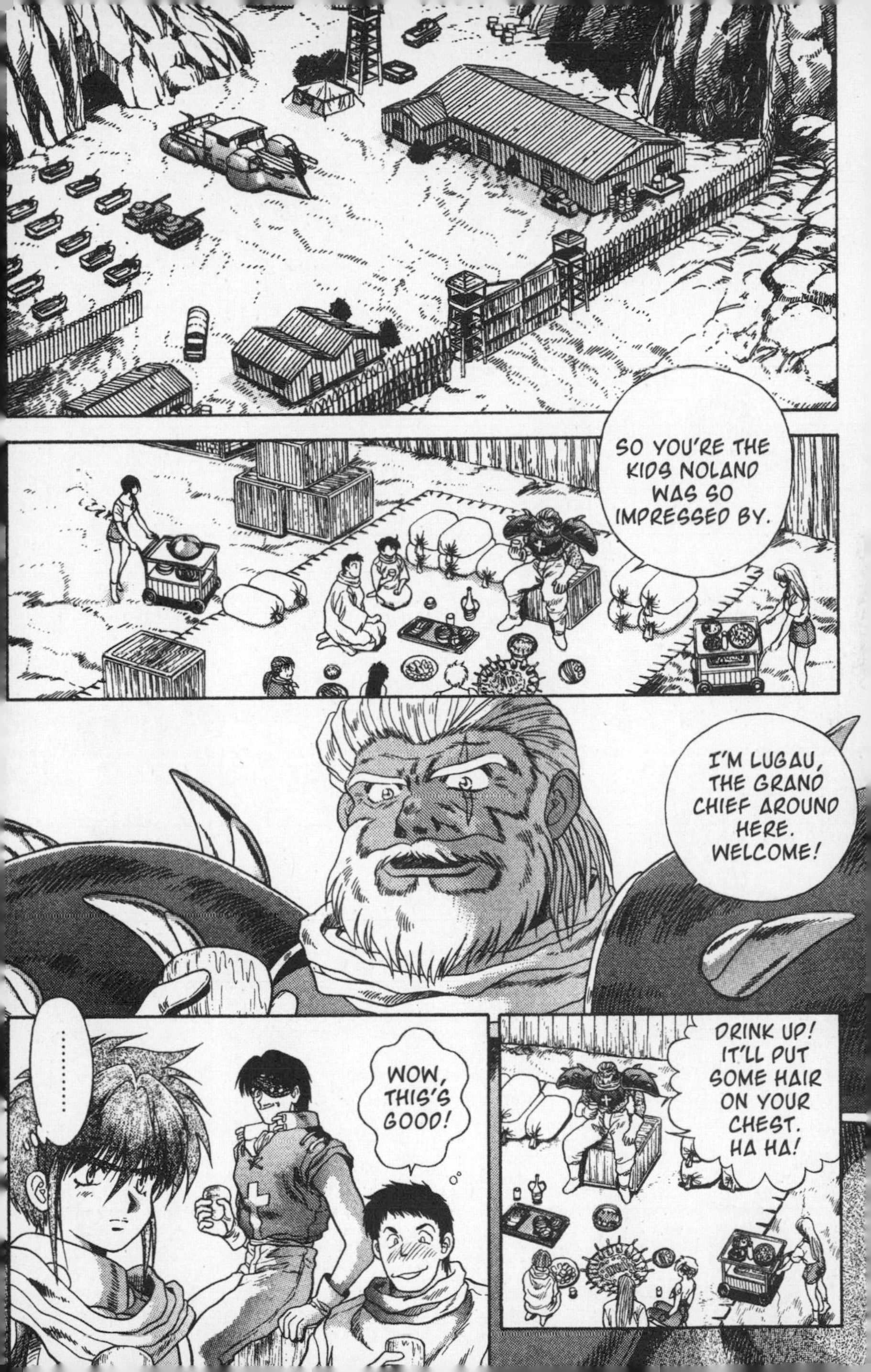
SO YOU'RE THE KIDS NOLAND WAS SO IMPRESSED BY.
I'M LUGAU, THE GRAND CHIEF AROUND HERE. WELCOME!
DRINK UP! IT'LL PUT SOME HAIR ON YOUR CHEST. HA HA!
WOW, THIS'S GOOD!
......

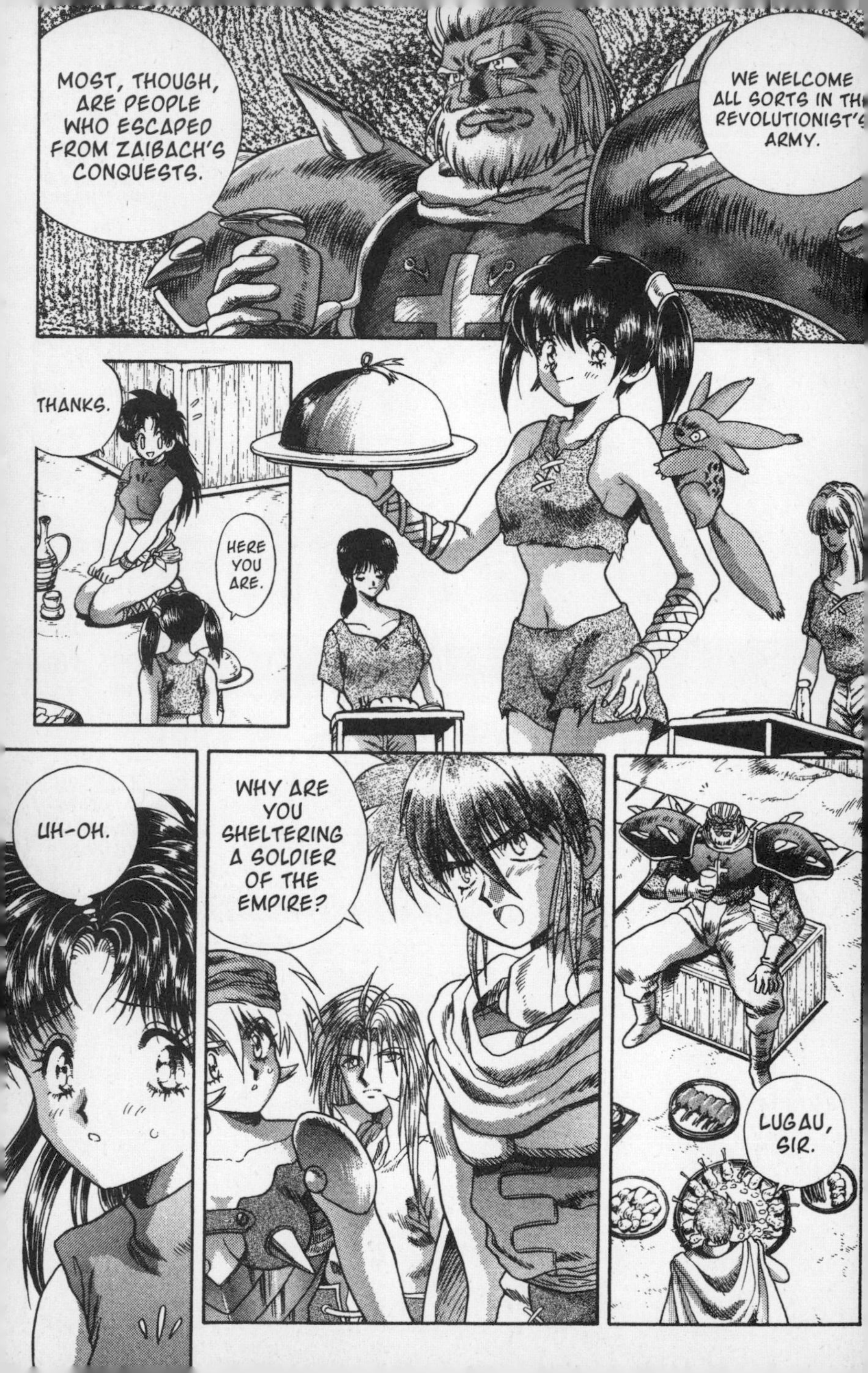
WE WELCOME ALL SORTS IN TH REVOLUTIONIST'S ARMY.
MOST, THOUGH, ARE PEOPLE WHO ESCAPED FROM ZAIBACH'S CONQUESTS.
HERE YOU ARE.
THANKS.
LUGAU, SIR.
WHY ARE YOU SHELTERING A SOLDIER OF THE EMPIRE?
UH-OH.

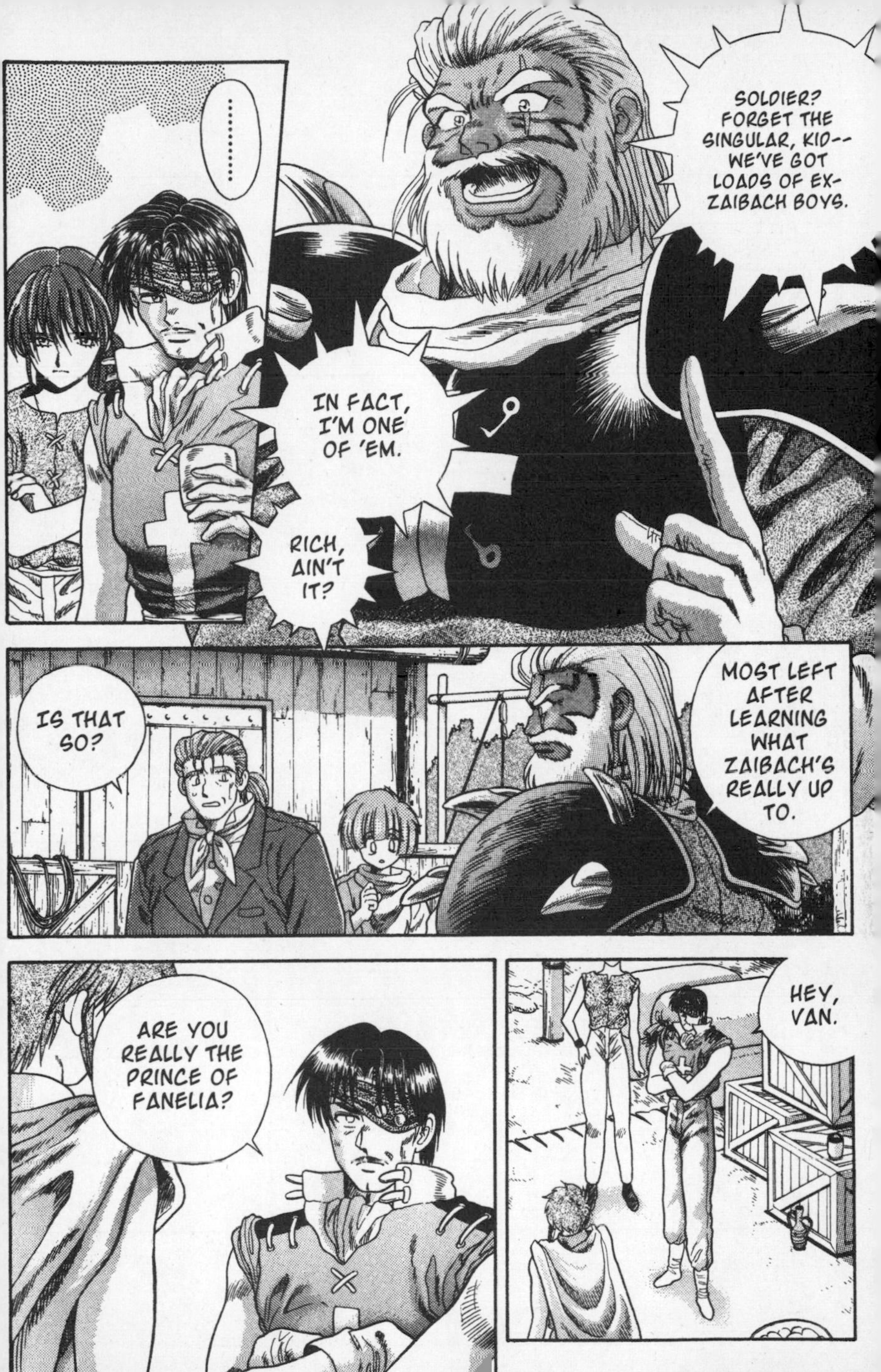
SOLDIER? FORGET THE SINGULAR, KID--WE'VE GOT LOADS OF EX-ZAIBACH BOYS.
IN FACT, I'M ONE OF 'EM.
RICH, AIN'T IT?
......
MOST LEFT AFTER LEARNING WHAT ZAIBACH'S REALLY UP TO.
IS THAT SO?
HEY, VAN.
ARE YOU REALLY THE PRINCE OF FANELIA?

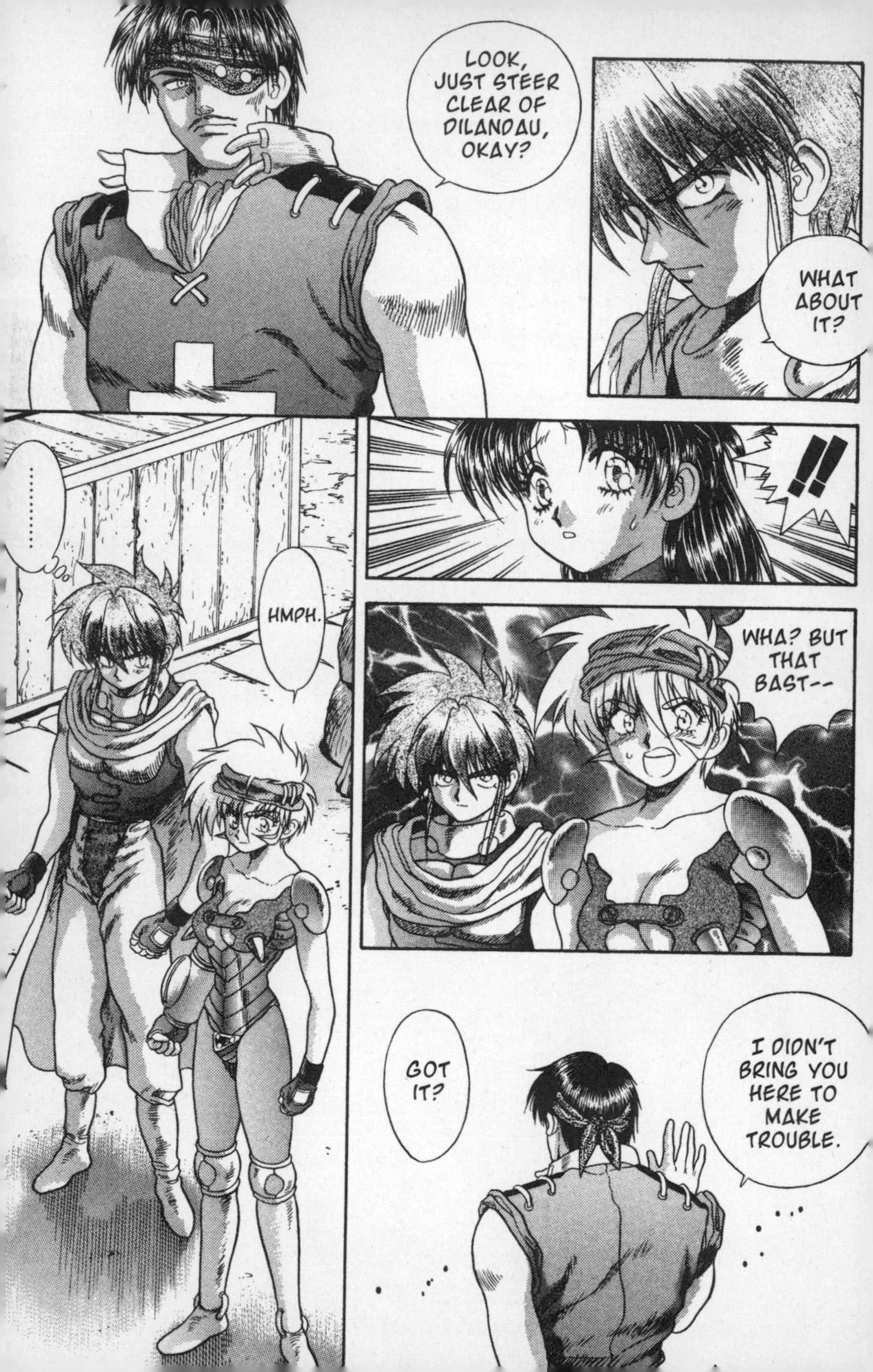
WHAT ABOUT IT?
LOOK, JUST STEER CLEAR OF DILANDAU, OKAY?
!!
WHA? BUT THAT BAST--
I DIDN'T BRING YOU HERE TO MAKE TROUBLE.
GOT IT?
...
......
HMPH.

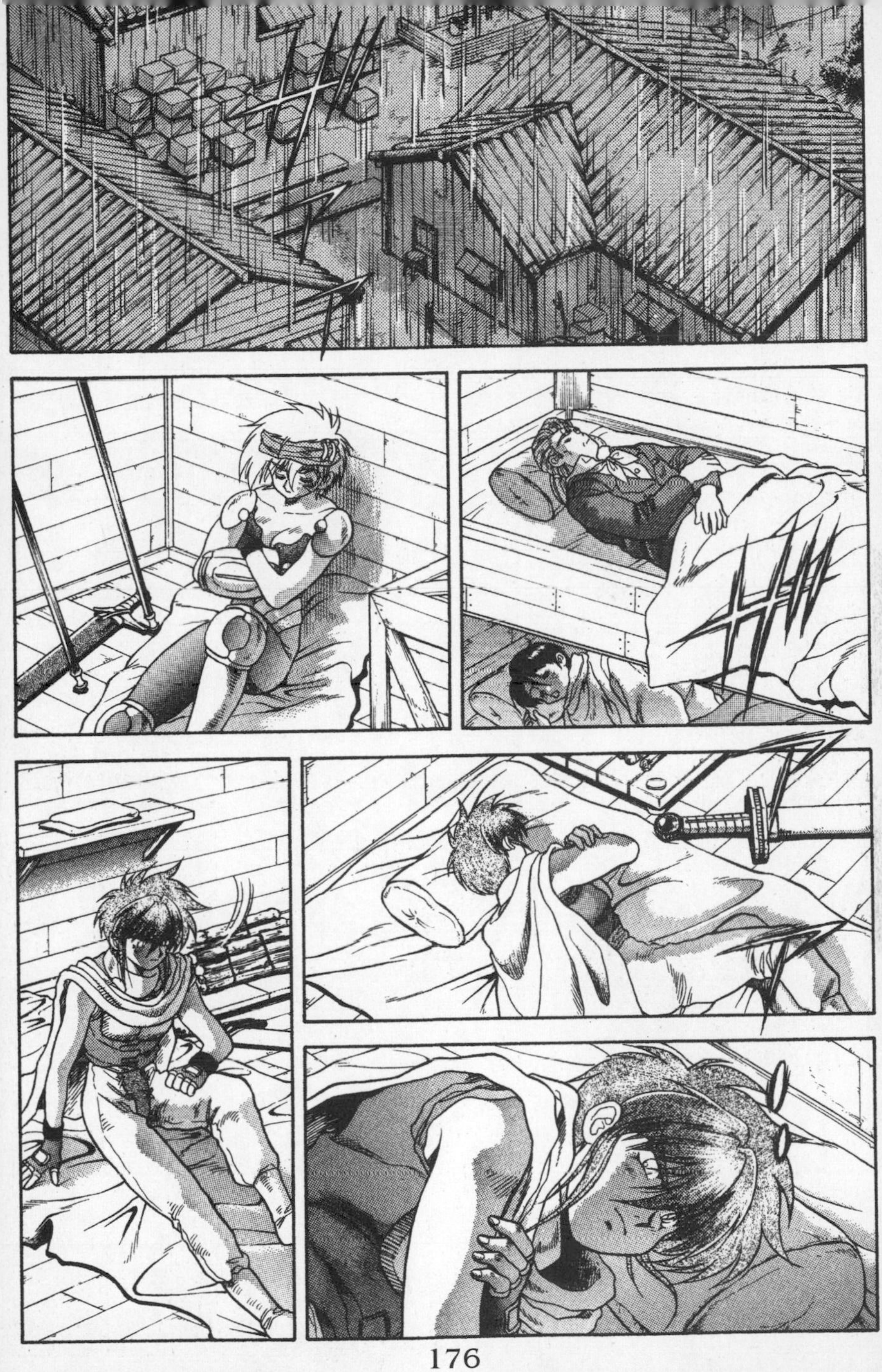

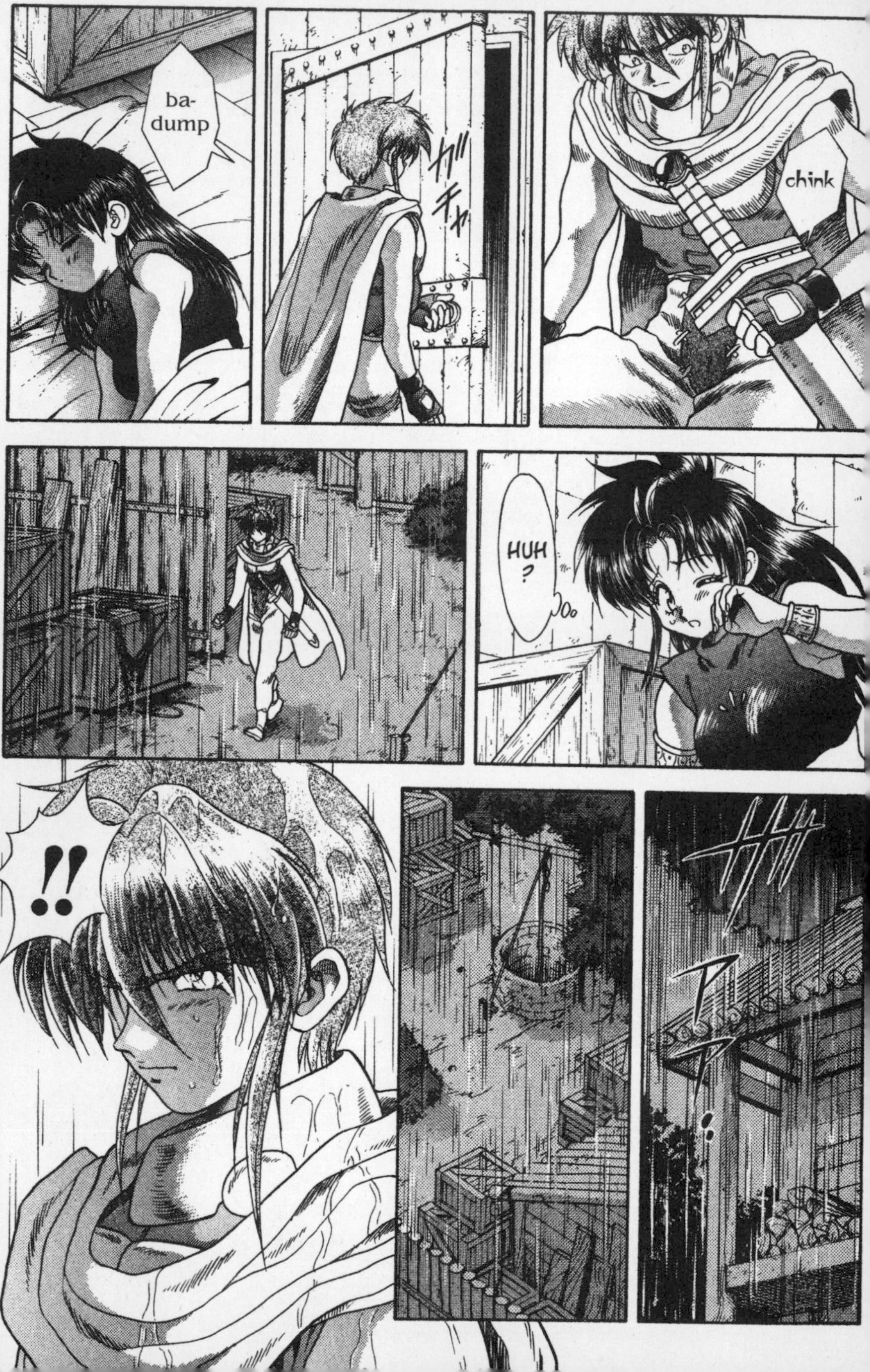
chink
ガチャ
ba-dump
HUH ?
!!

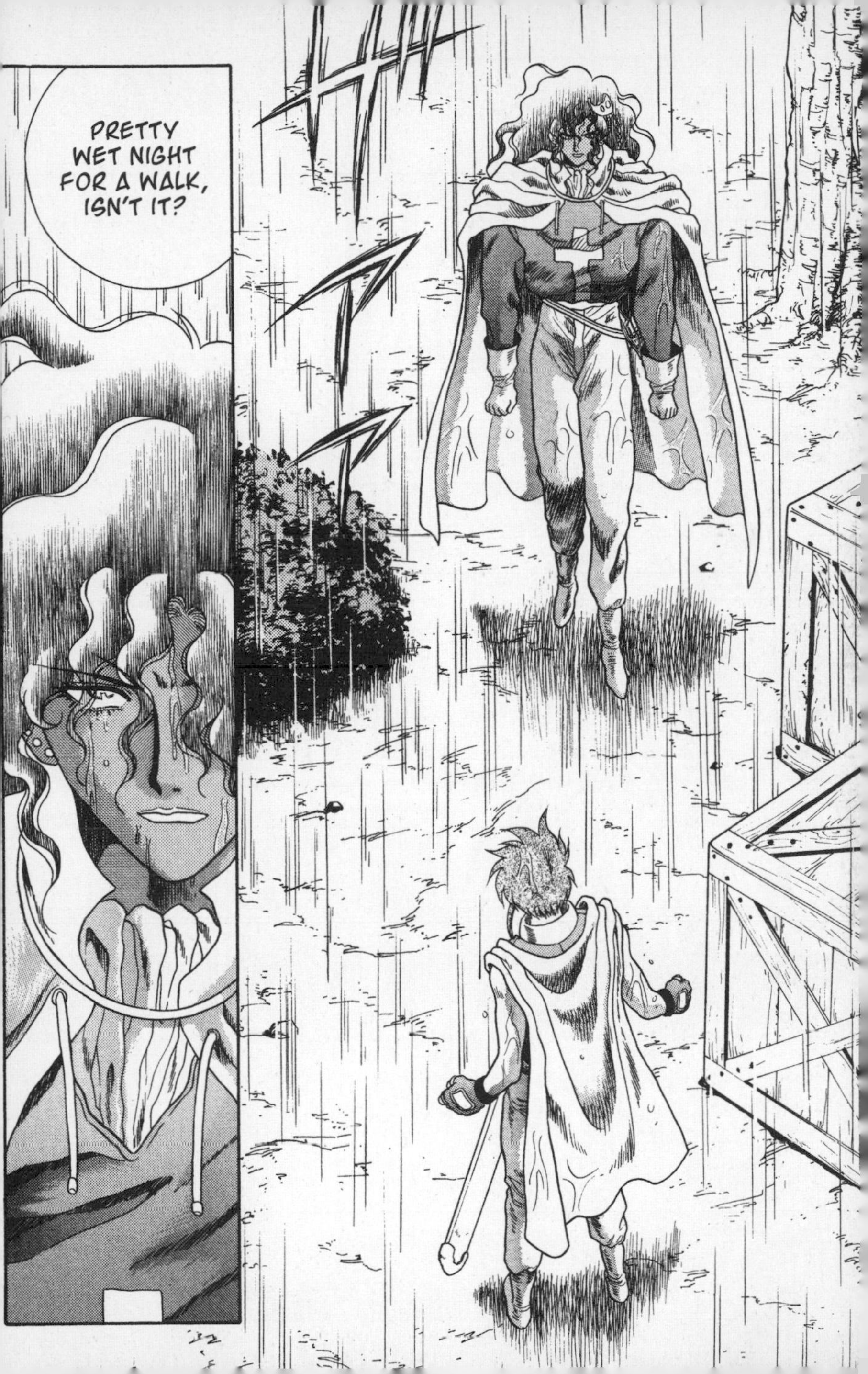
PRETTY WET NIGHT FOR A WALK, ISN'T IT?

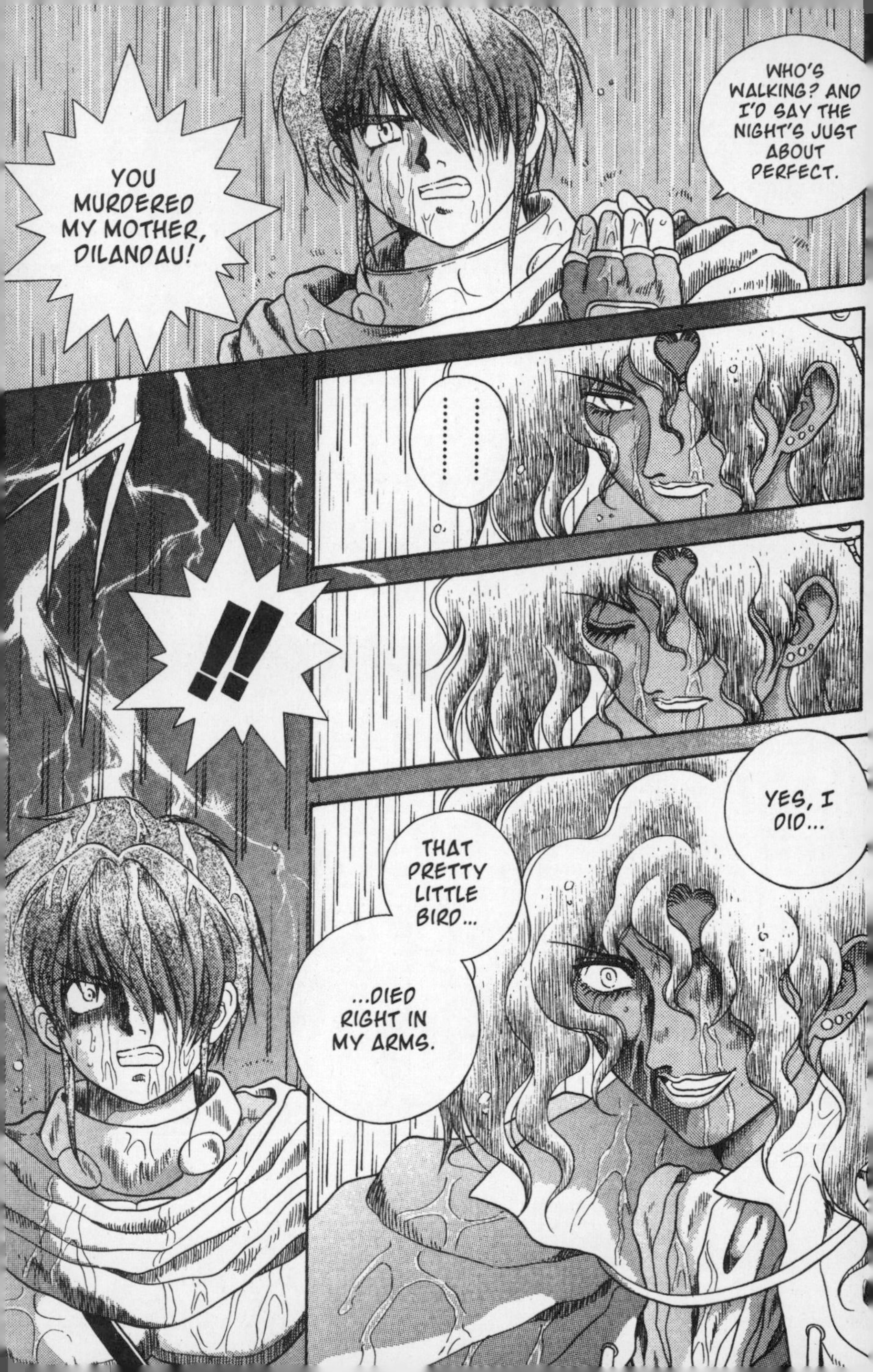
WHO'S WALKING? AND I'D SAY THE NIGHT'S JUST ABOUT PERFECT.
YOU MURDERED MY MOTHER, DILANDAU!
......
YES, I DID...
THAT PRETTY LITTLE BIRD...
...DIED RIGHT IN MY ARMS.
!!

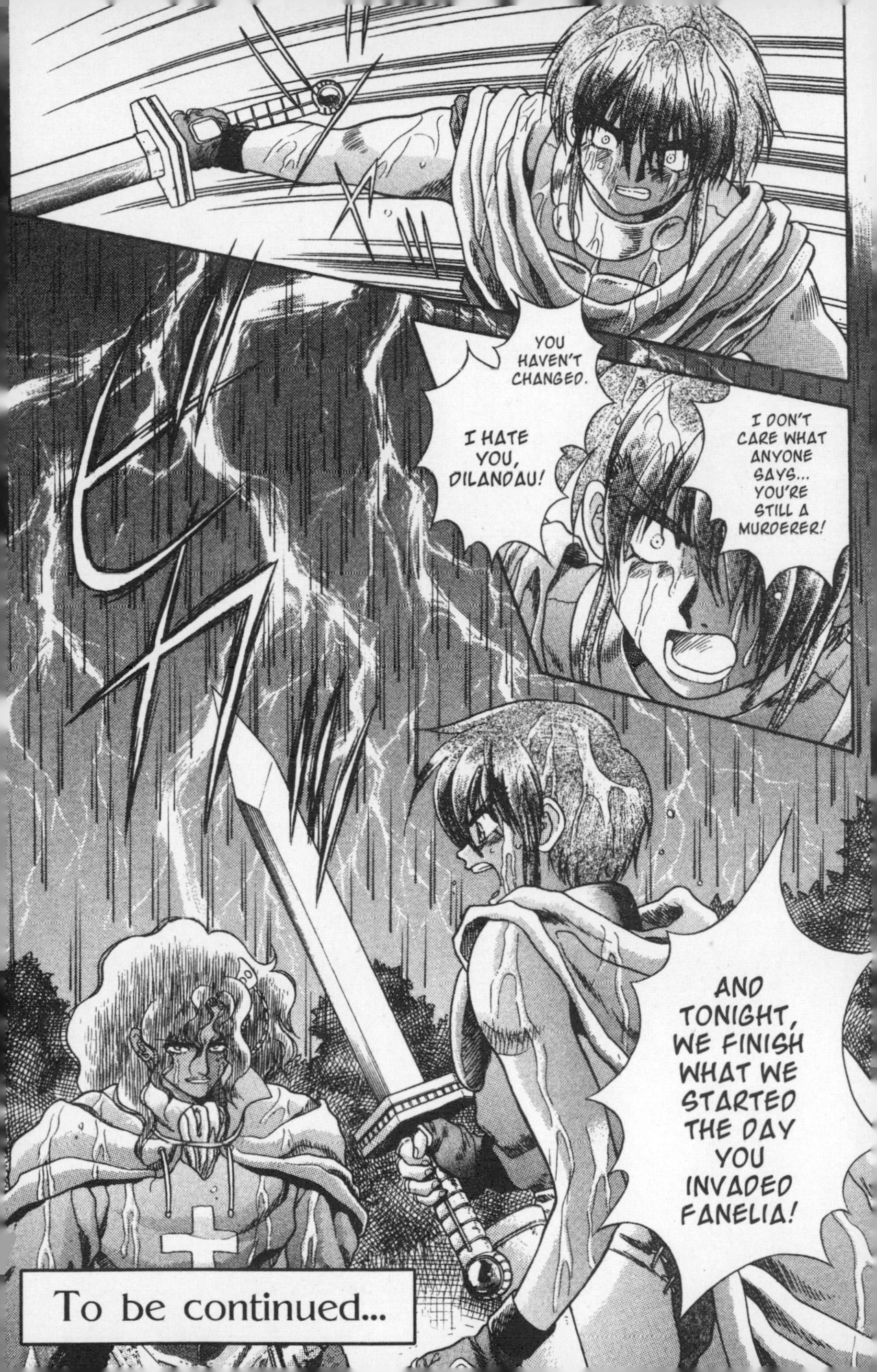
YOU HAVEN'T CHANGED.
I DON'T CARE WHAT ANYONE SAYS... YOU'RE STILL A MURDERER!
I HATE YOU, DILANDAU!
AND TONIGHT, WE FINISH WHAT WE STARTED THE DAY YOU INVADED FANELIA!
To be continued...

In the next volume of

THE VISION OF ESCAFLOWNE

It's the moment you've been waiting for! At last, Prince Van confronts Dilandau Albatou, the brutal captain who murdered his mother. Blood will undoubtedly spill, but will Van be the spiller or the spillee? Meanwhile, Emperor Dornkirk rallies his forces for an attack on the Duchy of Freid, the peaceful dukedom that also holds the last significant deposit of "super fuel" on Gaea. The Revolutionist's Army will do whatever it takes to defend Freid, but their only hope of victory rests in the hands of a very confused Hitomi!

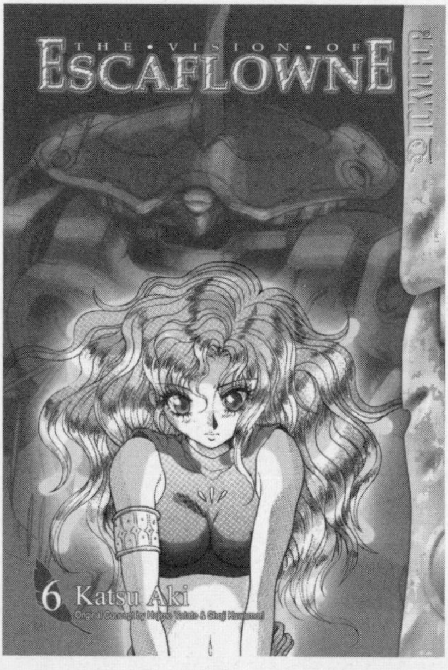
THE VISION OF
ESCAFLOWNE
6 Katsu Aki

ALSO AVAILABLE FROM TOKYOPOP.

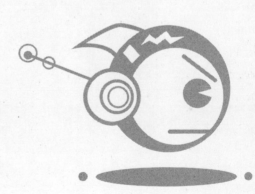

**For more
information visit
www.TOKYOPOP.com**

01.09.04T

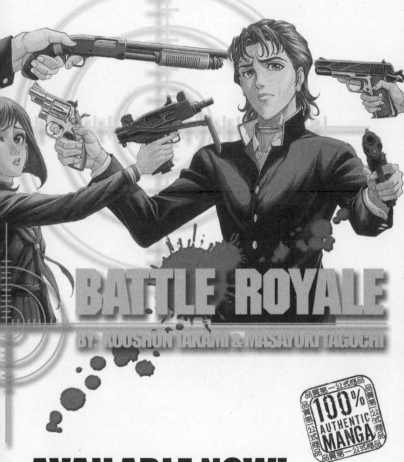

When the curriculum is survival... it's every student for themselves!

TOKYOPOP

BATTLE ROYALE
BY KOUSHON TAKAMI & MASAYUKI TAGUCHI

100% AUTHENTIC MANGA

AVAILABLE NOW!

MATURE AGES 18+

www.TOKYOPOP.com

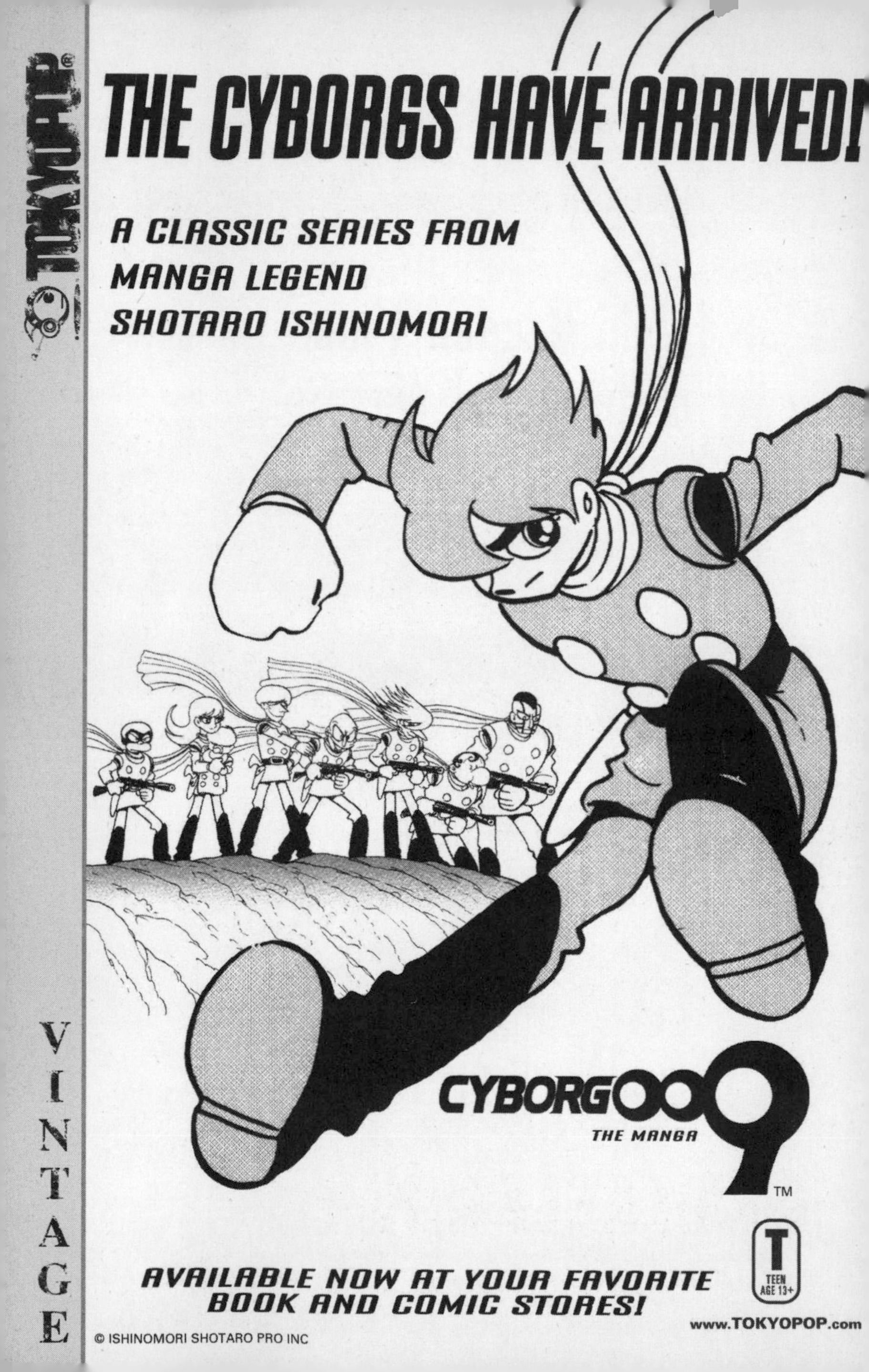
TOKYOPOP
THE CYBORGS HAVE ARRIVED!
A CLASSIC SERIES FROM
MANGA LEGEND
SHOTARO ISHINOMORI
CYBORG 009
THE MANGA
TM
T
TEEN
AGE 13+
AVAILABLE NOW AT YOUR FAVORITE
BOOK AND COMIC STORES!
www.TOKYOPOP.com
© ISHINOMORI SHOTARO PRO INC
VINTAGE

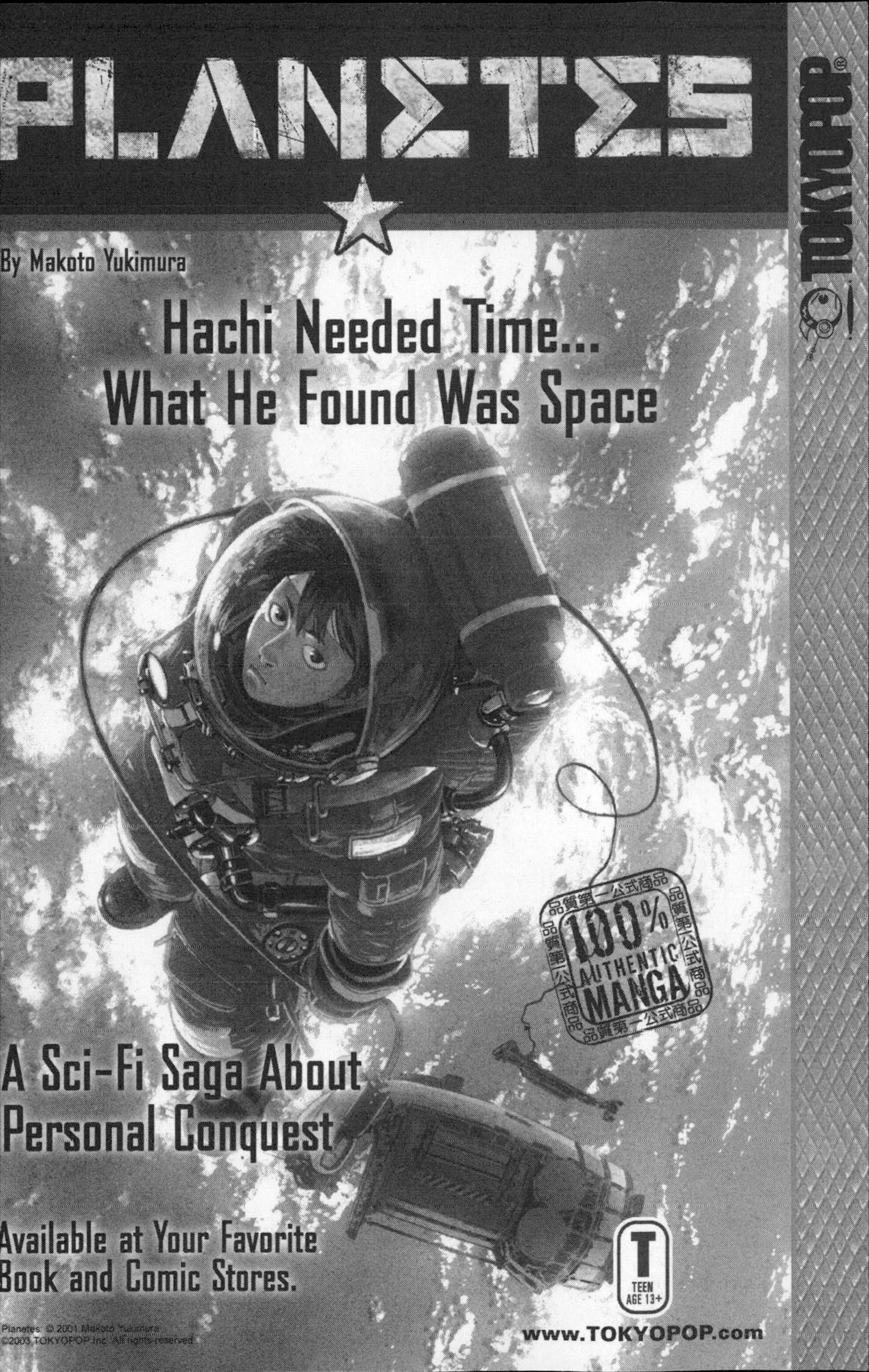

PLANETES
TOKYOPOP
By Makoto Yukimura
Hachi Needed Time...
What He Found Was Space
100% AUTHENTIC MANGA
A Sci-Fi Saga About
Personal Conquest
Available at Your Favorite
Book and Comic Stores.
T TEEN AGE 13+
Planetes © 2001 Makoto Yukimura
©2003 TOKYOPOP Inc. All rights reserved.
www.TOKYOPOP.com

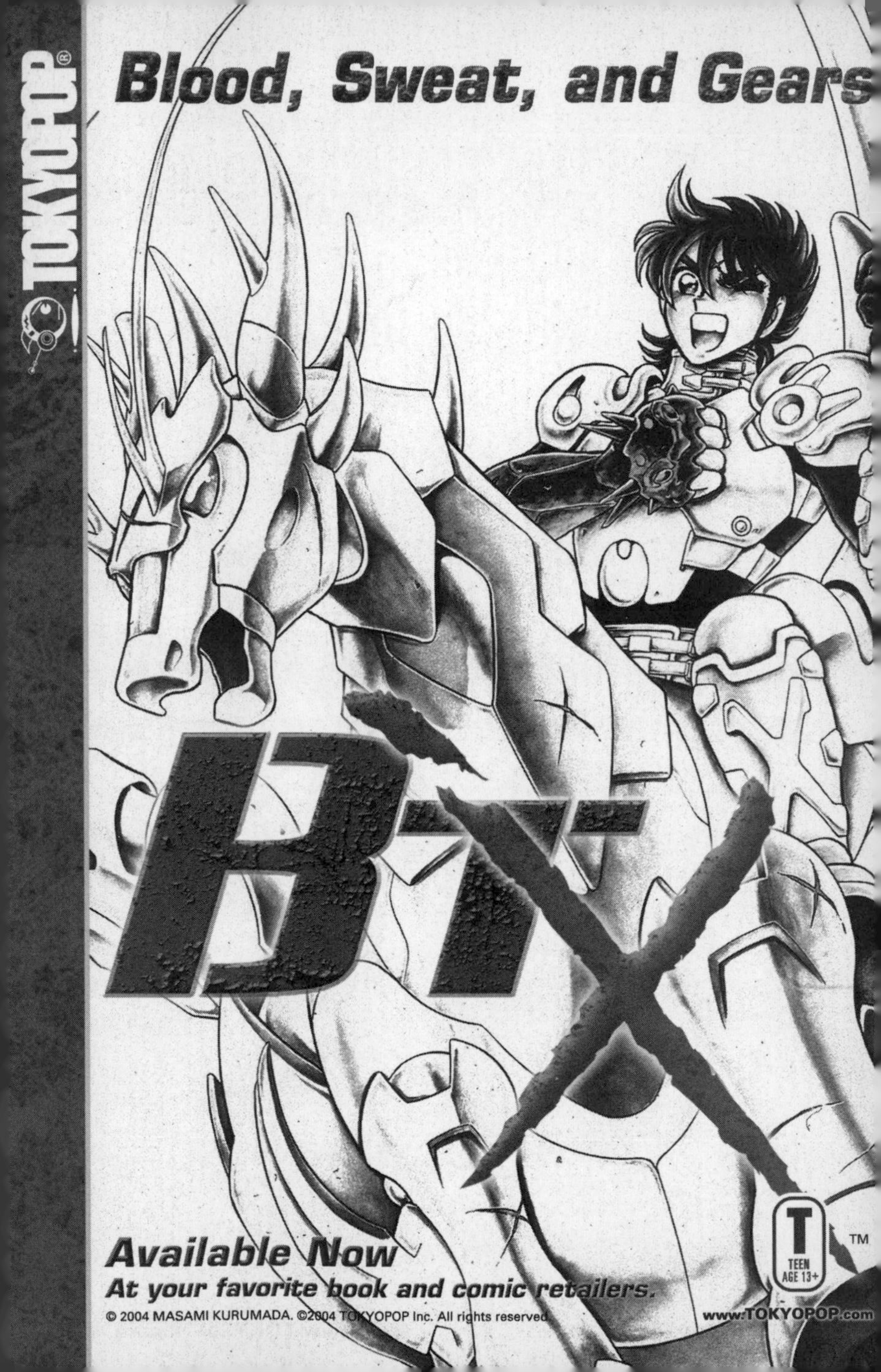
TOKYOPOP
Blood, Sweat, and Gears
B'T X
TM
Available Now
At your favorite book and comic retailers.
T
TEEN
AGE 13+
© 2004 MASAMI KURUMADA. ©2004 TOKYOPOP Inc. All rights reserved.
www.TOKYOPOP.com

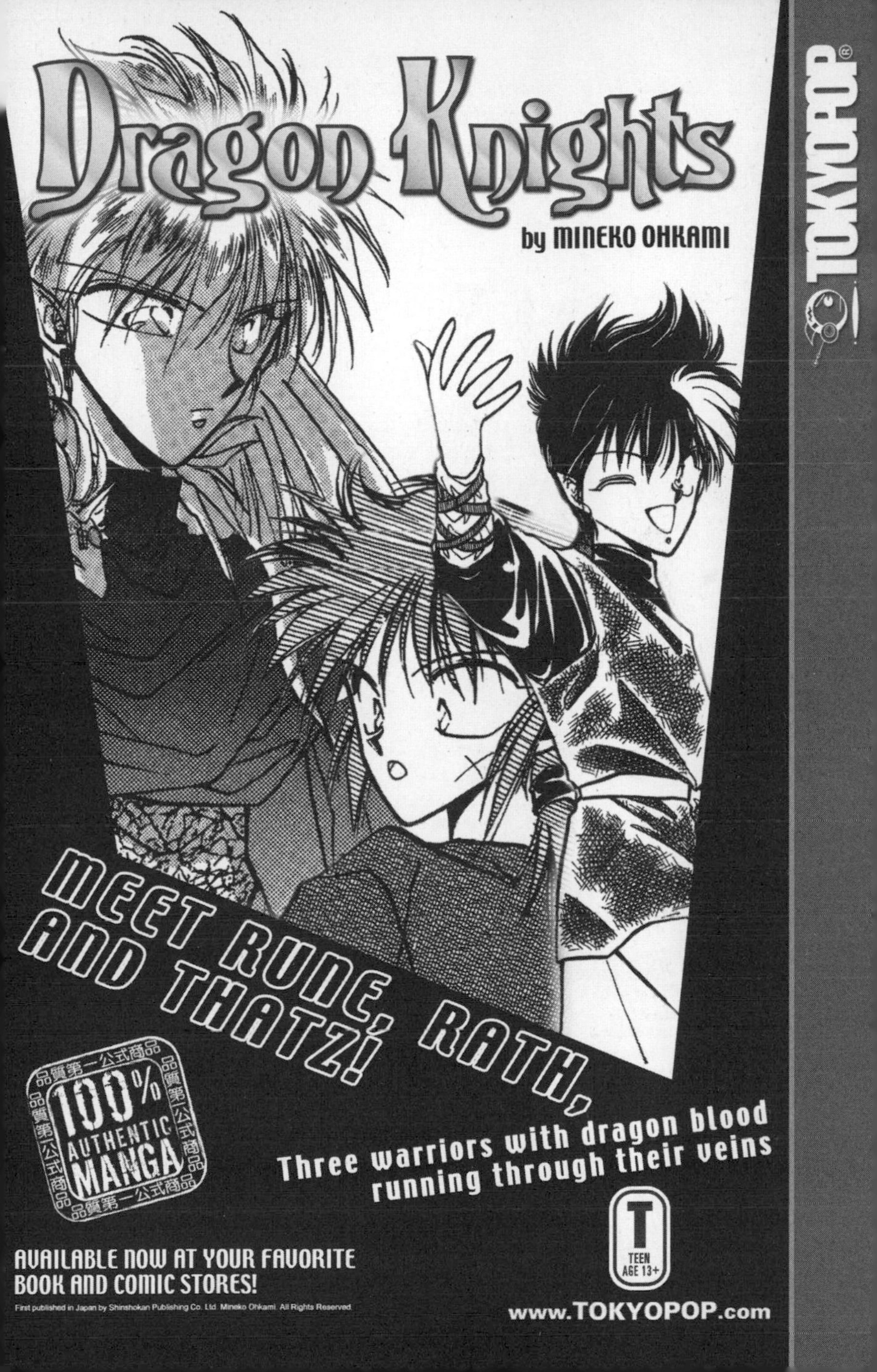
Dragon Knights
by MINEKO OHKAMI
TOKYOPOP®
MEET RUNE, RATH, AND THATZ!
Three warriors with dragon blood running through their veins
100% AUTHENTIC MANGA
品質第一公式商品
T TEEN AGE 13+
AVAILABLE NOW AT YOUR FAVORITE BOOK AND COMIC STORES!
First published in Japan by Shinshokan Publishing Co. Ltd. Mineko Ohkami. All Rights Reserved.
www.TOKYOPOP.com

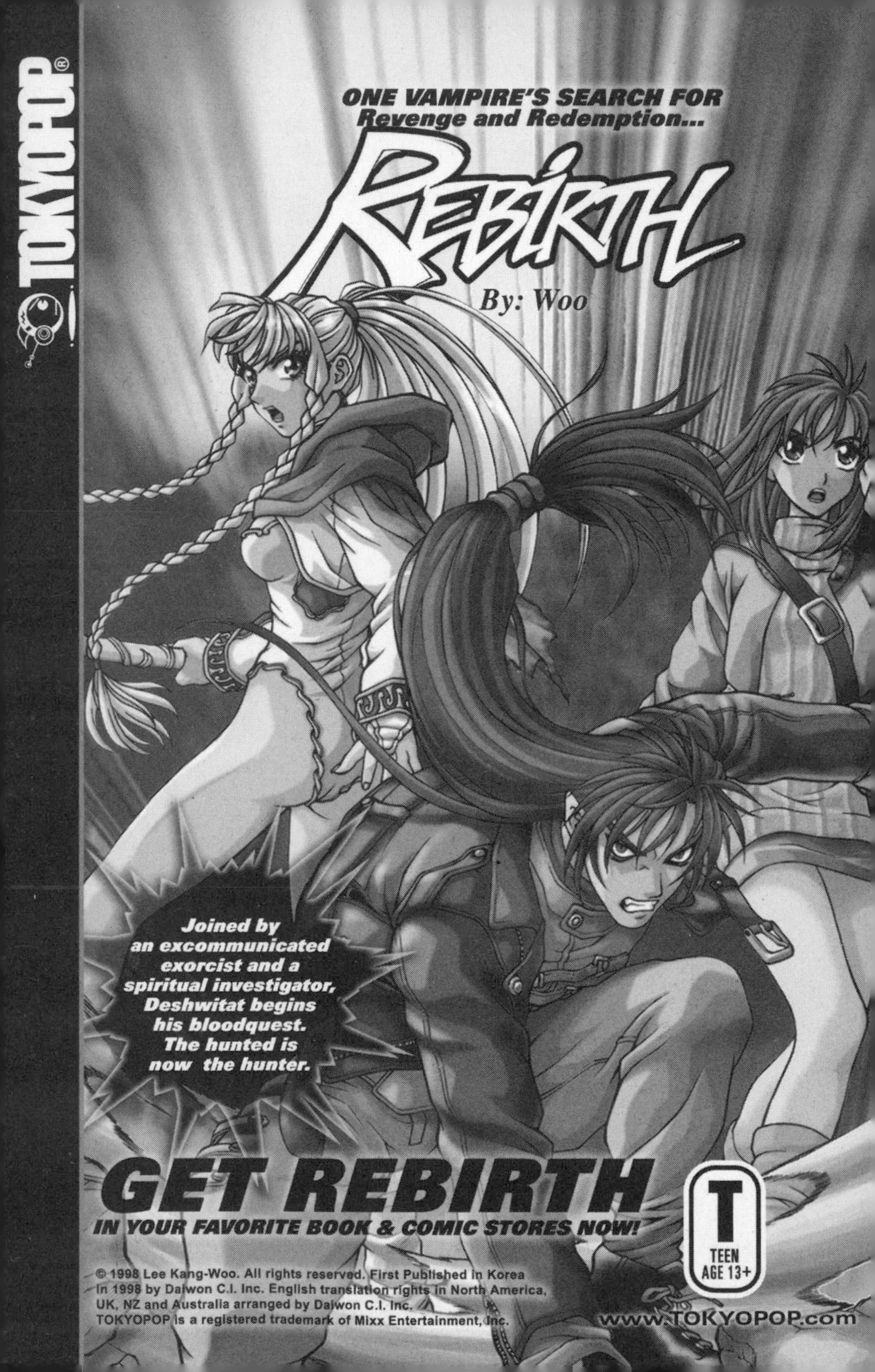
TOKYOPOP®
ONE VAMPIRE'S SEARCH FOR
Revenge and Redemption...
REBIRTH
By: Woo
Joined by an excommunicated exorcist and a spiritual investigator, Deshwitat begins his bloodquest. The hunted is now the hunter.
GET REBIRTH
IN YOUR FAVORITE BOOK & COMIC STORES NOW!
T
TEEN
AGE 13+
© 1998 Lee Kang-Woo. All rights reserved. First Published in Korea in 1998 by Daiwon C.I. Inc. English translation rights in North America, UK, NZ and Australia arranged by Daiwon C.I. Inc.
TOKYOPOP is a registered trademark of Mixx Entertainment, Inc.
www.TOKYOPOP.com

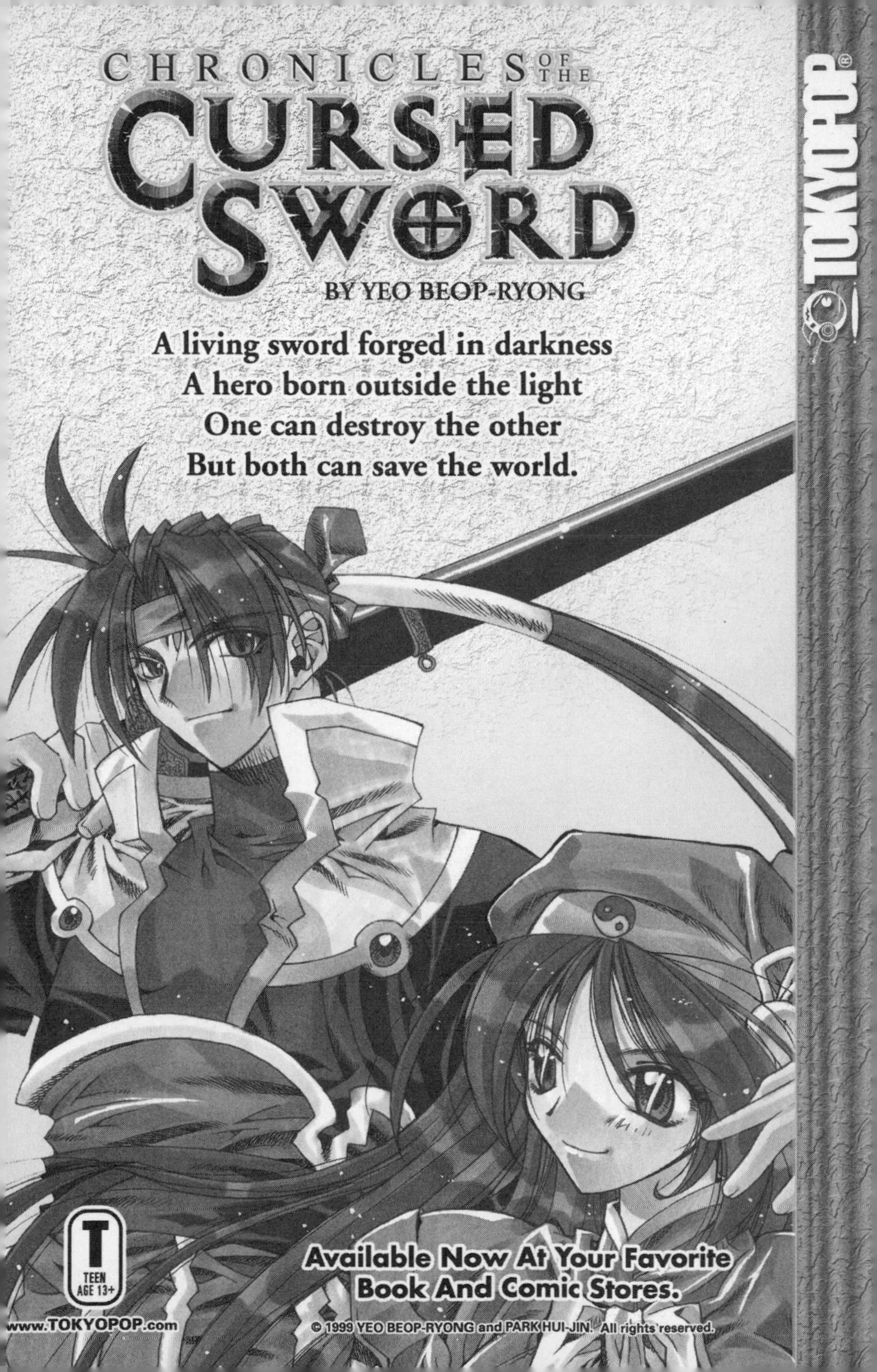
CHRONICLES OF THE
CURSED SWORD
BY YEO BEOP-RYONG
A living sword forged in darkness
A hero born outside the light
One can destroy the other
But both can save the world.
TOKYOPOP®
T
TEEN
AGE 13+
Available Now At Your Favorite
Book And Comic Stores.
www.TOKYOPOP.com
© 1999 YEO BEOP-RYONG and PARK HUI-JIN. All rights reserved.

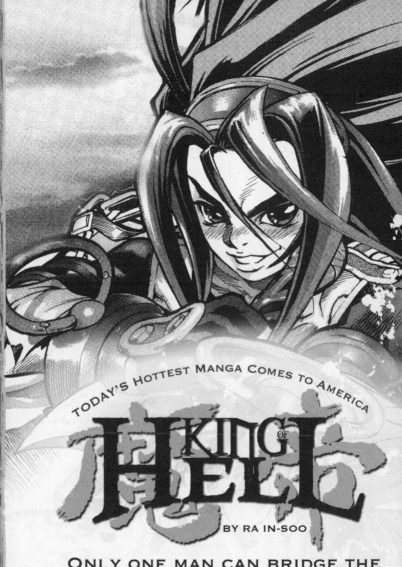
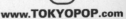

D0019192

STOP!
This is the back of the book.
You wouldn't want to spoil a great ending!

This book is printed "manga-style," in the authentic Japanese right-to-left format. Since none of the artwork has been flipped or altered, readers get to experience the story just as the creator intended. You've been asking for it, so TOKYOPOP® delivered: authentic, hot-off-the-press, and far more fun!

DIRECTIONS

If this is your first time reading manga-style, here's a quick guide to help you understand how it works.

It's easy... just start in the top right panel and follow the numbers. Have fun, and look for more 100% authentic manga from TOKYOPOP®!

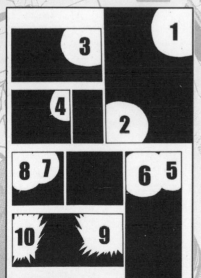

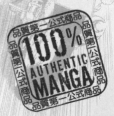